READINGS
IN
ADOPTION

READINGS IN ADOPTION

I. Evelyn Smith

PHILOSOPHICAL LIBRARY

NEW YORK

Copyright 1963 by Philosophical Library Inc.

15 East 40 Street, New York 16, N. Y.

All rights reserved.

Library of Congress Catalogue Card No. 62-9773

Printed in the United States of America

CONTENTS

CONTRIBUTING AUTHORS

ROBERTA G. ANDREWS, *Associate Director,* Children's Aid Society of Pennsylvania
LOIS R. BEEMER, *Assistant District Director,* Los Angeles District Office,
        Children's Home Society of California
VIOLA W. BERNARD, M.D., New York
BERNICE BROWER BOEHM, Ph.D., *Research Consultant,* Child Welfare Division,
        Minnesota State Department of Public Welfare
JOHN BOWLBY, M.D., The Tavistock Clinic, London, England
DONALD BRIELAND, Ph.D., *Director of Children's Services,* Illinois State
        Department of Mental Health
FLORENCE G. BROWN, *Executive Director,* Louise Wise Services, New York
FLORENCE CLOTHIER (WISLOCKI), M.D., *Assistant to the President,* Vassar College
ANITA COLVILLE, Child Adoption Service, State Charities Aid Association, New York
LELA B. COSTIN, *Assistant Professor,* School of Social Work, University of Illinois
EILENE F. CROSIER, San Antonio, Texas
SARA DUBO, M.D., *Associate Director,* Hawthorn Center, Northville, Michigan
RITA DUKETTE, *Director,* Adoption Division, Illinois Children's Home and Aid Society
ALEX ELSON, Chicago
MARY ELIZABETH FAIRWEATHER, *Supervisor,* Adoption Service,
        Children's Services, Cleveland
RICHARD FRANK, M.D., Chicago
E. ELIZABETH GLOVER, *Director of Publications,* Child Welfare League of America
CHARLOTTE L. HAMMELL, *Director,* Child Care Service, Delaware County
        Institution District, Media, Pennsylvania
MILDRED C. HAWKINS, *Supervisor,* Placement Division, Lake County Department of
        Public Welfare, Gary, Indiana
LYDIA T. HICKS, *Supervisor,* Child Adoption Service, State Charities
        Aid Association, New York
GRACE LOUISE HUBBARD, Formerly Supervisor of Intake, Child Adoption Service,
        State Charities Aid Association, New York
DOROTHY HUTCHINSON, Formerly Professor of Social Work, New York School of
        Social Work, Columbia University (deceased)
VALERIA R. JURACSEK, M.D., *Psychiatrist,* Michigan Children's Institute
ANNE LEATHERMAN, *Director of Social Services,* Methodist Home, Waco, Texas
ELIZABETH I. LYNCH, *Casework Director,* Bureau of Adoptions,
        Los Angeles County, California
ARNOLD LYSLO, *Director,* Indian Adoption Project, Child Welfare League of America
H. GORDON MACKAY, *Executive Director,* The Adoption Institute, Los Angeles
SARABELLE MCCLEERY, Langley Porter Neuropsychiatric Institute, School of Medicine,
        University of California
ALICE E. MERTZ, *Family Service Consultant,* Bureau of Public Assistance,
        County of Los Angeles, California
RUTH MICHAELS, Brooklyn, New York
MORRIS H. PRICE, San Diego, California
BEATRICE PRUSKI, Vaughn, Washington
RALPH D. RABINOVITCH, M.D., *Director,* Hawthorn Center, Northville, Michigan
CONSTANCE RATHBUN, Director of Casework, Boston Children's Service Association
ARTHUR L. RAUTMAN, Ph.D., *Chief Clinical Psychologist,* Mental Hygiene Clinic,
        Veterans Administration Regional Office, St. Petersburg, Florida
JOSEPH H. REID, *Executive Director,* Child Welfare League of America
JULIUS B. RICHMOND, M.D., *Professor and Chairman,* Department of Pediatrics,
        Upstate Medical Center, State University of New York, Syracuse
FRANCES H. SCHERZ, *Director of Casework,* Jewish Family and Community Service, Chicago
WILLIAM D. SCHMIDT, *Executive Director,* Children's Services, Cleveland
H. L. SHAPIRO, Ph.D., *Chairman,* Department of Anthropology,
        The American Museum of Natural History, New York
RUTH TAFT, *Director,* Adoption Department, Children's Services of Connecticut,
        Hartford, Connecticut
STUART W. THAYER, New York
NEVILLE B. WEEKS, *Director of Social Service,* Brookwood Child Care, Brooklyn
EMILY MITCHELL WIRES, Formerly Supervisor of Child Welfare, Westchester County
        Department of Public Welfare, White Plains, New York
LEONTINE R. YOUNG, *Professor,* School of Social Administration, Ohio State University

ACKNOWLEDGMENTS

Acknowledgment is gratefully made to the following for permission to reprint from their publications:

The Child Welfare League of America: *Adoption for School-Age Children in Institutions,* by Neville B. Weeks, 1953; *Fee Charging for Adoption Service,* by Eilene F. Crosier, November, 1949.

The Columbia University Press and World Health Organization: "Substitute Families. Adoption," by John Bowlby, in *Maternal Care and Mental Health,* 1951.

The Family Service Association of America: *Casework Papers 1955, from the National Conference of Social Work,* 1955, "Supervision after Adoptive Placement," by Lois R. Beemer.

International Universities Press: "Application of Psychoanalytic Concepts to Adoption Agency Practice," by Viola W. Bernard, in *Psychoanalysis and Social Work,* edited by Marcel Heiman, 1953.

McGraw-Hill Book Company: "The Unmarried Father" from *Out of Wedlock* by Leontine R. Young, 1954.

The Child: "What Shall I Do with My Baby?" by Bernice Brower Boehm (12:166-169, April, 1948); "Who Am I?" by Grace Louise Hubbard (11:130-133, February, 1947); "If a Baby Is to Be Adopted," by Mary Elizabeth Fairweather (16:40-43, November, 1951); "When a Couple Plans to Adopt a Baby," by Beatrice Pruski (17:127-129, 134, April, 1953).

Child Welfare: "The Adoption Worker's Role and His Personality in the Professional Adoption Process," by Sarabelle McCleery (31:3-8, 12, October, 1952); "The Community and the Adoption Problem," by William D. Schmidt (31:3-7, May, 1952); "Today's Controversial Clients: Married Parents Who Place Legitimate Children for Adoption," by H. Gordon MacKay (37:18-22, January, 1958); "Helping Children Move into Adoptive Homes," by Charlotte L. Hammell (28:9, 12-14, January, 1949); "The Transitional Method in the Adoption Placement of Older Infants and Young Toddlers," by Roberta G. Andrews (40:15-21, May, 1961); "Placing the Second Child for Adoption," by Lydia T. Hicks (39:15-21, May, 1960); "Adoption for the Handicapped Child," by Anita Colville (36:10-14, October, 1957); "Negro Adoptions—Challenge Accepted," by Mildred Hawkins (39:22-27, December, 1960); "Adoptive Placement of American Indian Children with Non-Indian Families," by Arnold Lyslo (40:4-6, May, 1961); "Adoptive Families for 'Unadoptable Children,'" by Ruth Taft (32:5-9, June, 1953); "Some Casework Implications in Adoptive Home Intake Procedures," by Rita Dukette (33:8-9, 15-16, January, 1954); "Supervision of the Child in the Adoptive Home," by Florence G. Brown (34:10-16, March, 1955); "Some Problems in Developing Research on Adoption," by Donald Brieland (35:17-21, February, 1956); "The Legal Profession's Responsibility in Adoption," by Alex Elson (35:21-24, March, 1956); "What the Adoption Worker Should Know About Infertility," by Richard Frank (35:1-5, February, 1956); "Criteria for Predictability," by Julius B. Richmond (35:7-9, January, 1956); "Anthropology and Adoption Practice," by H. L. Shapiro (34:1-4, December, 1955).

Thanks also to E. Elizabeth Glover, editor of *Child Welfare,* who contributed a discussion to "Adoption for the Handicapped Child" by Anita Colville.

Child Welfare League of America Bulletin: "The Adoptive Foster Parent: A Basis for Evaluation," by Constance Rathbun (23:5-7, 12-14, November, 1944).

Children: "Placing the Older Child in Adoption," by Anne Leatherman (4:107-112, May-June, 1957).

Journal of Social Casework: " 'Taking Sides' in the Unmarried Mother's Conflict," by Frances H. Scherz (28:57-61, February, 1947); "Placement for Adoption—A Total Separation?" by Emily Mitchell Wires (30:283-288, July, 1949); "Adoptive Placement of Infants Directly from the Hospital," by Elizabeth I. Lynch and Alice E. Mertz (36:450-457, December, 1955); "A Plan for Improved Service to the Adoptive Applicant," by Sarabelle McCleery (34:73-78, February, 1953); "Competence and Conscience in Homefinding," by Dorothy Hutchison (36:365-368, October, 1955); "Casework Considerations in Rejecting the Adoption Application," by Ruth Michaels (28:370-376, December, 1947); "The History-Giving Interview in Adoptive Procedures," by Lela B. Costin (35:393-400, November, 1954); "Implications of Psychological Testing for Adoptive Placements," by Lela B. Costin (34:68-73, February, 1953). (The name of this journal has been changed to *Social Casework,* under which title some of the foregoing articles appeared.)

Mental Hygiene: "Placing the Child for Adoption," by Florence Clothier (26:257-274, April, 1942); "Adoptive Parents Need Help, Too," by Arthur L. Rautman (33:424-431, July, 1949).

Proceedings 53rd Annual Meeting, New York State Welfare Conference, 1952: "Psychiatric Considerations in Foster Home Placement and Adoption," by Ralph D. Rabinovitch, Sara Dubo and Valeria F. Juracsek.

Social Service Review: "The Adoptive Applicants See a Child," by Morris H. Price (26:423-427, December, 1952).

Social Work: "Principles, Values, and Assumptions Underlying Adoption Practice," by Joseph H. Reid (2:22-29, January, 1957).

Yale Law Journal: "Moppets on the Market: The Problem of Unregulated Adoptions," by S. W. Thayer (59:715-736, March, 1950).

PREFACE

Preparation of this book of readings in adoption was both a pleasure and a responsibility. Selection of articles for an anthology is difficult and decisions were hard to make in view of the many excellent articles available. I tried to choose articles which make a significant contribution to the various aspects of adoption. It is my hope that other adoption workers, who might have made different choices of articles, will understand the difficulties and forgive my having failed to include many helpful contributions in this field. The book is not intended to be all-inclusive but to provide an introduction to some aspects of adoption which will lead to additional and more comprehensive reading in special areas.

In the last ten or fifteen years adoption thinking and policies have been changing so rapidly that it is impossible for any collection of articles at a given time to represent completely all the latest ideas on adoption. Furthermore, there are still differences of opinion in some areas. In selecting the articles I have tried to cover many different facets of the adoption program and to present various points of view. This book is not intended as the last word in adoption principles and philosophy but I hope it will be helpful in providing a groundwork of knowledge on which to base future planning and policies. It was Seneca who said that "our forefathers have done much, but they have not finished anything." From our experience we know this is applicable to adoption in the past and today. Surely it will be equally applicable in the future.

To all the authors and publishers who have graciously given permission for the use of their articles in this book, I extend my personal thanks. Without these contributions this book would not be possible.

I wish to acknowledge the encouragement and advice given on preliminary material by Dorothy Bradbury when I first thought of working on this project. Without her encouragement I would not have started the book. I am particularly grateful to Elizabeth Deuel Chapman who read the manuscript for the introductions and made many helpful and thoughtful suggestions. A special note of thanks is due Grace Darling whose expression of continuing interest is largely responsible for the final publication of this book.

In the present scientific age with its contemplated trips to other planets some may think it inappropriate to spend so much thought on one individual child's welfare as adoption workers must. If one has misgivings of this kind, he would do well to remember what Arthur H. Compton has pointed out so aptly: "Twenty thousand years ago the family was the social unit. Now the social unit has become the world, in which it may truthfully be said that each person's welfare affects that of every other." And to that I would add, each child is worth our thought and care for himself alone.

I. Evelyn Smith

General Concepts and Basic Philosophy

of Adoption

Introduction

Adoption was the ancient and remains the modern method of establishing by law the relationship of parent and child between individuals who are not related. It is the process by which a child becomes a member of a family with whom he has no immediate blood ties.

Adoption was originally thought of as a way to provide heirs in a childless family. In modern times the emphasis in adoption is on the interests of the child rather than of the adopters. It is primarily a means of creating parent-child relationships for homeless children.

Adoption is, therefore, never a first family relationship in a child's life. It can only be a beginning again with new parents after a total breakdown with his natural parents whether or not they shared any living together.

With the universal interest and curiosity that exist in the addition of children to family groups, it is not surprising that adoptions have stimulated the interest of most people, even those who will never be personally involved. Nor is it surprising that misconceptions and prejudices are prevalent.

1

The prevailing lay concepts in regard to adoption are: people are generous and kind to take unknown children into their home; adoptions are the most desirable and economical way to provide for homeless children in a community; it is natural for married people wanting children they cannot bear to be given those others cannot care for; it should be as simple a process to adopt a child as it is natural to want the child; adoptions are personal matters and the less outside interference the better.

Child welfare agencies are sometimes accused of filling institutions and boarding homes with children who are adoptable, and holding on to children who should be placed in adoptive homes. Sometimes the public even thinks that agencies contribute to the shortage of children available for adoption by their unwillingness to release children for adoption. But unless parental rights have been terminated legally, agencies are not authorized to place children for adoption.

The professional service of child placement is not consistently defined nor generally recognized. Such service is still considered a hindrance by some in getting children; but fortunately it proves a help and protection for increasing numbers.

With regard to the sources and numbers of children available for adoption some facts, not generally known, are available.

The number of full orphans being cared for by agencies and institutions is small. Most of these children have one or both parents still living. Many are in foster care because their own homes have been broken as a result of death or chronic illness, separation or divorce or mental incapacity of parents, the necessity for the mother to work outside the home, or physical or moral neglect of children by parents. Even when parents do not keep in touch with these children or give them parental love and care, legal custody which would enable the agency to place these children in permanent adoptive homes cannot always be obtained.

Nation-wide statistics are not available on the number of full orphans and half-orphans in foster care. Certain individual studies do contain such figures. "Foster Care of Children in Michigan", a report of a Joint Legislative Committee issued in 1951, shows that of the 8,607 children in foster care of institutions and agencies on December 31, 1949, only 3 percent of the children were fully orphans; about 16 percent had one parent dead. Other statistics in that report show that over 70 percent

2

of the children in foster care were more than 5 years old; 45 percent, more than 10 years old. Thirty-eight percent of the children were in institutions; 62 percent, in foster homes. The largest group (45 percent) were in paid boarding homes; 11 percent were in adoptive homes.

A study made in Pittsburgh under the auspices of the Health and Welfare Federation of Allegheny County of 4,013 children under foster care in 1947 showed that about 4½ percent of these children were full orphans; children with one parent dead, almost 22 percent. Twenty-three percent were children of unmarried mothers and 32 percent were children whose parents were divorced or separated.

"Child Placement and Adoption", a report of the Joint State Government Commission to the General Assembly of Pennsylvania, Session of 1951, contains information on children under agency care outside their own homes in selected counties as of December 1949. This report indicates that the number of fathers who are deceased ranges from 1.4 percent in one county to 50 percent in another; the number of mothers deceased ranges from 7.8 percent in one county to 34.2 in another. Figures for Philadelphia in the studies of unadoptable children, together with the reason why they were determined unadoptable, give the following percentages for 1,312 children; 40 percent, consent of parents or guardians unobtainable; 2.2 percent, abandonment cannot be established; 24.5 percent, age factors (too old for adoption); 11.1 percent, physical or mental condition; 11.1 percent, behavior problems, 11.1 percent, other reasons.

In spite of the low percentages of children available for adoption among those in foster care, adoptions are on the increase. In fact, one of the social phenomena of our times is the great increase in adoptions during recent years. In 1959 the number of adoption petitions filed in the United States was approximately 102,000. This estimated total represents an increase in adoptions of 6 percent over 1958. These estimates are based on adoption reports from state public welfare agencies. In 1959, 47 states reported and provide the base for the estimate made by the Children's Bureau, Department of Health, Education, and Welfare, for that year; in 1944 with 22 states reporting the estimated number of adoption petitions was 50,000.

This increase occurs in adoptions by stepparents and other relatives as well as in adoptions by nonrelated persons. Factors contributing to this growth in adoptions include the large number of homes broken by death, divorce or desertion, and the subsequent adoption by stepfathers of children after marriage to the mothers; the greater emphasis by child welfare agencies on getting children into adoptive homes rather than allowing them to remain in institutions and boarding homes for long periods of time with no continuing relationship with parents or other relatives; more children born out of wedlock who represent a major source of adoptable children; and greater confidence on the part of the public in adoption agency services as the result of help given to adopting parents in selecting suitable children for them. Then too, our increasingly complex social life stimulates formalized legal relationships with dependency status becoming significant for income tax, military service-connected dependency, social security benefits and other rights.

With the increasing numbers of adoptions and the prevailing lack of knowledge of social procedures and philosophy, it is understandable that many adoptions are completed without any social service.

Detailed information furnished by 32 states for 1959 showed that in these states approximately one-half of the children were adopted by persons not related to them. Over one-third were adopted by their step-parents. Of the children adopted by unrelated persons 39 percent were placed for adoption without the assistance of a social agency, 37 percent were placed by voluntary social agencies and 24 percent by public agencies. Thus 61 percent of all the adoptive placements in these 32 states were by social agencies. In 1951 when annual reporting started the proportion of agency placements was only 52 percent.

In adoptions many functions of organized society mesh in the complicated process that creates legally and socially this new union of child and parents. Legal, judicial and social functions, distinct in their methods and content, combine to achieve the adoption. State vital statistics departments add their function to record the adoption and issue birth certificates with name changes.

Each of these functions operates within the framework of a different body of knowledge and organization—practitioners of law, courts, child welfare agencies, and vital statistics bureaus. Jurisdictional questions should not arise since the functions are distinct and coordinate rather than duplicating or overlapping.

This book considers primarily the social service functions in the adoption process in which the professional child-welfare worker is the expert.

The knowledge and skills social work has in the area of understanding and furthering social relationships, and particularly in child placement, form the basis for the social service function in adoptions. The child welfare content draws heavily upon other specializations within social work and upon other fields such as medicine, psychiatry, psychology, religion, education, recreation. In fact a major contribution of the child welfare function is understanding the totality of the child and his situation—both individual and social—while still focusing upon his welfare.

The overall purpose of the welfare program is to prevent the break-up of families and the child welfare program including adoption is an integral part of this program. All parents have tremendous meaning for a child even though some may be very "bad" parents.

As Dr. John Bowlby has said, "It must never be forgotten that even the bad parent who neglects her child is nonetheless providing much for him. Except in the worst cases, she is giving him food and shelter, comforting him in distress, teaching him simple skills, and above all is providing him with that continuity of human care on which his sense of security rests. He may be ill-fed and ill-sheltered, he may be very dirty and suffering from disease, he may be ill-treated, but, unless his parents have wholly rejected him, he is secure in the knowledge that there is someone to whom he is of value and who will strive, even though inadequately, to provide for him until such time as he can fend for himself."[1]

In the past emphasis was on physical neglect in deciding that children needed to be removed from their own families, and the meaning of the family to the child and its real value for him were sometimes overlooked.

Today agencies distinguish more clearly two forms of neglect —physical neglect and emotional neglect. The present trend is to keep children who are physically neglected in their own homes by giving the parents sufficient supportive help if possible, so that they can maintain their home without having their children suffer in their physical development. This enables the parents to

[1] Bowlby, John: Maternal Care and Mental Health, p. 68.

5

continue providing for their children's emotional needs so essential to the child's total well-being.

To preserve the child's own family for him and to keep him living within its circle is always the prime objective of child welfare. The social service supplements and strengthens parents in their care of their children but never supplants them nor assumes any part of parental responsibility so long as they carry it alone or with available help.

In those instances in which separation of children from parents is necessary, parental responsibility continues in the plan for the children and hopefully in restoring the family as a unit. The parents' role is significant in placement whether it be temporary or permanent.

The parents must recognize that the child is their responsibility, that the agency cannot give satisfactory care to their child unless they participate and share in all planning for the child. The parent must feel that any information he gives will be kept confidential, that he has a right to make his own decisions, that the agency's concern is the welfare of the child, and that the worker understands and appreciates his feelings of inadequacy and guilt in needing placement for his child, whether that be voluntary or mandatory through court action.

Since the child's own family means so much to his welfare, what conditions or set of circumstances justify separation of children and parents?

The reasons parents are unable to maintain a home for their children may include any or several of the following: illegitimacy, chronic illness or incapacity of parent, instability or psychopathy of parent, alcoholism, mental retardation, death of one parent, illness requiring hospitalization, imprisonment of a parent, desertion by one or both parents, separation or divorce, and economic factors.

Emotional instability and the inability of parents to make effective family relationships are today a major cause for children requiring care outside their own homes. Personality disturbances, especially in mothers, play a large part in this need for foster care. Personality disturbances of parents may contribute to neglect of children, physical cruelty, prolonged ill heath of a parent (especially mental illness or neurosis), lack of parental control, unhappy marriages, desertion, separation

6

and divorce. Neurotic and unstable parents are irresponsible, may be unable to learn from experience, are often inaccessible to help, capable of only superficial relationships, and promiscuous in their sexual behavior. They have usually been deprived of mother love in their childhood and consequently are unable to give love and consistent care to their own children. They are neglected children who have grown up to become neglectful parents.

Since emotional neglect of children is usually due to the emotional instability and psychopathy of the parents, this is more serious for the child than physical neglect. The emotionally neglected child comes into foster care primarily for his protection and welfare.

Understanding some of these factors helps us realize that we cannot expect normal parental attitudes from some parents and that they are too immature themselves to fulfill their children's needs. Their past experiences and environment have made them unable to meet life's responsibilities in an adult way. The caseworker's attitude toward these parents is not one of blame but of understanding. Although the caseworker recognizes the ways in which parents are failing to meet the needs of a child, he respects the parents as individuals and is not hostile toward them. Otherwise, he is unable to help both the parents and the child.

The caseworker in his relationship with parents must help a parent, married or unmarried, make a decision to place or not to place a child, and to understand the meaning of placement whether on a temporary or permanent basis. The unmarried mother is especially in need of guidance and should not be forced into a hasty decision without full knowledge of facts and consequences of her decision. When a separation is not voluntary and a child has been removed from the parent by the court, the caseworker has the responsibility for helping the parent understand the reality of placement and his role in the plan for separation.

In brief, a knowledge of what children need in the way of good health, physical development, personality development, emotional security and belonging to a family and being loved, is essential if a child-welfare worker is to help parents with their plans for their children's needs. Wherever possible the caseworker helps the parents preserve the natural parent-child relationship, maintain regular contacts with the child, give him the emotional support he needs to remain in foster care, and also

7

helps the parents use whatever strengths they have to reestablish the family and take the child home again.

Experience proves many of these children in foster care can never be returned to their own families. Their parents frequently cease to show any continuing interest in them or even to visit them in their boarding homes. Such children suffer the loss of their parents both physically and emotionally, do not feel they belong anywhere, are confused about their own identity and parentage, about their relationship to the agency and to the succession of workers and boarding parents who pass in and out of their lives.

Having seen what happens to children in foster care whose parents desert them, it is clear that foster care is at best a substitute measure and should never be an end in itself. Neither foster homes nor institutions can provide the security and affection children need. A child cannot defend himself against the tragic loss of his home and family. So it is the agency in whose care he has been placed that must take responsibility for helping him build a new life. Many of these children need a permanent home and family such as adoption offers.

For the scope of this book emphasis is upon adoptions. Our focus, therefore, comes to be upon the small group of children whose chance for a "normal" life is salvaged after family breakup. If separation from parents could be avoided, there would be no adoptions. And if we did not believe that the child's own home was of the greatest value to him, we could not hold the convictions we do as to the worthwhileness and seriousness of creating a new "own home" for him.

Present practice considers adoption a good plan for many of these children but not necessarily a perfect plan, nor the only possible one. Adoption concerns the child, the natural parents of the child, the adoptive parents, and the community.

Who among these homeless children is adoptable? The standards for considering a child adoptable have changed over the years. Formerly agencies believed that the child was adoptable if "normal" both physically and mentally. But a physician recently said that we must not search for the mythical goal of normality in children; none of us can define what "normal" is. We must help each child in his own way to develop his potentialities.

Adoption agencies now believe that even a handicapped child with no home of his own is entitled to be placed for adoption if the right home can be found for him. In a workshop on adoption held in 1948, the Child Welfare League of America defined the adoptable child as "any child who needs a family and who can develop in it, and for whom a family can be found that can accept the child with its physical or mental capacities".

In adoption the welfare of the child is of paramount importance. With the advance in knowledge of what is essential in childhood for healthy physical and mental growth the concept of what constitutes a "fit and proper" home has changed also. The evaluation of families for adoptive placement of a child is becoming more flexible and less arbitrary. The "perfect family" is no longer the objective although the prospective adoptive home must be one in which a child can develop a healthy personality. The adoptive parents must be compatible and have a reasonably stable relationship. They must both fully accept the idea of adopting a child.

The prospective adoptive parents must also have confidence in the agency's ability to select a child for them. They need to be free to share with the agency their past experiences, their feelings, their attitudes, problems and goals as well as their desires for a child. Such honest sharing is possible if there is a joint conviction that a successful, happy parent-child relationship depends upon their combined efforts. Mutual confidence between agency and adoptive applicants can then exist.

To achieve this confidence the agency worker needs to acknowledge that each family is different and that the agency is not seeking perfect families; to explain agency policies and procedures; and to share each step as they move along so that the family knows what the worker is doing and why. Only when this kind of relationship exists can the caseworker use this period of getting acquainted with the adoptive family to help them become better prepared for a child by adoption and thereby facilitate the placement and later integration of a child into the adoptive family.

While adopting parents should assume the normal risks involved in natural parenthood, a careful assessment of the potentialities of the child and of the adoptive home is essential. This practice increases the probability of the development of satisfactory relationships in the newly established family.

9

The community, too, has a stake in seeing that good adoption resources are available and children placed in suitable homes through approved procedures. If such resources are not available, many children who could be placed for adoption will remain in foster care so long that they are too old for adoption or are unable to adjust to a substitute home. There is also the danger that individuals will attempt to meet the lack of resources by themselves trying to serve as placement agencies. Some of these individuals are motivated by the desire to help an unmarried mother or a prospective adoptive family. Others, prompted only by a financial motive, dispose of the baby to the family willing to pay the highest price. Neither of these situations assures that a proper evaluation of the home and the child has been made and placement considered on the basis of desirability for this child.

Community responsibility for effective service rests upon the cooperation of doctors, lawyers, ministers, hospital administrators, nurses and members of other groups serving parents. Community interest needs to be expressed in good legislation and the demand for competently administered programs which keep the public, including unmarried parents, aware of all the services that relate to the complex adoption process.

Social service must be identified in the community. It is the thread that is woven throughout the adoption process and links the child, his natural family background, the adopting parents, and the community participants.

Good placement of children available for adoption depends upon good social service. Continuity and consistency in planning for the child are not possible without it. Agencies offering adoption service should have enough well-trained workers to help natural parents at the time service can be most useful in working through their problems and planning for their children. These workers should obtain appropriate information about the child, his background, physical health, emotional stability and intelligence. The social agency should also be the contact point for adopting parents. The homefinding workers should assure a reservoir of approved adoptive homes so that no child available for adoption will be held in a boarding home because a suitable home is not available for him. They should study the prospective adoptive parents to determine their physical and mental health, motives for wanting a child, their personality characteristics, relationships with one another, and capacity to be parents.

10

Only on the basis of such information can the adoption agency bring together the child and the family who show the best promise of mutual happiness.

In addition to having funds for adequate staff, social agencies need sufficient financial resources to provide or arrange for medical care, hospitalization and shelter care or foster care for unmarried mothers, as well as temporary boarding home care for a child available for adoption until a plan for his placement is completed.

Communities need social agencies staffed to perform these functions. Their services in the community need to be widely interpreted and understood.

No one article can cover all the concepts in the basic philosophy of adoption underlying the practice of approved agencies. The following articles have been selected because they discuss pertinent principles and processes of adoption placement as related to the community, natural and adoptive parents, the child and the appropriate social agencies.

The Adoption Worker's Role and His Personality in the Professional Adoption Process

SARABELLE McCLEERY

When I accepted the responsibility of discussing the role of the adoption worker and his personality in the adoption process, my thoughts raced over a wide variety of factors and circumstances: the work with the child, with his natural parents, and with prospective adoptive parents; interrelationships between these people; interrelationships between the social worker and these people. With impatience at our mortal limitations, we seek the improved skills and the greater knowledge that will make this possible. The goal is to establish a constructive love relationship between individuals who are strangers. What does the adoption worker do?

The Story of Gretchen, Jimmy and the Grahams

About a year ago a 20-year-old unmarried girl came to our office accompanied by a distant relative. Gretchen was only 4'2" in height. She was pregnant and was suffering with edema, so that she seemed excessively misshapen. She was carrying a large suitcase which almost dragged on the floor. Her obvious distress aroused the sympathy of everyone who saw her. As the adoption worker put it, "She had the saddest expression—as if the misery of the ages rested upon her." Gretchen was in urgent need of

12

help. She had not been to a doctor; she had to find some place to live until the baby came; she was in a state of panic over her condition. We were able to relieve some of her anxiety about the future and get her established promptly in a foster home, under the care of a doctor.

As we came to know Gretchen better in the weeks that followed, she told us she had become an orphan at the age of three, had lived in a children's institution until she was eight, and then had lived in a series of foster boarding homes. She had never felt that she belonged to any of these families and had sought out her own relatives as soon as she was free to do so. The baby's father was a boy she had known for years in school, but he was offering no help to her. She did not want any plan but adoption for the child.

In the foster home Gretchen became an immediate favorite. The foster mother and the other girls staying there commented on her bright and sunny disposition, and her ability to put others at ease regarding her handicap.

Gretchen was the only member of her large family who was not of normal size. She was dwarfed by a congenital handicap of short arms and legs. She told us that her dwarfism had never interfered with anything she wanted to do except, as she added with a smile, she had not been accepted as a telephone operator. She was a high school graduate, and up to the time she came to us she had been taking a post graduate course in secretarial work.

Gretchen's baby was born by Caesarean section. He was a fine, 9½ pound boy, a healthy youngster with a good cry and a strong body. The medical examination revealed that he was a dwarf like his mother.

So here we have a newborn infant with the need that all babies have for tender, consistent, loving care. Here we have Jimmy, a child relinquished by his mother, belonging to no one except as the agency can find for him his place in the world. Here is Jimmy, a child with a permanent physical handicap, requiring a special adjustment process if he is to become a constructive and useful member of the community. Here is Jimmy—and here is the adoption worker.

Now couples applying to an agency make plans and they daydream even as do families who have their babies in the usual way. Many will say longingly, "We want a child who can go through college," or, "We want a girl for the first one," or, "We want a boy who will enjoy outdoor life like we do." In

13

getting acquainted, the adoption worker is faced with the difficult task of deciding whether the family's description of the desired child means, "We want a child and we hope he will be thus and so," or, "We want a child only if he is thus and so." Some families will explain that they are not particular; "All we want is a healthy, normal child." However, when this wish is explored, one usually finds that each person has his own definition of "normal" which is quite different from the wide variety of "normal" children found in most school and church groups. There are some families who say that they will take any child, and while this can mean a basic acceptance of a wide variety of children, it can mean many other things, even that they have been so defeated by life, or their attempts to adopt, that they expect no more than second, or even fourth, best.

In looking for a home for Jimmy, we reviewed all of our most promising applications, and finally decided that we would approach the Grahams, who seemed to have qualities basic to good adoptive parenthood, that is,—warmth in personality; secure and loving marital relationships; a mutual desire for children; reliable employment, income, housing; and wholesome attitudes toward adoption. Although they wanted a young child the Grahams had asked to be told about any child who might need them and there seemed to be a genuine spontaneity and flexibility in their attitude. The adoption worker was convinced that had Jimmy been born to the Grahams they would have made excellent parents for him. Nevertheless, they were not expecting to adopt a child with a severe handicap, and probably would question their own ability or wish to take on such a responsibility.

The adoption worker knew he could place Jimmy in a temporary foster boarding home for observation and study, and while this would not offer the child the advantages of unbroken and continuing parental ties, good care could be assured. However, one of the factors that contributes to the depth of love felt by many parents is the emotional realization of the complete dependence and helplessness of the infant and his need of them. The impact of this often is greatest as they assume responsibility for their newborn child. For Jimmy, even more than for children less obviously handicapped, every assistance would be needed to help him find a place in the hearts of new parents. Therefore, after much earnest discussion within the office, the adoption worker decided to inquire about the Grahams' interest before Jimmy was moved from the hospital.

In his initial telephone call to the Grahams, about Jimmy, the adoption worker explained that he would like to discuss with them a newborn infant who had a severe handicap. The family naturally wanted more information over the telephone, but they were asked to postpone the discussion until the office interview. This was done to avoid any decision being reached prematurely without an opportunity for full expression of feeling.

When the Grahams came in to keep their appointment the adoption worker described the situation in simple, factual terms, avoiding technical language. He explained that although the shortened arms and legs as yet were not noticeable to any but the expert, the condition would become apparent as the child grew older. He stated that Jimmy's physical handicap had nothing to do with the mentality or other personal characteristics except as these are affected by attitudes. The Grahams were delighted at the prospect of having a child, but, as one would expect, they were very uncertain about this condition. They asked many questions and discussed their feelings with great frankness. When Mr. Graham recalled a fellow townsman, also dwarfed, who earned an adequate living as a filling station operator, they said they wanted to see the child and that they thought they would want to take him. They knew that other children would be available to them if they decided against taking him.

Jimmy at five days was an unusually pretty baby, and the Grahams were delighted by the personality he already seemed to have. They discovered with pleasure the dimple in his chin, and the feel of his soft brown hair. They asked innumerable questions about the immediate care of a young infant, laughed at themselves for their earlier confidence in theoretical knowledge and their present fear at the sight of a tiny breakable body. Finding themselves increasingly sure that they wanted to take the baby, they returned to another discussion of how to handle the handicap. They were prepared for the words that would be used by doctors and other professional persons and the meanings of these words were explained. Suggestions were given for telling relatives and friends most intimately acquainted with them. The family decided they wanted to take the child immediately, and described practical arrangements. These were satisfactory and the Grahams were allowed to proceed as they suggested.

In the months that followed, the family found that they had many complicated feelings and used the adoption worker consistently. Their attachment for Jimmy, however, did not lessen and love ties grew deeper. To the adoption worker they described with delight the magic they saw in a child's growth. They were encouraged to use other community resources also. A local college professor was teaching a course on working with the handicapped child and the Grahams enrolled, explaining that they were adopting a handicapped child. The attitude of their doctor was helpful to them. Although he did not minimize the condition, he told them that in an independent arrangement this condition might not have been noticed until much later and that the family taking the child would have been caught unprepared.

Jimmy's adoption has not yet been completed in court, but there is every indication that he has a secure place in the hearts of his new parents and that everything possible will be done to help him. Aside from the shortened arms and legs, he has been a healthy youngster, and one much praised by friends and relatives. As the Grahams tell the adoption worker of the problems they are preparing to face, these seem minor to their joy in having him. They describe in detail how much richer and more meaningful life is to them now than ever before.

Planning with Natural Parents

What did the adoption worker do? First, of course, came the work with Gretchen. Not all agencies are like the one in which I work in having both an adoption service, and a full program of maternity and case work service to the unmarried mother, whatever her plan for the child may be. How best to help the confused or hostile unmarried mother, and at the same time to protect the interests of the child, is a full topic in itself and will not be discussed here. However, when an agency's function with the natural parents is limited to work regarding possible adoption, the adoption worker still has the responsibility of preserving and strengthening constructive relationships between parent and child when they exist; or, if separation is the plan, he has the responsibility of taking the relinquishment in the most helpful fashion.

In Jimmy's situation the child himself had little meaning to the mother. He was incidental compared to the overwhelming disappointment she was experiencing in her desperate attempts to secure some real place for herself in the lives and hearts of other people. Not even in her fantasies was she seeing herself as mothering a child. Relinquishment was accepted at the time

16

she wanted to give it, and work both before and after was directed toward lessening her sense of defeat and building toward a belief that she could have some control over her own destiny.

Planning for the Child

In our case illustration, what else did the adoption worker do? Obviously the main focus of his work was toward safeguarding Jimmy's future. In adoption service, the welfare of the child must come first. The primary responsibility of the adoption worker is to represent the interests of the child. He must know the needs of each youngster for whom he is responsible and be unswerving in his determination to secure for that child the best possible chance to grow up healthfully and happily. If Jimmy's worker had not known with deep emotional conviction both the needs of the infant who had lost his own parents and the special needs represented by Jimmy's handicap, his difficult task could have become an impossible one. He could have read into the condition of dwarfism a handicap over and above that of very short arms and legs. He could have felt such a conflict between the needs of the child and his conception of the needs of adopting parents that a stalemate would have resulted.

To relate to a number of children on an individual basis and with positive feeling requires a maximum of flexibility, but it is the only way to avoid the pitfalls in generalizations or labeling. Children needing adoption cover a broad range. There are infants and older children, members of majority and minority races, healthy and sick, handicapped and with superior bodies, slow learning and quick, those with emotional problems and those without, knock-kneed, crosseyed children, and children with musical talent and a good sense of rhythm. All of these terms fail to picture the child just as the hospital doctor's reference to "the kidney in Ward 3" fails to describe the whole patient. The caseworker's ability to see past the words to the child himself, to feel with the child, and not just about him, will, in a large measure, set the limit for his effectiveness in adoption work.

On occasion some aspect of the child's situation arouses the kind of personal feelings that make it hard to plan well. It may be difficult to consider on its merits the situation of a child, apparently white, with a mother who is white and a father who may be Negro, if the worker's feelings about race and prejudice divert his energies away from the child's need for a new home. Words like syphilis, feeble-minded, and insanity may evoke a response quite different than if descriptive statements were used. Jimmy's handicap is an open invitation for the adoption worker to project whatever unsolved problems he might have in that area.

When children become hard to place because of the worker's personal feelings, certain things can be done. The opportunity for projections will be lessened as speculation is replaced by knowledge. The knowledge that one is not expected to know all about a child nor to predict the future will bring relief from anxiety for many. For others, it will help to know in specific detail the meaning of a particular condition that exists or is expected to develop. For instance, when Paul's epilepsy is recognized as "a tendency to convulse which can be controlled by medication," it may assume the realistic proportion of a particular illness and be less likely to create the fantasy of the poorly dressed man writhing on the sidewalk, foaming at the mouth, surrounded by a crowd. Being specific in making descriptions and avoiding generalizations will help the worker individualize the child and his particular situation.

Probably some elements of projection will always be present in inter-personal relationships, but they assume great importance in adoption work. In many respects the child is an "X" quantity, an unknown. Until the life is lived no one knows what it will be. No amount of information can guarantee a certain appearance, a hidden talent, or a specified rate or kind of development. Physical condition, whether it be good or poor, a handicap and the way it affects a child's functioning, the ability or lack of ability to learn, are all things that apply to the current situation. Except for a very few circumstances, they are subject to change. In addition, modern genetics teaches us that while much is inherited, no tests have been devised to make it possible to predict in advance which genes will be carried by an individual offspring. Into this unknown, it is natural for the adoption worker to project whatever may be his own attitudes. His expectations regarding a child will be influenced by his feelings about handicaps, heredity, backgrounds different from his own, and social classes. Even in areas where facts are available, projections will be at work, and the worker's handling of a situation will be influenced by feelings stemming from his own early experiences. For instance, in the study of prospective homes, a worker may seek to find for children the things he felt missing in his own upbringing, or he may try to duplicate for the children what he had felt to be happy and satisfying. Obviously, the goal is not to avoid personal feelings but to guide them into channels most useful to the children the adoption worker is trying to help. He will want to use all resources available to bring this about. These would include supervision, use of psychological and psychiatric consultants, and psychotherapy, if indicated.

Planning with the Child.

Jimmy's story tells little of the preplacement work which is essential to help the older child move comfortably into adoption. Jimmy was an infant with his life ahead of him, but many children available for adoption are three, six, eight or even thirteen years old. They bring to the situation a tangled accumulation of experiences and attitudes that can interfere with the capacity to respond to new parents with positive feelings.

The older child needs to come to an understanding of his past and to a sure knowledge that he cannot remain with his natural parents, or with the foster parents with whom he is living. He needs to know this definitely or he can feel, in a sense, kidnapped. To free a child from the clinging hands of the past, and to equip him to go on to a more constructive, happy future, requires skill of the highest order. The whole process must be designed to increase his sense of self-worth and to keep him from feeling helpless in the grasp of strange, even unfriendly forces. To do this the worker must have the courage to face the truth with him without evasion, even if it involves pain. The worker may be the first person in his experience to give the child honest facts and help him find his own sense of direction.

I remember the work with one six-year-old girl who urgently wanted to belong to someone and more than the average youngster was able to express her wishes in words, begging the worker to hurry and find the new home. The worker was keenly aware of how much the child was suffering by being the least favored one in the temporary foster boarding home, and he knew that if placement were delayed she might fall back into unrealistic fantasies that her own mother would re-establish a home for her. Already the caseworker had faced the difficult task of helping the child face the painful truth that while the mother made many promises and brought beautiful presents, she would never take the daughter to live with her. Despite these facts the adoption worker, in arranging the meeting of child and new parents, was able to keep himself free to handle developments as they arose and not to promise an emotional relationship before it developed. This was imperative if the child was to learn to put her trust in real values and not relegate the worker to the role of the mother who promised things which might or might not develop.

Planning with Adoptive Applicants

In addition to the work with natural parents, the planning for and work with the child, what additional responsibilities does the adoption worker have? As we saw in the story of Jimmy, there is the work with the prospective parents, with adoptive applicants. Although the Grahams may not have been average, neither were they atypical. During the study a constructive relationship based on mutual trust and confidence developed between the worker and the family. While this was put to a greater test here than in some other situations, such a relationship is always the goal.

It is significant, however, that although the adoption worker liked the Grahams very much, he did not lose the focus of his professional task. He was sympathetically attuned to the family's interests and wishes, but, although he felt with them, he did not confuse their wishes with his own. This too easily could mean finding for a family the child one would like to have oneself. We see the dangers there. If as a child, an individual had received a great deal of pressure to achieve in intellectual areas, he might basically feel, even though he knew better, that to be loved a child must be bright and must achieve. The same thing could be true of other qualities. Each family will be different, each caseworker will be different, in the variety of personal qualities considered important.

An attorney once posed the question to me, "If you have a family equally suitable for an average infant and for a problem four-year-old boy, which child would you give them?" The implication, of course, was that the family might be penalized for the breadth of their interest by being given the difficult child. I talked with him about how these confusions are lessened when first consideration is given to the needs of the child. If, as he said, the family were equally suitable for the four-year-old and the infant, it must mean that they had the capacity to love each child deeply and to gain satisfaction from the care of each. In that event we would work toward the placement of the child who most needed them. It might mean the infant or the older child, depending on other homes available. As well as benefiting the child, this approach gives the greatest advantage to adoptive applicants. If a family with an interest in a broad range of children takes the child which can readily be accepted by many families and it is impossible to find a good home for the other child, the result is one couple instead of two receiving children.

However, the role of the adoption worker with prospective parents is a much more complicated one than might seem from a statement of first principles,—that the child comes first. The adoptive applicant is more than a resource for children to be taken on or discarded casually as he is or is not needed. The adoptive applicant is a client of the social agency and the method of receiving his application, the method of acceptance or denial of the request, can play a helpful role in his life or a destructive one. In addition, as the adoption worker is able to feel with the applicant, to clarify and hopefully dissipate hidden anxieties, to build on strengths already present, the individual is prepared for his role of adoptive parent, and the worker finds secure homes for the children he has to place.

As was stated earlier, many families in coming to an agency limit their application much more than did the Grahams. This is inconsistent with the conscious thought of most that they only want the opportunity for parenthood that nature has denied them. Occasionally families have some awareness of this as they say, perhaps in jest, "We really take less risk in adopting a child than in having one of our own." This is true, of course, for defective children needing custodial care are not offered for adoption, and in addition, families have the right to take or reject any child offered to them. However, in and of themselves, the children available for adoption are no different than children not separated from their own families. The crosseyed child, the child with a clubfoot, or even the defective child, could have been born to the adoptive applicant. The new parents might or might not have the internal resources to deal adequately with the situation, but in trying to have a child by birth that was the risk they took.

Since most families do not overemphasize the risk involved in having a child of their own, what is it about adoption that is different? We must recognize that most conscientious families bring to parenthood some degree of anxiety. The term, "little stranger", frequently used to describe the expected or newborn child, expresses some of this. Parents can worry about what this

21

new member of the family will be like and they can worry about their own ability to live up to the demands of good parenthood. The feeling of strangeness is diminished, however, as husband and wife dream of the child carrying the features or the qualities of one another. Because they feel they know themselves, to some extent they feel they know the child. Out of their self love and their love for one another, and out of their desire to complete their union with children, a little nest of protective love can be already prepared by the time the child arrives. Should a handicap be present, the new parents will be sorry, but will do everything they can to overcome the difficulty. The child is part of them.

Consider the difference in adopting a child. These prospective parents cannot reassure themselves by looking at one another. In fact, their beliefs and feelings about the kind of people who release their children for adoption or have them taken away by courts can make their speculations anything but reassuring. Their attitudes toward adoption may be further complicated by their feelings about their inability to have children of their own. Sterility, the inability to carry on life to the next generation, offers a basic threat to many persons. The adopted child may be a constant reminder of failure, instead of being a reminder of happiness. There are many sources for parent-child conflict when children are born into a family. When children are adopted, few of these are removed and several new ones are added.

Families may not recognize the anxiety but feel relief when all goes well. Some do not apply for second children, saying they feel they "hit the jackpot" with the first one and do not want to "push their luck" too far.

Some couples will compensate for their underlying uneasiness by denying all worry. Others will set rigid qualifications for the child they would accept. Sometimes the attitudes toward the natural parents, toward sterility, toward children's problems, toward illegitimacy, lie deep in personality structure and are not readily accessible to change. Other times feelings shift as the adoption worker has an accepting attitude and at the same time gives true facts regarding the events that lead to a child's needing adoption and about the influences of heredity, facts which sometimes fill in the unknown and make the process seem less strange.

Depending on the evaluation of the prospective parents and their deep needs in an adopted child, on the number and kind of children needing homes, and on the number and quality of other applications, a family may or may not receive a child. Although the attitude of the adoption worker may serve to relieve some of the applicant's feelings of self blame or failure if a child is not placed, the focus is not therapy, and care must be taken to preserve the defenses a couple may have built up to protect themselves.

The Placement Process

When the adoption worker is aware of the needs of the child to be placed, and the needs of the prospective family, he is ready for the next step, which will bring these lives together, hopefully in ever-deepening bonds of love and respect. To discuss a particular child with the family is to continue the process begun in the study. Facts about background, health, and development of a specific child in some instances may help the new family to feel acquainted. Sometimes couples who have been very comfortable in thinking in general terms about adoption find unexpected and indeed unpleasant feelings coming to consciousness when confronted with the prospect of a flesh and blood child. Here the adoption worker can help by taking time to explore the meaning of these reactions, to free the family to turn down the child, if indicated, or to help them to resolve their feelings in other ways before the new relationship is established. Just as Jimmy's worker did not attempt to answer for the Grahams, so always the adoption worker must leave the family free to reach its own decision. This does not mean a cold or uninterested attitude. Warmth and sentiment help to tide over the interval before the "little stranger" becomes the son or daughter, but an urgency on the part of the worker can confuse the family's natural feeling for the child.

The time of placement usually is a compromise or adjustment between the needs of the child and the needs of the family. Jimmy, as you recall, was placed directly from the hospital, because for him and the Grahams this promised the most security for the future. For most infants fully relinquished by the natural parents, placement from the hospital without a break in love ties for the child might be desirable, if it were not for the fact that many adoptive applicants do not feel sufficiently comfortable with adoption to deal without rejection with whatever complications may arise. Many new parents are less anxious when they know how a child has developed up to a certain point while under study. In addition, the time limitations imposed by hospital placements do not permit the relaxed consideration of a specific child that often is needed, nor is the planning with the natural parents often completed that early. With older children it may be necessary to have considerable time in a study situation before the children are ready to take on new parents.

Post Placement Work

During the period of supervision in the home before the adoption is completed legally, although the adoption worker still represents the child, he can be helpful only as he has equal respect for the feelings of the new family. In the case of Jimmy, the worker needed to help the Grahams with their feelings and to guide them toward the best methods of dealing with the situation. The family knew that the adoption worker would not be disappointed in them if they were ambivalent, and they knew he would not in any way force them to complete an adoption. Sometimes, particularly with older children, direct work with the child is still necessary after placement and here, too, the adoption worker cannot take sides, as it were, with either parent or child.

The Adoption Worker

As we look over the things the adoption worker is expected to do, we can see that, in addition to professional knowledge, definite personality qualities are required within the professional discipline. The nature and variety of his responsibilities often are such as to put him under considerable pressure. There may be more to do than the time available allows. Regardless of volume, the work being done often takes a heavy toll of psychic energy. For some the weight of responsibility has this effect. For others, it is the necessity of forming an individual relationship with a constantly shifting group of very different people who do not present ther needs in an orderly fashion. One person may find it takes considerable effort to assume a leadership role with parent substitutes because the natural tendency is to be passive. Another may have to push himself to move a child from the study home and expose him to possible rejection. The adoption worker must find a way of handling his anxieties so that they will not be passed on to the children or the parents. He must have confidence in the values of adoption. He must have a warm interest in other people and yet not place fetters on their emotions. Psychological hurdles will vary with each adoption worker. Crossing them always takes energy, and when there is any volume of them he may be too emotionally fatigued to make the best use of his professional skills.

In addition, community attitudes, methods of financing, financial limitations, and state laws regarding guardianship have a direct bearing on what the worker can do. For instance, in some places it would not have been possible to work freely with Gretchen in terms of planning for the baby until the ultimate plan was definitely known.

Both supervision and administration have a direct contribution to make to the effectiveness of performance. Decisions regarding specialized or diversified caseloads or procedures in handling the volume of adoptive applicants in a large agency require total agency action and cannot be the sole responsibility of any one caseworker. Competent supervision can provide a framework to relieve some anxiety, to share responsibility and to help the adoption worker see trends in his work which may indicate personality bias.

All of these things—professional information and skill, dynamics of agency functioning and personality factors go into making the future for thousands of Jimmies. Jimmy was used to illustrate the role of the adoption worker, not because of his handicap, but because he is essentially an ordinary child. He is ordinary even in the fact that there is something very special about him—even as there is something special about every child.

CHAPTER 2

Principles, Values, and Assumptions
Underlying Adoption Practice

JOSEPH H. REID

No field of practice in social work is more before the public, more sensitive, or more controversial than adoption. It is a subject that arouses strong prejudices, suspicions, and emotions. A senate committee investigates adoption. Many medical and bar associations have established committees on adoption or have taken stands pro and con. Columnists who rarely turn to social welfare for subject matter, such as Sokolsky, Pegler, and others, write heatedly and at length concerning adoption. Practically every national magazine has within the last year carried one or more articles on this subject. TV and radio have found the subject of such public interest that in addition to many public service programs, several commercial programs have appeared, with at least two producers considering commercially sponsored series. Adoption unquestionably touches upon the basic interests and values of the American public.

Much of the writing about adoption is hostile to adoption agencies, and it seems fair to assume that such writing reflects the common opinion of at least a large segment of the American public. Either the public disagrees with the assumptions, principles, and values that are held by social work in respect to adoption or else they do not understand them. I choose to believe that the latter is the case: that it is not clear to the public what social agencies stand for in their adoption practice, and why they believe that certain conditions are more conducive to the welfare of the child and the public than others. For that matter, it is also true that social workers themselves have often been confused about their values and practices and only in recent years has a clear rationale been developed that can be supported with conviction.

Adoption agencies are a creature of the public, not just in the sense that they are financially supported by the public, but more importantly, that society has created agencies to fulfill its responsibility to children. If for no other reason, adoption agencies, and the profession that is engaged in adoption, have a pressing responsibility to clarify their values and principles and to make them known. The only way that adoption services can be strengthened and extended to every child who needs them is for the public to understand clearly and to accept the rationale that lies behind the practices of social agencies. Are the values on which we build a basic professional practice unacceptable to the public? Are social workers completely out of line in their thinking? This seems doubtful. Though there is confusion and lack of clarity (as in any other developing scientific discipline, there have been false starts and false premises), the basic things that the profession stands for deserve and can get support from the body politic.

Assumptions

Let us examine some of the assumptions on which the practices of adoption agencies are based.

1. The necessity of having adoption agencies rests on the fact that adoption is not and should not be a private matter. Society in general is concerned with every adoption and has a responsibility to protect all concerned. Children should not be passed privately from hand to hand without society, through the state as *parens patriae,* taking responsibility to see that the child is protected.

2. The three parties involved in every adoption have rights and must be assured certain protection, both through legal measures and the responsible administration of services by social agencies, to which the state, acting in its welfare function, has delegated the responsibility for the welfare of children.

3. The administration of social agencies requires professional

27

skills and understanding that have been developed historically in the field of social work. Therefore, basic responsibility for the administration of such agencies rests with professionally trained and experienced social workers who utilize the help and professional knowledge of several other disciplines.

4. Every child needs and has the right to have his own parents and the first obligation of society is to make it possible for him to grow up with his own people in his own home. No child should be unnecessarily deprived of his own parents.

5. The child's need for continuous and loving care and guidance is essential to his well-being and development and to the future of the nation. If the child's own parents are unable or cannot be helped to give the care that is expected for children, it must be provided by others.

6. The purpose of adoption is to provide for each child who has been permanently deprived of a family of his own and who can benefit by family life a home in which he will have the opportunity for healthy personality development.

For many reasons these assumptions are not always clear and have not been sufficiently interpreted to the community which itself created adoption services and to which the administering agencies are accountable.

Principles

Out of the knowledge and experience gained from social work and other fields dealing with children, parents, and child-parent relationships, certain principles have evolved that are guides to practice. Their aim is to carry out the purpose of adoption as conceived by the community which has created adoption services. Among these is the belief that, as a practice, there needs to be casework determination of the needs of the child, the natural parents, and the adoptive parents before a sound adoptive placement can be made. Second, that it is sound practice to place the infant in his adoptive home just as early as possible, consistent with the determination that his parents have come to a firm decision concerning his release. Third, that there are certain essential qualities for parenthood and potential adoptive parents should possess these qualities. And, finally, that the agency has responsibilities to the child, to the adoptive parents, and to the natural parents.

Everything that is done must be in the child's best interest, but the natural parents must be free from duress or pressure in making the decision. The adoptive parents must have an equal chance with others as they seek a child. All three parties to the adoption must be protected in regard to confidentiality.

Values

Social workers hold certain ideas of what is good for children. These represent their own values, which may or may not be consistent with the values of others, and often are, in fact, in conflict with them. For example, the capacity of adoptive parents for giving love and receiving love, for exercising parental responsibility is placed far above wealth or social status. Wealth or status is not accepted as an indication that a couple will be good adoptive parents. Therefore, we attempt to free adoption agencies from all outside pressures. We believe that the only sound motivation for adopting a child is the desire to live a full life, to accept parental responsibility, to love and be loved. We reject as invalid such motivations as providing an heir for a childless family or attempting to strengthen a shaky marriage. Our focus is on the well-being of the child. Sometimes this focus is in direct conflict with the values of religious groups which, though just as concerned with the well-being of the child, may place spiritual considerations far above temporal considerations. For example, many social workers reject the concept that if a home cannot be found for a child of his own religious faith, he should not be placed in a good home of another faith, even though it means that he will be permanently deprived of living in a family group as their own child.

There is, of course, a long list of other assumptions and principles and values that surround adoption practice, some of which are just emerging clearly. Many of them have grown out of historical accidents and the community and culture in which we live because social workers are part of that community and that culture. The existence of conflicting principles and practices can be accounted for in part as we look at the history of adoption and the culture out of which it has grown.

Historical Background

Perhaps the area that reflects the greatest confusion in the minds of adoption workers, and for that matter the general public, is the role of the agency in regard to the adoptive parents themselves. Are they clients? Are they people who are doing the child and the agency a favor by agreeing to adopt him? Or are they people for whom the agency is performing a valuable service? Before that question can be answered, it is well to look at history.

Only a few short years have transpired from the time when agencies did not have adoptive applicants rushing to adopt every normal white infant that became available. Twenty or thirty years ago, agencies had to go out and recruit adoptive parents for white infants; they had to try to "sell" the country on adoption. Attitudes toward illegitimacy, toward bringing children of different "blood" into the family set up strong barriers to adoption. So it was only natural for many social workers to believe (consciously or unconsciously) that the adoptive parents were doing the child and the agency a favor by adopting him. At that time agencies were certainly child centered and believed the purpose of adoption was to find a home for the child, and not children for homes. But regardless of their professed convictions, many probably had difficulty in resolving this principle with the shortage of adoptive applicants. Today we find the same attitude existing in respect to those who will adopt a so-called "hard-to-place" child—one has only to read the newspaper publicity given to a family that adopts several Eurasian children or a blind child, or a family of two or three children. Cultural attitudes, as reflected in the newspapers, indicate clearly that these adoptive parents are regarded as performing an extremely valuable public service. And who would question that parents who will go to great expense to correct a serious physical defect in a child or knowingly struggle through several years of difficult adjustment with a seriously disturbed child are not worthy of praise and are not doing something for their fellow men?

When this situation existed, not only in respect to the handicapped child but the normal white infant as well, it was only natural, in the effort to "sell" adoption, that agencies developed the "blue-ribbon attitude" which still, unfortunately, exists in many quarters. Agencies were convinced and attempted to convince the public that they could guarantee them a perfect child; that by coming to an agency, adoptive parents could be sure that the child was without physical, emotional, or mental defect; that his heredity was sound and adopting a child was a far less risky procedure than having one normally. If adoptive parents were doing a child a favor, it was only fair to guarantee them as good a child as could be found. Out of this attitude, or perhaps concurrent with it, developed a rationale, consisting of a series of rationalizations, that it was in the best interest of the child for him to be perfect and to match perfectly with a family. Agencies felt that, if the child was imperfect, if his physical defects or his emotional difficulties would make it difficult for him to be accepted by the adoptive family, he was in a sense unadoptable and it was better for him to be raised in a form of foster care other than adoption.

Principles and values got all mixed up with convictions, but to be fair, it is also true that other disciplines buttressed the attitudes of social agencies during this period. Noted psychologists, Gesell among others, assured the agencies that their tests did permit accurate prediction of what the child would be like in later years; in other words, guaranteeing the adoptive parents a perfect child. Certain geneticists also led adoption agencies astray and there is no question that for many years doctors, particularly pediatricians, were very conservative in recommending the adoption of any child with a physical defect.

But unfortunately this mixture of realities—a shortage of adoptive parents, prejudice in respect to illegitimacy, and invalid predictions on the basis of psychological testing—was not seen as transitory. Rather, adoption agencies developed from them certain very strong convictions. Out of them came certain principles of practice relating to adoptability that we now reject. The fact of our rejection, however, will not enable agencies to escape condemnation for the public's belief that they will not, for example, place cross-eyed children. It will be a long time before the general public is aware that agencies have changed their principles and convictions.

Shifts in Cultural Attitudes

Broad cultural considerations have deeply affected the principles and convictions of agencies. It may be trite to say that all of us live within our culture and cannot divorce ourselves from it, but it is important to recognize that attitudes toward children in the United States have changed quite rapidly in the last three or four decades. Children have an unusual place in our culture compared with others. It is not too far-fetched to say that we are comparable to certain primitive cultures in the South Seas in the way we view children as the *raison d'etre* of our civilization. Paradoxically, as the child lost economic value, he gained social value. Children are no longer thought of as chattels to be passed by deed from one family to another. The parents' rights in regard to their children are sharply curtailed by public opinion and law, even though some people believe they should be still further curtailed (*e.g.*, Pearl Buck). A family in the United States is not considered complete or meaningful unless it has children. Childless couples have a multiplicity and diversity of pressures upon them to have children while large families are becoming respectable. In fairness, it can be said that it is not socially acceptable not to have them. But on a deeper level, in a troubled and anxious world, we have come to realize that there are few things more basic than the pleasure of contributing to the development of another human being, to love and be loved by a child. All religions of our Western civilization regard the reason for the family as being for the nurture of children.

The child, too, is actually a symbol that our cultural opportunities are not static. It is not only the immigrant who believes that in his children he will find fulfillment, that his child will have opportunities and therefore accomplishments far beyond those he could have had. Again it is not trite to say that in our culture children are the hope of the future (and at times an escape from the present).

These and many other shifts in cultural attitudes have contributed to a shift in the attitudes of agencies. The adoptive parents today are not doing a child a favor by adopting him. Rather, they are seen as people who are fulfilling themselves and enriching their own lives by the process of adoption. But because agencies see it this way is no reason to believe that the average adoptive parent sees it this way, too. Many do, of course, but many others approach adoption agencies feeling generous and philanthropic. Therefore, when they cannot find a child or are rejected, their reaction is strong. The press has already reflected this in articles headed, ''Why You Can't Get a Child,'' or ''Why You Can Get a Child,'' which have replaced, ''Open Up Your Heart to a Child,'' or ''Have You Room for One More?''

Principles Have Changed

And so principles have changed with these attitudes. Today most good agencies have completely dropped guarantees of a perfect baby. The ''blue-ribbon'' concept is outmoded. But more important, the agencies themselves have developed the conviction that they do not have a responsibility to guarantee a perfect child. Rather, they see what the general public probably saw before they did—that having children naturally or through adoption involves risk. There are no guarantees in life and there is no reason for adoption to be an exception. So we have articles on ''Babies for the Brave'' or we have agencies with confidence explaining what can be ascertained through medical and other examinations and what cannot. We have agencies encouraging people to take risks, and not minor risks, but very serious ones. Through the help of geneticists, anthropologists, and others, agencies can enable the parents to see precisely what the risk is.

Another influence, of course, is our present knowledge that known methods of psychological testing of infants have little predictive value except in identifying gross pathology. Therefore, even if agencies wanted to guarantee blue-ribbon babies, they could not. This is not to say that it would not be desirable to be able to predict with some accuracy what the child's mental capacities will be in later life. Perhaps some day psychological tests will be devised that will be of greater use. But the fact that they do not exist does not for a moment cloud adoption as a process of helping children and families. In essence, we have recognized the strength, the courage, and the fiber of families in America to accept what comes and also to be really accepting of less than perfect children. In essence, we have recognized the power of love.

There are other parallel influences that have affected the convictions and practices of agencies. A major one has been the research emanating from child development, psychiatry, and social work that has so clearly established during the past twenty years the importance of early mothering to a child. John Bowlby's brilliant summarization of this research has had a deep influence upon agencies.[1] As conviction developed of the paramount need to the child for an early and sustained one-to-one mothering relationship, other considerations were placed in perspective. For example, were a psychological test developed tomorrow that could predict when the infant was eight months of age what his later development would be with accuracy, it is doubtful that any good agency would use the test. The reason is that we realize how much more important early mothering is, and therefore early placement. Out of this conviction the principles of agencies are changing rapidly and all progressive agencies in the country are doing their utmost to lower the average age of placement to its irreducible minimum. That minimum still has very different meanings, as has been revealed by recent studies. For some agencies it means an average of three weeks of age. For others it is still unfortunately

---

[1] *Maternal Care and Mental Health* (New York: Columbia University Press, 1951).

four months, but a time will come very soon in which, except under unusual circumstances, an agency that has not managed to place its children well before three months of age will be considered guilty of poor practice.

Unmarried Mothers

Sometimes social workers hold a position that is essentially more conservative than that of a segment of the public. Some in our society for example, would remove children from all unmarried parents at birth because they cannot provide proper nurture for them. Such a procedure would not, however, be consistent with American principles, law, and culture. In spite of this, however, it is necessary that agencies examine all the values that exist in our culture and develop convictions of practice, points of view that take them into consideration. For example, the pendulum of social work attitudes in respect to the unmarried mother has swung wildly during the past few decades. There was a time when the attitudes of many of our churches and agencies were extremely punitive toward the unmarried mother. The scarlet letter of Hawthorne has still not disappeared from view.

Perhaps as a reaction to this in the thirties and early forties, there was a too-permissive and nondirective attitude toward the unmarried mother. Agencies believed they were guilty of prejudice if they did anything but let the mother make up her own mind. Now, as can be observed in most good agencies, it is necessary to have a point of view in respect to work with unmarried mothers. An agency has a responsibility to point out to the unmarried mother the extreme difficulty, if she remains unmarried, of raising her child successfully in our culture without damage to the child and to herself. Such a fact must affect our principles in working with the unmarried mother in respect to the disposition of her child. It is not an unwarranted interference with the unmarried mother to presume that in most cases it will be in the child's best interests for her to release her child for adoption. There still exists a great deal of fuzzy thinking around this subject. The concept that the unmarried mother and her child constitute a family is to me unsupportable. There is no family in any real sense of the word.

The concept that the unmarried mother has an absolute right for self-determination is to me fallacious, too, because there are many situations in the case of a family of an unmarried mother,

34

in which the interests of the various members of the family so conflict that the agency has to make a choice in counseling the family in order to protect one member as against the other. In our set of values, we have to accept the fact that when a child is involved and there is a conflict between the interests of the mother or father and the child, the situation must always be resolved, if possible, in the child's favor. In work with the unmarried mother, her emotional needs, her motivations, her desires cannot be given paramount consideration as against the needs of the child and in some situations, perhaps in many, the mother herself may suffer a loss for the sake of the child. Of course, we strive to help the mother see that her interests and the child's interests are indivisible and that she should proceed from this base in making her choice. However, without a point of view on this an agency flounders.

Agencies have also reached conviction about the position of the adoptive parent. Certainly, as child welfare agencies, they have not been established primarily for the purpose of providing services to help the childless. Basically, they are child-centered agencies to find homes for children needing adoption. To be sure, when the adoptive applicant first comes to the agency, he comes for a service and the agency has to interpret what service it can render for him and differentiate it from giving or withholding a child. As long as adoptive parents feel that agencies exist for the purpose of giving or withholding a child and that essentially agencies will simply look the adoptive parents over and decide whether they should have a child, the agency is not making its point of view clear, nor will it ever have a chance to build decent public understanding.

The job of the agency is to help adoptive applicants determine whether adoption is a solution for the needs and desires that brought them to the agency, and whether they are able to meet the needs of the kind of children for whom the agency needs homes, not whether they will be good parents. Helping the applicant decide and become an adoptive parent is a real service. The agency can also offer him the real service of selecting a child, within the knowledge and the limitations of that knowledge, whose needs this family can meet.

A third service the agency can render, which no one else is in a position to render, is to make certain that the child is really relinquished, that the adoptive parents are protected against intervention by the natural parents. Here its work with unmarried mothers or other natural parents is the key. It is not just a legal matter, but essentially a psychological one that requires the professional help of casework.

However, the agency must also have a real interest in the adoptive family's problem. For example, it should have expert knowledge concerning medical resources for helping the adoptive parent have children naturally. It is the agency's responsibility to assist the applicant in obtaining such help.

We could, of course, examine many other aspects of the assumptions, principles and values in adoption practice and of cultural and historical considerations that affect them. One that deserves mention is the influence of law upon adoption, particularly our common law which developed during a period of English history in which the parent was granted more absolute rights than we are willing to concede today. Agencies must have conviction about their principles—if the law needs changing, they have the responsibility to spearhead the movement to do so.

Clarification

Our first responsibility is, of course, to clarify our own position. Fortunately, the evidence is clear that adoption agencies regard this as a priority task. The National Conference on Adoption (1955) in which the practices of agencies were submitted to other disciplines was an important step toward clarification. The Adoption Standards Committee of the Child Welfare League, which has been meeting to enunciate standards and their rationale, clearly and unmistakably is another. Widespread efforts in many localities by agencies to meet with the two other professions most intimately involved in adoption (law and medicine) to examine varying principles and values is of deep importance. Citizens' committees, such as that in California, are another major step in the right direction, and the frankness with which social agencies, such as the New York State Department of Social Welfare, have discussed in the press the problems that confront them in finding homes for children, is extremely healthy.

When we seek to clarify our own principles and our own assumptions, it does not mean that we seek complete uniformity of practice, a solid front of procedure. Conformity is not desirable at this stage of human knowledge and should not be promoted as such. But to clarify values, to test them against the culture in which we live, is of major importance.

Most of us believe that children in a community will be

served best if all adoptions are completed through licensed adoption agencies. This makes it all the more necessary to make our convictions and beliefs clear to the public. When we ask society to vest one of its most fundamental responsibilities in any one type of organization, we can do so only if we have tested the way in which we propose to discharge that responsibility for the public. No delusion is easier to come by than the delusion that one's own values and principles are held by others. It is not to be regretted that social workers in adoption agencies are made rather painfully aware that their convictions are accepted by only part of the public.

To achieve what we want for children, we must proceed with deep and determined convictions, and we must not be afraid to express those convictions clearly, even though they may conflict with those of others. We must have a point of view, and that point of view must be clear since we have accepted a professional responsibility that society has vested in us on behalf of children. We must also, then, accept the responsibility of advocating strongly to society how it must carry out its responsibilities if children are to be served.

CHAPTER 3

The Community and the Adoption Problem

WILLIAM D. SCHMIDT

It has been estimated that there are 60,000 adoptions occurring each year in the United States. One authority states that approximately 38,000 of this number are adoptions of children who are not related to their adoptive parents. Adoptions by step-parents and blood relatives represent the balance. There has been a sharp increase in the number of adoptions since the onset of World War II. The number of adoptions was by contrast very low in the mid-depression years. Although at first glance the 38,000 adoptions each year appears like a sizable number, it is really quite small when we consider that there are more than 38,000,000 families scattered throughout the more than 3,000 counties in our country. This is an average ratio of one child adopted annually for every 1,000 families in the country. To those of us working in adoption agencies, this ratio hardly seems possible. The nation-wide interest in adoption is out of all proportion to the number of children and families actually involved. No other social phenomenon has resulted in greater interest or sharper emotions, considering the numbers involved. Very few adults in our nation have no opinion whatsoever on adoptions. Many possess a smattering of information on which prejudice is built. There are comparatively few who possess sufficient knowledge to assess the adoption problem with intelligence and objectivity. This is a fact to be reckoned with in any consideration of the adoption dilemma.

Whose Best Interests Should Be Served?

There are wide extremes in viewpoints on adoption. Most everyone agrees that children are this country's most precious resource. Because of this basic belief, it would seem that the highest in ideals and success would accompany every effort of society to place the best interests of children above all else. This is unfortunately not the case. For too many people there is confusion between the best interests of children and the interests of adults. If some of you think that this is a hard and unjustified comment, let us look at a few historical facts:

The enactment of laws for the protection of children in the United States almost universally post-dated laws for the protection of animals. This social lag in providing legislation for the protection of children reflected the philosophy that the rights of parents over and against their children were unbridled and not to be interfered with. Statutes prescribing penalties for cruel punishment, non-support, abandonment, neglect, and contributing to the delinquency of a child have come into being during the past seventy-five years. A very specific example of the country's slowness in providing protections to children, because of confusion with the interests of the adults, lies in the proposals for a child labor amendment to the Constitution. This amendment did not become law until October 1, 1938, and then only despite bitter opposition generated against it.

Special Facilities Finally Obtained

Our entire American history in the struggle for the protection of children is one of delay and belated attainment of goals sought. We have succeeded in establishing children's courts, children's correctional institutions, and special facilities for the care of orphaned chldren, so that they and their problems were not lumped together with adults.

As to adoption, some of our states have laws which go back to colonial days. For many years, however, the only statutory requirements involved registration of the fact of a new parent-child relationship created with adoption. This registration process was similar to that required for the transfer of chattel. It was not until the last years of the nineteenth century that states became concerned with the manner and the circumstances under which adoptions were made, and a degree of regulation was established by statutes.

There is a great deal of variation in the adoption statutes among the states. A few have attempted to provide controls over the adoptive placement of children, but most states emphasize protecting the rights of natural parents and adopted parents, and omit similar protections for the children. Relatively few states require as a protection to the child a determination of the suitability of an adoptive home for a particular child.

It is possible to set forth certain standards for the measurement of good adoption laws and practices. In any adoption, there are three parties who are involved—the child, his natural parents, and his adoptive parents. Any adoptive planning which does not contemplate protection to all three parties is faulty. Safeguards must arise for the natural parents so that their rights are not terminated summarily, hastily, or under duress, and assurances must exist so that they will not have their lives upset in the future by adoptive planning which goes awry. The adoptive parents must be assured first as to a child's adoptability; next, that there will not be interference from natural parents at any future time; and, last, that the child selected for them will fit into their home and their lives. As to the child, there must be assurance that he is being placed with people like him who will love him and provide for his needs as society expects of parents, to the fullest extent of his capabilities and within his limitations.

Babies Can't Be For Sale

As we reflect on these standards, is it not clear that the greatest assurance for good adoptive planning occurs when it is undertaken by qualified agencies which operate on the basis of these standards? Do we not find that makeshift planning for adoption done by independent persons or poor social agencies is clearly not in the best interests of children? We have heard much in recent years of gray market babies and black market babies. The gray market refers to placements done by well-meaning persons who lack the skill or the facilities to undertake such placements. The black market refers to those transactions in which adoptions are made for a consideration without intervention by any qualified public or private children's agency. Edwin J. Lukas in an article, "Babies Are Neither Vendible Nor Expendable", in the Record of the Association of the Bar of the City of New York, February, 1950, describes well the operations of the black market:

"It is a misnomer because the majority of states do not foreclose such transactions. In those states—particularly in large urban centers—sums ranging from $500 to $5,000 have been reported as having been paid to willing 'sellers' by willing 'purchasers' for the acquisition of babies concerning whose physical and emotional health virtually nothing is known—by the seller or the purchaser. These transactions take on the character of under-the-counter sales of merchandise in times of scarcity, not unlike nylon stockings or cigarettes during the war, and theatre tickets for a popular musical comedy. They have the aura of what Rebecca West calls a 'rich, dark rottenness'.

"But more than that, they partake of the selling of humans into a species of feudalism. That the infant has no choice nor the public a voice in the selection of the child's natural parents is probably an unavoidable biological phenomenon. But that the public should be equally helpless in the selection of his foster parents is a social disaster of unmeasurable magnitude, the implications of which, ramified and obvious as they are, need not be elaborated. The very nature of infancy or childhood is such that a child is incapable of protecting himself."

I am asked occasionally if these dramatic stories on black market babies could possibly be true. From first-hand experience I can attest to the truth of some of them. Two years ago at one of our specialized maternity homes in Cleveland, a well-dressed business man appeared, stating he was from West Virginia and that he wanted to take home a baby that day for his son and daughter-in-law who were childless. The superintendent explained to him that babies were just not placed for adoption that way. Not to be deterred, the man said, "I know it costs money, and I'll pay you $3,000 for one."

What makes people act this way? Very likely this man was a respected business man in his own community. Have we become so accustomed to buying our way into everything that we've lost all our sense of values and reduced our concern for children to the level of the market place?

A study made by the United States Children's Bureau two years ago showed that the greater number of adoptions throughout the country occur as a result of independent arrangements by parents, friends, relatives, doctors, lawyers, and others. Only in about 25 per cent of the cases are adoptive placements made by authorized child welfare agencies. This is a national average, and the percentage would be higher for any given urban area where social agencies operate.

In view of the universal acceptance of the thesis that our children are our nation's most precious resource, why is there such a wide variation in adoption practices, and why is there such a sharp difference of opinion on the importance of placement by qualified agencies? Perhaps the answer can be found in the fact that adoptions are highly charged with emotion. When people apply to adopt a child they usually feel quite strongly about the matter. Their friends and associates frequently share their hopes and aspirations. Identification with their progress in pursuit of a child is a natural result. Unconsciously, for some reason, many people consider the declared wish to adopt a child as being prima facie evidence of adequacy to be a good adoptive parent. They find it unnecessary that this wish must be looked at to see if it is compatible with the best interests of a child. While this wish to adopt is usually indicative of everything good that we look for in adoptive parents, actually, the wish to adopt is no more proof of parental adequacy than is the expressed desire to join a particular church proof of one's belief in that church. The underlying motive in each instance is the important thing. A person joining a church to acquire an air of respectability to cover up certain questionable actions in his own life is not likely to be a good church member. Adoption applicants seeking a child to hold together an unhappy and unstable marriage are not likely to be good adoptive parents. And if we consider the interests of the child to be involved, we are compelled to be sure of the adoptive applicants for the child's sake.

Public Sides Against the Agency

These are the matters that concern adoption agencies as they plan for the children entrusted to their care. Are these things understood by the general public? The answer is "No". We found this out four years ago in our community when newspaper publicity broke on a certain case situation. The story of our services to this child and his parents and the developments as a result of the publicity spoke clearly of the lack of public understanding.

A little five-year-old boy named Johnny had been under the care of our agency because of difficulty his natural parents had in maintaining their home. When all help to the parents was of no avail in re-establishing the home for little Johnny,

42

the parents relinquished legal custody of him to our agency, so that we could plan an adoption for him. Johnny had been cared for in one of our foster homes for several months. At this point, his foster parents expressed the wish to adopt him. This wish was given careful consideration but was not granted, primarily because there were dangers involved to the child. His natural parents knew where he was and out of our experience with them, we were concerned that they might well re-enter Johnny's life in the future. The foster parents were very disappointed in our decision. They sought legal help and public support through newspaper publicity, so that their hopes might be realized despite our decision. The articles by the reporter and the editorials by the newspaper hit hard at our agency. Out of deference to the natural parents, we could not reveal the confidential factors concerning them which formed the basis for our decision on Johnny's adoptive placement.

This publicity and the questions it raised made us realize that interpretation of our adoption practices needed attention. Instead of proceeding alone in formalizing plans for interpretation, we asked our Welfare Federation to establish a community committee for the purpose of studying and interpreting adoption practices. Such a committee was established with broad citizen representation from the press, the bar association, the academy of medicine, the nursing association, the ministerial association, business, the public relations field, housewives, and adoption agency representatives.

Our committee first occupied itself with a study of adoptions and agency procedures. Several meetings were held, and procedures in detail were presented to and studied by the committee. After this study, the committee found itself in essential agreement with the standards, principles, and procedures of the agencies in the community. It found, however, that good interpretation of adoptions was seriously lacking and that the facilities of the agencies were clearly insufficient. Adoption staffs were found to be overburdened and unable to cope with the job they had to do. Home studies were delayed because of staff shortages. Foster care resources were too limited to provide interim boarding care for all children needing it prior to adoptive placement. Casework services were inadequate to serve all unmarried mothers. As a result of these findings, the efforts of the committee were directed toward securing expansion of

43

agency staffs and resources, which assisted the agencies materially in expanding their adoption activities.

Next, the committee on adoptions organized a program of interpretation to combat misinformation and to provide positive information on adoptions. The interpretative phase of the committee's work has been under way for almost two years. The following projects have been undertaken and carried to completion:

1. An article prepared by a physician who was a member of our committee appeared in the publication of the Academy of Medicine.
2. An article prepared by a lawyer from our committee appeared in the publication of the Cleveland Bar Association.
3. An article prepared by a registered nurse appeared in the nurses' monthly journal.
4. An article prepared by a clergyman from our committee appeared in the monthly publication of the ministerial association.
5. A film on adoptions released a few years ago by the March of Time has been made available to local groups.
6. A pamphlet was prepared, giving questions and answers on adopting a child in Cleveland, and distributed in quantity at every opportunity.
7. Several television and radio interviews and dramatizations have been arranged.

What has been the significance of these cumulative efforts? In 1949 it was estimated that the adoption agencies placed 43 per cent of all adoptions of unrelated children in the county. In 1950 this estimated figure rose to 60 per cent. The dissemination of information to professional groups, to clients, and to the public at large clearly resulted in a greater proportion of adoptive placements by social agencies.

Waiting Period Source of Concern

In our own agency we found ourselves sorely in need of facts. Often it was necessary to gather information never previously collected. We were quite concerned about the time interval between the date applications to adopt were received and the date a child could be placed. We set about to gather the facts so that they could be shared with our applicants. We found several interesting things which corresponded with our own general impressions.

44

In our study we related the children legally available for adoption on a certain date to the applicants on file to adopt a child as of that same date. There were sharp extremes. We found Negro and other minority group children legally available for adoption without a single corresponding application to adopt. We found the ratio of Catholic children of all ages to Catholic applicants desiring such children to be approximately one to two. We also found that the ratio of white Protestant applicants wanting infants of superior ability to such children legally available for adoption was twenty to one. Here was the core of our difficulty, and we finally had the facts. Our study showed one thing clearly: that we had too many applicants of one kind and no applicants of another; and that we had a responsibility for stimulating applicants for some groups of children, and an obligation to explain to other groups why placement for them was so slow. One other thing showed up in our study. As is typical of our entire population, our children covered the broad range of intelligence or ability, with a concentration in the "average" range. Our applicants, however, were mostly in the range wanting "superior" children. The possession of factual information like this helped materially in planning for our children's needs, as well as helping to clarify our relationships with couples applying to adopt.

Dilemma of Confidentiality

I would like to mention one more problem which we might entitle "The Dilemma of the Adoption Agency". It deals with the matter of confidentiality. I know of no quarrel with the policy followed by adoption agencies that information secured from or about adoptive applicants is treated in strict confidence. The agency is obliged to follow this policy as a protection to its applicants, even though it may suffer in the process. This sometimes becomes burdensome when a rejected applicant gives friends some false reason for rejection, because the real reason cannot be shared with comfort. Under these circumstances the applicant must be protected, even though the agency suffers. Whenever the opportunity arises to share true facts, which will not be of harm to the applicant, they should be given out in order to protect the agency. One such opportunity came to us recently when a lady wrote a letter to the editor of a local paper complaining bitterly about adoption agencies not giving her a child, with specific mention of the agency I am associated with. I immediately sent a letter to the editor in reply, which appeared the next day. It read in part as follows:

45

"Sometimes disappointed applicants make misleading statements as to why they did not receive a child. When this happens, agencies usually must remain silent, because they cannot state publicly the true reasons. However, in this instance we are able to reveal a fact not stated in Mrs. Anderson's letter, because it is not uncomplimentary to her, which throws a different light on the nature of her complaint.

Mr. and Mrs. Anderson applied to Children's Services for a child on August 13, 1947. They then had two young children of their own—a boy and a girl. In view of the many applications of childless couples which far exceeded the number of babies legally available for adoption, Mr. and Mrs. Anderson were told that it was unlikely that the agency could place a baby with them. It is understandable that this was a great disappointment to them."

Interestingly enough, that afternoon I received a telephone call from a man who identified himself only as a neighbor of Mrs. Anderson. He was profuse in his commendation of my letter, stating, "Only it wasn't strong enough. She's doing a poor job of raising her own children."

Times are more frequent, however, when the agency cannot similarly protect itself. Another case comes to mind which happened several years ago in my public experience. A young couple applying to adopt gave indications of being good prospects for a child until references were seen. The family's minister strongly recommended against placement with them because of their incompatibility. The minister had been trying to persuade them to seek psychiatric help with their difficulties. He did not want this fact to be used as a basis for denial of application and requested that his participation as a reference be kept in the strictest confidence. Our home study subsequently supplied supportive information to the minister's evaluation. We could not deny application on the grounds of incompatibility, but we did actually deny on another ground—unstable financial security—since the man's earnings were characterized by sharp fluctuations. The applicants for the moment accepted the decision. Subsequently, however, they became dissatisfied with it.

Governor Backed Agency's Decision

They sought out friends active in political circles to exert pressure in their behalf. Specific complaints soon reached the governor, who asked us for a report on the matter. The governor was given the essential facts on which our rejection was based, together with an explanation of the importance of confidentiality in the matter. He affirmed our decision, and confidentiality was respected when the governor advised the complainants that the matter had been handled to his satisfaction. I am sure that there are still people concerned with this event who impute to this governor political and human irresponsibility because of his action in this case.

Agencies periodically find themselves in this position. They cannot reveal the facts in deference to their applicants, despite the onus it sometimes brings on the agencies. Although we cannot share with the public the facts in each such case, we can from time to time explain why an agency must remain silent, and we must be ready to seize each opportunity to explain the dilemma of the adoption agency.

There is one more thing I would like to say on interpretation. As we proceed to tell the story of adoptions, there are positive and negative aspects to be told. Undue emphasis must not be given on one to the exclusion of the other. The tragedies of independent placements which have gone wrong should be revealed without identification. Our public trust requires it. Some of them are very dramatic. We had one a few months ago which I would like to tell you.

Mrs. Jones was about to give birth to her sixth child. She and her husband had a hard time of it making ends meet. The new baby was not expected or planned for. As they reflected on another mouth to feed, they were overwhelmed. They had heard of an attorney who placed children for adoption. They decided that they would seek out this attorney to place their expected child. So that friends and relatives would not heap criticism upon their shoulders, they conceived a plan to announce that the baby was stillborn. Upon the baby's birth, the attorney placed the child with a couple, as had been planned. Three months later the adopting couple came hurriedly to see the attorney. They had learned from a pediatrician that their baby was a moron. They insisted that the attorney take the child back, since they wanted nothing further to do with him. The attorney called the natural parents, informing them that he was returning the child. The parents were distraught. How could they face their friends and relatives? What should they do? They found their way to one of the social agencies. Plans were finally made for the care of the child under public agency auspices, to the great relief of the natural parents. It takes little imagination to realize the suffering experienced by these parents and the couple receiving the child for adoption.

This case is a good one to illustrate the harm that can be done to adoptive parents and to natural parents by ill-conceived and ill-advised adoptive placement. The use of true case illustrations which play upon fear has its place in interpretation. The positive aspects of interpretation, however, need equal emphasis. The assurance that careful planning for the natural parents, the adoptive parents, and the child can be done by qualified adoption agencies will go a long way toward obtaining public acceptance and support.

ADOPTION SERVICES
AS RELATED
TO NATURAL PARENTS

Adoption Services As Related To
Natural Parents

Introduction

Most people believe that practically all adopted children are those of unmarried parents. While the majority of children placed for adoption in non-related homes are children born out of wedlock, a surprisingly large number are children born in wedlock. In some instances the parents of these children are living together at the time of placement and continue to do so. Children registered as legitimate include those whose mothers are widowed, divorced, or separated from their husbands, or whose fathers are not the husbands of the mothers. There are also a few whose parents are living together but who do not wish to assume the responsibility of parenthood for one or more of the children born to them.

According to the publication of the Children's Bureau, Department of Health, Education, and Welfare, "Adoption in the United States and its Territories, 1955," 73 percent of the children for whom petitions were filed by unrelated petitioners in 1955 had unmarried parents and about 27 percent had married parents.

Children born in wedlock who are adopted are usually from broken homes. Frequently they have been in foster care and separated from their parents for long periods of time prior to the decision to surrender them for adoption. Sometimes the parents have asked for the initial foster home placement for their children thinking it would solve their problems, including such complicated ones as physical or mental illness, marital difficulty, rejection of children, immaturity of parents, or inability to accept parental responsibilities.

Sometimes courts have made the decision for initial separation of the children from parents because the parents have misused their rights and failed in their responsibilities as parents with the result that the rights of their children have been threatened.

There will always be some parents who misuse their parental rights, just as there will always be some individuals who violate the rights of others. It is essential, however, for a community to provide sufficient services to enable parents to meet the minimum needs of their children if they have the desire and ability to do so.

The community needs to understand that placement is not the answer for all children whose parents have difficulty in caring for them, and that for many children, placement creates more serious troubles. Separation from his family is a grievous blow to a child's emotional life and causes anger, disillusionment, despair, resentment toward his parents, guilt, frustration, anxiety, shame, and a deep sense of his own unworthiness. Children handle these feelings differently and a variety of "behavior problems" emerge. Children are ill-equipped to understand these feelings or handle them constructively. Aggressive, hostile, threatening behavior may develop which the community resents. Or equally damaging behavior problems may show in the child's inability to accept reality, in withdrawn, fearful, self-negating relationships, and in a retarded rate of development for his capacities.

Children's thoughts and feelings are absorbed in what they are losing when they are separated from parents. They are seldom able to anticipate a new home or environment, or to use it constructively without a great deal of help. They need to understand the reasons for the placement, to be assured repeatedly their feelings are natural, to be able to express their feelings openly in talking about their problems and in acting out some of them. Most children blame themselves for the failure of their family life. Accepting love and security in their new environment is not easy for them even though they want and need both. Their anxiety-filled experiences to date make them incapable of reaching out or trusting what is offered to them. And is it any wonder when they have already lost their "very own home"?

If children cannot be helped to accept the necessity for placement, recognize their own feelings and be able to talk about them, they cannot accept love and security in their new environment and will receive little benefit from placement.

The reasons for adoption of children in those instances in which both parents are living and together at the time the child is placed, grow out of such circumstances as the illness of one or both parents, the feeling that they cannot adequately care for additional children, or possibly their inability to face family disapproval if their marriage occurred shortly before or after the birth of the child. In these situations the services of a social worker are essential if children are not to be separated from their families unnecessarily.

Most parents whose children need to be cared for by others feel that they are failures as parents and have a sense of worthlessness. Often a sense of guilt over their failure in parental responsibilities prevents their being able to accept a plan for permanent placement of a child. Social pressures emphasize parental responsibility and the "unnaturalness" of giving up children.

Parents need help in evaluating their situation and circumstances to be certain relinquishing their child is what they wish to do. Often a temporary crisis makes married parents seek to place a child for adoption. They feel incapable of dealing with their problems and think of the child as an additional problem or burden. Whether their problems relate to difficulties in marital relationships, to individual emotional insecurities, to immaturity, to mental or physical ill health, or to economic strains, every effort is needed to rehabilitate the family so that their children need not suffer permanent separation from their natural family. The right help at the right time may enable parents to assume their parental responsibilities again. Custody cases reported by newspapers with great frequency show that many parents, having given up children willingly to friends or relatives, later become able to care for the children and try to regain their custody.

The child welfare agency can fulfil its purpose of serving children only if it recognizes that helping children begins with service to their parents. Many parents need help in being responsible parents. In fact society has continually increased its organized services to supplement the effort of parents in their care of children. It is generally acceptable for parents to seek help in educational, health and physical problems, or in recreational needs outside the family. Similarly it should be equally acceptable for parents to supplement their own strengths in the areas of social relationships and general behavior of their children and family unit. Mature and trained caseworkers can help parents think through some of the problems relating to their child's care more adequately.

However, sometimes parents' own needs are greater than their need to be adequate parents. In those instances in which parents cannot provide directly the physical care the child needs, or are too immature to meet their child's emotional needs, they may accept some responsibility by cooperating in a plan for the child which will provide a new and permanent family.

Since a large number of children available for adoption in nonrelated homes are children of unmarried parents, an adoption program necessarily involves services to unmarried mothers and fathers. There were 201,700 children born out of wedlock in 1957.[1] Seventy thousand eight hundred were white; one hundred thirty thousand nine hundred were non-white. Services in these cases must reach the unmarried mother and her needs as she sees them. The viewpoints and requirements of all professions serving unmarried parents, such as medicine, law and social work are related and all should be compatible with the needs of unmarried mothers and their children.

We know services to unmarried mothers are essential to meet the problem of independent adoption placements. Nation-wide more people express interest and concern. State legislatures consider many bills to assist needy unmarried mothers so these mothers will not be forced to make hasty and ill-advised plans to dispose of their children. More adequate legislation providing for and financing services is needed. The practice of independently arranged adoptions will continue so long as adequate medical and social service for mothers and their babies, and adoption placement services are not available.

The unmarried mother in her desire for secrecy often goes to a community where she is not known. There she may find that she is unable to obtain the service she needs—medical care, shelter care, boarding care for the baby—because she is a non-resident. Only if she is able to pay the full cost of these services, are they usually available to her. Otherwise there is generally a requirement to approach her family or her home community, or both, to see if they will assume financial responsibility. The fear of the community is that the child may not be adoptable and may become a long-time charge on that community. There are numerous situations, however, in which it is not desirable for public welfare officials in the girl's home community to know about her pregnancy. To meet such problems a few states have arranged for state funds to care for unmarried mothers and their children.

Communities and agencies are doing much to individualize the service of agencies in line with the individual needs and circumstances of unmarried mothers. One of the most obvious needs

---

[1] Illegitimacy and its Impact on the Aid to Dependent Children Program, U. S. Department of Health, Education and Welfare, April 1960, p. 10.

of the unmarried mother is for medical care during the prenatal and postnatal period, at the time of delivery, and in the care of the newborn infant. Agencies must have cooperative arrangements with clinics and hospitals, and funds to enable a mother to make or continue plans for private medical and hospital care when she desires this.

Along with the provision for medical care, is the need to make temporary living arrangements during pregnancy. Maternity homes, shelters, and private boarding homes serve this purpose. A flexible program should provide various living resources to meet the varying needs of unmarried mothers.

The unmarried mother also presents complicated problems in her relationships. At best she is anxious and uncertain in relation to her own family group or individual members of it, is insecure in her relationship to the baby's father, is in conflict about the new family group which the birth of the child creates without social sanction, and is confused in her feelings toward her child. To help the mother clarify these relationships calls for a high degree of casework skill.

With the mother's cooperation and permission early and informal contact with the unmarried father is desirable. He needs an opportunity to discuss the situation confidentially and objectively with a social worker. He needs to know what alternates are open for the expectant mother, their child and himself. This helps the worker understand his attitudes and feelings toward the mother and the child. It also clarifies what responsibility he is willing to take in planning for the future. In contacts with the father the social and emotional aspects of the problem need as much consideration as the economic status of the man and his ability to help financially. Frequently the father is maladjusted and in as great conflict as the mother.

Any decision about court action in regard to paternity and financial support rests with the mother, not the agency. She may also need help in understanding her motives in pressing for court action. She may be motivated by a need to punish the man, by her own inner conflicts, by a sense of her own unworthiness, or by a desire for support of the child. Frequently court action is undesirable from the standpoint of the mother and the child. It is unfortunate that some governmental agency policies require court action if the mother needs financial help from the tax-supported agency.

Often the unmarried mother uses an assumed name during her pregnancy in an effort to keep the fact of her illegitimate pregnancy from becoming known. Sometimes the name she assumes is that of the baby's father. The mother should know the legal difficulties involved in changing one's name, as well as the need to have the child's birth record correspond to the correct name of the mother. It is any child's birthright to know his own legal identity if this becomes necessary at some future date.

The early family relationships of a girl who becomes an unmarried mother always include problems that were not constructively solved and resulted in a less than normally satisfying pattern of relationships. Many unmarried mothers are emotionally sick. Usually they follow certain basic personality patterns. With unmarried mothers as with all other people, their behavior is an attempt to satisfy their needs and desires. Often they are unable to reach more constructive forms of behavior even though their illicit experiences are not satisfying to them. The lack of continuity in their relationships enhances their need for social relationships and so their problem. They act without conscious knowledge of why they act as they do and with no awareness of the underlying motives for their behavior. When the caseworker helps the unmarried mother understand how unhappy family relationships or other circumstances have caused her to act as she has, she may use her understanding to build a greater sense of her own value as a person and recreate her own life pattern. The caseworker helps her know herself better, her own needs, feelings and problems, helps her examine the whole of her situation and accept the realities of it. Only in this way can the mother be assisted to make a responsible plan for the baby and have the strength to reach a mature way of managing her own life.

The mother who relinquishes her baby is trying to give her child what she knows he needs and what she wants him to have —love, care, and security from two parents in a normal home situation such as she cannot provide. With the agency's help she is able to assume her maternal responsibilities and make a constructive plan for her child. Casework service helps the girl come to peace with herself so that she will not express her conflicts and desires in unwholesome ways and so she will not need to have another child out of wedlock. Because of the emotional needs of an unmarried mother, it is highly important to the community that she receive skilled casework service so that she may have this chance of becoming better adjusted.

Before placing the child for adoption, the agency needs, with the cooperation and help of the natural parents, to study the child's background. This usually includes information about the physical, mental, social and emotional development of the parents and their families, and the developmental history of the child. Social histories are necessary from both the mother and the father since selection of the most suitable home is difficult if only half of the child's background is known. If more than one person may be the father, an evaluation of the level of interests and abilities of the men is helpful.

Parents should participate in making plans for adoption of their child. They may participate in various ways—by supplying the necessary social and medical history, by sharing in financial responsibility for temporary care, and by cooperating with the agency in working through complicated legal obstacles. This participation increases their self-respect, helps them feel they are being responsible parents even though it is a difficult situation for them, and lessens their sense of guilt over relinquishment of the child. It also indicates to the agency their readiness to accept permanent separation from their child.

The child's heritage from his natural relatives, when passed on to the adoptive family, helps them connect him as a person to his past, helps them know the family characteristics which they should minimize or accentuate in their relationship with the child, and enables them to answer questions which the child may raise about his natural relatives in later years.

Unmarried mothers are less reluctant to have paternal history obtained if they understand that the medical and social history is needed for the good of the child.

Casework services help both unmarried and married parents determine, without pressure, the best plan for the child and themselves when they seek adoption for their child. These services require sufficient workers and sufficient funds to pay for temporary boarding care of the child, if this is indicated, to give parents time to consider carefully the best plan for their child. Children should not be permanently separated from their own families simply because the community lacks the resources to help a family through a temporary crisis. The social agency must also help the parents with plans for the child if he proves to be unadoptable because of serious defects.

Although agencies do not wish to rush the unmarried mother into a hasty decision, they recognize that it is not in her interest, and certainly not in that of her child, to allow her to delay her final decision too long. Present practice, therefore, tends to set limits—giving her a reasonable but not an indefinite period in which to make up her mind.

Adoption is not the best solution for every child born out of wedlock just as it is not best for every legitimate child whose parents are unable to care for him in their own home. However, when parents wish to relinquish their rights to a child after full consideration of all interests, they must understand the legal requirements for transfer of guardianship, including any continuing responsibilities and duties they may have under the law.

Termination of parental rights may be voluntary or mandatory. A written agreement for the voluntary relinquishment of a child is in common use throughout the United States; judicial termination of parental rights when instigated voluntarily by parents is also possible. Termination of parental rights because of their unfitness is accomplished only by court action. Courts are reluctant to terminate parental rights against the wishes of the parents except for grave reasons.

In the past many agencies were unwilling to accept a relinquishment from parents until the agency determined that the child was adoptable. Voluntary agencies with limited financial resources were responsible for the continued support of children whom they had accepted on relinquishment from the parents and who subsequently proved unadoptable. If a backlog of such children existed in the agency caseload, a major part of all financial resources would be required to provide for these long-time care cases. In such a situation the agency could not accept and serve other children needing care for a temporary period before placement for adoption.

Many parents are psychologically ready to relinquish their child before completion of the study of the child and before the agency knows that the child will be adoptable. Relinquishment should be timed in terms of the parents' readiness rather than in terms of the agency's completion of the study of the child and determination of his adoptability.

In the case of an unmarried mother, relinquishment is desirable as early after birth of her child as she is ready to give it, provided there are no gross physical or mental defects. Even when there are gross defects, a governmental agency should take a surrender if the permanent separation of the mother and child is the most suitable plan, i.e. a child of incestuous background who is unacceptable to his natural family.

Agency failure to accept relinquishments when parents are ready creates difficulties for them. Parents remain in a state of uncertainty, not knowing what to expect, and are unable to re-establish their own lives on a stable basis. Consequently, agency service is less helpful to them. Independent placements may result as well as delays in placement of the children.

Liberalization of laws making a child, relinquished and later found unadoptable, eligible for public support, would enable voluntary as well as governmental agencies to accept relinquishments when parents are psychologically ready to sign. The laws covering termination of parental rights need continued analysis and revision: (1) to provide for a relinquishment procedure that protects both the child and parents; (2) to define termination of parental rights as it relates to the child and parents; (3) to define rights and responsibilities granted the social agency; (4) to provide for transfer of parental rights and responsibilities to adoptive parents; and (5) to provide for transfer of responsibilities and rights from one social agency to another resource.

Of the many articles on the needs of unmarried mothers and their children those chosen for inclusion here relate to the mother's decision to give up her child and the parental history of the child essential for proper placement. There are numerous articles discussing help to parents with various family problems but the editor was able to locate only one article dealing specifically with the problem of helping married parents decide whether or not to give up a child. Written material concerned with the study of a child's background is extremely limited; and very little literature exists which helps in working with the unmarried father and in obtaining paternal history.

What Shall I Do With My Baby?

BERNICE BROWER BOEHM, Ph.D.

We, as social workers, have long felt that one of the most complex problems facing us is the task of helping the unmarried mother reach a decision about plans for the future care of her child.

Our close contact with the unmarried mother makes us quickly aware of the conflicts and anxiety that she feels when faced with the necessity of making a decision about her child; and her vital emotional stake in the problem is clearly evident to us.

At the same time, the worker is equally aware of what society as a whole feels about the problem, and the stake that society has in the future planning and well-being of the child, as well as society's concern with the problem of the unmarried mother herself, a concern which has been sometimes punitive and other times reformist.

Frequently, because of our understanding of the emotional disturbance of the unmarried mother, and our anger against the harshness of society's judgment, we have set out to combat these judgments by aligning ourselves with the client and sometimes even propelling her into a plan that ignored the basic factors in the situation.

In this way we sometimes impeded the ultimate adjustment

of the mother and the child into society, despite the fact that we were so anxious to have society accept them.

Still later in the development of our professional skills, we became aware of a third stake in the problem—the stake of the case worker herself. We realized that our experiences and feelings toward our own parental relationships frequently colored our attitudes toward the mother and her child, and in many cases played a significant role in shaping the client's decision.

This growing awareness brought with it additional hazards in our work with unmarried mothers. In an effort to make certain that the mother was free to make her own decision uninfluenced by the attitude of the case worker, the worker also frequently failed to participate in this vital decision. And failing to give her client the necessary support, the worker left her to face the entire burden of the decision alone.

Our developing perspective on the problem has been shown in the historical pattern of dealing with the unmarried mother and her child. For many decades the foundlings' home was the major solution offered by society to rid the mother of the evidence of her guilt and at the same time to offer the child a chance of survival. But this was a harsh solution, wherein no heed was given to the needs of the mother, and the existence of the child in both physical and emotional aspects was grim.

Later, with the emergence of case work as a planned procedure, emphasis was placed on the desirability of the unmarried mother's keeping her child with her. This was in part due to the social worker's earnest desire to modify the harsh attitude of society, and in greater part due to the growing understanding of the importance of family life in the emotional development of the child.

Mothers who were undecided about plans for their babies were urged and encouraged to keep their babies with them.

Maternity-home procedures were planned so as to encourage formation of an emotional bond between mother and baby, and from this developed such requirements as compulsory breast feeding by the mother, an insistence that all mothers give personal care to their babies, and requirements that the mother and child live together in the maternity home for a stipulated period of time after delivery.

In our zeal to secure the advantages of a mother's love for the child, we tended to assume that the mere act of living together necessarily would give the child the security and affection that goes with satisfactory family living.

Many people today, both in social work and in the outside community, feel that the unmarried mother should be encouraged to keep her child, just as there are many people who believe that the only adequate solution for the future of the child of the unmarried mother is placement away from the mother in an adoptive home.

For a long time, however, most of us have been aware that neither of these answers can be applied in all situations. We have striven for our answers on a case-by-case basis, knowing that it was only through understanding the dynamics of each situation that we could determine the meaning that *this* child had for *this* mother, and thereby help her make a plan that would best meet her own needs as well as the child's needs.

We in Chicago have been giving a good deal of thought to the problem of helping the unmarried mother in her decision about the baby. An institute was recently held here under the auspices of the Council of Social Agencies, dealing with the problems that we are talking about today.

Do we emphasize mother or child?

In our planning for this institute, the members of the committee sat down together to discuss and clarify their own thinking about the relationship between the unmarried mother and her child, and to see what reconciliation would be needed between divergent points of view.

Since service to the unmarried mother is given by various types of agencies, we found that our thinking about the problem was frequently affected by the function of our own agency.

The major point of discussion seemed to be whether our primary emphasis lay with the interest of the mother or the child. Which of the two was the major responsibility of the agency? And upon which was the primary emphasis of our work to be placed?

As we talked further, the points of difference seemed to lessen and we emerged with the definite feeling that not only was there no single plan of action that was preferable in all situations, but also, except for rare instances, there was no basic conflict between the best interests of child and mother.

We realized also that our best possibility for working out a sound plan for the future welfare of the child lay in helping the mother to work out her own problems, since it was only

61

in this way that she could be free to make a sound plan for her child.

We have long recognized the complexity of emotions and behavior, and we know that for this reason the decision regarding the child could not be an isolated factor in the life of the unmarried mother.

We know that this decision would be influenced by the same emotional factors that had entered into the pregnancy and the total behavior pattern of the unmarried mother, and that it was through an understanding of these factors that we and she could best ascertain the meaning of the child to her.

We have seen this in many situations where a thorough exploration of the present situation has clearly indicated the inadvisability and even the impossibility of the mother's keeping her baby.

The mother herself has participated and is in agreement with this conclusion. Nevertheless, she finds herself completely unable to carry out the decision that she herself expresses as being best for herself and for her child. We know then, that reality for this girl contains other elements than those in her present life situation.

This does not in any way imply that external realities should not be given full consideration, or that they should not be presented by the worker and carefully explored with the mother. On the contrary, it is vitally important that this be done, since the girl herself may be so strongly motivated by inner psychological pressures that external realities have little meaning for her.

It then becomes the function of the case worker to help the girl understand the psychological pressures and to relate them to the realities of the present situation. We know that no plan can offer happiness for the mother or the child if the plan ignores the present reality, but it is important to expand our concept of reality so that it includes the psychological realities of the girl's situation as well as the external realities.

Let us briefly consider some of the plans that these girls bring to us.

Many of the girls who come to us state with fixed determination that they plan to keep their babies. Some of them have the backing of their families in this decision, and the circumstances of their lives indicate that despite many hazards the baby may have some degree of security in living with its mother.

Many more, however, have little mature warmth or security

to offer the child, and the plan seems to offer serious disadvantages both to the girl and her baby. What, then, impels these girls to cling to their babies?

Dr. Margaret Gerard of the Institute for Psychoanalysis in Chicago recently pointed out that many of the unmarried mothers coming to us for help are impulsive and infantile individuals, whose own dependency needs may lead them to hold tenaciously to their babies. Sometimes this is because the girl feels that her family, or perhaps the worker, expects it of her. Or she may cling to the child through inability to relinquish any possession for fear that she may regret its loss at some time in the future. One factor that Dr. Gerard pointed out is of particular importance for us who must help the mother in making a decision.

Repeated experience has shown that the more dependent, immature women whom we know to be inadequate mothers practically always choose to keep their babies once they have seen and handled them. This choice grows, not out of an ability to care for the child, but out of the wish for pleasure for herself. We have all known mothers who, long after taking the baby, have found the difficulties which faced her overwhelming, and have come to us, saying, "If I only hadn't seen my baby I could have given him up." They have blamed the worker for not having helped them to make a plan that would have made this possible.

Medical social service helps

In Chicago we have been able to secure the cooperation of many of the hospitals in carrying out such plans, particularly those hospitals that have medical social-service departments. In these hospitals the mother does not have to see her child if she does not wish to, and in that case the baby is placed on a formula immediately after birth. This, of course, is done only with the mother's approval, and the baby is brought to her if at any time she changes her mind. In this way the girl has the support of her worker and the hospital in carrying through the plan that she basically desires, but which she might not be able to carry through if her feeling of guilt were increased by enforced personal contact with her baby.

Many other unmarried mothers need to cling to the child because of their attachment to his father, and the hope that through the baby they can still maintain a tie with him. Others who have been led into pregnancy as a result of their own disturbed family relationships, need to keep their babies as a help in working out these relationships. Some need to reinforce their dependence upon their families; others, to bring about their emancipation from an overly dominating family. The latter problem is illustrated as follows:

Dorothy J. was referred to our agency by a worker in the social-service department of the court, who felt that she needed help because she was greatly distressed over the pending adoption of her baby. This adoption had been privately arranged by Dorothy's physician, and she had already signed relinquishment papers before the clerk of the court. However, in the process of the adoption study which was being made for the court, Dorothy was interviewed and was most emphatic at that time in saying that she wanted to keep her baby and that she had signed the adoptive consent only because of coercion from her mother and the doctor.

She was under a great deal of tension when seen by our social worker and spoke with considerable excitement. She told of the pressure that had been put upon her by the doctor and her mother to consent to the baby's adoption, and of their threats to take her to court to prove her an unfit mother if she persisted in keeping the baby. She said that the doctor had even had telephone service cut off from her hospital room and had told her that she would not be able to go home with the baby unless she had money to pay the hospital bill and the bill for his services.

However, although she repeated her anxiety to keep the baby she could offer no tangible plan for his care. Dorothy was still living at home with her mother, and felt that it would be impossible for her ever to leave home. She was earning an adequate salary as a secretary, and felt that she could support the baby, but that it would be impossible for her to take him home because of her mother's opposition. There was some fantasy of a later marriage to the baby's father, but when this was discussed Dorothy herself expressed considerable distaste for such a marriage, feeling that the man was considerably beneath her, socially and educationally.

Since it seemed probable that Dorothy's consent had been obtained through duress, she was assured that legal assistance would be given through our legal-aid department. At the same time arrangements were made for her to have regular interviews with the social worker to help in making future plans.

The worker felt that there was great conflict in Dorothy's mind about plans for the baby, despite her verbalized insistence on keeping him, and she felt that Dorothy's inability to consider tangible plans, as well as her need to remain in her parents' home, might indicate that she did not actually want to keep her child. What then was the meaning of this child to Dorothy, and why did she need to cling so desperately to him?

As the interviews progressed Dorothy was able to bring out a great deal of her feeling toward her family. As an only child she had been the absorbing interest of her dominating mother, a mother who at the same time had not given her a great deal of warmth. Her father was a pleasant but passive person who had played an unimportant role in the family, the same kind of role that the baby's father played in Dorothy's mind.

Mother has conflicting desires

The root of the conflict became more clear. She had a desire to emancipate herself from her mother's control and become independent, coupled with a desire to remain dependent upon the family and win her mother's affection in that way. This conflict had led to the relationship that resulted in her pregnancy, and also to her desire to keep the baby, against her mother's wishes.

As the interviews progressed, Dorothy herself became more aware of the confusion in her feelings toward her family, and her need to hold on to her child seemed to be decreasing. One day she spontaneously sent a letter to the legal-aid bureau attorney stating that she wanted to drop the action for the custody of the baby since she felt that the child would have no real security with her and would undoubtedly be better off with the adoptive parents.

She is still continuing her interviews with the worker, and although her relationships at home are not happy, she has shown a capacity for greater activity and increased friendships outside the home. This of course came about not only through her understanding of her own feelings, but also because the worker in many ways served as a mother substitute for Dorothy, a mother who was less restrictive and without need to control.

This may seem a strange case to present as an illustration of problems concerning keeping the baby, since it starts and ends with an adoptive situation. However, it is illustrative of the kind of motive that frequently impels a girl to keep her baby when she does not actually want him.

Adoption brings child some security

The next large group we meet is made up of girls who plan to have their babies adopted. Social workers always feel some security in dealing with this group since they know that if a placement is made through an authorized agency the baby at least will have some security for the future.

Sometimes, however, because of our reassurance about the baby we tend to neglect the emotional needs of this group of mothers. This is understandable in many ways since the pressure of work frequently forces us to use our time and effort on situations where the mother is undecided about plans and the future of the baby is in jeopardy. However, we are frequently surprised when all the plans are made, and the mother then changes her mind or is thrown into a panic of indecision. Sometimes this happens because we have not been sufficiently sensitive to her conflict about adoption, and have not helped her deal with her feeling of guilt. Sometimes, even when this kind of mother goes ahead with the adoption plan, her feeling of guilt may lead her into another pregnancy.

The extent to which this can be carried is shown in the situation of Gloria, an attractive, quiet, intelligent girl of 22, who came to us one summer asking for maternity care. She said that she was married and separated, but that her husband was not the father of the expected child. She told us that she had one son by her marriage, who was living with relatives of her husband. She spoke to the worker in a frightened tone, and looked as though she expected punishment or criticism. The worker quickly sensed her need for reassurance, and discussed practical plans for her. Before Gloria left that day plans had already been worked out for hospitalization, financial assistance, and living arrangements.

Later, in checking on the records of other agencies, we discovered that this was really Gloria's fourth pregnancy, and that all four pregnancies had been illegitimate. The first two children had been placed in adoption by an agency, and the third had been placed privately. The worker felt that with this secret standing between them there was no possibility of helping Gloria; and she told the girl what she had learned, but reassured her of our continued interest. At this point Gloria dissolved into tears and could not discuss it any further. She was not pressed to talk, and we continued to plan to help her.

In the third interview Gloria began to talk about wanting to keep her baby. She showed great distress over giving up the first child. The other two children seemed more shadowy in her mind, but the giving up of the first child was still so vivid that it might have happened only yesterday. It was agreed that the important thing was to work out the plan that Gloria really wanted.

There had been no security in Gloria's early family life. Her parents separated when she was only 2, and she was shifted from one relative to another, spending several brief periods with her mother. Records indicated that Gloria had suffered real cruelty from her mother. On one occasion the mother had burned the little girl's hand for a slight misdeed, and relatives stated that the mother had really tried to starve her.

There was also evidence that the mother was promiscuous, but she was also very hostile to Gloria because the girl had been involved with men. Gloria had had a better relationship with her father's family, who had a more respectable status.

It seemed apparent that Gloria's relationships with men were largely on the basis of reaching out for a family relationship. Most of the men involved were older, and she spoke frequently of the kindness and consideration they had shown her, although for various reasons they had been unable to marry her.

Gloria kept her baby and gave him excellent and devoted care. Because of our concern over the welfare of the baby, as well as Gloria's past history, we discussed the situation with our psychiatric consultant. It was felt that the situation was hopeful, and that the girl was now reaching out for help because she had been allowed to keep her child.

In her mind the agency was not associated with the punitive, depriving attitude of her own mother. We had shown her by our attitude that we did not condemn her, nor did we see her as a worthless person; and because of this she was now able to reach out for help in other areas.

Gloria has continued under care, and now that her baby is older, plans are being made with her for vocational counseling, with the possibility of day care for her child when she returns to work.

Child's happiness at stake

The group that concerns us most is composed of girls who ask for long-time foster-home placement for their babies. These girls neither want to keep the children nor are they willing to give them up, but hold on to them through the nebulous tie of keeping them in foster homes. We are all aware of the unhappy situation of such children, children who grow up in a foster home, knowing their own mothers. These children are prevented from forming close ties with the foster parents, but at the same time do not get the affection and security that they crave from their own mothers. Frequently the child feels divided allegiance, and a rivalry is created between his own mother and the foster mother. As this goes on, the child may be impelled to repeat the neurotic pattern of the mother which had been the cause of the original situation.

As for the mother, this kind of solution has frequently enabled her to put off facing any of her own problems, because she is able to escape into this indefinite plan for long-time placement of the baby. In the past many agencies frequently entered on such planning without thorough consideration of all the motives involved. This is now less likely because of the extreme shortage of foster homes. This shortage has now forced us to sharpen our skills so that the foster home can be used to the best advantage. It is true, of course, that long-time foster-home care is sometimes necessary, but this is usually a last resort.

If we accept the basic premise that the focal point of planning is to help the mother meet and solve her own problems, what implications does this have with regard to the agency program and the role of the case worker? There are a great many implications to be considered: The first is the need for flexibility in the agency set-up. This implies flexibility both in legislative provisions and in agency procedures.

It is important that assistance and service be available for nonresident unmarried mothers, since the very nature of their problem, and their ultimate rehabilitation into their own group, frequently makes it necessary that these mothers seek help in a locality where they are known to no one.

It is also important that various types of living arrangements be made available to the girls. In many localities maternity homes are the only resource, although we know that many of the more disturbed girls are unable to adjust in a group and because their emotional needs are not met in such a situation they are not responsive to case-work help.

Rigorous requirements for paternity hearings should not be insisted upon, since it is frequently desirable for the girl and for the future welfare of the baby that all ties with the father be broken. Unless the future welfare of the child seems seriously jeopardized, it is important that the mother be given the right to determine whether or not she wishes to institute such hearings. This is particularly important of course in situations where adoption is considered, since a clean break with previous ties is clearly indicated here.

In considering the role of the social worker it is important that she be prepared to accept her own responsibility for helping the unmarried mother reach her decision about the disposition of the child.

Worker should not shirk duty

In our eagerness to permit our client the right to self-determination, we have frequently avoided our own responsibility in helping her to face one of the most vital problems that a girl can be called upon to meet. In many records we read such examples as the case worker who insists upon discussing alternate plans with the girl who has already resolved upon adoption for her baby, thereby confusing the girl and making her feel that the case worker, and therefore society, looks upon her as a bad mother for wishing to give up her child. We have all also read records where the mother specifically asks the case worker for advice and counsel, only to be turned aside by the worker who states, "It's all up to you."

We have all learned that one of the most important tools of case work comes through the relationship that is developed between the client and the worker. If we accept this premise, how then can we remain aloof and apart from so vital a decision? It is important to realize that any decision which the girl makes will have some painful aspects, and that it will be necessary to help her work through the feelings that may arise before and after her decision. It is also important that we fully convey to her the fact that even if she does not make the decision that we feel is best, we are still interested in her, and she can still turn to us for help.

The responsibility for making a decision for the future of an unborn child is indeed a grave one. We are all awed by the consciousness that here is an individual who as yet has been untouched by the problems of the world. What will his future be, we wonder? But as social workers, we have always had to carry grave responsibilities, and if the great amount of thinking that has recently gone into this problem is any indication, we will not hesitate to meet these responsibilities in their turn.

CHAPTER 5

Placing the Child for Adoption

FLORENCE CLOTHIER, M.D.

Every social worker recognizes the importance of security for the dependent child, but many social workers retreat from the finality of adoption, which experience shows is full both of gross and of subtle hazards. Yet it is generally agreed that it is the permanence and the finality of legal adoption that make possible the security and sense of belonging that should be associated with child placement. There is risk in adopting a child and there is risk in being adopted. None the less, since adoption is the procedure that, in the light of our present knowledge,[1] offers the greatest protection to the dependent child, our entire effort should be directed toward expanding our adoption program and improving the efficiency of our adoption technique.

We can no more eliminate the hazards of adoption than we can eliminate the hazards of marriage, but we can struggle ceaselessly to minimize them. We do not yet know enough to be able to lay down didactic laws about adoption placements, but we can all study, by direct observation, the effects of placement on children and on adopting parents. We can also scrutinize and evaluate what research workers in the fields of psychology, genetics, medicine, sociology, and education have to

---

[1] See *Social Aspects of Adoption,* by Sophie Van S. Theis. New York: Child Welfare League of America, 1937.

say that may be applied to our immediate problems. The worker who limits her interests either to direct clinical work or to theoretical, academic concepts cripples herself and her clients.

The adoption worker's chief concern is how to find the right home for the right child with such efficiency that the child is placed early and permanently and the adoptive parents are satisfied that he will be in truth one of them and not a stranger among them. The social worker must be courageously aware that the placement she makes will determine the future course of the life of the child and the future happiness of the family. Her adoption placements must, therefore, be made thoughtfully, but promptly after an evaluation of the child and of the adoptive home.

I.

In the evaluation of children for adoption, the social worker is faced with two distinctly different problems. The first is the evaluation of the socially inaccessible, newborn infant, not yet influenced by experiences or emotional relationships. The second is the evaluation of the older child whose performance can be observed and who can perhaps give some account of himself, but whose personality is complicated by the inclusion in it of elements of the personalities with whom he has grown up, as well as by reactions to the experiences through which he has lived. The private physician or the nonprofessional agency usually concerns itself only with the adoption of infants, but the social worker is faced with dependent children in both age groups. She can, and she often does, hope to simplify her problem by allowing the infant to grow up in a "controlled environment" to an age of greater accessibility. Though the child can now be talked to and tested, he is by no means a more "sure bet" for adoption; in fact, new hazards have been introduced.

If the adoption of a newborn infant is contemplated, the study of him is perforce limited to a study of his heredity and to medical examinations. Of the two, the latter is far the more convincing and satisfying. A good pediatrician, with adequate laboratory facilities, within the first few weeks after a child's birth can state whether there are any gross abnormalities of structure or congenital disease processes. Certainly no baby should be placed for adoption who has not been examined by a competent physician—or, better, by a pediatrician—and this examination should include laboratory studies. Thoroughgoing physical and laboratory examinations, combined with an adequate medical family history (usually absent from social records), should rule out from blind adoption placement a group of grossly handicapped children. This group includes children suffering from hereditary degenerative disease of the nervous system, Friedreich's ataxia, congenital blindness and deafness, Huntington's chorea, congenital syphilis, and hemophilia.[2] Concerning the unsuitability for adoption of this group of children, except under peculiar circumstances, there has been little controversy.

Most of the babies for whom social workers must plan do not represent any such definitely pathological familial history, and most of them pass muster by the pediatricians as healthy specimens, free from congenital disease. But many of these babies have factors in their family histories that, in the present state of our knowledge, cannot be evaluated. These factors some regard as definite deterrents to adoption, others disregard them, and still others are on the fence about them.[3] These include (1) psychosis that cannot be explained on an organic basis (manic-depressive psychosis and schizophrenia); (2) familial feeblemindedness; (3) epilepsy; (4) alcohol and drug addiction; (5) criminality; and (6) general emotional instability.

Family histories weighted with these conditions do give one cause to consider carefully the steps to be taken. There is as yet no definite knowledge as to how great a role heredity plays in any of these conditions. Theis emphasizes that "laws of heredity are complicated, and care must be taken not to let a little knowledge of this point play too powerful a part."[3] Indications, still far from final, are that psychosis, as defined above, some types of feeblemindedness, and perhaps epilepsy[4] may have significant hereditary factors. Whether these factors operate to an important extent entirely apart from the environmental situations that, in the natural family, are their concomitants, we do not know. The importance of identifications or extreme reaction formations in the children of psychotic, feeble-minded, and epileptic parents cannot be overlooked. Alcohol

---

[2] On this point see the following: "Suitability of Children for Adoption," by Hyman Lippman (*American Journal of Orthopsychiatry*, Vol. 7, pp. 270-73, April, 1937); "Adoption Practices and the Physician," by R. L. Jenkins (*Journal of the American Medical Association*, Vol. 103, pp. 403-8, August 11, 1937; also published as a reprint by the Child Welfare League of America); and *Eugenical Sterilization*. (Report of the Committee for the Investigation of Eugenical Sterilization, the American Neurological Association. New York: The Macmillan Company, 1936.)

[3] See Theis, *op. cit.*

[4] See "The Inheritance of Epilepsy as Revealed by the Electroencephalograph," by W. G. Lennox , E. L. Gibbs, and F. A. Gibbs. *Journal of the American Medical Association*, Vol. 113, pp. 1002-3, September 9, 1939.

and drug addiction, criminality, and emotional instability have even less definite evidence to support them as absolute contraindications to adoption.

More studies are needed patterned after that reported in Theis's *How Foster Children Turn Out*.[5] Among the 910 children studied, covering the period from 1898 to 1922, 269 were adopted. Of these 269 children, 145 were foundlings and 45 more came from families about whom very little was known. Among the 235 adopted children who were followed up, 207 were found to be making an adequate adjustment. "More than two-thirds of those children who had what seemed to be a most unpromising of all possible starts are rated as capable" (making an adequate adjustment). Theis's study indicates that children placed early in life tend to adjust more successfully than those placed after the age of five.

In this early study, details as to true family background are, for the most part, lacking. Extensive follow-up studies of adoptions of infants of known heredity who were placed fifteen or twenty years ago would make valuable contributions to our knowledge as to the adoptability of children whose true family histories are generally regarded as unfavorable. Workers in adoption would do well to apply to their field the careful evaluation of past work that is to be found in the field of delinquency in the Gluecks' *"One Thousand Juvenile Delinquents,"*[6] or in the field of child welfare in *The Rehabilitation of Children,* by Baylor and Monachesi.[7]

The adoption of the newborn infant is a ticklish business, but, when skillfully and thoughtfully carried out, it probably offers a better prognosis than does the adoption of an older child. Social workers should question carefully, but not arbitrarily rule out, the possibility of adoption of infants whose hereditary history is weighted with psychosis, feeblemindedness, epilepsy, addiction, criminality, or general emotional instability. When these conditions occur in the family history, nothing is to be gained by waiting until the child is two or three years old before deciding whether or not he is eligible for adoption. Of these conditions, only feeblemindedness would definitely and surely show itself within the age period when the child would still be likely to be adoptable, and the disadvantages of institutional care or replacement outweigh the advantages

---

[5] New York: State Charities Aid Association, 1927.

[6] Boston: Harvard University Press, 1934

[7] New York: Harper Brothers, 1939.

gained by postponing the decision as to adoptability. A one-, two-, or three-year probationary period would protect parents from assuming responsibility for a feebleminded child or a child whose epilepsy or emotional deviation was grossly apparent early in life. The social agency's aim for every newborn dependent child should be for the earliest possible permanent placement, either with relatives or in an adoptive or permanent boarding home.

The dependent child of pre-school age may be the agency's first client, rather than the unmarried mother who seeks for a plan for her unborn baby. These children of one to five years are not infrequently the illegitimate babies whose mothers retained custody of them, either at the mother's own insistence or in response to maternity-home or other external pressure. These children not only are dependent, but also have been neglected physically or emotionally. They have suffered rejection and usually replacements. Their social, intellectual, and emotional development has been either inhibited or warped. Personality reaction patterns or ego defenses have already been established, but fortunately are not yet rigid and fixed.

This more finished product, on the surface, appears to be easier to evaluate than the newborn, wrapped in the cocoon of infancy. Medical examination of a pre-school child, however, reveals relatively little more than medical examination of an infant, except as regards physical appearance and structure. The family history is about equally important for the two age groups.

The pre-school child can be subjected to a battery of tests and can be given an I.Q. rating, but the meaning of that I.Q. is by no means obvious. During the past three years a series of startling papers have come from the Iowa Child Welfare Research Station concerning the tremendous changes in I.Q. observed in children under certain environmental conditions.[8] These findings would seem to have been to some extent confirmed by those of a study conducted by the child-caring agen-

[8] See the following three papers by Beth Wellman: "Mental Growth from Pre-School to College" (*Journal of Experimental Education,* Vol. 6, pp. 127-38, December, 1937); "Our Changing Concept of Intelligence" (*Journal of Consulting Psychology,* Vol. 2, pp. 97-107, July-August, 1938); and "Guiding Mental Development" (*Childhood Education,* Vol. 15, pp. 108-12, November, 1938). See also "Mental Development of Children in Foster Homes," by Harold Skeels (*Journal of Consulting Psychology,* Vol. 2, pp. 33-43, March-April, 1938) and the two studies by Marie Skodak, "Mental Development of Adopted Children Whose True Mothers Are Feebleminded" (*Child Development,* Vol. 9, pp. 303-8, September, 1938) and *Children in Foster Homes* (Iowa City: University of Iowa, January, 1939).

cies of St. Paul, Minnesota.[9] Although the Iowa studies have been severely criticized,[10] workers in the field of adoption would do well to remember that the extent to which the I.Q. is capable of modification has not as yet been definitely determined.[11] There is evidence that the I.Q. does change and that it may represent an evaluation of the child's environment and experience rather than of his inherent possibilities. Many of us have dealt with cases in which a child's intellectual development proceeded normally through infancy and early childhood, and then, after some major traumatic experience, came to a standstill or was markedly slowed down.[12]

The I.Q. of the pre-school child has significance only as an expression of the child's present state of development, which has been conditioned not merely by constitutional factors, but also by his life experiences. Theis[13] asserts that workers must have "imagination about the potentialities of children and their capacity to grow and develop and a conviction that change is inevitable. . . . Children can and do expand and grow, each in his own individual way, to an amazing degree under favorable circumstances."

Gesell,[14] in his defense of psychometric tests as valuable guides and protection in the field of adoption, says:

"The infant, to be sure, is very immature, which tends to make him inscrutable; but, on the other hand, he matures at an extremely rapid rate, and this tide of maturation brings him more repeatedly and more cogently within the purview of systematic observation. . . . The rate and limits of his growth may also be foreshadowed by the manner and the fullness in which he makes the first stage of his developmental journey, say from 4 months to 12, or 18, or 24 months. . . . The reader, however, must not be left with any misconcep-

9 See "Effect of Foster-Home Placement on the Intelligence Rating of Children of Feeble-minded Parents," by Jessie Wells and Grace Arthur. MENTAL HYGIENE, Vol. 23, pp. 277-85, April, 1939.

10 See the two papers by Florence Goodenough, "Look to the Evidence!" (*Educational Methods*, Vol. 19, pp. 73-9, November, 1939) and "Can We Influence Mental Growth?" (*Educational Record Supplement*, Vol. 22, pp. 120-43, January, 1940).

11 Florence Teagarden, in her recently published book, *Child Psychology for Professional Workers* (New York: Prentice-Hall, 1940) devotes considerable space in her second chapter to a review of the nature-vs.-nurture controversy. At the end of that chapter, she presents a bibliography on this important, but still unsettled, subject.

12 See "Some Aspects of the Problem of Adoption," by Florence Clothier. *American Journal of Orthopsychiatry*, Vol. 9, pp. 598-615, July, 1939.

13 See *Social Aspects of Adoption, op. cit.*

14 See "Psych-clinical Guidance in Child Adoption," by Arnold *Gesell*, in *Foster Home Care for Dependent Children* (U. S. Children's Bureau Publication No. 136, revised edition). Washington: Government Printing Office, 1926.

tions concerning the automatic precision of the diagnostic procedures. They do not operate automatically at all; their final usefulness hinges upon trained clinical judgment. The normative developmental schedules furnish an objective basis for the construction of a considered estimate and for a comparative evaluation of successive examinations. In this sense they favor verifiable as opposed to intuitive appraisal. It must be remembered that all diagnosis deals with probabilities and not with absolute prophecy. It is here the aim to reduce the likelihood of error in such important situations as placing a child in a foster home.''

The pre-school child is also subject to appraisal by the intuitive or psychiatrically trained observer. Theis[15] states that ''in practical adoption work it is the child's own readiness to accept new relationships and his capacity for relating himself emotionally to his new parents that determine his placeability more than any one other factor.'' And Jenkins[16] says: ''The behavior of the child should be noted with an eye to estimating his aggressiveness or timidity, sociability or seclusiveness, adaptability, emotional stabilty, response to various measures of control and other characteristics that may be of importance in determining his adjustment in a home.''

The worker who is responsible for recommending for adoption a child of pre-school age or older must take into account not only the poorly understood influences of heredity and constitution, but also the subtle influences of environment and experience, so difficult to determine. These two forces exist in the presenting personality or ego of the child as compromises, conflicts, or contradictions. The child's physical well-being, as well as his mental status, is deeply modified by them. Constitution offers broad limits as to physical and intellectual endowment, but achievement in either sphere of life depends on other factors than heredity alone. It is not unlikely that the favorable intellectual response to environmental stimulus reported in the Iowa studies is to be explained by the child's identification of himself with new love objects in his expanded horizon.

In general, it seems to be true that the child whose psychosexual development has been frequently interrupted by changes of environment that have limited his capacity for identification with love objects is unlikely to be able to form the emotional

---

[15] See *Social Aspects of Adoption, op. cit.*
[16] *Op. cit.*

relationships necessary for healthy social development.[17] These children do not easily make the transition from an orientation toward their aggressive demands to an orientation toward tender, loving impulses. They remain restless, impulsive, demanding, and unsatisfied. They cling to infantile sources of gratification instead of reaching out for the responsibilities of maturity.

II.

No less difficult than the evaluation of the child is the evaluation of the prospective adoptive parents. Theis[18] points out that "after suitability as to usual standards of good character and living conditions have been established, there will be subtler elements for consideration. . . . Subjective, as well as objective factors in the home must be understood. . . . The crux of good adoption work probably lies in the adoption worker's ability to give wise and imaginative assistance in the selection of the right home for the child who can accept placement."

The prospective adoptive parent comes to a social agency as a client in need of help. Whatever his motive may be, he is taking what is, for him, a big and important step which will modify his entire future life. The step he contemplates is one that he thinks will bring him deep satisfactions. From his point of view, the application to adopt a baby has been carefully considered. The action he is taking has usually followed a long period of thought and discussion with relatives, neighbors, or family advisers—i.e., doctors, lawyers, or ministers. To many who apply for a baby, the role of client of a social agency is not easy.[19] A barrier of reticence and shame must often be overcome before a prospective adoptive parent can put himself in the hands of a social worker. Initial self-consciousness, with its accompanying tension or defenses against anxiety, must be recognized by the social worker. Sometimes the adoptive parent may cover his anxiety by expressions of an altruistic wish to be of service to neglected childhood. It is the responsibility of the skilled social worker to understand and to evaluate not only the superficial motives that the adoptive parents present, but

---

[17] See "The Problem of Frequent Replacement of the Young Dependent Child," by Florence Clothier (MENTAL HYGIENE, Vol. 21, pp. 549-58, October, 1937) and "Social Development of the Young Child," also by Florence Clothier (*Child Development*, Vol. 9, pp. 285-97, September, 1938).

[18] See *Social Aspects of Adoption, op cit.*

[19] See "Adoption as the Community Sees It," by Mary F. Smith, in *Social Case-Work with Children*, edited by Jessie Taft. (Vol. 3, No. 1, of *The Journal of Social Work Process*). Philadelphia: Pennsylvania School of Social Work, 1939.

also the deep, underlying needs that have driven them to attempt to work out their inner dissatisfactions through the adoption of a baby.

After ruling out obviously inadequate prospective adoptive parents, there are no rule-of-thumb methods that the social worker can use to judge the suitability of a home for receiving an adoptive child. Physical fitness, absence of gross mental disease, some measure of economic security, and an adequate social and community adjustment are essential, but they offer only minimal protection to the child. Adoptive parents whose fitness on the scores listed above cannot be questioned may apply for a child for grossly improper motives, concealed behind a honeyed love of children. Such a motive may be connected with the inheritance of property or the fulfilling of the conditions of a will. This sort of client rarely comes to the attention of social workers, preferring the anonymity of nonprofessional agencies.

Other clients with motives that make them unsuitable for the responsibility of a child are those who apply for a baby as a last resort in the effort to patch up a crumbling marriage. Occasionally prospective parents apply for a baby because they think or have been told that the responsibility of a baby would be the best treatment for a wife's "nervousness."

After a good initial rapport has been established with the client who applies to adopt a baby, the gross fitness of the home and the superficial suitability of the adoptive parents can readily be established by social investigation. This investigation, as it proceeds, should bring to light any serious personality defects in the prospective parents and any evidences of marital incompatibility that, with the passing of time, might threaten the child's security. Before placing a baby, the social worker will want to be sure that all members of the child's future immediate family will welcome his admission to the family unit—especially that both the husband and the wife want him.

The social worker must be able to determine whether the prospective parents are really interested in the child they plan to adopt or whether their interests are exclusively and permanently focused on a beloved child whom they have lost and whose place they are trying to fill. Some clients apply for a child in order that a child of their own may have company. This motive does not necessarily rule them out as suitable adoptive parents, but the social worker must be very sure that the adopted child does not come into the family merely as a pet for a lonely or spoiled only child. Where there are "own children," the adopted child's situation is apt to be precarious by comparison.

Elderly couples who have waited for years in the hope of having a child of their own, and who finally accept it as inevitable that they cannot, must be considered carefully before they are given a child. Their routine of a well-ordered life will be interrupted, and rigid personalities, travelling in deep grooves, cannot accept a rude upheaval with complacency. The cheerful, companionable, well-brought-up child of their phantasy may be very different from the noisy, untidy, often cantankerous, ungrateful, flesh-and-blood hoodlum who manages always to be underfoot. On the other hand, elderly couples who have longed for many years for a baby may, when they receive one, cling to it as an infant. They may limit its capacity for development by an oversolicitous, overprotective attitude.

When a single person applies for a baby, social workers are justified in hesitating before making a placement.[20] To attain what we regard as psychosexual maturity in our culture, the child needs close association with both a mother and a father during the early years of life. Normal Oedipus development cannot occur in an environment in which one parent figure is lacking. Masculine and feminine attributes are both found in all individuals. The boy has need of a father figure on whose personality, by the process of identification, he can strengthen his masculinity. He has need also of a mother figure to awaken and call up his love impulses and tenderness. His relationship to his mother will serve as a prototype of his future love relationships. The girl, too, needs happy relationships with both a mother and a father, if she is to attain a feminine identfication and, in adult life, a tender relationship with a man that is not overshadowed by fear and aggression. The girl who becomes illegitimately pregnant is all too often a girl who, in childhood, has been denied a wholesome father-daughter relationship. The unmarried adoptive parent is in danger of investing all her (it is usually a woman) emotional interest in the child and thus smothering its individual growth. The role of adoptive parent is easier if there is a stable marriage as a background for the interplay of feelings.

---

[20] For an excellent discussion of this topic, see Chapters IV and V of *An Adopted Child Looks at Adoption*, by Carol S. Prentice. New York: D. Appleton-Century Company, 1940.

Very often childless couples adopt a baby believing that they are sterile, and then, within a few years, have a child of their own. The psychology of this phenomenon is complex and but poorly understood. When it does occur, there are sometimes tragic results for the adopted child. Where sterility is the motive for adoption, every effort should be made by the prospective parents, and encouraged by the social worker, to elucidate in so far as possible the cause of the sterility. Medical examinations of both the husband and the wife are indicated, and in some cases consultation with a psychoanalytically trained psychiatrist will be of help.

Jenkins,[21] in discussing the investigation of the prospective adoptive home, gives the following advice:

"Perhaps the crucial criterion is the ability of the parents to see in the child something more than a satisfaction of their own needs; the ability to recognize in the child a separate personality, with needs of its own. While some desire to relive through the child is perhaps usually present in, and normal to, parent-child relationships, prospective adoptive parents who give the clear and immediate evidence of a predominant desire to work out their own thwarted ambitions through a child should be considered unfit. On the other hand, a degree of parental pride in the achievements and accomplishments of a child is natural and desirable. It is, therefore, advisable, so far as possible, to place children with parents who will value the degree of achievement of which the children are capable.

"The recognition of motives is often not easy. Prospective adoptive parents may not recognize their own motives in seeking a child, or, recognizing them, they may seek to conceal them. To estimate motives requires an adequate acquaintance with the prospective parents to sense the goals, values, and frustrations that determine their attitudes and color their lives. . . . Of particular importance is the type of family organization in which each of the prospective parents grew up and the attitude he held toward his own parents."

III.

Having determined what children are eligible for adoption in some home, and what homes are capable of rearing some child, the social worker faces the responsibility of deciding

---

[21] *Op. cit.*

what child to recommend to what particular adoptive parents. As the child grows up and approaches maturity, it will be easier for him and for the adoptive parents if his appearance and constitutional type are not too foreign to that of the family of which he is a part. The racial antecedents of the child and of the adoptive parents should be the same or as like as possible. Physical characteristics of the true mother and father should be borne in mind when adoptive parents are being considered for a child. In a general way, the temperaments of the child's true parents should not be in complete contradiction to the temperaments of the adoptive parents. But temperaments cannot be measured, and the social worker's sensitivity and intuition must guide her evaluation of them.

Antonio came to the attention of a study home for children at the age of nine. He had been presenting serious behavior difficulties in his adoptive home since the age of six. He ran away, stayed out late, was destructive of his adoptive parents' possessions, and stole from them. His stealing had begun with rummaging through his adoptive mother's desk and bureau drawers.

Antonio's adoptive parents were middle-class, naturalized citizens of Italian birth. They lived in one of the better Italian neighborhoods of a large city. They had adopted Antonio in infancy from a Catholic maternity home, allegedly because of the adoptive mother's sterility resulting from an operation. Antonio had been a cunning, alert, responsive baby. The maternity home in which he was born kept only the sketchiest of records. His mother was known to be French-Canadian, but nothing was known of his father.

As Antonio grew older, his hair became an auburn mop and his eyes deep blue. His skin was fair, and his definitely pug nose was covered with freckles. The name of Pat would have fitted his appearance and manner far better than did the name of Antonio. From the point of view of his particular adoptive parents, he was an ugly duckling. The adoptive mother really had wanted a "Little Lord Fauntleroy" of a child as a plaything and as a possession to show off to her Italian-American friends. In the culture in which he was growing up, Antonio was an absurdity and an anachronism, and he quickly sensed this situation and reacted to it by ever more difficult behavior.

His rummaging, I think, can be explained by his unverbalized desire to find out who he was and where he really belonged. Emotionally frustrated and deprived, he resorted to stealing in an effort to find satisfaction in taking material things from his parents to replace much-needed intangibles. He was aggressive and destructive in order to punish his adoptive parents for letting him down. For both Antonio and the adoptive parents, it was an impossible situation and one that might have been avoided by painstaking selective placement.

Though there are no scientific data on the point, and though heredity may play but a slight role, there may be some validity to the lay concept that breeding or cultural tradition will show itself. Fiction and folklore are full of examples of the princely born who, brought up by peasants, manifests his nobility in his personality and bearing and eventually attains the position to which his birth entitles him.[22] The reverse of this situation can also be found, and many workers in the field of adoption may have had contact with what seemed to be examples of it. (The cultural tradition and personality characteristics referred to here are not to be confused with intelligence level.)

To what degree, if any, there may be an unconscious identification of the self with cultural antecedents will probably remain a mystery for many years. The universal "family romance," whereby the child identifies himself with phantasied parental figures—the counterparts or opposites of the reality figures with whom he lives—may be the explanation of the apparently complete lack of harmony between the adopted child's personality and his home.[23] It is seldom possible to find a child from a family of exactly the same cultural tradition to place in a home. All that one can do is avoid contrasts that are too glaring between the background of the true and that of the adoptive parents, especially if in both cases that background has been constant or characteristic for many generations.

We come now to some consideration of the technique of placement. Practice varies widely as to how much information about the background of the child should be given to the adoptive parents. In Lippman's study,[24] an attempt was made to determine how different people "engaged in mental-hygiene work deal with the problem of child adoption." He states that almost all of the answers to his question as to how much of the family

---

[22] See *Myth of the Birth of a Hero,* by Otto Rank. (Nervous and Mental Disease Publishing Company, 1914.

[23] See "Some Aspects of the Problem of Adoption," by Florence Clothier, *loc. cit.*

[24] *Op. cit.*

history and background should be given the adoptive parents "emphasize the need to treat each case according to its needs. They find it impossible to set down any rules that can apply to all cases. For example, one parent will demand that he be given all information. Another will want to rely entirely on the judgment of the agency. Some parents appear able to accept the child in spite of any negative factors in the family background." Thirteen of those who answered his question believed in telling as little as possible, particularly in the case of material of an unfavorable nature; one told nothing; nine held the opinion that the adoptive parents should be told everything they wish to know, except the names and addresses of the true parents; one stated that he told what the child would need to know later on; and three told as much as they felt could be accepted.

Whatever the policy about giving information to adoptive parents, there can be no question but that all the pertinent facts concerning the child's true family history, his birth and medical history, and his personal history (if he is not a newborn infant) should be recorded and filed by the agency as a valuable private document. It is also the obligation of the social worker always to tell prospective adoptive parents of any pathological condition in the child's family history that is suspected of having a strong genetic basis—*i.e.*, psychosis with no organic basis, familial feeblemindedness, or epilepsy. It is also mandatory to give adoptive parents free access to full knowledge concerning the child's medical history. If a child of pre-school age is retarded in development, adoptive parents should know it, but without the label of an I.Q. A single psychological examination of a pre-school child whose environment has not been conducive to good intellectual development can be grossly misleading.

Few social workers will question these basic essentials of agency adoption practices. It is when we discuss how much more of the data included in our records we should lay before adoptive parents that we reach controversial ground. It is a question that is perhaps best answered individually, according to the educational backgrounds and personalities of the adoptive parents and also according to the philosophy and personality of the social worker concerned. There are some adoptive parents whose honesty is such that they are in an easier position with relatives and neighbors if they can say: "We adopted him through a reliable agency, so we know that nothing was

83

found in his history that would make him an unsuitable child to grow up in our home. Our respect for the judgment of the agency has been fully confirmed by our love for and satisfaction in our child.'' These parents, without sacrificing their honesty—a sacrifice that children sense intuitively—can tell the child that they do not know about his own people. If the child has a burning curiosity to know more about himself, such information as can be given him is not lost, but can readily be obtained.

An adopted adolescent girl once said to me: ''I know that if I thought my mother really loved me, I wouldn't care a hoot about who my own people are, but, as it is, I know she is hiding something from me always. She knows more about me than I do, and I can't stand it.'' At a subsequent interview, the adoptive mother told me that for sixteen years she had been hoping that she would forget some details about her adopted daughter's true mother, who lived in the same large city. The true mother had some social prominence and occasionally her name appeared in the newspaper. The adoptive mother was terrified for fear she would let slip some bit of information that would lead to her daughter's discovering her true identity. For adoptive parents to have access to the names of real parents must often have untoward results.

To sum up, we can say with emphasis that all pertinent information should be available, that no child with a grossly pathological family or medical history should be given to adoptive parents without their full readiness to accept such a responsibility, and that what further detail is laid before them must depend on the individual situation. My personal feeling is that no adoptive parent should be prevented from obtaining pertinent information about the child for whom he assumes responsibility, but that the agency should not insist upon every adoptive parent's reading the child's entire record. I suspect that where the policy is to give out no information, an adequate history is often not available, and that where the policy is to insist upon the adoptive parents' reading the full record, there is a wish on the part of the agency or the social worker to divide the responsibility for the step that is contemplated.

After the child is placed, there is, in twenty-two states,[25] a most important protection against an obvious misplacement— namely, a probationary period before the adoption becomes

---

[25] See *Adventuring in Adoption*, by L. M. Brooks and E. C. Brooks. Chapel Hill: University of North Carolina Press, 1939.

final. The advantages of this in protecting the interests both of the dependent child placed for adoption and of the adoptive parents far outweigh the disadvantages which become apparent in some cases. It is argued that the uncertainty and insecurity of the probationary period vitiates the supposed advantages of an adoptive home, and that continued supervision by a social worker makes it impossible for adoptive parents to feel toward the child as they would toward their own.[26]

In regard to the first point, if so much insecurity and uncertainty exist, it may mean, not that the probationary period is at fault, but that the home is not measuring up to the child's needs. Concerning the second point, if a social worker's supervision is utterly intolerable, it probably indicates that she failed to build up a helpful rapport early in her contact with the adoptive parents.

The probationary period can serve as far more than a gross protection of the child and the adoptive parents. It can be a period of infinite value, both to the adoptive parents and to the social worker. During this time, the social worker should be helping to prepare the adoptive parents to deal with the inevitable problems that arise in the life of an adopted child. The most obvious of these is when, what, and how to tell the child of his adoption. On this subject Jenkins writes:[27]

"Many adoptive parents seek to conceal from their adoptive children the fact of adoption. The motive for the concealment is apparently the fear that they will not be accepted as parents by the child if it learns of its adoption. If concealment were likely to be successful, the element of deception might be overlooked. Experience indicates, however, that even when the adoptive parents move to another neighborhood or to another city, the adopted child, with few, if any, exceptions, ultimately learns of his adoption. The knowledge, usually coming relatively late, from an indirect and sometimes unsympathetic source, often produces an emotional crisis in the child's life, frequently with damaging results. The estrangement of child and parents may take its origin from this crisis, sometimes without recognition by the parents of the cause. The child who has been told of his adoption when young, at the age of 4 or 5, is forearmed against this type of damage. The knowledge need not interfere with the child's sense of security in his parents; indeed, clever parents some-

---

[26] See *The Adopted Child*, by E. G. Gallagher. New York: Reynal and Hitchcock, 1936.
[27] *Op. Cit.*

85

times capitalize the fact to add to the child's security by pointing out that he was selected because they wanted him especially. It is highly important, in order to avoid future perplexing doubts, that an adopted child be told of his identity and given any possible favorable information about his parents."

Valentina P. Wasson's little book[28] is probably as good an introduction to the whole subject as any, if used at the proper age, four to six. It will not answer the child's deeper questions as to his integrity as a person. It may well be that the strength of a child's impulse to know about his true parents varies indirectly with the strength or depth of his identification with his adoptive parents. If his identification with his adoptive family is slight, he will return repeatedly to his phantasy of his natural parents. If his identification with his family is complete, he will have little need of his true parents.

How much the child should eventually be told of his own parents is again a highly individual matter. Some contend that access to such information is a "birthright" that should not be denied the child, but the family background of many a child who has adjusted successfully and happily in an adoptive home is such that it seems to me that knowledge of it might create more distress than is justified.

For the social worker, the probationary period is of inestimable value. It serves her as a preliminary check on the validity of the long, painstaking work she had done in selecting the child to be adopted, the home to receive the child, and the matching of the two. The ultimate success or failure of her work, to be sure, cannot be known for years, but if she is perspicacious she can learn more from such a follow-up period of observation than from all the books and papers written. Only if she has the benefit of seeing the results of her work in the probationary period can she have complete experience in the field of adoption. Only through follow-up experience can she individually, and we as a group, learn to be less bungling and more shrewd and expeditious in our decisions as to what child to place in what home.

Adoption will remain a hazardous relationship, but it is far less hazardous for the child than its usual alternatives. Our goal must be to know more without allowing increased knowledge to limit our scope instead of broadening it.

---

[28] *The Chosen Baby,* by Valentina Wasson. New York: Carrick and Evans, 1939.

CHAPTER 6

Today's Controversial Clients: Married Parents Who Place Legitimate Children for Adoption

H. GORDON MacKAY

Michael Schapiro, in his study of adoption,[1] has stated that in 1953, of the total number of children placed for adoption in the United States, approximately 50 percent were born in wedlock. Of these, 28 percent were placed with non-relatives and 72 percent were placed with relatives. Also, to declare the "full orphans" myth outmoded, Mr. Schapiro points out that only 2 percent were children both of whose parents were deceased. Fifteen percent had one living parent. Finally, the most startling statistic presented here is that, of the children born in wedlock, 25 percent have both parents living together.

In his total presentation, Mr. Schapiro gave rather brief attention to the causative factors in the placing for adoption of children of married parents. His two major reasons seemed to be "financial need" and "emotional instability." Although financial need is part of the picture in many such instances, it has been found not to be the basic dynamic force in the final breakdown of relationships. The second factor, "emotional instability," will be considered in this article.

---

[1] *A Study of Adoption Practice*, New York: Child Welfare League of America, Vol. I, April 1956, p. 41.

Charlotte Towle[2] has stated that the profession of social case-work can be described as the "conscience of the community." In an effort to gain some knowledge of the experiences and attitudes of communities, agencies, and social workers as they come face to face with married couples who seek agency serv-ices toward adoptive placement of their legitimate children, this statement has indeed been validated over and over again. The agency is, in its practices and philosophy, reflective of the community conscience. This, of course, varies with communities and with the relative strength of the agency in its community. However, there is a rather definite pattern of distaste, disbelief, and, in many communities, an almost complete denial that such client needs do indeed exist.

If we, as a profession, are to seek methods and provide serv-ices to meet our clients' needs, we must be aware not only that such clients do exist, but that adoption agency intake services are meeting married client needs in greater numbers through-out the country.

These initial observations have not been drawn from exhaust-ive research. Rather, in preparing to present an institute at the South Pacific Regional Conference of the Child Welfare League of America (San Francisco, April 1957) I selected for inquiry twenty-six Child Welfare League member agencies in-volved in adoption throughout the United States. I requested information concerning the community's attitudes, agency prac-tices and philosophies, workers' attitudes, and any case material which the agencies might feel pertinent for institute discus-sion.[3] The response was immediate. In a seven-week period, twenty-three of the twenty-six agencies responded not only with thoughtful comments and observations, but also with deep-seated convictions supported by appropriate case material.

The most dramatic element in this mass of material was the "crying out in the dark" of adoption agencies at this moment. The inconsistencies in attitudes and convictions of agencies which are equally established evidence the fact that we are in the throes of professional growth. Each agency in its own way, seemed to be striving for a satisfactory and "conscience-free" stand to take on this obviously controversial set of clients. Sev-eral agencies were most emphatic in their conviction that they have been doing a disservice to children and parents by involv-

---

[2] Charlotte Towle, "Client Centered Casework," *Social Service Review*, Vol. 24, 1950, p. 451.

[3] I was unable to gain any statistical data beyond the year 1953. However, this infor-mation seemed particularly significant and demandingly noteworthy.

ing them in long-time institutional or foster care in the idealistic hope that all parents could "with casework service assume
responsibility for their children . . . and thus, allow children
to grow up without adequate parental ties." These agencies
stressed their belief that some parents are pleading to be relieved of parental responsibilities and that, when helped with
their guilt, they can often function more adequately as individuals, and sometimes as parents to children born to them at
a later time.

Other agencies made just as strong statements emphasizing
that they were unable to accept married couples who request
adoption for their children. They stressed the need to work
desperately to rehabilitate and re-establish family circles "if
the home can possibly be helped to provide anywhere near a
wholesome life for the child." These agencies also stressed the
violent community reactions to agencies accepting the decision
of married parents to place their children in adoption.

Another type of response was the statement of one large
adoption agency that their experience with such clients was so
limited they had been unable to reach any conclusions.

Protecting the Child's Rights

In the midst of these agency reactions, let us examine the
statement that we are "child-centered" agencies. We are indeed interested in the natural and adoptive parents' needs,
but what of "child-centeredness" where rejecting parents are
forced to keep an unwanted child? What are the child's rights
in this situation?

In the field of adoption, for many years we have been pre-
occupied, and justly so, with how to serve the unwed mother
and her child. Years ago, were not our communities and our
agencies facing the same kind of controversy with the unwed
parent client as we seem to be facing today with the married
client? Communities may not have moved to a total acceptance
of the unwed parent, but there is increasing evidence of the
acceptance of the reality that such clients do exist. There is
also evidence of the community's sympathies and desires to
help the unwed mother and her child. Will we ever reach the
time when we are ready to help married parents who request
adoption services? How deeply can a problem strike at our
basic social unit—the family?

Perhaps the most logical initial step is to acknowledge that
such disintegrating family units do exist and then attempt to

gain some understanding of them as clients in need of the adoption agency's professional services, which may or may not lead to ultimate adoptive placement of their children. Let us then consider the dynamics, and see if we can explore some of the ensuing conflicts which must be faced by the social worker himself as well as his clients.

From the reports received in this inquiry, it would appear that the usual pattern for many adoptive agencies' counseling service to married couples who request adoptive placement for their child is an almost immediate referral to a family counseling agency. Many of these parents ultimately make their way back to the adoption agency after extensive casework service. They have obviously been unsuccessful and the picture is now further complicated by their increased confusion and abounding residual guilt. It would seem then that the adoption agency social worker, in considering the clients who have come to him saying that they are unable to continue as parents, must have a sound awareness of the factors which make for stability in marriage and in parenthood. He must also assume his responsibility to offer casework services.

So often, the caseworker himself may have inner conflicts aroused when faced by parents "rejecting" a child so totally. This, of course, is not necessarily the case. The social worker who has not himself considered his own attitudes toward parent-child separation may feel an almost overwhelming sense of frustration and confusion, and make a hasty referral to a family counseling agency. This quick dismissal of a situation could be avoided if the adoption worker recognized that a request to place a child for adoption may be a single symptom of dislocation in the family that may actually be resolved in a number of ways, only one of which is adoptive placement.[4] If the worker can consciously feel and know that the fact that parents come to a placement agency merely means that discussion of placement is where the casework process starts, he can approach it with a proper and constructive perspective.[5]

In addition, if the caseworker understands his attitudes towards his own parent-child relationships, it will certainly allow him to approach the client with a minimum of guilt on his own part, guilt drawn from his sudden involvement in the potential permanent separation of parent and child.

---

[4] *The Training of Child Welfare Workers for Placement Responsibilities* (Report of Sub-Committee of Citizens Committee on Adoptions in California) Children's Bureau, 1953, p. 10.
[5] *Op. cit.*, p. 11.

Understanding Family Breakdown

Since we in adoption agencies are faced with families in the process of disintegration, it would seem logical that we have some understanding of the process of family destruction. There seems to be very little written about these specific clients in social work literature. However, there is considerable material on marriage and family relationships.

Nathan Ackerman, M.D., in his article "The Diagnosis of Neurotic Marital Interaction,"[6] had set up some exhaustive criteria against which a marriage might be measured. He states that when a man and woman join in marriage, a process of reciprocity immediately starts to take place. These people are individuals with two separate life experiences and although their initial emotional relationships seem to make them "as one," the individual needs of each member, of course, persist. So, the couple begin to build a relationship upon their ability to reciprocate in the mutual satisfaction of each other's needs. The caseworker, as he is involved with each marital partner, must repeatedly seek answers to these questions "Where is this reciprocity breaking down?" and "How are they compensating for this interruption in the smooth pattern of reciprocity?"

If the individual cannot create proper compensation and thus establish a new sense of reciprocity in his relationship with his marital partner, a destructive element enters in the marriage. An unhealthy repression of hostility ferments and grows, nourished by the frustration and denial which the individual feels in the marital give-and-take. Otto Feneschel,[7] some time ago, stated that repression and denial are the principal defense mechanisms of the infantile ego. They are ways of handling guilt inadequately. When a matter becomes repressed a constant expenditure of energy is required to maintain this repression. A person does not just submerge a distasteful emotional reaction but must constantly strive to keep it there, or the breakdown in relationship moves a step further, into open conflict.

Of course, no interpersonal relationship can be described by a few general terms. For a social worker this is not only the time to react to a situation but also, as Dorothy Hutchinson

---

[6] *Social Casework,* Vol. 35, April 1954.

[7] Otto Feneschel, M.D., *The Psychoanalytic Theory of Neurosis,* New York: W. W. Norton and Co. Inc., 1945, p. 150.

says,[8] "the time for skill and knowledge of pathological behavior and of the inevitable dynamics of behavior." We are dealing not only with individuals but with interaction which the worker is attempting to help move toward some state of balance. This is certainly not the usual clinical situation of patient and worker in a therapeutic relationship since it has the additional catalyst of decision making. The element of finality in relinquishment is ever present. It can be almost overwhelming to a worker to feel that the future of a child rests upon his skills and upon the outcome of his series of contacts. Discussing temporary care, Miss Hutchinson wisely states that social workers must have "tough minds" to protect them from their own "too tender impulses." This applies especially in respect to the separation process in adoptive planning.

Often the married client is unable to move toward a meaningful relationship with the caseworker. The caseworker must realize the implications of the tremendous guilt this person feels, both in his attitude toward his mate by saying that the marriage is no longer "perfect," and also recognizing that he is planning to "give away" his child. Thus, it takes on a threefold aspect: self-punishment, punishment of the mate, and the alleged rejection of the child.

Parents' Unresolved Ties

The worker may find in these situations that one or both of these personalities are built upon an inadequate or immature ego. The marriage may superficially work well until pregnancy or the presence of the child, then the unresolved parental ties in one or both of the parents' own life takes over, often making this individual unable to act as a parent to his own child.

How often have we seen in other casework situations the adult who is still trying to seek a love relationship with his own rejecting parent, even though he is now in his maturity? Often it is not until such a person is called upon to give of himself as a parent that this rather drastic picture of inadequacy presents itself. Thus, in a marriage that seems to be destroying itself, it is not always a case of the partners' inability to relate to each other but a more subtle unresolved problem within one or both of them. If this can be brought to the surface and worked with, there is a basis upon which caseworker can hope for the re-establishment of the family. With

---

[8] *The Placement Worker and the Child's Own Parents,* Dorothy Hutchinson, *Social Casework,* July 1954, p. 29.2

sound casework support, gradual insight on the part of both clients can lead to a new set of compensations. These, in turn, may ultimately develop into a different form of cooperation than was present at the beginning of the marriage. The marriage then may have a foundation for re-establishment.

Throughout all of this strain in the family relationships, the child himself, of course, is strongly affected. The needs of this child must be considered paramount since he is the "innocent victim." However, this should not drive the worker again into a sense of over-identification which can be far more damaging than helping. The child can be an active and rewarded participant in the re-establishment of the family unit. This certainly is not easy, but the child if allowed to participate, secures the dignity and self-satisfaction of re-establishing himself in the role of a loved child with his natural parents.

However, if the process of disintegration has moved to a point where there is no possibility of re-establishing a secure family unit, the social worker has to help these parents and children separate in the most constructive way possible. If parents can feel that they are actually giving the child something by providing him with a secure future in adoption, they are able to leave this experience with less damaging guilt. This may be a first responsible act.

When couples relinquish a child they need not themselves be going their separate ways. Rather, it is far more typical to find that the parents are able to use this separation positively in re-establishing their own relationship and perhaps become adequate parents to later offspring.

Helping Parents to Help Child

In assisting the parents, can we help them feel a sense of giving their child a chance rather than a sense of rejection, thus helping the child to use this service. This has a positive effect upon the child himself. If he feels that the parents want the best for him, his own fears and anxieties about permanent adoptive placement will be somewhat alleviated. One of the factors in letting the parents feel the soundness of their decision is that their concern for their child will be passed on to the adoptive parents. The fact that the agency feels that the adoptive parents should have a positive identification with the biologic parents is extremely rewarding to them. This, of course, is just as rewarding to the child in later years, whether he separated at a time of infancy or when he was older. The child who becomes aware in later life that there was another set of parents in his background is far better able to adjust to the new realization if he can feel that he was not "thrown away," or "left on a doorstep," but rather that he was planned for with a sense of concern. Thus, in this process of separation, the worker can use a casework technique which can have lasting effect on the child while it helps the parents act responsibly.

Now, in a final look at the national picture presented by the agencies who participated in the author's inquiries, it seems obvious that our profession must not only admit that there are such clients in our communities but that they feel dire need of assistance and for the sake of their children, they should have it. Agencies can be more child-centered if they aggressively interpret to their communities the need for action in providing consultation and adoption services to such families.

CHAPTER 7

"Taking Sides" in the Unmarried Mother's Conflict

FRANCES H. SCHERZ

What is the nature of the helping process in relation to the decision the unmarried mother must make in keeping or relinquishing her child? To what extent should the caseworker "take sides" in the decision? What social or emotional factors should be considered before she can align herself with or against a plan for placement?

These and related questions are being examined by local agencies that are working with unmarried mothers.[1] The pregnant girl presents a special social problem, because of society's attitude toward her. Despite advances in acceptance as shown in eligibility to Aid for Dependent Children programs, our culture still penalizes the woman who has a child outside the bounds of marriage. We have only to recall this country's repudiation of Germany's encouragement of illegitimate births to realize how deeply ingrained are these taboos in our social structure. By and large the unmarried mother and her child face overt and subtle condemnation from family and community.

The experience of a family agency that has worked extensively with unmarried mothers may be helpful in indicating a treatment approach that seems to be valid. In 1944 the Family Wel-

[1] See "The Unmarried Mother's Decision About Her Baby," by Leontine R. Young, *Journal of Social Casework*, January, 1947, p. 27.

fare Society of Atlanta was asked by the Board of the Florence Crittenton Home to take over the latter's casework program. The Home gives service to unmarried mothers from two counties that have agencies with membership in the Atlanta Community Chest, but it also accepts applications throughout the state of Georgia and occasionally from outside the state. The Family Society is responsible for all intake and for continued service while the girl is in the Home. The Home has a capacity of twenty-four girls, is generally full and frequently has a waiting list. About one-half of the girls come from farms or communities outside the two counties. Since taking over the casework program the family agency has given service to almost three hundred unmarried mothers. It is not possible within the limitations of this paper to present the setup of the Home or the details of the relationships among the Home, the Family Society, and child-placing agencies.

Material gathered during this experience has led us to believe that the caseworker should take an active, "steering" role in helping the unmarried mother to make a good decision for herself and the child. She should "take sides" in the conflict by opening areas for consideration that will help the client to view the total situation. In general, we have found that the unmarried mother shows less conflict about the pregnancy than about keeping or placing the child. In some situations the pregnancy itself has served the emotional need, temporarily or permanently, and is no longer a source of disturbance, whereas the child is a reality that must be faced.

The caseworker should try to understand, and use in treatment, knowledge of the precipitating factor in the pregnancy, underlying behavior patterns and conflicts, and the social, economic, and cultural setting from which the girl has come and to which she is returning. The latter should perhaps be emphasized because our experience has shown that caseworkers frequently focus their interest in the emotional elements of the conflict without giving sufficient recognition to environmental forces which may have an equal degree of impact on the decision the unmarried mother makes. There are some cultural groups and some social and family situations in which illegitimate pregnancy is accepted as a normal form of behavior but, since that is not the usual pattern of behavior in our society, most girls who come to a Florence Crittenton Home or to a large city from smaller communities do so because they cannot face social or parental condemnation. They seek the shelter and anonymity provided by the institution or the boarding home. If the caseworker stresses those elements of the conflict which stem from emotional reasons for the pregnancy and does not place adequate emphasis on social elements, the client may make a decision that becomes untenable when she is ready to resume her ordinary way of living. This means that the caseworker should take active responsibility for discussing attitudes of parents and community, for presenting social and economic problems in raising a child born out of wedlock. Through this method, the client is given an opportunity to examine and evaluate the reality aspects of her situation and to weigh their meaning and importance in her decision.

Although I have emphasized the social implications of keeping or relinquishing a child, it is not done with the intention of depreciating emotional areas. The caseworker should help the client to uncover and evaluate those emotional needs that are related to the pregnancy and the coming decision. We know from psychiatric orientation and from casework experience that most unmarried pregnancy has a neurotic base. It is frequently a symptom of unresolved love-hate parental relationships, originating in early childhood. If the caseworker, in her genuine wish to leave the client free to make her own decision, does not strengthen that part of the personality which is struggling to make a wise decision, the unmarried mother may remain fixed in the very ambivalence of love and hate which helped to create the pregnancy. In helping the client to discover and work through emotional needs, the caseworker should "take sides" by pointing out those elements that make it desirable or undesirable to keep the child. She may go a step further by aligning herself openly with the healthier part of the client's personality and state what she believes to be the best decision. Such treatment will, of course, be timed to the client's pace and presupposes a good relationship between caseworker and client. Failure of the mother to resolve the conflict, either because of our lack of direct participation in the decision, or because of the mother's degree of neurotic involvement, leaves her in the predicament of not being able to keep and care for the child or to relinquish it. These children frequently are taken in and out of foster homes or institutions and are deprived of a secure love relationship, which is coming to be accepted as the basis of an integrated personality.

When a good decision has been reached by the client, she should be supported and encouraged by help in concrete and emotional areas. Support should be purposeful and consistent lest the client be thrown again into a state of anxiety and indecision.

The caseworker is in a peculiarly fortunate position to help the unmarried mother make a good decision. Since we believe that such pregnancies are a response to an emotionally starved or distorted parental relationship, then the caseworker can become, in many situations, a parent substitute. In particular, she can become a substitute mother, an "amended," loving mother. Conscious assumption of such a role gives the client a feeling of acceptance and—of equal importance—a feeling of dependence. This is particularly important since early childhood deprivations leave the client with unsatisfied dependency needs which play a significant part in causing unmarried motherhood. Also, when the pregnant girl admits the pregnancy by coming to the agency, she is frequently in a shocked and traumatized condition and requires a period of dependency on the caseworker before she can begin to work on the problem realistically. This new kind of mother can help to make and sustain decisions, can use her role to help the client to give up the baby to *her*. Thus the unmarried mother is enabled to identify the baby with herself in having an accepting parent who will see that the child has a loving home when it is placed.

Miss A was shocked when she was refused admittance to her mother's home. Instead her mother suggested that Miss A have her landlady call the family agency for help in planning during pregnancy. This stunned surprise lasted for most of the first interview, yet to the caseworker the mother's behavior did not seem at all unusual in the light of Miss A's life history as she told it in this and subsequent interviews.

Miss A, 17, was the youngest of five children who were deserted by the mother when Miss A was three years old. The father tried to hold the family together but six months later placed all of them in an orphanage. Miss A left the institution at 15 to live with two older sisters who danced at night clubs, in a neighboring state. She described these sisters as being good to her but "they were only 18 and 20 and couldn't take care of me." She didn't blame them for not keeping her in school or for not attempting to control her choice of friends.

Miss A had very little to say about the putative father; she had known him several weeks, thought she was in love with him but later decided he really had not been interested in her. After she knew she was pregnant she had a brief relationship with another man she thought she loved. Her sisters couldn't take care of her and she somehow felt her mother would, so she returned to her own community. She knew her mother had remarried several years before and had two young children. At no time did Miss A blame her father for placing her in the orphanage. "How could a man be expected to take care of five little kids?" She thought her stepfather was "nice" too, although in reality she had only seen him once. Toward her mother she showed intense resentment for deserting her and for refusing to help her now. She expressed a strong desire to keep the baby. "It's something that belongs to me and I'll love it and be a good mother."

After discussion, the caseworker and Miss A agreed that she would be given money to live in a private boarding home instead of entering the Florence Crittenton Home, because she could not face another institutional living arrangement. In a series of interviews the caseworker encouraged Miss A to look to her as a giving, "different" mother. The worker was able to help Miss A to recognize that she had built a fantasy picture of her parents which had conditioned her behavior and was affecting her feelings about the coming baby. Having felt that the father's effort to keep the family together was a sign of love (in reality he had deserted also), Miss A misunderstood casual interest by men as real love. She had not had enough affection to know how to evaluate relationships. Also, Miss A had needed to become pregnant to try to force a dependency relationship on her mother as well as to punish her. By keeping the baby she could show her mother that she could be a "good" mother, one who did not throw her child away. Through such gradual interpretation, the caseworker helped Miss A to realize that she did not love the baby for itself. The caseworker also helped Miss A to see that the baby was not a "thing," but a real person. She pictured the life of the mother and child in the future, the difficulties of working and caring for a child without a father, the community's disapproval, Miss A's lack of training for an adequate job. At the same time the caseworker held out to Miss A the possibility of training for work, of a happy marriage, with children who would be wanted for themselves.

This illustration shows the degree of activity and responsibility the caseworker took in helping the client to evaluate social and emotional forces and to relinquish the child for adoption. This situation, although different in details from others, is not atypical in work with unmarried mothers. We see in Miss A an example of early love deprivation, of constant hungering for affection, of accumulation of anger at not getting it. We see the usual normal intensification of biological and psychological sexual needs in adolescence distorted by a neurotic base. Where there has been an early love deprivation, especially by the mother, we frequently find that the relationship of the girl to the putative father is a casual one, that he is a "tool" by which to achieve the pregnancy. We also find that the girl sees herself, unconsciously, as a depreciated person, one who is not deserving of normal love since she may have been responsible for losing the mother's love through her own ambivalent feelings toward the mother.

The caseworker, by being a "good" mother, showed the client that mothers could be loving, that Miss A was worthy of love, that it was possible for Miss A to become a "different" mother later through marriage. This points to the need for caseworkers to stress, as with all clients, the possibility of constructive personality change.

The worker helped Miss A to see that she was using the baby as a symbol of neurotic need and that she did not have to keep it on that basis. The worker also evaluated Miss A's ability to support and rear a child in a community that would not accept illegitimacy. She took responsibility for helping the client to know that her contribution as a mother would be to relinquish the child. Although Miss A wavered at times, the caseworker consistently pointed out that Miss A was doing the best thing for herself and the child. Following placement of the baby, Miss A successfully completed a course in beauty culture.

Despite casework knowledge and skill, it is, of course, not always possible to help an unmarried mother make a wise decision. Some clients are too involved emotionally to use help. With many, the time factor operates in limiting the caseworker's usefulness. The majority of unmarried mothers who come to an agency are advanced in pregnancy because of the need, conscious or unconscious, to keep their secret as long as possible. Many wish to forget the experience and to break contact as soon as the child is born, and therefore make hasty decisions. Many wish to return to their homes in other communities as quickly as they can and do not work through the conflict. The time factor points to the need for early evaluation and for active direction by the caseworker.

Miss M, 22, was referred from a near-by camp by her commanding officer. She was six months' pregnant by a man with whom she had had one sexual relationship. She told the caseworker that she had decided to try to become pregnant as a means of getting out of the navy with an honorable discharge. Miss M, the oldest of eleven children, had been raised on a farm. She expressed some fondness for both parents but had considerable resentment over the amount of responsibility she had to take for the younger children and for household and farm tasks. This resentment came out indirectly, as did her feelings about the parents' rigidity in religious and moral areas. Although she said she liked all this responsibility, feeling against it was near the surface.

After graduation from high school, Miss M left home determined to become an aviatrix. She came East, worked in airplane plants, and took some flying lessons. She fell in love with a man not of her religious faith, and lived with him for a year, knowing he would never marry her. After a quarrel over this, she impulsively joined the WAVES. She hated the regimentation and the authority of the officers.

Miss M was determined to keep her child because she felt "responsible" for bringing it into the world without a father. She was certain the baby would be a girl and was already planning to have her "well behaved and disciplined." Miss M was not planning to inform her parents about the child, felt it would "work itself out somehow" if she were to return home eventually.

The keynote of Miss M's personality seemed to be impulsiveness born of rebellion. She seemed to have a highly developed system of reaction formation, as evidenced by periods of adequacy, responsibility, and good organization, followed by outbursts of impulsive self-destructive acts. The period of contact had to be brief since Miss M planned to return to her home shortly after the child's birth. The caseworker worked quickly in trying to interpret behavior to Miss M, in raising questions about her return to a small, rigid community and family, in trying to minimize the guilt that was so large a part of the client's determination to keep the child. Despite this Miss M left with the baby, ostensibly to return home. Several months later the caseworker received a letter from an agency in another state indicating that Miss M was asking for placement of the child. She seemed undecided about requesting a temporary or permanent plan.

Although the caseworker failed to help Miss M make a good decision, this illustration again points to the fact that the caseworker was actively concerned in exploring and treating the emotional and social situation and in trying to "take sides" in the decision.

The question may be raised as to whether or not interpretation of conscious or near conscious material, when given at a faster pace than the client can assimilate, has any constructive value or whether it tends to arouse greater anxiety. We have felt that, because of pressure of time with many unmarried mothers, if interpretation is based on understanding and sympathy and is handled skilfully, it has real value. The caseworker needs to gauge the force of the neurotic impulse and the strength of the ego. But the understanding that the client gains in working through a crisis situation has lasting therapeutic effects. Even if accepted on an intellectual level, this helps the client to participate actively in assuming responsibility for her share in the decision. In some instances intellectual understanding later becomes integrated into the personality.

Another question that may be raised is the kind and extent of activity a caseworker should undertake in anxiety-provoking areas during pregnancy. Should working with emotional material and concrete planning for the child be postponed until after the birth of the baby? Our experience as well as material gathered from conferences with psychiatrists has led us to believe that exploration and interpretation of conscious emotional material and discussion of concrete plans are less anxiety provoking and help the client to face a decision with greater strength if handled during the entire time of contact than if limited to the post-natal period.

Both illustrations used in this paper have indicated that we are more "on the side" of having the unmarried mother relinquish her baby. Our experience has shown that with rare exceptions it is the more neurotic girl who keeps the child. Occasionally we have found that an unmarried mother, whose pregnancy is comparatively free from neurosis, can be helped to rear her child in the face of social difficulties. Most of the clients, however, ask for help with adoption plans when they come to the agency. If the social and emotional history indicates that placement is the best solution to the mother's conflict, the caseworker's role should be that of helping the unmarried mother work through to acceptance of this plan and to support her in her decision through the inevitable period of uncertainty and wavering. This assumes that the caseworker is herself free from emotional and social taboos, and free to give the unmarried mother a maximum degree of help.

CHAPTER 8

The Unmarried Father*

LEONTINE YOUNG

Until recently, the unmarried father has been pretty much an adjunct to the problems and complications surrounding the central fact of illegitimacy. That he had a part in creating the situation was, biologically speaking, incontestable; but beyond that his chief importance was considered to be his capacity to give financial assistance and the question of his willingness to do so. To a marked degree he was considered a potential but probably unreliable resource, to be ignored, appeased, or bullied as the occasion required; few of the ordinary human emotions and reactions were attributed to him, with the exception of his possible if not probable attempt to deny any participation in the situation and to evade all responsibility for it. In short it was more or less taken for granted that he was in any case a pretty worthless character probably without scruples or conscience, from whom little could be expected, and that little to be exacted for the most part only by compulsion. That he was a human being with needs, problems, fears, and potentialities of his own was an idea only rarely considered and still more rarely acted upon.

There are, of course a number of reasons why this was, and

* Reprinted by permission from OUT OF WEDLOCK by Leontine R. Young, copyright, 1954. McGraw-Hill Book Company, Inc.

for that matter still is, true to a considerable extent. Biologically, the man's role ends with conception, and physically he is free to go his own way. Without the emotional and social interests and ties of marriage he has in many cases no basic incentive or interest in maintaining a relationship or assuming any long-time responsibility. Even where such incentive and interest do exist, the attitude of courts, agencies, and in general the community as a whole is scarcely conducive to encouraging his interest in the direction of action. The punitive nature of our laws, court decisions, and official rulings places even the most conscientious man immediately on the defensive, a position resented by every person as undignified, embarrassing, and injurious to self-esteem. In a great many cases the so-called "alleged father" is in effect accused of trying to escape responsibility before he can so much as open his mouth. It is tacitly taken for granted that he would flee unscathed from the whole problem if permitted. Hence often from the beginning pressure, official or otherwise, is imposed upon him to compel financial assistance for the girl and later financial support for the baby. There may be little if any interest in his side of the story, and the official attitude toward what he does say is often one of suspicion.

Under these circumstances it is scarcely surprising that many men promptly deny paternity or take refuge in that classic and unprovable retort, "How do I know I am the father? She may have been out with half a dozen men for all I know." While in many cases the man may be quite aware that this is not true, he acts like someone accused of a crime seizing upon the undeniable ambiguity inherent in the situation as an alibi. It is certain that what he fears is usually far more than financial responsibility. The threat of certain if undefined punishment is ominously present and is enhanced by the unsympathetic attitude with which he is often met. His own conscience may contribute to his fear and can serve to magnify for him the amorphous danger which he is sure awaits him if he makes any damaging admissions. The extent to which this can influence his actions can be seen in the man who will admit his paternity of the child to the girl directly and will even give voluntary financial assistance but who denies officially any responsibility and warily side-steps any action that could be construed as an official admission of paternity. Of course by this refusal he also avoids any clear and binding commitment and keeps himself theoretically free from continuing and specific obligation.

All this creates a synthetic and poisonous atmosphere injurious to everyone concerned. Its original premise is false and involves everyone in a false situation. If every unmarried father is considered guilty until proved innocent, the man who might under different circumstances wish to participate and help is lumped indiscriminately with the man who wants only to escape the whole business. From the man's standpoint he is being punished for the sexual act, and this is the crime to which he must not admit. Obviously there is no possibility of knowing what the unmarried father is like as a person, no chance of his real participation in the situation, until this accusing and punitive attitude toward him is abandoned.

The man so accused has little opportunity to consider anything but his own defense. His feelings for the girl, for the child, and his obligation to them are subordinated all too often to the artificial and largely unnecessary problems raised by this attitude of condemnation. That some men would under the most favorable circumstances seek to evade any responsibility is certain, but inability to face unpleasant realities and do something about them is not unique to this problem. It is also certain that many men, if left free to concentrate their attention on the problem itself, would be far more interested in helping, both financially and otherwise, than is now the case.

Because of this punitive attitude we have had little opportunity to learn what the unmarried father as a person is like, even when the unmarried mother has identified him. His very defensiveness has been a shield which has tended often to make him act in conformity with the prevailing stereotype of his personality. When he expects to be condemned or exploited, he has first to be convinced that this will not happen. His physical ability to escape consequences has naturally contributed materially to the difficulty of establishing contact with him. In addition the problem has been complicated by the unmarried mother's own attitude. Many girls regard the man seemingly as no more than a biological adjunct and do not want him involved in the situation. They give his name, if at all, reluctantly and discourage his active participation. Other girls are actively hostile to the man, and his reaction is more often one of fear than of interest. Both these circumstances increase the difficulty of knowing the man at all and of knowing what he is like, what his feelings and problems are. When we divest the problem of prejudice and of moral judgments, it is clear that there are two people involved in a difficult and unhappy situation, both of whom must have their own problems, fears, and desires. The question is not who is to blame or which of the two carries the greater moral responsibility but what can be done to understand and help both of them.

As we have come to know something of the unmarried father as an individual, one factor has emerged clearly. He is in almost every case a counterpart of the neurotic personality of the unmarried mother. Their problems complement each other with precision, and unconsciously each has sought in the other an answer to his own neurotic needs. Thus, the girl who wishes to eliminate the man totally from any share in the baby picks someone who is irresponsible or disinterested in her as a person or someone she never really knows. In these cases the man rarely if ever appears in the picture at all. We can only conclude from such sketchy information as is available that he is usually an immature and quite promiscuous person who is no more interested in the girl than she in him. He is not concerned with protecting her from possible pregnancy or in what may happen to her afterward. His action is often an impulsive one and seems to remain for him an incident of little importance. In adolescent fashion he seems to be experimenting with sex but under circumstances which will leave him free of consequence.

In many cases, of course, he never knows that there has been a baby. Whether or not consciously he ever considers this possibility is not known. In other cases the girl has informed him of her pregnancy, but he has ignored the fact.

During the war a number of girls wrote to the men concerned but never received any answer from them. Since at that point all contact was discontinued, nothing more is known of the men's reaction than that they fled all responsibility and wanted nothing to do with the problem. This has happened so consistently that it seems apparent that this type of girl has selected unconsciously the type of man who can be depended upon to abandon her. Emotionally childish, he may be a drifter without roots, moving from job to job and from one community to another. Unlike the girl, he is aware of his sexual interest but does not combine it with any affection for her as a woman. He is quite possibly afraid of women and hostile to them. The sexual act itself may well have become to him an act of hostility rather than affection, which would explain his willingness to exploit the girl, his failure to use contraceptives, and his refusal to share the consequences with her afterward. Consciously

107

or not, he seems to want to hurt her and to fear any woman who might make demands upon him.

This certainly plays a part in those situations where he has known the girl for some little time and has expressed interest in her until he learns of her pregnancy—at which point he deserts her. Some couples have even discussed marriage tentatively. One intelligent young woman, in discussing the father of her expected baby, said that she had known him for some months and that they had discussed marriage. They had talked about it in general terms as something that might take place at some vague date in the future. At this time they had not had sexual relations. When the girl became pregnant, she told the boy; he reacted with shock and dismay and shortly afterward left town. She had heard nothing from him and had no wish to see him or to attempt to secure help from him. She remarked that she had always known he was irresponsible and unreliable. Clearly the boy was frightened of responsibility and of the demands the girl might make upon him. His hostility to her was demonstrated in his behavior toward her and is particularly striking in the light of her basic lack of interest in him. Far from making any stringent demands upon him, she seemed to be relieved that he had gone. What he had feared lay within himself, not in the reality. In a sense each had what he had wanted: the girl a baby, and the boy the knowledge that he had impregnated a woman and escaped without ties or personal involvement.

To know why this was important to him one would have to know him, what he wanted, and what he feared. By the very nature of the problem this kind of man is not known directly and is rarely seen by the case worker. It cannot, however, be simply assumed that he thereby forgets the whole incident or that physical freedom implies automatically psychological freedom from consequences. Work with soldiers during the war brought out the fact that a number of men were deeply concerned by their abandonment of a girl whom they had impregnated. They had a strong sense of guilt because of their behavior, and while no one knew what had happened, they discussed it voluntarily, impelled by their own unhappiness. What they had done was a part of their total personality problem, which had created turmoil and unhappiness for them in many areas of their lives. The man in these situations needs help just as the girl does, but it is rarely possible to give him that help except as he is seen in relation to other manifestations of his basic difficulties.

In cases where the unmarried father is known, the corollary between his problems and those of the girl is even more apparent. Mr. B. was a married man, but childless. Brought up by a dominating and possessive mother, he had always been uncomfortable with girls and unsure of himself. He had married a cold, rather aggressive woman, and over a period of years had become almost completely impotent with her. Both he and his wife were severely inhibited with each other, and there was little warmth in their relationship. Then he met Irene, a girl many years his junior. Irene had also grown up in a home dominated by an aggressive and rejecting mother and had never been able to work out a happy life adjustment for herself. The death of her mother had left her more than ever adrift. Mr. B. became very attached to Irene, and they had sexual relations. He was not impotent with her, and he expressed a strong need for their continuing relationship. Neither of them took any precautions, and when Irene became pregnant, Mr. B. suspected the fact before she did.

Despite the practical problems they faced, Mr. B. was deeply pleased by Irene's pregnancy. He took immediate responsibility, gave her financial support, helped her make arrangements for shelter care, and participated actively in plans for the baby. Yet at the same time he continued to affirm his love for his wife and refused to consider separation from her. He attempted to keep the whole affair secret from her and would see Irene only in hidden, sporadic meetings. For awhile he toyed with the idea of trying to persuade his wife to adopt the child without letting her know of his relationship to the baby. When Irene refused to consent to this, he still tried to persuade her to place the child in a boarding home. Ultimately Irene surrendered the baby for adoption, a plan which Mr. B. was reluctant to accede to. He continued, however, his interest in Irene and felt he could not let her go out of his life. Neither could he face the possibility of separation from his wife.

Deeply unsure of his own masculinity, Mr. B. wanted the baby as tangible proof that he was a man. He wanted to continue the relationship with Irene for the same reason. With her he could be strong and adequate; with her he was not impotent. Yet this was seemingly possible for him only so long as the relationship remained illicit. The permanent structure of his life was still with his wife, who was in a sense his defense against

109

his own sexual urges, against the challenge of his own manhood. He did not see that he was strongly hostile to both women, that he deprived his wife of emotional satisfactions and Irene of security, respect, and companionship. Like a child, he wanted everything on his own terms. He was aware of his fear and his unhappiness, and he tried desperately to keep an untenable situation in balance. Like the unmarried mother, he could not combine love and a sexual relationship with marriage, and like the unmarried mother he wanted a child out of wedlock. He married a woman like his mother, a dominating and depriving woman upon whom he was very dependent, and with whom he was impotent. He had a girl who was very masochistic, who was dependent on him, and who beneath her dependence feared and distrusted him. His fundamental rejection of her met her neurotic need and confirmed the validity of her hostility to him. In his family background, as in his personality structure, Mr. B. had in masculine form the counterpart of the unmarried mother's problem. Even his wish to give the child to his wife, who was also psychologically like his mother, has a reminiscent ring. One might almost say that but for the accident of biology he would in fact have been an unmarried mother.

Although quite different in personality, Mr. G. had some of the same basic problems. A man in his late thirties, he had grown up in a well-to-do home where his father was very much the autocrat. The youngest of three boys, he had turned to an older brother for protection and understanding. When he was still a young boy, the family lost most of its money and shortly afterward the father died. His mother had worked to support herself and the boys and had died when they were young men. Mr. G. always spoke of her as the most wonderful person in the world and was bitter that she had died before he could make up to her for her sacrifices for him. Of his father he rarely spoke.

Although he had a good education, Mr. G. had never held a permanent job. He usually took jobs far inferior to his ability and training, and there were often long periods of unemployment between them. During these periods he turned to his brother for financial assistance. He had continued to be very devoted to and dependent upon his brother, although his situation had been sharply complicated by his brother's marriage. He resented his sister-in-law and described her as a neurotic and demanding woman. She in turn despised him and resented his demands upon his brother.

An unhappy, bitter man, Mr. G. had avoided all but casual

relationships with women until he met Miss L. The youngest of
three children, Miss L. had felt overshadowed all her life by a
more brilliant and successful older sister. Her mother was dead,
and she had grown up in a home dominated by a strict, stern,
and rejecting father.

The relationship between Mr. G. and Miss L. was a brief and
unhappy one. The very needs which had first brought them together engendered conflict between them. When Miss L. became
pregnant, she insisted that Mr. G. marry her. Frightened at
this, he became openly hostile to her and refused even to see
her. He did help her to some extent financially and was very
concerned about the child, toward whom he felt very guilty. He
participated actively in plans for the child and at first wanted
to place the baby in his brother's home. When this idea was rejected by both Miss L. and the brother's wife, he discussed
with the case worker the advisability of adoption. He continued
to reject any consideration of marriage with Miss L. despite
her pressure on him to do so. Furious at his refusal, Miss L.
became very punitive toward him. Although she had at first decided to place the baby for adoption, she now announced firmly
that she would keep the child; she instituted court proceedings
against Mr. G. to compel his support of the child. The more he
urged adoption, the more firmly she determined to keep the
baby. She placed her son in a private boarding home and turned
her primary attention to forcing permanent support from Mr. G.

While neither of them realized it, there is a definite similarity
in the personalities and problems of these two people. Each
was bitterly hostile to the opposite sex; each was fundamentally
dependent upon someone stronger than himself; each was incapable of giving to another person or considering the welfare
of another person apart from his own. Mr. G. feared and hated
women and for years avoided any involvement with them. Unconsciously he may have felt that they threatened the precarious balance of his own masculinity and that he must defend
himself against them. The extent of his neurotic conflict is revealed in his selection of Miss L., who could only attempt out
of her own anger and jealousy to destroy the very masculinity
he had so long tried to protect. In effect, Mr. G. chose a woman
who could only confirm and validate all the fantasies and fears
he had had about women in general. He had conclusively proved
to his own satisfaction that they were his mortal enemies.

He never saw Miss L. as a troubled, unhappy person like
himself, pushed by her own fears and the victim of her own

111

conflicts. She was a powerful and evil ogre in his fantasies, as he was in hers. What he never recognized was that he was trying to destroy her in the same way that he accused her of hurting him. He had ignored the possibility of a child despite the fact that he was an intelligent man and well aware of the consequences that could ensue. When Miss L. did become pregnant, his first wish was to take the baby from her and give it to his brother, who had remained throughout the years a father to him. Certainly at this point he saw the baby as wholly his, and like the unmarried mother he wanted to give it to the dominant parent. Like the unmarried mother, he apparently wanted this child for a purpose—to act out his own childhood fantasies.

In a sense, Miss L. was really for him a means to an end. When she refused to give him the child and pressed for marriage, he was appalled. His one wish then was to retaliate, to hurt and humiliate her, and at the same time he feared her. Like two destructive children, these people were so swamped by their own hatreds and fears that they were blind to the realities of their situation, blind to the fact that in the process they were damaging themselves irreparably, blind to their obligation to the child, who was now a pawn in their futile battle with each other.

The unmarried father seems to come from the same type of background as the unmarried mother. The dominating mother or the dominating father has created a neurotic home situation in which the personality of the boy has been warped. Blocked in his emotional development, he has as an adult attempted that impossible task of reconciling infantile needs and confusions with the realities of the adult world. Like the unmarried mother he has often seemingly an unconscious desire for a child out of wedlock; he finds it difficult and often impossible to combine love and a sexual relationship within the structure of a happy marriage. And like the unmarried mother he wants the baby, not for its own sake, a child to love and protect, but rather as a symbol, a means to an end. The baby may be proof of his virility, but he does not ask himself why this must be achieved outside the confines of marriage. More than has been generally realized, he has a personal stake in the fact of the baby. Occasionally this is high-lighted when an unmarried father sues for custody of the child, sometimes after he has married a woman other than the mother of the child. One suspects that the pattern of giving the baby to the mother or to a mother substitute is not confined solely to the unmarried mother. In some cases the father has been successful in securing a surrender from the mother and has himself adopted the child. Sometimes he has taken the baby home to his mother, and sometimes he has placed the child in a boarding home with a hired substitute mother.

To what extent his own neurotic needs enter into the situation is difficult to ascertain because, comparatively speaking, so little attention has been devoted to the study of his psychological part in the problem. Considering the fact that he has no legal right to the child, that his interest is frequently discouraged both by the unmarried mother and by the generally unsympathetic attitude toward him, one can safely assume that his needs play a far greater part than usually appears on the surface.

The desire for an out-of-wedlock child and hostility toward the woman seem to be closely allied. With some men this is also tied up with a strong masochistic urge. This is particularly noticeable in many married men who have legitimate children, a steady job, and a secure position in the community. That this is more than an extramarital fling at romance or the unthinking impulse of the moment can be seen in the fact that these men select neurotic girls who do not really like men and that they ignore any question of consequences.

One young man, a successful doctor with a wife and children, became interested in a very narcissistic girl who had a punitive and aggressive mother. At no time apparently did he consider the question of contraceptives or the practical consequences for him of an out-of-wedlock child. When the girl became pregnant, he found himself at the mercy of her mother, who was intent on revenge as well as practical assistance. Another man with a large family and an established position in a small community carried on a brief and unhappy affair with a girl strongly tied to her stern and dominating father. When the girl became pregnant, the man rejected her completely, but he had overlooked the potency of the baby as a weapon over his head. The girl not only insisted upon keeping the child but planned to place it in a boarding home in the same small community where the man and his family lived. The answer to why men like this seem so intent upon bringing their own world down about their ears must lie in the shrouded conflicts of their childhoods.

Some of the factors involved can be seen in Jim, who was so caught in the toils of his own masochism. Jim was the only child of a neurotic and possessive mother and a passive but rejecting father. When he was a child, his mother made all decisions for him, indulged him to excess, and excluded so far as possible his relationships to anyone else. She became for all practical purposes his world, and he was almost totally dependent upon her. His father was a stranger whom he alternately feared and despised. They could not talk together, and Jim took all his problems to his mother. As a young man he remained dependent upon his mother, a state he both resented and desired. Often irritable at her domination, he made some tentative but abortive gestures toward friendship with his father. He was unable to keep a job and was bitter about his failure, placing all the responsibility for it upon his employers.

In his early twenties he met Nora, an unhappy young girl, who felt rejected by her mother and pushed aside by a more successful sister. Like Jim, she had never been able to keep a job, make friends of her own, or achieve independence. Jim's mother opposed their friendship and wanted the boy to stop seeing Nora. When Nora became pregnant, both the young people were frightened. At Nora's insistence they were secretly married, but Jim refused to let anyone know of either the pregnancy or the marriage and insisted that the baby be placed for adoption. He feared that the truth would upset his mother so seriously as to damage her health, and he could not tell his father because he was certain that would shatter what little relationship existed between them. Angry at Nora, he was depressed, discouraged, and bitter. He felt responsible for Nora and the baby; yet he blamed Nora for the pregnancy and their whole predicament.

Actually Jim felt guilty toward his parents, toward Nora and the baby, and he was unable to make any decision or assume any real responsibility. A very sick personality, he had attempted to assert his manhood, only to find himself crushed by responsibilities he could not carry, punished for his very attempt at independence, and thrown back into his dependence upon his mother, with his guilt only an additional tie to her and burden upon him. His feeling for the child was lost in the insatiable maw of his own needs, and Nora had become only an additional menace. Jim has remained a small child despite his physical maturity. In extreme form he exemplifies the problems which involve many unmarried fathers even when, as more mature personalities, they are better able to handle the consequences. Doubt of their masculinity, dependence upon and resentment against women, guilt over their relationships to their own parents, self-punishment for their hostile feelings and actions—however the ingredients are combined, the result is a psychological picture that matches that of the unmarried mother.

One thing is clear. We need to divest ourselves of the misconceptions and the condemning attitudes which have made the unmarried father a resource, not a person. It is not by any means certain that his more active participation in working out the problem would result in help for the girl and the baby. This could well be true in some cases and equally untrue in others. But to limit our interest in the father to this area is to use him as a means to an end. As a human being with needs, feelings, and problems of his own, he is entitled to help on his own merits. Even where he has given financial support or taken an active part in planning, he has been seen largely in terms of his contribution to the main problem of the girl and baby. That he has himself felt often that his only importance, his only raison d'etre in the situation has been what he can contribute is unquestionable. The unmarried father as seen by a social agency often approaches the interview either apologetically or defensively. He cannot talk naturally about himself and his own feelings, and he attempts usually either to justify himself or to settle the matter as speedily as possible for a financial consideration.

One man approached the case worker in a maternity shelter as if he were literally entering a lion's den. Obviously feeling himself hopelessly condemned in advance, he attempted neither explanation nor justification; but hastily, as if he were appeasing a dangerous enemy, offered to pay the expenses of the unmarried mother at the shelter. Since the case worker's remarks up to that point had been confined to a simple greeting, his attitude was based on the response he expected to get. When the worker neither criticized him nor regarded him as an unsatisfying stand-in for a checkbook and showed an interest in him as an individual, he was at first frankly incredulous, then suspicious, and finally candidly relieved. When the interview ended, he remarked with a rather pathetic attempt at jocularity, "I'm alive and unhurt, and I never expected that to happen." The general attitude of censure combined with his own neurotic fear of women had conjured up for him a fantasy of terror that only his guilt and the pressure of his conscience had prevailed upon him to face. His need was first to be respected as a person, with recognition that his problems were responsible

115

for his part in the situation as surely as were the unmarried mother's role for her involvement.

It is probable that we would be much better able to help the unmarried father if he were seen by a man case worker. Since most unmarried fathers regard a woman as probably sympathizing exclusively with the unmarried mother, normally there are initially fear and resistance in their attitudes. With the resentment that they often have toward women anyway, they must regard the woman case worker with suspicion. This is particularly true when she is also working with the unmarried mother. When there is a great deal of hostility between the man and the unmarried mother, the man's tendency under these circumstances is to think in terms of "whose side" the case worker is on; and the law of self-preservation dictates that he should be wary unless he can be convinced the worker favors him. Obviously there is little possibility of his using help so long as he attempts to involve the case worker in his tug of war with the girl. So little experimenting has been done with the plan of using a male case worker that it is impossible to know what its advantages and disadvantages might be, but it seems worth trying in an attempt to give some reassurance to the unhappy and confused people in this group.

There has been a tendency to consider the unmarried father, the unmarried mother, and the child as a unit, as the unmarried family. This is on the evidence a fallacy, and one that ignores the fact that legally, socially, and psychologically this is not a family group. It becomes involved with the erroneous idea that the unmarried father will, if he becomes interested, help in the solution of the problems of the unmarried mother and the baby. While this may occasionally be true, it is a dubious premise that one emotionally sick person can help another emotionally sick person with the problems common to both of them. There lingers about the idea a faint aura of the old-fashioned romanticism that saw in this situation two lovers separated by a cruel fate. The facts are that the unmarried mother and the unmarried father have rarely had a happy relationship; they are more often either indifferent or actively hostile to each other. Both the unmarried mother and the unmarried father may seek to use the baby to fulfill neurotic purposes of their own, and unless protected the child may become no more for them than a pawn in their mutual struggle. They differ sharply from the extralegal family, with which they are often confused. A man and a woman may live together outside the legal tie of marriage for a variety of realistic reasons, the most common being an undissolved marriage on the part of one or both. In many such situations the couple establishes a home and raises a family of children. Except for the legal factor, this may be a family like any other. Psychologically, the parents are not an unmarried mother and an unmarried father, and they do not show the same personality problems or act out the same behavior. The very fact that they are parents in the social and emotional as well as the biological sense distinguishes them immediately from the unmarried mother and the unmarried father who establish no real or lasting relationship with each other. Whatever the problems of the extralegal family, they cannot be understood or solved unless they are recognized as family problems having little or nothing to do with illegitimacy per se.

Help for the unmarried father as for the unmarried mother lies in seeing him as he is with his own needs and problems. He has a responsibility in this situation, as does the girl, and like the girl he needs help in assuming and carrying out that responsibility. While he may escape from it more easily than the unmarried mother, he does not by that token escape from his own problems; and these problems will continue to involve him in difficulty, to cause him unhappiness, unless he is able to face them and is given help with them. The attitude of assessing moral guilt and confusing realistic responsibility with punishment for sin has acted effectively to obscure the real problem for the unmarried father, as it has so often for the unmarried mother and the out-of-wedlock child. The real question is not which of the two carries the heavier weight of moral responsibility but what their problems as individuals are and how they can be helped to live happier, more constructive lives for themselves in the future.

ADOPTION SERVICES
AS RELATED
TO THE CHILD

Adoption Services As Related To
The Child

Introduction

Children available for adoption placement include those of unmarried mothers, those of married mothers whose husbands are not the fathers of the children, those born in wedlock who are permanently separated from their parents for various reasons, and orphans. The majority of these are infants but there are also older children.

They range in intelligence from the dull normal to the superior; they have varying physical inheritances from those who are perfect physically to those with one or more handicaps; they are of different racial and nationality backgrounds. They are in short a cross section of all children in the country.

Most agencies agree that a child should be placed with his adoptive family as soon after birth as possible and repeated changes of foster homes avoided. There is agreement too that group care of infants is undesirable. Adoptive parents are also anxious to have a child as young as possible. They feel that he is more a part of their family when he does not consciously remember another home and family. Early placements also facilitate the establishment of warm relationships between the child and parents, and the integration of the child into the family is a shorter and easier process.

In the past early placement has not prevailed in agency placements although practically all placements made independently of agencies are of this type. Agencies felt that the difficulty of assessing a new-born baby's chances of normal physical and mental development involved too great a risk for them to offer the child to adoptive applicants. This practice grew out of their conviction that a child must be "perfect" before he could be offered to an adoptive family. This meant long delays to correct physical weaknesses or to determine the child's intellectual capacity.

Since many adoptive families are willing to accept a child who has some defect, this policy has been altered. Families have accepted children with physical handicaps such as club foot, harelip, congenital hip dislocation or disfiguring birth marks, and even children born with congenital amputations of some external portion of the body as a hand or outer ear. Some children partially or totally blind or deaf, mentally retarded, or with congenital heart trouble have also found permanent families at an early age in spite of these handicaps.

In the past young children experienced delayed placement because agencies held infants for psychometric tests. At present we question the value of such an assessment of a young infant for predicting his future intellectual capacity, although it does provide information about the child's development on a given date. As a result agencies have generally discontinued the practice of holding children for long periods of time in order to be more sure of the probable capacity of the child.

Most parents whose children are offered for adoption are unable to care for them even temporarily. Some agencies will place an infant directly from the hospital with the adoptive family if there was good casework service prior to birth of the child, full information on hereditary factors was obtained from parents and everything pointed to a normal and healthy development on the part of the child, if the mother gave due consideration to the factors involved in relinquishment and was doing it for the child's best interests, and if the pregnancy and birth were normal. This practice arises from the fact that a child's emotional well-being requires satisfactory mothering as an infant and as few changes in homes as possible.

In the majority of cases, however, some kind of temporary foster care is necessary for a child before a final decision about adoption. This period helps determine whether adoption is in the interests of the child and of his natural parents. Parents need time to make their decisions soundly so that they can live with them indefinitely. Their cooperation in planning for their child is an important factor in evaluating their readiness to relinquish the child.

Circumstances do not always give the agency opportunity to know and work with the parents prior to the birth of a child. The agency needs time to evaluate the potentialities of the infant in order to select the most suitable home. Study of the child helps the agency determine the kind of parents who will be able to accept and love the child and make him happy.

Since infants should reach their permanent homes at an early age, temporary care should be kept to a minimum. Affectional ties built with a family group during his infancy increase the child's security. Both the child and the adoptive parents benefit if the child is placed at from two to four months of age. Sometimes earlier placement is possible. But many children are held for a longer period because of questionable factors either in relation to the child or to the legal right of the agency to place him. However, agencies try to obtain as early as possible the information necessary to select the home in which the child's adjustment will be most favorable as well as to complete the legal procedures required for placement.

During the period of temporary care the child receives necessary medical examinations and tests, corrective work, and developmental tests depending upon his age. The agency worker remains in touch with the parents, keeps informed of their attitudes toward permanent separation, completes the social history and arranges for the legal steps required for transfer of guardianship.

During this period too the worker helps the child, especially the older one, express and resolve the conflicts he has about his situation. If there are behavior difficulties the worker gives help with these and observes the child's capacity for growth and change. This experience with the child assists the agency to predict the possibility of a successful adoption placement and to determine on what basis the child can love and relate to new parents.

The worker also helps the child understand what is happening to him, gives him confidence in the agency's concern for him, prepares him for the acceptance of new parents, arranges for his gradual introduction to the adoptive parents so that he may know them before going to their home, and helps the move to the new home become one of his own choosing rather than a transition the agency has made for him.

The demand is for infants, so it is more difficult to find homes for older children. An "older" child has different meanings to different people. To some who are willing to adopt an "older" child, "older" means a child of about two years of age. To agencies looking for homes for older children, an "older" child usually means one of school age, with the range being upward through minority.

Older children who become available for adoption are usually children whose parents cannot take care of them because they are divorced, separated or mentally ill, children whose parents have lost their parental rights because of neglect or desertion of the children, and children whose unmarried mothers have kept them for several years because the mother could not make up her mind to surrender the child or because she has found that she cannot successfully keep her child born out of wedlock.

The adoption of older children requires especially skillful handling since they still have emotional ties with their own parents or with their foster parents; they may have been replaced so many times that they are unable to relate satisfactorily with any substitute parents; or they may have become so insecure because of their experiences that their behavior is too aggressive or withdrawn for adoptive parents to accept. Nevertheless, experience shows that many of these older children with help can accept adoptive parents and gain new security with a permanent family.

Increasingly in the past few years, adoptive agencies have become concerned about placements for older children. However, still too few agencies accept this responsibility. Therefore, they do not have older children being planned for when families seek them; or they do not know adoptive homes interested in older children as the need for placement occurs.

Another difficulty arises in the case of older children placed away from home perhaps because of divorce or separation of their parents, whose families have gradually lost interest in them, and finally fail to keep in touch with them at all. By the time these parents accept the idea of relinquishing their legal rights to their child, the search for a home may turn out to be a long and unsuccessful one, even though the agency recognizes the need of the child to belong to and be part of a family.

Difficulties in placement arise not only from age but from other factors such as personality disturbances that develop from troubling experiences. Changes in home situations inevitably give rise to severe emotional disturbances. Many children for whom agencies seek homes are suffering from the devastating experience of being removed from their own homes and families, and also many times from several boarding homes.

Children of minority races and nationalities have the same characteristics as other children plus the added difficulty of being part of a relatively large number of children available for adoption in relation to the supply of adoptive homes in their group.

Children who are retarded mentally are also considered for adoption now provided they are sufficiently intelligent that they do not need institutional and custodial care.

Some of the methods used to recruit homes for difficult-to-place children include: (1) making full use of families who apply by redirecting their interests to children who need homes,

(2) setting up lists of children for whom homes are not available, (3) listing approved adoptive homes for whom children are not available, with effective professional circularization of such lists and pertinent information about both families and children, and (4) assigning a worker to visit homes of applicants who might be suitable in an effort to interest them in one of these children.

Relatively few children are unadoptable today. Probably the largest number of children in the unadoptable group are those who are grossly retarded mentally. When a child has such limited mentality that he needs institutional care for his own protection and training, there is little chance for a successful adoptive placement. Infants who are hydrocephalic or microcephalic, children with inheritable diseases in their background such as muscular dystrophy and others with very severe physical handicaps are usually considered unadoptable.

Service to the unmarried mother is an essential part of an adoption program and the agency has a responsibility to help the mother make the best plan for a child whether or not he is considered adoptable. If the best plan calls for the separation of the child and the mother or parents, the fulfillment of this plan should not depend on the adoptability of the child.

There are children who have become too old, before surrendered or legally available, for an adoptive home to want them. Children 10 years of age and over are especially difficult to place for adoption. Such children are not unadoptable even though adoptive homes may not be available. Agencies can become more successful in recruiting homes for such older children if sufficient effort is made. Agencies can also become more alert to recognize when parents are abandoning their children emotionally and work with them intensively to try to ensure the security of a permanent home for the child before years have passed and he is too old.

Some children have been emotionally damaged by experiences in their own homes, by the necessity for removal from their parents, or by numerous replacements while in boarding care. Therefore, problems related to their deep insecurity are often evident, and some may never be able to relate to adults well enough to adjust successfully in an adoptive home even if such a plan could be worked out. For some of these children, however, it is possible to make adoption plans.

The goal of adoption is to have the child make deep and lasting ties to his adoptive family so that he gains as nearly as possible the same sense of belonging and being wanted as an own child. Sometimes the child being placed for adoption has suffered from rejection by boarding parents as well as by his own parents. While he has a great need to have a warm affectional relationship with permanent adoptive parents, he may have become deeply distrustful of any relationship. His previous experiences with people have impaired his ability to relate to others.

Therefore, the success of the adoption and the child's acceptance of his adoptive family depend to a large extent on his proper preparation for placement. The worker must be familiar to the child and must have established his confidence in her through previous experiences such as office visits, trips to the doctor, shopping trips, or pleasure excursions. An older child needs help to express his feelings about separation from his own parents and understand and accept it before he can have a meaningful relationship with adoptive parents. The worker can help him express and clarify his feelings about adoption before he actually sees the adopting parents.

The boarding mother can be of great help to the agency in preparing a child for adoption. Her ability to encourage the plan of adoption and to let the child go freely will be reflected in the child's ability to make this change to a new and permanent home. Such a move should usually be made gradually and at the child's own pace. When he is ready to accept the new home, even though his acceptance may have come more rapidly than anticipated, the agency should move with him. Agency practice should relate to the child's individual needs and his ability to move into the new home.

After placement in the adoptive home, the worker remains the tie with his past experiences until the child is firmly established in his new family and no longer feels the need of this tie. The worker gives reassurance to adoptive parents regarding behavior of the child which may cause anxiety in the new relationship, and helps both the child and his new parents understand each other and become an integrated family.

When legal adoption has been completed in court, the agency's services to the child are generally ended. However, adoptive parents may wish to consult the agency about a child at a later date and the agency remains ready to help at any time. The child may also consult the agency about his family history (without being given identifying names and addresses) when he is an adult.

When the adopted child grows up with the knowledge of his adoption, feels free to talk with his adoptive parents about his status and has a happy relationship with his adoptive parents, he often has little need for a more detailed picture of his past. When he is not happily adjusted with his adoptive parents, even putting him in touch with his natural relatives is seldom the solution to his feeling of insecurity.

Since the interests of the natural relatives also deserve consideration, it necessitates a similar desire or willingness on their part before an adopted child should be put in touch with natural relatives. The reasons for the child's interest and inquiry are important. If he desires actual contact with natural relatives, the protection of natural parents, particularly of an unmarried mother, needs to be pointed out.

The numbers of children returning to agencies for information about their families are not large. Sometimes it is because a placement has not been satisfactory that a child seeks information about his natural relatives. More often a child may return at time of marriage, when taking out insurance, or to increase his feeling of security about his own background in knowing more about his natural parents. There is need for further studies to show the primary causes of the return and the time in life when such children are apt to return to the agency.

Just as it is generally desirable for children to learn facts of human relationships from their parents, so it is most satisfactory for explanations about his natural family to come from the adoptive parents as the child's questions arise. This is an area in which adoptive parents need help. It involves too the giving of adequate information at the time of placement to the adoptive parents.

When an adopted child becomes an adult and seeks to approach his natural parents, it is better for the agency to serve as an intermediary and work out plans rather than to force an adopted child to explore vital statistics and court records and make direct contact with his relatives. The agency should usually make clearance with the adoptive parents and respect their rights in the matter, especially when the child is still a minor.

The agency also has responsibility for protecting the natural parents. There are instances in which it would be embarrassing for the natural mother to have the situation of this child reopened years after she considered it closed.

The existence of large numbers of children away from their own homes is due in part to the lack of basic community services to assist children and their families while families are still intact, and to rehabilitate their homes so children in foster care may return to parents after a temporary separation. Adoption services that are inadequate also create a backlog of children who, with good adoption planning, might have been placed in permanent homes instead of growing up in institutions or boarding homes after their families ceased to show interest in their welfare.

Adoption is part of a total program for the welfare of children. But good adoption services do depend upon the availability of related family and child-welfare services to children who may or may not need adoption, and to their natural and adoptive parents.

The articles selected for inclusion in this section relate to aspects of adoption which pertain primarily to the adopted child's welfare—the suitable age for placement; his placement; helping him in the temporary boarding home and in moving to the adoptive home; the contact with his previous environment; placing of handicapped and so-called "unadoptable children"; and the agency's responsibility in meeting inquiries for information about his natural family.

CHAPTER 9

Helping Children Move Into Adoptive Homes

CHARLOTTE L. HAMMELL

A child's first meeting with adoptive parents is an experience of great import. The very air seems charged with excitement, tension, and with feeling to be expected at the brink of fulfillment. It is the culmination of an operation begun by the own parent's request for release from parental responsibility, and the prospective adoptive parents' need to create a home for a child. Casework help in an adoption service is always connected with a living situation which the agency provides and for which it is responsible. Regardless of the age of the child, through a period of temporary boarding care the agency establishes the child's capacity for adoption by observation and knowledge of his background, constitutional equipment, and development. The temporary boarding care must include sufficient affection and encouragement to promote normal growth and development since the agency is responsible for furthering the child's adoptability. Through an adoption home study the agency has established confidence in the capacity of prospective parents to adopt.

The knowledge of the child and prospective adoptive parents is then used by the agency to form the casework judgment that these particular adoptive parents can meet the child's particular needs and offer opportunity for his continued growth and development. The decision to introduce child and family is fortified by the confidence of the agency in the ability of each to move into the relationship which begins when they meet. This confidence should not be confused with determination that the child and family like each other since each needs to be free to accept or refuse the relationship. The meeting of child and adoptive parents further tests and increases the knowledge of each and either confirms or negates the judgment of the agency. As skill and knowledge are developed and employed, there is decrease in the number of children who are not placed with adoptive parents after meeting them. The agency owes the child the protection and adoptive parents the consideration of asking them to participate in an experience in which they can find confidence in each other.

The Pre-adoptive Boarding Mother

Casework supervision in a pre-adoptive temporary placement differs from that in other forms of temporary care in that it carries the continuous thread of study of the child's suitability for adoption. The foster mother is the focus of supervision and participates in the determination of adoptability by helping the caseworker to know the child. It is important for her to have recognition of her contribution and knowledge of the steps used to know the child. The foster mother is asked to mother the baby but not to become his mother. Psychologically this is a difficult responsibility to carry. Foster mothers differ in personality and so in their way of taking, caring for, and releasing babies but they do need to feel their part in the general agency purpose in offering adoption service in order to take a succession of babies, give them affectionate daily care and then to let them go into adoption homes. This identification with the agency purpose of preparing babies for adoption placement is essential for foster parents who offer this kind of temporary care since their need of an individual child becomes less as they are able to feel their full contribution to a service to children. Acceleration of the tempo of pre-adoptive care, payment of the foster family in terms of service and availability, exchange between caseworker and foster mother regarding daily living care and medical and psychological examinations—all these define the role of foster mother as co-worker rather than as client.

Trouble is most keenly felt by many foster mothers in the experience of giving up the child. Supervision by the caseworker cannot remove the loss and pain in this experience for the foster mother but it can help by protecting the child from the full brunt of its expression. The caseworker presents the decision that it is time for the child to meet an adoption family and in order to be fully responsible needs to be able to accept the foster mother's feeling both for and against the agency's action in behalf of the child. The supporting element is that both have concern *for* the child. Although the boarding mother does not participate in the child's actual meeting with adoptive parents, she can either further or interfere with its purposes.

Placing the Infant

The age at which the child is introduced to adoptive parents is only one factor though an important one. The main difference in focus derived from the age of the child is that there is more direct casework with the child as his age increases. The predominant need of the baby six months or under is to be known by the caseworker. Knowledge which includes not only the results of psychological and medical examinations but also the foster mother's experience with him as a growing being. For the very young baby received directly from the hospital, the casework help consists of first selecting a good foster home where he can have human relationships and secondly in the help to the foster parents who fulfill his needs. The focus of casework is the foster parent and not the baby.

Sammy met his adoptive parents at the age of six months. A week before his boarding worker had brought him to the playroom to meet the adoptive family's worker. At the time of this trip he was a relaxed, happy, trusting baby who cuddled down in an affectionate way in whosever arms were about him. On the day Sammy came for the visit with the family the foster mother reported that he had been fretful, difficult to dress, although he is usually so easy to manage. The foster mother thought he was aware that something was about to happen. I suspect that he was reacting to the tension and anxiety with which she handled him because *she* knew what was happening. He was relaxed and comfortable with the caseworker, made no protest when she changed his diapers. When the adoptive parents came into the playroom, Sammy was on the couch by his caseworker. The adoptive father was beaming, went right to Sammy, and said, "How's my boy?" Sammy responded with a bounce, began to jabber, dropped the toy on which he was chewing, and held up his arms to be taken. Sammy did react against the adoptive mother's first attempt to change his diaper by crying vigorously. She

129

was tense, self-conscious, unsure in her handling of him, and he knew it. After he had been in the new home for four days, the adoptive family reported that he was eating and sleeping well and had settled down with them. The second night he was fretful, did not want to eat. They discovered two teeth about to come through. The adoptive father had been running around trying to find something to relieve him and finally hit on a few drops of rye whisky which he rubbed on the baby's gums. This immediately soothed him and he went off to sleep. The adoptive father thinks caring for a new baby may require more adjustments on the part of the parent than of the child.

Normally babies show the first specific emotional response to the mother between 3 and 4 months. At 6 months we need to watch the baby's reactions as indication of the degree of his loss in going to a new mother person. This varies with individual babies but it is my experience that at this age a baby can be moved from one home to another without serious disturbance to him. Much of the help is in the careful transfer to the adoptive parents of information about his care—not only medical information, formula, and his daily schedule, but what the baby has been used to in the way of individual response to his patterns. The purpose of this is to provide as much continuity as is possible in the care of the baby since at this age the mother still functions for him in so many ways. The young baby does need care and skill in handling from the caseworker and visits should be carefully planned to avoid feeding and naptimes so that the regularity on which he depends will not be upset. All of these are of inestimable value in helping the young baby preserve his equilibrium as he meets an adoptive family. Unless the adoptive mother has had experience or natural ease in caring for a baby her first efforts will be fumbling, insecure, and the baby has to experience her newness as well as her difference from his familiar mother. In the placement of babies 6 months and under, the important casework help lies in aiding the foster mother to release the baby and in helping the adoptive parents to take on the care of a new baby rather than in direct work with the child.

The Toddler

As the baby grows, consciousness of himself and other people increases as does his emotional response to them. The 6-month-old infant begins to discriminate strangers, the 12-month-old is often shy of them. By 18 months, the child has begun to express growing independence through motor activity and connection with "things." Casework help to an older infant or toddler in moving into an adoption home requires more direct work with the child in preparing him to meet adoptive parents.

Sally was 17 months old when she met her adoptive parents. Her need of adoption was not established earlier because her father made an extended attempt to keep her following her mother's death. Sally had been in one boarding home from the age of 3 weeks until she was placed for adoption. She is a child of sensitivity, strong determination, and excellent ability who had established strong roots with her foster family. The tempo of her placement was slow and geared to Sally's needs. The adoptive family could have taken her more quickly. The boarding worker brought Sally in for two visits to the playroom, a week apart, the last one being the day before she met her adoptive family. On each of the preparatory playroom visits, the adoptive family's worker saw Sally but the boarding worker remained with her, leaving her for the first time after she had found a beginning comfort with the adoptive parents.

From the adoptive worker's record of the first visit: "Sally was self-contained and non-expectant. Her worker and I initiated some play indicating a willingness to include her if she wanted to join us. Slowly Sally showed interest and curiosity with some tentative advances but never any real participation. During the next visit, Sally was more relaxed, able to play with toys, laugh with the workers and began to show some of the free activity of a toddler. Sally was cautious in meeting her adoptive family who had been prepared for her slowness and could give her time. Sally had a long visit with her adoptive family in which she had begun to show herself off proudly, was very active and even said a few words, but she seemed to sense the finality of the good-bye from her boarding worker. She seemed physically to droop and shook her head in protest. After her worker left, Sally cuddled down against her adoptive mother and seemed a little comforted."

These bits from the placement of a 17-month-old girl give a glimpse of the difficulty for her as she moves from one home to another. At this age it is expected that a child's behavior will show strong reaction against the strange and new as he knows well the difference between familiar adults and strangers.

Sally is an unusually alert, sensitive child and was frightened by this beginning. It is in spots like this that the caseworkers need to weigh and balance a child's immediate need as shown by the feeling she is expressing and her need of a home. The whole placement had been tentatively planned with consideration of the needs of both family and child but freedom to vary the plan needs to be maintained if it becomes evident that a child has had all she can take. Relaxation of fear is seen through increasing familiarity with the new. Sally's fear shows her need of the caseworker as a known familiar person to carry her through this experience of leaving the boarding home if she is to maintain her ability to respond to new people. The caseworker supplies the supporting base for the child until she can establish a beginning comfort with adoptive parents.

The Older Child

Comparison of the casework help needed in the placement of a toddler with that of a younger baby shows the increased importance of direct work with the child so that his fear and resistance to change do not predominate over the surge of independence so natural at this age. The importance of help to the foster mother in releasing the child and to the adoptive parents in preparing to receive the child is not lessened, but added to this is the child's need for casework help as he moves into an adoptive home. Casework with the foster parent, child, and adoptive parents cannot remove the experience of loss for the toddler but it can provide a transitional support and so lessen the shock of complete change.

The fact that a child has more difficulty in moving into an adoptive home as his age increases seems too obvious to need proof. Most normal infants can be successfully placed for adoption. What about the possibility of adoption for the two, three, four, five and six-year-old children who have passed the period of infancy without having secured a permanent home? It is my belief that adoption placement should be chosen for children of this age on a highly selective basis. The core of the criteria is the child's capacity to withstand the change and to establish satisfying relationships with new parents. The previous living experiences of older children for whom adoption is considered have often been disconnected, consisting of many changes of home and of care which have either interfered with or failed to support the natural growth process. When the normal early infantile need to relate to parent people has been seriously thwarted, adoption placement can be more destructive than helpful in its requirement of the child to accept new parents which psychologically he may not be able to do. Other children have established such deep emotional ties with their parents that they are unable to experience the loss and deprivation of complete separation and still move from it to an adoptive home which carries some need for unity if it is to be successful.

There are, however, some older children who still have the capacity to change and to use casework help as support in moving from one home to another. The content of casework with older children varies from that with an infant or toddler because the child's feeling is more actually and evidently conscious and his participation is not possible without his knowledge.

Susan, a six-year-old girl, whispered to her caseworker on the way back to her boarding home after a visit to adoptive parents, "Will they be good to me?" "I think so, do you?" Susan's face was troubled and serious as she said, "Sometimes I slip and wet the bed." I thought they could understand about things like that, but it is hard not to know for sure. Susan then recalled her other experiences in foster homes of which she had had several, ending with, "This one is supposed to be the last but I wonder if it will be." I said her new parents wanted a girl to live with them until she grew up and I knew they wanted *her* but I guessed she would have something to say about that too. Susan gave a sigh and then said, "I may not like it there." I agreed that she might not. Susan's face softened as she said, "I did like the people."
This bit shows all of a child's longing to belong, her fear of another rejection, suggesting the traumatic effect of experience on deep-seated personality patterns.

Direct work with the child is an important part of the casework help for older children whose language is well established. The method is varied to include the interview. Younger children can get some realization of change through the caseworker's repetition of "bye-bye," "new mommy and daddy," at appropriate times but the actual experience of being taken away from the boarding home and of meeting with adoptive parents largely carries the realization of change for the child under eighteen months. This is not so for the older child who faces change consciously. The worker has the responsibility of letting the child know the destination and people to be met on each trip. Other content of direct work with the child varies with the individual child but usually includes reference to the past. As the child faces the prospect of change or begins to experience it the feeling about former changes frequently recurs. Questions about the new home, feeling about leaving the present home, decision about which toys, clothes, and possessions the child will take are usually part of the content of casework with the child. The criterion of the child's readiness to actually move into the adoptive home is that he has begun to choose what the caseworker has chosen for him.

Conclusions

The nurture of children by their natural parents is deeply rooted in our society and in our psychology of individual growth and maturity. Adoption separates the child from the people who carry his biological heritage and substitutes parents consciously evaluated as capable of offering a favorable environment for his growth and development.

As caseworkers, I suspect we know less than we should about the continuous or recurrent problems for those whose living existence is divorced from those who gave them life. We do know that it is more difficult for the child to move to adoption as his age increases. If we really understand and believe this, we cannot escape the consequent responsibility of searching our programs of child care for ways of offering adoption to the children who need it before they have outgrown the capacity to make new, permanent ties with adoptive parents. Are we sometimes afraid to let own parents choose adoption for their child as soon as they can? How often do children suffer damage through our delay in planning for them both before and after they have been received into the care of the agency. As far as the child is concerned, the reason is less important than the fact. If he needs adoption he should get to it when he is young and his potentialities for using it are greatest. The responsibility of an adoption service is as great to provide living experiences for children which contribute to their adoptability as it is to determine it and to offer them casework help in making adoption their own.

"Who Am I?"

GRACE LOUISE HUBBARD

Who am I? is a question that cannot be answered completely by any birth record, no matter how expertly devised or carefully handled. Every individual has a right to accurate and complete identification of himself, but he has also the right to understand his identity in its broadest meaning.

Webster's dictionary defines identity as "unity and persistence of personality"—a dynamic concept, implying something that comes from within, something made by the person himself.

A right to our identity really means the right to be able to create for ourselves that degree of unity and persistence of personality that gives us a sense of self-direction, of relatedness to people, and to our environment. It includes what we know about ourselves and about our origin, and also what we have been able to take out of our life experience. Lineage alone does not create one's identity. But to discover suddenly that one's family foundation is not what it has always seemed to be may bring a shock and a need for readjustment.

This experience may sometimes come to a person who was born out of wedlock but has been protected from knowing that fact, whether living with his own relatives or apart from them; or, in fact, to anyone who has been brought up in some form of foster care.

The amount of help available to a young person in this position depends upon what his situation has been in relation to his family and friends, and to the social agency that had a part in determining his early life.

A person who as a child was placed by a social agency in a foster-family home, whether for adoption or for permanent supervised care, is assured of a record of his origin and identity, and of a source of help in finding out not just what the record shows but what human experience lies behind it.

The agency knew the mother who had to choose how her child would live—with her or apart from her—and is in a position to give him not only the facts but some interpretation of the pressure of circumstances that led to her choice.

A young person who is trying to fuse an unknown past with his present, needs more than to know his ancestry. He wants to know his heritage.

First Clue from Birth Certificate

If he has been completely uninformed about his birth history, he may get his first clue to it from what is recorded or omitted on his birth certificate. He may be made unhappy by what he finds and he may feel that the certificate itself is responsible for his unhappiness because it does not tell him enough. But the real cause of his distress is that he cannot understand the circumstances that created his present situation. There is always a story behind the record, and it is that story that he really wants. Not facts alone, but interpretation of facts, will help him.

Adopted children do not seem, on the whole, to have a very great need to look into their past connections, but when they do the need may be urgent. The workers in my agency have found that a small proportion of children do come back, asking for information about their parents or their lineage in general. The degree of their interest is related closely to the success of the foster-home experience. Children adopted as infants, who become well integrated into foster homes and have happy, satisfying lives there, do not as a rule feel great concern about their original families.

Sometimes, however, they want to know about themselves, and when this happens their interest may range from a sort of general curiosity about such things as their nationality and the first names of their parents and how they looked, to an active desire to find out all they can, and perhaps even locate and meet their relatives.

My agency has always recognized the right of the child to know about his own family, if he wants to—at a time when he is adequately prepared for the knowledge—and if the foster parents sympathize with his interest and are ready to have him know. The foster parents have a real stake in this, and they have a right, which the agency recognizes, to a share in determining the point at which a child is given the story of his own family and the way in which it is given. This is not a conflict in interest, for the child turns naturally to his foster parents with his first questions, and usually it is through them that he reopens the contact with the agency. In fact the foster parents often make the first move and in doing so seek the help of the social worker for themselves as well as for the child.

Foster parents do need help in this situation, for to them it may seem to threaten destruction of all that they have built up. It reminds them that this child, whom they have made their own, had an origin apart from them. They fear for themselves as well as for the child when they are faced with the necessity for explanations. There is reassurance for the foster parents in the social worker's recognition of the part they have played in the child's consciousness of himself as a person and the extent to which this consciousness contributes to his sense of identity.

At the time that war conditions began to require many persons to show proof of age and citizenship, the New York law providing for correction of birth certificates after adoption was relatively new, and many foster parents in that State did not have corrected certificates for their children. Consequently the agency that had placed these children for adoption at least 18 years before received many requests for information. The requests came through foster parents and directly from the grown children. The agency handled all these requests on an individual, casework basis, and, in recognition of the emotional significance which this renewed contact might have for both child and foster parent, assigned to this service an experienced case worker. This worker made every effort to establish with each individual a relationship based on the assurance of the worker's continuing interest in his achievements and his welfare. Often, but by no means always, a latent concern about family history emerged, revealing a mixture of the wish to know and some dread of what the knowledge would be.

There is bound to be some conflict between the individual's imaginary picture of his unknown parents and the reality. His divided feeling, of hope and fear, may include reluctance to have the dream picture destroyed and replaced by a reality less agreeable.

The individual may wonder what responsibility he would be expected to take if he should find his relatives in trouble of some sort, or whether he might have to bring them into his present life. He may unconsciously resent his parents' desertion of him. He may never have accepted his separation from them as necessary, particularly if he was old enough to remember it.

At the same time he may be very much interested in knowing why the separation took place, what sort of people his parents really were, and how much he will think of himself as a different person when he has this more complete picture of his origin.

Will He Seem a Different Person?

This will bring him face to face with himself as another person, as the child of parents different from those he has always known and to whom he has given his affection. It is natural for him to wonder whether he can fuse the two aspects of his identity into a coordinated whole, his real self. We can understand that he may want help in getting through a disturbing experience.

The individual who decides that he wants this information arrives at this decision very gradually. Renewal of contact with the agency may have revived for him some earlier desire to define and clarify his identity. And in the agency worker, whether or not she was the person who actually participated in his placement, he has someone with whom he can discuss his feelings freely and from whom he can get both the information he wants and some interpretation of the situation that led to his separation from his family. The worker knows him as he is now, and represents the agency that knew him even before his foster parents did.

The social worker's responsibility is not only to the young person who is seeking the establishment of some relation with his past, but also to the mother who may be asked to reopen a long-closed chapter of her life. Naturally, the worker will proceed with great caution. The fact that a grown child wants direct contact to see for himself does not necessarily mean that the mother will want it. Even when both want to meet, and when the adoptive parents are in sympathy with this wish, the mother and child need help and support. Much careful preparation must precede any actual meeting.

Such meetings are on the whole infrequent. Unless the foster child's own life has been unusually lacking in emotional relationships, his interest seems to be in the satisfaction of knowing, rather than in trying to rebuild something that never really existed.

When I say that the individual needs help, I do not mean to imply that his learning about the past is necessarily an upsetting experience. The way in which the information is given determines this. The quality of the own parents' interest which went into their original planning for the child, the extent to which their plan represented a genuine desire to obtain security for him and to overcome his early handicap, even the limitations that kept his parents from caring for him—these are important. Little things such as what the mother or father is like, the color of eyes or hair—the things we all know about our own families—help him to get a feeling of his parents as people—of their human attributes—and that is what he really wants.

The situation facing the young man or woman about whose past nothing whatever is known, who was abandoned in infancy, is both easier and harder.

If there is no past, there is no problem of assimilating it into the present, no threat to one's present personality.

On the other hand, it may be difficult to accept the fact that one has no past. Some of these young people find themselves unable for a long time to believe that there is no knowledge anywhere of their origin. The skill of the worker can be used here in helping the individual to realize that the source of true identity is within oneself. What comes out of the past may be strengthening or weakening, but it does not in itself create individuality or identity. It is not easy to feel that one started from nowhere, and must make a life entirely out of one's own living of it. But what comes out of it in ultimate perception and awareness of identity is in the end a self. Thus it was expressed by one who had been through the experience: "When all is said and done, I would not change my state for that of any one I know."

The social worker today will recognize, from her first contact with a mother who asks to have her child placed, the responsibility, not only to make the best possible plan for the child, but to preserve for him as fully as possible the information about his heritage. Much of this information will rest undisturbed in the files, but consciousness of our purpose in gathering it together will help us to use it if it is needed.

The worker must bear in mind not only the mother's situation, but also the importance to the child in the future of knowing his mother's feeling about him, and how this entered into the choice the mother made.

At that point the mother herself is rarely able to think much about what the child will know about her in the future. In fact she is apt to hope he will not have to know anything at all. It is a frightening idea to her, for it suggests that the anonymity that she now sees as essential may be destroyed.

If she thinks of the birth certificate, she thinks of it as protection for herself rather than as identification for the child. She wants as little as possible to be on the record, lest it be used accidentally to disclose the facts.

She at first distrusts the social agency, and even though she comes to accept its good faith, she may doubt its power to protect her. She feels that her whole future is at stake. And if she uses an assumed name when she enters the hospital, and allows it to be put on the birth certificate, we need not wonder why.

The social worker will accept this if necessary. But she will help the mother to see that the agency does have the power and the will to protect her, though it can do this only if she will trust it with her full story.

Concern for Child's Future Comes Later

The mother may not realize this while her own problem is foremost in her mind, but after the child is born she begins to be concerned for his future, particularly if she has decided not to be a part of that future. By the time she has come to a decision to place him for adoption, she can understand better his right to his heritage and can help to preserve it for him.

She often feels that it would be better if her child did not know about her in the future, not only because she fears being disgraced, but because she thinks the child will resent her abandonment of him. She usually wishes that he need not know he was adopted, but she often asks whether he will be told this, and also what he will be told about her.

After she has signed a legal surrender she begins to see the child as a person apart from herself, for what happens to him will no longer be happening to her. Now she can help us to preserve some of her family tradition for the child if and when he wants it. If the case worker and the mother have built up a mutual understanding, the mother will see that she can help the child in the future by telling about the kind of people from whom he comes. The giving of this information to help the child later may also ease some of her feeling that she has failed as a mother by surrendering her child.

It is, of course, harder to get a true picture of the child's paternal ancestry. The mother may not know much about the father, or, if she does, may not tell. But the worker will bear in mind that information about the father is a part of the child's right no less than knowledge about his mother. If we are really convinced of this and can make this conviction a part of our approach, we can hope to show the father, as well as the mother, what comfort the child may get not only from the facts, but from the feeling that he was not cast off, and that his father as well as his mother took part in the effort to get security for him. This is probably of more real value to the child in the long run than legal establishment of paternity or formal acknowledgment of it.

When the child goes into his foster home, the worker sees that the story of his family background—of course without identifying information—goes with him. This is not only to give the foster parents a means of deciding whether or not they want this particular child, but also to help them prepare to answer the questions the child may ask when he is older. In giving this information the worker realizes that the child will turn first to his foster parents for information if he becomes curious about his earlier life. She will try, while giving the essential facts, to give also some evaluation of the parents' feeling in relation to the decision to provide a future for the child through adoption. Foster parents usually do think about this, and when they are taking a child they try to prepare for it, but as time goes on it becomes harder for them to realize it.

Part of the agency's contribution to the child's security—the purpose for which he was originally placed—is to strengthen and build up the bond between the child and his foster parents and to treat the story of the child's earlier life so that it becomes a part of experience shared with his foster parents rather than something differentiating him from them. The foster parents, particularly in the child's early life, largely determine when and how his questions are answered—in fact, they are often a factor in determining whether questions are ever asked.

141

Social agencies place greater emphasis now on the importance of integrating the child's past, as well as his present into that of the foster family, through letting him understand from the beginning that he has been adopted.

This makes for a very different situation for these children as time goes by, and it will be much less often that a young adolescent discovers suddenly, and probably at a time of some family crisis, that he has been adopted.

Having grown up knowing that he was adopted, having been free to talk of this with his foster parents while he was growing up, his need for a more detailed picture of the past will be less important. Or if it becomes important, the reasons will be clearer.

Because the agency carries its conviction of the child's right to his identity in the largest sense into each stage of its care and planning for the child, it does much to prevent the anxiety and apprehension that we have found in persons who were separated from their own families without knowing why.

We do not, of course, know how many children born out of wedlock are kept by their own parents, or at least by the mother, and grow up within their natural family groups, but the majority are so kept.

Some of these children eventually have fairly complete family life, when the mother marries the actual father or another man who accepts more or less genuinely the fatherhood of the child.

Of this group we know little as they grow up, for the social agency that aids the mother at the time of the child's birth rarely continues to be in contact with her until the child is grown. Thus there is less chance to help either the mother or the child with the eventual questions concerning his birth and his real father. But such children are likely also to have less need of this kind of help. Some do not ever have to face the facts of their birth. Others do, and face it without the help they need. Yet, even so, their situation is easier than that of the child who has been completely cut off from his family.

If the mother plans to surrender her child for adoption, the agency focuses its interpretation primarily on something that, when it actually occurs, will not be a part of the mother's own experience.

If, on the other hand, she is keeping her child, and she herself is to be the one to answer the questions, her attitude will depend largely on the extent to which she has integrated herself and her child into her own community, and her own feeling toward the father. She may simply tell the child the truth. Or she may say that the father is dead, because that represents her own feeling. We can be sure that it will be, not the facts themselves, but the values given them in the telling, that will determine the child's response.

When a child asks, "Who am I?" he does need to know his name and lineage, but what he is really seeking is to sustain his awareness of self so that he can achieve a unity and persistence of personality, in spite of the break in the continuity of his life. This is his right, a right that we are under obligation to secure to him to the greatest extent we can.

Careful and accurate recording of one's birth is a basic step, and the right of every person. But a sense of one's heritage is also every person's right, and if a child does not have his own parents to give him a sense of his heritage as well as his birth identification, interpretation should be given by someone with understanding, as well as knowledge, of the facts.

A child's identity is his sacred right.

CHAPTER 11

Placement for Adoption—A Total Separation?

EMILY MITCHELL WIRES

Much has been learned in recent years and been made available in casework literature about the disturbing effect upon a child of separation from persons and places to which he has become attached. There are the studies made by Anna Freud and Dorothy Burlingham of English children separated from their parents and homes by reason of the war, and the studies reported by Margaret Ribble, showing the results of separation as no less disastrous to the infant than to the older child, and, in the case of both younger and older children, irrespective of the reasons for the separation. For the infant, the possible physical consequences of the resulting emotional disturbance engendered by separation may, in extreme instances, even threaten his existence. For the older child, separation from affectional ties nearly always holds an element of blame for himself, of badness and punishment therefor, as well as an element of desertion and failure on the part of the persons from whom he is being separated.

This knowledge of the effect of separation on the child has been incorporated in some degree into casework practice by child-placing agencies in bringing about better foster-home placement. We have applied it by reserving foster care for only those children for whom our best skills leave no alternative, and by rendering the separation as free from hurt to the child as possible. In accomplishing the latter aim, we have recognized that the manner in which the separation takes place is of greatest psychological import to the child and that it should include preserving constructively for him in the new life as much of the old as possible. It is not so much the fact of change itself which works havoc with a child's sense of certainty and security as it is the degree to which it disrupts the continuity of his life, the flow and relatedness of his memories, and his tangible associations with his past. For the evacuated child the continuing family ties—in the shape of frequent visits, letters, and gifts from the parents and relatives, the retention of customary routines, of favorite toys, of pictures and mementos of home and family—were of outstanding value in lessening the ill effects of separation and in making available for his use the positive values of placement. For the placed child they are equally meaningful. In former years visits by parents were not allowed in the first weeks following placement, with the idea of first giving the child a chance to "settle down" in his foster home; subsequent visits were often regarded as upsetting to the child and a nuisance to the worker and foster parents, and were therefore often indirectly or openly discouraged. In most child-placing agencies all this has been changed. Recognizing the value and the meaning of the parent to the child, we are challenged to use our skills to see that these are, whenever possible and to the greatest extent possible, preserved for the child by giving the parent not only an active part in the separation but often in the actual placement itself. He participates by going with the worker and child to the new home, and not so much yielding up his parental right as using it in meeting the foster parents, transferring the child to their care, and seeing him established as a part of their family.

How about the adoption placement? Do the psychological facts regarding separation have application here, too? Do we, or should we attempt, for the child being adopted, the preservation of his past? Or should the separation be, or must it of necessity always be, total and final? In practice it is usually just that. True, the worker is present with the child as he moves from the foster home to the adoption home, and all that can be of value to him in the worker's presence before and during the transition is generally utilized in helping him to leave the old and pass on into the new. Toys, other meaningful objects, and daily routines are preserved for him as much as possible.

But of persons formerly near and dear, his deprivation generally is complete, abrupt, and final. Is such a total separation necessary? Does it not involve the loss of some values which we might like and sometimes be able to preserve for the child?

The following case material concerns the adoption placement of a little boy.[1] Born August 9, 1945, Robert had been placed from the hospital with a foster mother, a widow with several children and an income only just sufficient for their support. The foster mother understood that the baby's placement was to be only until it was determined whether his mother could make plans for his care or would release him for adoption. It was not until Robert was nearly 3 years old, however, that he was surrendered and an adoption home selected.

The adoptive parents gave many evidences of their ability to fill the role of parents to Robert. The plan for his placement was in the meantime developed by the worker to include not only the foster mother's aid in preparing the child psychologically for his move to the new home and new parents but, because of Robert's having been in this foster home for this important and considerable part of his life, and because of his strong attachment to the foster family and theirs to him, also to include the foster mother's actually going with the child and the worker for the initial visit to the adoption home. In a preparatory interview with the adoptive mother, the worker described this plan and solicited the adoptive mother's understanding and co-operation:

I told something of Robert's foster home situation, explaining that he had been in this home since he was a baby and that the foster mother, Mrs. W, and her two daughters were very much attached to him and that he had been showered there with attention to the point where he was probably a bit spoiled. I explained, too, that the foster mother understood that Robert had been surrendered and that we would be planning for an adoptive placement and that she loved Robert enough to want him to have the security of a family of his own, even though the separation would be difficult for him. I explained that the foster family's home was quite isolated and that the foster mother was a widow with few contacts aside from her immediate family, so that Robert had not had much experience in meeting new people and tended to be quite shy, clinging to the foster mother. He usually warmed up to

---

[1] This case was handled by Isabel Romm, caseworker, under the supervision of the writer.

strangers after a period of becoming accustomed to them, but was extremely fearful of going anywhere without the foster mother. She had always accompanied him when he needed to go to clinic or anywhere else. Because of all this I had discussed in general terms the problem of replacement with the foster mother, even though we had no specific adoptive home in mind. We had both agreed that perhaps we could introduce Robert gradually into the new foster family, as we were sure that he would be tearful and upset if he were suddenly uprooted. Also, because of Mrs. W's understanding and her real wish for an adoptive placement to succeed, we believed we could follow a plan whereby she could come with him to the adoptive home and so give him the security of being introduced to it by someone he really trusted.

The adoptive mother, Mrs. C., rather resisted this whole plan on two accounts. In the first place she did not believe that the change would be nearly as difficult as I was anticipating, even in the face of the situation as I described it. She had so much experience with little children and her whole family was so accustomed to making them feel at home. She felt Robert would very quickly adjust but it would be much better to "make a clean break quickly." I pointed out that much experience has proved that it is false to assume that children forget things because they cease to talk about them, and that a good deal of emotional harm could be done by an experience that would violate so seriously all a child's attachments and feeling toward those he had always regarded as his family. Mrs. C was not unaware of this and agreed that one could not expect a child to forget those with whom he had lived so happily for so long, but she still felt his new associations would be more quickly supplanted by dealing more boldly with the situation; however, in her great desire to please me and to secure the baby, she expressed a willingness to go along with any plan that I thought best. She brought up a second point, however, in which she identified very closely with the foster mother, because of her experience with a little girl whom she had cared for. She felt my plan would subject Mrs. W to a rather cruel experience. She did not mean that all contacts should forever be cut off, and she expressed a wish that the little girl mentioned before would always remember her and her family fondly, so she could certainly understand Mrs. W's wish that Robert would remember her fondly too. But she did think it would be asking too much of the foster mother to expect her wholeheartedly to create an atmosphere in which the replacement would be kept inviting to Robert over a long period of time.

When it was agreed that Mrs. W and I would come together with Robert, that we would see how the situation developed in regard to further procedures, Mrs. C and her two daughters with some relief brushed this whole discussion aside with an eager inquiry as to what Robert looked like, and what he was like. I described his appearance to them and said he was an active, bright little boy, quick, playful, full of ideas and questions. I told them, too that there had been some health difficulty and that he still had a condition which I wanted to discuss with them very fully. I spoke of the attacks which had been variously described as bronchitis and asthma or a combination of the two, and described them and their effects on Robert. Mrs. C and the girls exchanged glances and together they exclaimed that it was exactly like the illness from which one of the girls had suffered for many of her early years. Mrs. C stated that she knew just how to take care of this and was in no way discouraged by my description of the seriousness of some of the attacks.

As I went on to talk about Robert and answer their questions, Mrs. C expressed the attitude of all of them when she said, ''Will we be in our glory when he's here!'' They made all sorts of plans to make him feel at home including inviting several of the children in the neighborhood in for little parties. I explained that Robert was not used to too much of this sort of experience, and as a matter of fact had not played very much with youngsters of his age. We talked on further about Robert and his special characteristics and they asked many questions, but persisted in assuring me that the whole situation would work out much more easily than I seemed to feel it would.

About a week later the worker visited the foster mother to tell her that an adoptive home was now available for Robert and to outline with her the manner in which she hoped to carry out his transfer and the part she wished the foster mother to play:

Visit to Mrs. W. On the telephone I had told Mrs. W that I had something rather important to discuss with her. When I now revealed that we had an adoptive family in mind for Robert, she smiled rather sadly and said she had somehow felt that this was just what I was coming to say. She shed a few tears and explained that of course I would understand how she felt about parting from him; but she assured me that this was what she was wanting for him and she had steeled herself to expect it. She explained further that she was expecting her family to come to visit from California and that she would be quite busy over the summer months so that she would be distracted from her grief at the parting. I told her how pleased we were with the care she had given Robert in the face of the difficulties with the asthma and we hoped in the future she would again take another baby and give him as good a start as she had given Robert. She assured me that in the fall, when her family had returned to the coast, she would like very much to take another baby for us.

Robert was outside playing and looking sun-tanned and well. I played with him and pulled him in his wagon for awhile and he became very playful and friendly. However, when I asked him if he would like to come for a little ride with me, he flatly refused and would not even hear of any plan to go for a ride at some future time, but when we discussed the possibility of going for a ride with his mommy, he was quite pleased and eager and we made an appointment for the following day.

I had spoken to Mrs. W of the need for preparing Robert in some way that would not leave him confused or resentful at being replaced. She said he had heard them discuss the relatives coming from California and possible plans for the W's to go with them when they returned. She thought she could place it on this basis and I suggested that she speak of the fact that she wanted him to have another new mommy who would love him and take care of him just as she had done. Mrs. W became very much more emotional about this than I had expected, and wondered if we could not go ahead with this plan as quickly as possible. I thought that perhaps the next day we could go for a short visit to the C's just so that Robert would spend a few hours there to become familiar with the family.

In the meantime the adoptive mother was seen and an appointment made for the worker to bring Robert and his foster mother for this visit:

I picked up Mrs. W and Robert, both of them all dressed up for their visit. Robert proudly showed me how his white shoes had been all cleaned to go to visit a nice new mommy. He seemed a little questioning about the whole venture but was willing to go for the ride and we spoke of the visit with so much enthusiasm that he began to look forward to it, too. On the way to the home he became very thirsty. Mrs. W suggested that when we came to the new mommy's home, she would give him a nice drink of water. For the rest of the drive he kept harping on this subject.

When we arrived at the C's home, Robert began to hang back a little and we did not ask him to go in but slowly walked ahead and he, of course, ran to catch up with us. Mrs. C and one daughter were at home and their faces lit up when they saw Robert; his appearance obviously delighted them. They greeted him very quietly and he hung back with a questioning, serious face. We sat down to talk and he immediately asked for a glass of water with this same slightly frowning expression. Mrs. C brought him a glass, knelt down as she gave it to him, and put her arm around him. He did not resist her. We proceeded to talk and Robert began to explore the house. The family's cat came in and this provided a great deal of distraction as Robert began to play with it boisterously; however, when Mrs. C and her daughter attempted to come too close to him, or make too much of a fuss over him, he would become shy again and withdraw from them. The daughter brought him a small ball which he proceeded to roll around and then he found a marble with which he played with the cat, rolling it for the cat to retrieve. He still resisted any particular overtures from us and would play in another room when any of us came to join him. Finally, from one of the back windows, he saw a chicken in the back yard and this interested him greatly. Mrs. C offered to take him out to see the chicken but he wouldn't go; however, when she offered to take him another time, he eagerly made arrangements to "go tomorrow." He kept wanting to stay by himself and play but when I asked whether he wanted to leave, he vigorously shook his head and said, "No, not yet." Mrs. C's other daughter came home with a friend and exclaimed over him so heartily that Robert again became more shy and withdrawn. When we left him alone again, however, he proceeded to play busily with the cat and to look out the window and generally explore the apartment. He found a box of candy and brought it in to Mrs. W, asking if he could have a piece. She told him to take it over to the new mommy and ask her and Mrs. C offered him the candy which he greedily took.

Later Mrs. C's son came in, in a baseball uniform and with

a bat and ball, all of which interested Robert tremendously. While the rest of us remained in one room, the son and Robert made very good friends in another room and he and Robert made plans for Robert to learn how to play baseball. Mrs. C finally got up and showed him a room, which would be his, with his own bed. Robert still seemed quite puzzled by all this and not quite sure what it all meant. While he still usually kept at a distance from most of us, he seemed to want to explore further this strange situation. He would sometimes come back to Mrs. W for reassurance and then go on with his various games and exploration. He heard the train whistle and Mrs. C explained to him that the trains went by quite near the house and offered to take him to see them, too. Again, he did not want to go at this time but enthusiastically planned to go with her "tomorrow." Finally, it was getting quite late, and as we got up to go and Robert still hung back, Mrs. C went over to him and again knelt by him and asked him whether he would like to stay overnight "right now." To our great surprise Robert agreed that he wanted to stay, although he looked to Mrs. W for approval. She nodded her head and said, "All right, Robert, you stay here and have a good time." We waved goodbye to him and Mrs. C and her daughter immediately started making other plans with Robert about things that they were going to do with him, and told him, "Daddy will be home soon and he will be so glad to see you." Robert waved to us, apparently very content to stay, although he still had a rather serious expression on his face.

A telephone call by the worker to the adoptive mother next day elicited a happy response. Robert, in spite of the unusual and exciting events, had slept quietly the night through. The news was relayed by the worker to the foster mother who was a bit tearful but very glad to know everything had gone so well. A few days later the worker called on the adoptive family with Robert's clothes. Again there were expressions of great delight in Robert and at the ease with which he seemed to have accepted this change. The worker felt that there were nevertheless implications for Robert which the adoptive mother needed to know and with which she would probably need help.

I told her that things had developed so much more quickly than I had expected, that I had not had an opportunity to discuss with her further the meaning of this removal to Robert and the way in which we could help him to understand it.

She showed a good deal of resistance toward opening the subject with Robert, apparently sure that the best way to handle the situation would be to ignore it. I pointed out the fears that such a procedure might bring to a child regarding the seeming disappearance of those whom he had loved, his fear of a recurrence of such an event again. We talked at great length and although I do not believe she was happy about my point of view, she acknowledged that it did seem plausible and we discussed possible ways of dealing with the problems with Robert. After discussing various alternatives, she thought and I agreed that she would wait for an oppor- tunity that would in itself give rise to a natural discussion with the child.

The worker's next visit nearly a month later allowed her not only to note with surprise Robert's freedom with her in contrast to the suspicion with which he used to regard her or any other stranger who first came to him, but revealed the adoptive mother's beginning acceptance of the worker's interpretation to her of the continuing meaning for Robert of the foster family:

Robert never showed the fright of strangers which I had led them to expect and according to Mrs. C became very comfortable in every aspect of the new situation almost immediately. The first day he had asked "when his mommy was coming back." Mrs. C seized this as the opportunity she needed and explained that his other mommy was very well but she had to go away just as she had told him, but he couldn't go along and of course he needed someone to take care of him. She wanted someone to take care of him who loved him and she knew that Mr. and Mrs. C and their family would love him very much. She ended with, "I'm your new mommy." She repeated this several times. Robert listened to her very seriously. Finally, after a pause, he looked up at her with a smile and said, "Oh, mommy." She then proceeded to explain about his daddy and his sisters and his brother at great length. After this one time Robert never brought the subject up again.

Mrs. C, having relieved herself of the necessity of this explanation with Robert, was again very resistive toward any mention of his former life to him. I told her I understood well why she felt this way, although she put it on the basis that she was afraid, with all these new relationships to keep straight, that Robert would be confused by mention of his former foster family. But she agreed now that when he had had a little time to become confirmed in his understanding of all these new relationships, she would again casually mention the former foster family to him in a reassuring way.

Although she insisted that Robert had never spoken of the W's again, implying that he did not think of them, when I reminded her of our former discussion about possible fears arising from such a situation, she thoughtfully related that Robert was unwilling ever to let her out of his sight to the extent that she must take him with her wherever she went. I commended her for her insight on seeing the connection between this behavior and our discussion.

The brief space of time within which Robert's placement was accomplished, the fact that he went to the adoption home on a trial visit and then that he remained there—all this may well raise questions around the worker's practice. The subsequent passage of time, though, and Robert's continued adjustment seem to have confirmed the soundness of what she did. Furthermore, examining it again, we find an element in it which may explain why this little boy's placement, which the worker feared was going to be difficult and traumatic, moved along with surprising acceptance and participation on his part. If, as usually happens, a child goes to a new mother-person (whether it is from his own mother to a foster mother, from one foster mother to another, or, as in this case, from a foster mother to an adoptive mother) and, in going, is cut off completely from the former mother he may not only feel the latter has deserted him, but he may also feel he has deserted her and that if he transfers his affections and allegiance to her successor he is indeed disloyal. The presence of the foster mother in his visit to the adoptive home meant for Robert the opportunity to test and secure from her for himself permission to make this transfer, and this, we believe, more than any other thing, enabled him to come so quickly to the decision to stay there.

These, perhaps, are what would be our worst fears around introducing a foster mother into the actual replacement or adoption home: a fear that the foster mother would not really give up the child to the new mother, and a fear that the new parents would resent her, resent her having had the child and resent her continued meaning for him. But, difficult though the demands on each mother may be, if we decide that it is much better for the child to have it done this way, then should not all our skills be mobilized and directed toward its successful accomplishment? And do we not believe that the foster mother (or adoptive mother) with whom the worker has a good relationship and to

153

whom the worker can give support in the accomplishment, can do things which under other circumstances she would find impossible? What is it that we need on the part of foster parents for success in such a venture as has been described? It is true that we cannot expect foster parents to possess professional skill but we can, I think, at least aim at helping them achieve a professional attitude toward their jobs in a child-placing agency. This attitude, however, cannot be expected to emerge all at once. It must find its beginnings in our own attitude toward foster parents, and must be present throughout the home finder's study, the placement of a child, and the worker's supervision—an attitude which sees the foster parents as a vital part of the agency and which credits them with being able to place the child's interests above their own. Surely no less should be expected of the adoptive parents, and their capacity to do less might very well be accepted as proof of their unsuitability. The degree to which we can hope to preserve past ties for the adopted child will, of course, vary greatly according to the individual circumstances. We can at least suggest that the older the child the more important it becomes to do as much of it as possible. The way in which it can be and is done will vary with each situation.

CHAPTER 12

The Transitional Method in the Adoption Placement of Older Infants and Young Toddlers

ROBERTA G. ANDREWS

Although articles by Spitz and Anna Freud describing the reactions of infants and young children to separation from the mother person predate Bowlby's monograph *Maternal Care and Mental Health*[1] by at least a decade, it undoubtedly was the latter work which more dramatically and forcefully focused the attention of child care workers upon methods of helping infants and young toddlers in the transitional move from one mothering person to another. Placement agencies, whatever their specific service, are in the business of separation. Caseworkers, by virtue of the nature of their work, must help young children leave one set of parents for another set, often under extremely painful and traumatizing circumstances.

Growth Versus Trauma

More has been written on the subject of separation than about the methods used in helping a child to manage a separating experience. Gerard and Dukette[2] in a chapter entitled "Tech-

---

[1] John Bowlby, *Maternal Care and Mental Health*, World Health Organization, Geneva, 1951.

[2] Margaret W. Gerard, *The Emotionally Disturbed Child*, Child Welfare League of America, New York, 1953.

niques for Preventing Separation Trauma in Child Placement'' cite only articles in early issues of the *Journal of Social Casework Process*.[3] In her introduction to Volume III, Taft points out that adults responsible for moving children are faced with the temptation to take too much responsibility or none at all. The papers in Volume III, particularly Gennaria's ''Helping the Very Young Child to Participate in Placement,'' describe a transitional process whereby the child is helped to participate in the separation from a foster family to an adoption family.

Whereas the title of the articles by Gerard and Dukette and by Gennaria, which are mentioned above, point up a difference in emphasis, i.e., the aspect of growth versus the aspect of trauma, there appears to be no disagreement between these writers that a transitional process is essential to enable a child to handle his pain in giving up a known set of parents to move to a comparatively unknown set of parents. Gennaria describes in detail the use of language, tone of voice, repetition of words in helping five different children ranging in age from about eight months to just over two years move from a foster to an adoption home. Gennaria puts value upon the repetition of words, specifically words which are part of a young child's vocabulary, as reassurance to the child. She also emphasizes breaking up the move from one home to another into parts to help the child manage the move without an overwhelming threat to his ego, which might result in serious regressive symptoms.

Gerard and Dukette state:

''. . . in utilizing the transitional method of placement the aim is to place the child in a new home only after he has developed some familiarity with it and gives evidence of a beginning affection for and dependence upon the new parents, at least upon the mother. . . . This method of placement involves the desirability of the child's having several and frequent visits with the new parents and with each parent alone to simplify the problem of developing interpersonal relationships.''

They comment on the value of relaxation, of the use of familiar toys, familiar foods. They state: ''. . . once the infant can associate the familiar sensations of the first relationship to the new face and person, the changes of behavior natural to the new mother can gradually take over and the child in turn responds to her whole person.''

[3] *Journal of Social Casework Process,* Pennsylvania School of Social Work, University of Pennsylvania, Vol. I (1937) and Vol. II (1939).

In order to avoid the kind of regression described by Anna Freud[4] and the kind of unsatisfied longing and state of tension resulting from a too rapid separation, the adoption department of the Illinois Children's Home and Aid Society, as described in the article by Gerard and Dukette, has worked out a transitional method of placement which may involve several trips to the foster home by the adoption parents, with a gradual assumption of daily care duties by the new mother until the child makes the move from one home to another.

A Modified Transitional Method

This kind of transitional placement, which provides emotional smoothness in the gradual transfer of child from one family to another, would be difficult for most adoption-foster care agencies to effect for a number of reasons: insufficient staff time, geographical distance between the home of the adoption family and location of the foster home, the emotional impact involved in bringing together foster and adoption parents, and the difficulty in maintaining the confidential nature of the adoption placement. Agencies pressed to provide adoption placement for minority children, siblings, older children, as well as infants, are faced with the practical limitations of time and money. Nevertheless, professional service rests upon sound practice.

If the method described by the Illinois Children's Home and Aid Society is without parallel and is the most desirable way in which to effect the replacement of a child, then all agencies should be striving to achieve that kind of practice irrespective of costs. However, if it is possible to place children using a modified and telescoped version of this transitional process without observable long-term deleterious results, the method, in principle, will become more universally practical.

This article grows out of an evaluation and case analysis of eight children who were between nine months and three years of age when placed with adoption families by the Children's Aid Society of Pennsylvania. My overall objective in this practice review was to weigh the growth potential for the child in the process of his separation against severe anxiety which might provoke serious regressive symptoms. In so doing, I attempted to differentiate between symptoms of grief which cannot be avoided and behavior which obviously was regressive —which was, in other words, a retrenchment or decompensation

---

[4] Anna Freud and Dorothy Burlingham, *War and Children,* Ernest Willard, New York, 1943.

of the ego resulting in the child's retreat to an earlier state of satisfaction and security.

Our concern as child welfare workers, possessing a knowledge of ego psychology and a psychodynamic perspective with respect to child development, is that a separation not be so traumatic as to lead to a malfunction in the child's capacity to love and to learn. We need to examine whether the defensive measures a child uses to handle pain and anxiety at the time of separation when there is a serious break in his continuity can affect his capacity for deep relationships and the development of spontaneity in his personal interrelationships. To quote from Bowlby: "Ego and superego development are thus inextricably bound up with a child's primary human relationships; only when these are continuous and satisfactory can his ego and superego develop."[5]

Charnley, in her book *The Art of Child Placement,* states, on the other hand:

"Once having recognized the fact that separation and pain are inter-twined, child placement workers need to sort out their feelings about pain. . . . It is necessary to focus on the ability of all—child and adults alike—to take in pain, to give it recognition and a part in their lives, to grow from it, to go on with it. To protect any child from all pain, physical and emotional, would be a highly questionable way in which to build a sound adult. Beginning with the moment of birth, life is a series of separation experiences and in each of these there is pain."[6]

Sustaining a Child's Ego

I selected the situations of children placed from a foster home between the ages of nine months to three years, in the belief that this is the most critical age for a replacement. It is the time when the child is forming and consolidating a discriminating attachment to parent figures. The child at this stage is aware of the loss of parents without having achieved the ability to protest through a sophisticated use of language.

Physical motility is non-existent or limited, depending upon age. The child is dependent upon powerful adults to provide protection, security, understanding, love and nourishment. The child in this age range also has begun to develop an oedipal attachment to a foster parent. He may be moved in the midst of

[5] John Bowlby, *op. cit.,* p. 53.
[6] Jean Charnley, *The Art of Child Placement,* University of Minnesota Press, Minneapolis, 1955, p. 12.

these libidinal attachments, or in other words before he has been able to consolidate his identifications, his sense of identity as the result of important relationships in his life.

In reviewing psychoanalytic literature, one reads that the ego may be regarded as having been developed for the purpose of avoiding traumatic states; that trauma is a relative concept depending upon factors such as the constitution and previous experiences, whether motor reactions are possible and how overwhelming the actual event may be. The child welfare worker, therefore, needs to evaluate the following: the innate health and strength of a child, his capacity to take love and nurture from the mothering person (who is not his biological mother), his awareness of himself and his ability to form discriminating attachments and to provide a responsive feedback to members of the foster family. Occasionally, known earlier deprivation—such as being hospitalized at four months for malnutrition—must be measured against the child's demonstrated capacity in a foster home to reverse the earlier deprivation and to attain a spurt in his physical and emotional development.

In planning for a child's replacement from foster to adoption home, certain transitional steps must be evolved in order to sustain his ego and thereby help him cope with the pain and fear involved in losing a known set of parents to take on relatively unknown, untried parents. Once a careful evaluation is made of all we know and can understand about a child, we use a telescoped transitional method in the belief that the child's capacity to cope with anxiety of separation can be strengthened by the professional activity of his own caseworker and the adoption worker, the former working also with his foster parents and the latter with the adoption parents.[7]

Steps in the Transitional Process

The effectiveness of the transitional process rests upon the following five ingredients, and how well they can be implemented:

1. The ability of foster parents to contain sufficiently their sense of loss so that they do not sabotage, subtly or openly, the agency's preparation of the child for meeting new parents: The foster parents must be identified with adoption as providing something better or more continuous for the child.

---

[7] In the adoptive work of the Children's Aid Society of Pennsylvania the same social worker seldom acts in both capacities, although exceptions might be made for older children.

Mary was twenty-eight months old when placed from the foster home in which she had lived from eight days of age. Of their many foster children, she was the only one to come to the foster parents as a new-born infant and they placed a special value upon this child. One reason for the delay in the placement of this normal, healthy, well-developed little girl was the foster parents' desire to adopt her, a sentiment in which neighbors and relatives actively joined. The agency holding custody wisely decided to give the foster parents sufficient time to make a realistic appraisal of their ages and health. Through casework counseling, these foster parents were enabled to cope with their sense of loss and to be able to give Mary emotional support in moving to new parents.

2. The capacity of adoption parents to understand the child's grief reactions, to provide loving comfort but not to overwhelm, and above all to be able to wait for the child's love and emotional feedback. Diagnostic appraisal of the couple as parents is the agency's insurance policy for the child's future.

The adoption parents chosen for Mary had learned much in raising their first daughter, Susan, adopted when a few weeks of age, now five and a half years old and ready for first grade. The adoption worker, based on her knowledge and understanding of the family, had trust in their capacity to understand Mary's reactions to her placement; she worked to help them achieve a relaxed perspective about how to handle themselves and Susan in the process of taking Mary into their home.

3. Preparation of the child by his caseworker for meeting new parents.

Trips to the doctor provided one of the chief means of enabling Mary to know and develop more trust in her caseworker, who was to be the one to precipitate intense pain for her but also provide what comfort and reassurance she could. The caseworker told Mary in the presence of the foster mother that she wanted her to meet a new mommy and daddy. Certain words were warmly and repetitiously used: " a new mommy and daddy to grow up with;" "a sister Susan who wants a sister to grow up with;" "Mommy Jones loves Mary and so does Daddy Jones but they want her to have a mommy and daddy and sister of her own to grow up with"; "Mary is a good little girl whom Mommy and Daddy Jones love but they want her to grow up with a mommy and daddy of her own, they have other children and now a new grandchild;"

"they want Mary to have a home all of her own;" "Mrs. Gardiner (caseworker) wants Mary to meet a new mommy and daddy and a sister Susan soon who will tell her about their house, their dog, toys. . . ."

Mrs. Gardiner visited Mary daily for a week to talk with her in the presence of her foster mother. As is so often the case, the foster father was away from the home during the day on his job, but his name was used. His pain in losing Mary made it difficult for him to discuss the move with her. The foster mother had to be the strong one in carrying the feelings of the family in helping Mary appreciate that she still was loved, that this move had nothing to do with being bad, that it was to give her a new mommy and daddy and sister to grow up with, etc.

4. The timing and handling of the meetings between child and new parents.

It was arranged that Mary's placement would take place in three stages; depending upon her emotional readiness she would drive home with the new family on the third day. In driving Mary to the agency for her first meeting with the new family, the child allowed herself to be placed in the car but sobbed in a completely heartbroken fashion. Her caseworker used comforting and reassuring words, told Mary she knew how sad she was, how unhappy and frightened but while accepting the child's grief, she continued to prepare her for meeting the new family and her words were a balance of recognizing what the child was feeling and at the same time reassuring her about the future. Mary also was told that after a short while she would be driven back to Mommy and Daddy Jones's house. In that first short meeting with the adoption family, the Masons, Mary was very frightened and would not respond to any of the advances made to her. She clung to Mrs. Gardiner, who after introducing the new family felt that this was all Mary could encompass in this first meeting. After they left, the adoption worker talked with the Masons who told her they thought Mary was a precious little girl, pretty and feminine. They were distressed by her reactions but could indicate their understanding of the painful separation from foster parents this move represented.

In planning for the following day, it was decided that Mr. Mason and Susan would wait in a nearby park, enabling Mary to have some time alone with Mrs. Mason. Mary, who had been able to tell Mrs. Gardiner how frightened she was of meeting the new family, did not cry on her second trip into the agency to be with them. When she saw Mrs. Mason, she began to cry at that point but did not refuse Mrs. Mason's offer to hold her. Mrs. Mason rocked her in the rocking chair, spoke to her softly and after about a half hour, Mary felt enough comfort and trust in the new mother to allow Mrs. Gardiner to drive the two of them to the nearby park where Mr. Mason and Susan were waiting. Mrs. Gardiner left them alone together when she felt Mary was comfortable enough for her to do so. In about two hours, the family appeared at the agency with faces beaming saying they had had a grand time together and that Mary had been able to ask them for what she wanted, such as the toilet, an ice cream cone, to be lifted up into a swing, etc. The Masons, feeling more confidence that Mary was beginning to like and trust them, had begun talking with her about her going home with them on the following day. Mary's reaction was one of interest and attention.

On the third day, Mary seemed to understand what was going on. The foster family had said good-bye to her, telling her just what was happening. She was able to leave the foster home in good spirits, but her grief was later reactivated when Mrs. Gardiner said good-bye to her. At the same time, she could take comfort and affection from the new family. The child seemed to gain reassurance from knowing how much they wanted her; she began to respond to some of the enthusiasm and eagerness in their plans to get started on the fairly long trip home. She watched as the new daddy loaded her boxes and suitcases of clothes and toys. Her favorite and familiar toys were transported as well as all of her clothing. She observed all this and nodded her head to explanations of what was happening. Although a sober little girl, there was no overt expression of distress as she was lifted into the Masons' automobile.

5. Close and continuous counseling to the new adoption family in the so-called period of supervision, provided for both in the agency's structure and in the legal waiting period.

The adoption worker kept in close telephone communication with the Masons for the first two weeks following upon the placement. She asked Mrs. Mason to describe in detail their trip home with Mary as well as the day's events from waking up to going to bed, in order to have a very clear picture of how Mary was handling her transition. Whereas

Susan and Mary had been able to play together in the back seat of the car on the drive home, the impact of her separation again hit Mary when she entered the new home. She dumped all of her possessions onto the living room rug, sorted them out, commented on many saying "This is my doll, my shoes, my dress." She was fretful and unhappy and responded to Mrs. Mason's rocking her. Fortunately, Mr. Mason and Susan were tired enough to take themselves off to bed. For several nights, Mary asked for the rocking time with her new mother and would ask her to sing particular songs to her. The Masons were rather delightedly appreciative of Mary's own particular way of handling the transition: the child insisted on going to bed with her shoes and socks on for ten days. Mrs. Mason stated that this did not concern her at all because sheets easily can be washed. They also related to the adoption worker the child's maintaining a distance between the new father and herself. Whereas they had understood that Mary had had a close attachment to the foster father, they were rather puzzled that she would not mention Mommy and Daddy Jones but would talk about other members of their family.

Six weeks following her placement, there were no indications of regression in her eating, sleeping and bowel functions. She had tested out the new mother in some badness and found her firm but loving. She made use of a toy telephone in holding conversations with Mrs. Gardiner, her caseworker, asking Mrs. Gardiner how the foster children in the Jones home were but never mentioning Mommy and Daddy Jones by name. The adoption worker, in her second visit to the family two months later, found Mary looking healthy and responsive; there was tremendous motor activity as she rode the hobby horse. She also indicated how much she felt a part of the family in discussing what fun she had had at Hallowe'en. Two and a half months after her placement, Mrs. Mason phoned the adoption worker to report on a new and satisfying occurrence: that previous weekend, when Mary, Susan and Mr. Mason were in the basement workshop, at one point she impulsively ran to him, clasped her arms around a leg, said, "You're my daddy, aren't you?" That evening, she sat on his lap and enjoyed his reading to her. On the following evening when he came home from work, both daughters rushed to the door to give him a gushy homecoming.

Three months after Mary's placement, the adoption worker

in her third visit to the home observes that there is less motor activity, a more settled quality in the child and more ability to concentrate in her play. Mrs. Mason reported that Mary was beginning to have dry nights, which she had not achieved in the foster home. She also was being more regular in letting her mother know when she needed to go to the toilet. There was some competition with Susan but apparently Susan, now becoming more engrossed in her school work, was not showing jealousy of Mary's bounding attachment to her new father.

Supporting Healthy Defenses

Was Mary's placement a traumatic one in the sense of producing immediate regression and in leaving permanent psychological scar tissue? The agency had evaluated her as a constitutionally strong, healthy child with a good ego; she had experienced good nurturing and good mothering from early infancy on. In separating her, the foremost concern was to prevent a state of shock or of withdrawal as described in "Children Who Do Not Cry."[8] Efforts were directed toward sustaining her capacity to cope with a painful situation without losing trust in adults, especially parents. She was helped to grieve, to express her fear, to protest in the various ways she had at hand. She was encouraged to ask for and take comfort. Her caseworker was the "middle man" who bore the brunt of the decision to move her. This was not placed on the foster parents in any way that would have been confusing to Mary.

In our opinion, these foster parents could not have sustained an acquaintance with the adoption parents. It would have been difficult to bring both sets of parents together to provide for the kind of transition described by the Illinois Children's home and Aid. The deep attachment of the foster parents to Mary, the geographical distance between the two families, the fact that the adoption father had to return to work, were practical considerations. Unless the practical matters involved in a smooth emotional transition can be managed well, more tension than relaxation can result and a child of Mary's age would be more confused than helped.

In this placement, the adoption parents were non-ambivalent in their desire for this child, and they received sustained help and support from their social worker in letting the youngster handle the transition as she needed to.

[8] Mary H. Emmons and Louis Jacobucci, "Children Who Do Not Cry," CHILD WELFARE, April 1960.

What defenses did Mary use in handling her important part in the transitional process? We know that a child's defenses are different from an adult's and that a child with a strong ego has different defenses from a child with a weak ego. A child of Mary's age uses different defenses than a much younger one. Perhaps Mary had to repress and deny the image and memory of her foster parents and quickly identify with and cathect the adoption family in order to ward off a sense of loss and helplessness, and restore to herself a sense of happy well-being. In the writer's opinion, these would be healthy defenses appropriate to the situation. The fact that Mary showed a minimum of regression indicates that the trauma, if it existed, was kept at a minimum.

Bernard in her article on adoption agency practice states:

"Sensitive timing of the various stages of adoption attuned to the particular child's inner pace is a vital ingredient of reassurance; destructive anxiety can mount when certain steps of the process are too prolonged, such as between a child's relation to prospective parents and his actual placement with them; by the same token however panic may stem from feeling rushed and stampeded so that a more graduated spacing and slowing down is the most effective reassurance."[9]

This writer is in agreement that a prolonged transition can provoke and increase anxiety in the child, in part because of the tension in his foster family, and also perhaps because of his need to identify with the new family to get the painful business over with so that he can settle down into a happier state of affairs. In our adoption practice at the Children's Aid Society of Pennsylvania, we strive to support the child's ego in coping with the pain and anxiety in his separation so that healthy growth will continue.

Nonverbal Communication

In placing the nonverbal child who is around one year old the same process is followed as in Mary's placement, with this difference: more emphasis is placed upon nonverbal communication in the preparation of the child for taking on a new set of parents. Escalona states that an infant's way of responding to external change may be based on his nurturing experience and how a mother enables the infant to "find optimal closeness to

---

9 Viola W. Bernard, "Application of Psychoanalytic Concepts to Adoption Agency Practice," in *Psychoanalysis and Social Work,* Heiman (ed.), International Universities Press, New York, 1953, pp. 182-183.

and to tolerate optimal distance from the comforting object."[10] These are useful concepts in achieving a deeper understanding of many ongoing aspects of the foster care of infants, particularly infants in pre-adoption care. A further concept of relevance concerns Escalona's description of contagion and communication, "contagion" referring to a feeling state which is transmitted to an infant and "communication" to a more purposive and conscious process.

Whereas the element of contagion probably is a part of human existence from birth on, communication is one-sided until the infant is able to feed back to the parent with his social and language responses. Probably by the time an infant has reached nine to ten months, certain patterns of mutual communication have been well established, such as smiling and laughing in response to being tickled, being talked to, being jiggled, swung in the air. Undoubtedly it is of great assistance to a child welfare worker in bringing about a transition that there is a common language between parents and babies, and that adoption parents by and large carry on with these patterns of communication. The placement worker tells the new family of specific rituals and methods of care for the infant, and in the placement itself attention is paid to the "islands of familiarity," also mentioned by Escalona, in that familiar clothing and toys become part of the child's dowry. The adoption family is given considerable data, verbal and written, regarding the child's schedule from waking to going to sleep at night, with particular attention paid to the kind of bed and bed clothing, the type of food, the way he is bathed, when he has social times, experience with the foster mother and father, foster siblings, and others.

Adoption practitioners have observed how important the adoption father is in forming an emotional bridge between the foster mother and the new adoption mother. We have observed in the Children's Aid Society of Pennsylvania that the older infant often shows a definite preference for the new father. This is true of both boys and girls but is only observed in the latter part of the first year of growth. Another observation made is that often the child who did not like a certain food in the foster home will eat it in the adoption home, or a child who does not eat much in the foster home has an increased appetite in the adoption home. Perhaps in some way the new adoption

---

[10] Sibylle Escalone, "Emotional Development in the First Year of Life," in *Problems of Infancy and Childhood*, Senn (ed.), The Josiah Macy, Jr. Foundation, New York, 1952.

parents definitely encourage the child in this kind of improvement in his daily schedule, in order to feel that they are better parents and that the child prefers them to the foster family.

An additional important observation is that in the majority of placements, somatic reactions are mild and very short-lived. We have observed different kinds and degrees of separation anxiety, such as not wanting the new mother to be out of sight during waking hours the first month of placement. More prolonged and serious separation anxiety when observed has been related to tension and uncertainty in the new adoption mother.

Learning from Our Mistakes

Not all adoption placements proceed as smoothly as the one we have described. In some placements, we have observed prolonged grief, withdrawal and some regressive symptoms. The problem may be that the child was too abruptly and insensitively moved without a proper diagnostic understanding of his vulnerability based on constitutional endowment and previous deprivation experiences. In the instance of such children, the use of the transitional method described by Gerard and Dukette would be preferred to a shortened method. The second common problem is found in the psychological unreadiness of the new adoption mother to be a mother. There may be a tension, a lack of confidence and a blocking which had not been understood well enough in the study of the family. Discussion at that time may reveal that the problem lies in the adoption mother's feelings towards her own mother. Sometimes these feelings can be adequately ventilated, and sufficient therapeutic resolution of the problem takes place to enable the mother to find a more giving relaxed relationship with the new child. At no time is the role of the adoption father lost sight of.

More study and research is required to understand adequately the comparative factors which differentiate emotionally smooth transitions from the difficult problematic ones. Whereas all adoption practitioners would agree that the earlier an infant can be placed in his adoption home, the less possibility of setback for him, we also know that for a variety of reasons, some children cannot be placed in early infancy. In placing this older group of children, a staff should never be unaware of the traumatic possibilities in such a placement. But experience also indicates that the kind of transitional method described in this paper can be in harmony with the child's capacity to take on new parents without being traumatized.

CHAPTER 13

If A Baby Is To Be Adopted

MARY ELIZABETH FAIRWEATHER

Fear of the unknown is a basic human characteristic of which case workers practicing in the adoption field have their full quota. Constructively used this fear can be a powerful incentive to careful study of the child, the natural parents, and the adoptive parents, which will transform the unknown to the blessedly secure known. Used otherwise, it can inhibit further learning.

As understanding of case work increases, generously supplemented by expanding knowledge in related fields, we who work in the field of adoption realize better, and have more respect for, the responsibility we assume in taking part in the permanent uniting of human lives. This respect is wholesome and necessary. It helps us to recognize dangers, and it convinces us of the necessity for greater exploration of unknown areas.

As a result of our sobering realization of the tragedies that can stem from badly put-together lives we have tended to remain within the protection of tested and tried methods, bolstered by all the scientific information at our command. This, too, is good in a profession that recognizes its youth. But if we are to grow, is it not high time that we take stock of the things we already know, face honestly what we do not know, and move together toward greater enlightenment by carefully observing our experience, our experiments, and their pooled results?

Inevitably, adoption practices are now uneven. Some of us have hewed closely to conservatism; others already have begun pioneering. The resources at our command are not evenly distributed, but our concerns are the same.

Let us take a glance at some of the territory we have covered and then let us train our sights on the country ahead. We may be sure that in any forward journey we shall have valuable companions. There are psychiatry, pediatrics, and psychology, with their growing knowledge of human personality and of healthy, maturing growth, and their tested standards for various stages of development. There are sociology and anthropology, with their contributions to the understanding of cultural patterns.

We can all think of others; but let us not forget our most vitally interested contributors, our adoptive parents. And let us not forget, either, the contributions of those unwelcome but ever-present attendants, the independent and—yes—the "black-market" practitioners. They, too, can teach us something by making us ask ourselves why so many unmarried mothers, and couples, who wish to adopt a baby turn to them.

Adoption Workers Influence Human Lives

Historically, social work has been concerned with the needs of the individual in relation to his environment. For many years our efforts were confined largely to our attempts to manipulate the environment to the greater advantage of the individuals about whom we were concerned. This is, and will continue to be, a major and respected responsibility of social work in general, and case work in particular.

Gradually, however, as psychiatric knowledge is applied more and more, we are learning about the effects of inner stresses upon the individual, and on his reaction to his environment. Our diagnostic skills are of necessity focused upon recognizing both inner and outer stresses, and their causes.

In no other aspect of social work does the case worker have such unlimited possibilities for selecting the environment of an individual as does the adoption worker. And if we believe that the personality, with all its emotional components, is largely shaped by the environment that nourishes it, then in the early placement of infants we must see an opportunity for skilled case-work services that is almost overwhelming in its significance.

It is, of course, this power to influence the lives of human beings that scares us and sends us scurrying for all the support and assistance our own and related professions can give us. Again, it is well that we are scared. It is well that we view this responsibility humbly and with awe. It is well to the degree that it produces in us an unquenchable thirst for greater and deeper wisdom upon which to form our judgments and discharge our responsibilities. It is well to the degree that it drives us to keener observation of facts, so that from pooled experience we can form a whetstone on which we can continually sharpen our skills. It is not well if this same fear reduces us to immobility and the overcautiousness that keeps us from careful experimenting and the ability to learn from it; if it blinds us to the significance of new knowledge in our own and allied fields.

For purposes of this discussion I should like to consider "early placement" as meaning placement of babies under 3 months of age. We know that comparatively few of our agencies are placing babies younger than that. Why? Because they know of families that accepted infants shortly after birth and have subsequently found that they had serious physical or mental impairments. This not only has given us cause for thought (as well it should) but has stopped some of us in our tracks with what appears, occasionally, to be permanent paralysis.

Because of those unfortunate placements we have wisely sought more careful and accurate advice from medicine and psychology. But have we always made full use of this advice? Medicine, for instance, tells us that there are comparatively few serious physical abnormalities at birth that cannot be detected in the first few weeks. Perhaps we have given undue weight to those comparatively few possibilities. We know that psychology is making rapid strides in testing. Are we keeping up with the psychologists?

Knowing full well the dangers of blind placements, we have looked down our noses at those who make them. Struggling to offset the evils of such placements, we have brought fear psychology to bear in appealing to the self-interest of couples who wish to adopt a baby, by saying: "Come to an agency so that you can be assured of mental and physical adequacy in your child!"

What Causes Adoption Failures?

Can we ever really guarantee this? And if we could, is this, or should this be, the primary function of sound adoption practice? And has this stopped or even slowed up the black-market and independent placements? The answers are all too clearly written, first in the statistics of adoption courts, and later in adoption failures recorded in family agencies, guidance clinics, juvenile courts, and mental hospitals. Are these failures due to mental or physical inadequacies of the child? Not predominantly. They are due usually to inadequate parents or inadequate help in the adjustment process.

Is it not time that we put our emphasis on other areas of our knowledge and concerns? Listen again to some of our other sources of advice: to psychiatry, to our own experience, to the adoptive parents themselves.

There is a triangular motif that runs through the design of all human life. Freud and his disciples point up its outlines in tracing the dynamics of emotional growth. Helene Deutsch, in her study, "The Psychology of Women," discusses a woman's profound need to love her child in a family triangle. Whether balanced or distorted, this triangle influences every psychiatric consideration of human experience from infancy to the grave.

In a sense, adoption practice is framed by another triangle, with the child as the apex and with the sides made up of his own parent or parents, the adoptive parents, and the agency. We have had the apex under the microscope for some time now and this is well, for we still have much to learn. But I suggest that if the apex is to be supported adequately the sides must be kept in balance and strengthened by our understanding.

We Learn from Other Fields

Reiterating my appreciation and admiration for what psychology has contributed, and promises to contribute, to the field of adoption, I believe we need to make careful use of everything it can offer and to be fully alert to its continuing contributions. But what of our other obligations? What of our other counselors?

What, for instance, does psychiatry tell us about early infancy? There is as yet no complete agreement about the significance of constitutional factors in the development of personality, but no one underestimates the influence of environment on these factors. I do not need to remind you of the constantly mounting studies that show the influence of family relationships from the moment of birth and the role that consistent mothering plays in the optimum development of the infant, not only physically, but emotionally and mentally as well.

Dr. Margaret Ribble, in "The Rights of Infants" points up the importance of the first 3 months of life in this respect and the damage that can be done to a child if mother love is lacking. Dr. Leo H. Bartemeier and his associates, who formulated the idea of the Cornelian Corner, emphasizes the advantages of earliest possible mother-child relationship. Doctors Arnold Gesell and Catherine S. Amatruda, in "Developmental Diagnosis," point out that children in faulty homes and in institutions are often retarded. Many psychologists expect children brought up in institutions to rate lower than their true potential levels. This is shown when the child is tested again after adoptive or foster-home placement. We have abundant evidence from our own experiences of how children who have been severely hurt emotionally can blossom if they are given love and security. We can and should obtain more scientifically compiled evidence of this, which is well known to every adoption worker. But we can never hope to measure how much more might have been attained if the hurt had not occurred.

We know that the very circumstances that make a baby available for adoption fill his earliest environment with conflict and rejection. We know how adequately and joyfully an adoptive couple, capable of healthy parental feelings, can meet a baby's needs in a way that is beyond anything we can hope to offer through other kinds of foster care.

First Adjustment Is All-Important

Looking at the adoptive parents, psychiatry underscores our conclusions by recognizing the importance of the complete dependency and helplessness of the very young infant as a factor in laying firm foundations for parental feelings in the adoptive family. We know the injury that change can cause to a child, and its effects upon his adjustment even in a happy placement. We know the disturbing effect a child's difficulties in eating, sleeping, and so forth, have upon adoptive parents, particularly the mother, and the vicious circle this can set up in the all-important first adjustment. This has urgent significance, not only in planning for early adoptive placement but, where this is not possible in planning for individualized rather than group care for infants.

Listen to applicants for a baby to adopt. "How early do you place?" "We want as young a baby as possible." "We are not afraid of taking some risks; we'd take some risks if we had a baby born to us."

Look at the throes of "psychological labor," always present at the time of placement. Aren't they lessened by the aspect of a young and helpless infant whose features have not developed the distinctive characteristics that have to be reconciled with those of the omnipresent fantasy child?

The coming of a child into an adoptive family has been described as a rebirth. This is not just a figure of speech. It has deep psychological reality. The birth pangs for both adoptive parents and child are notoriously greater in direct proportion to the age of the child.

Listen to adoptive parents who have had their baby from the first few weeks of his life: "Already he seems like ours. We know we can help him develop his personality as well as his physical powers and in that sense we are creating him and he is really ours."

Look at the majority of children placed by "black markets" and independent agents. In what age group do they fall? Infancy, of course. Why?

But what about protection? Well—what about it? Whom are we protecting by delaying placement? Is it the child, who is our paramount responsibility? According to psychiatrists, no. Is it the adoptive parents, whom we have chosen because of their indications of maturity, good life adjustment, and mutual happiness? Not usually at their request. Is it the child's own parents (frequently the unmarried mother), who have not found a more ready and willing answer through the "black market" or other independent sources? Psychiatric and our own case-work literature are filled with warnings of the neurotic conflict that may result from delayed decisions.

Here, again, is the adoption triangle. Our responsibility for protection lies within it, but that responsibility is not usually discharged in the best way by delayed placement of the child. When careful social diagnosis indicates adoption for an infant, we must remember that the welfare and protection of all concerned are inextricably interwoven. And I believe that their best interests are served by the earliest possible placement. Let us concentrate less on our fears of unknown factors in a child and try harder to develop greater ability to know our adoptive applicants and to realize what they can offer as healthy, nutritive soil in which a new life can develop. Normal, well-adjusted adults, given the opportunity, can weigh the risks of reasonable unknowns, arrive at a decision, and find a healthy way to adjust to the results of their decision. Basic case-work principles proclaim that the adoptive parents have a right to this kind of self-direction. If our professional evaluation has been sound we have no need or right to overprotect them.

Our energies might be spent to better advantage in careful casework services to natural parents in helping them reach an early and clear decision when adoption is indicated; in helping them to give as complete and accurate information as possible about their babies' backgrounds as one of their contributions to this plan. Between the natural parent and the child placed for adoption there is a psychological as well as a physical cord to be cut. If it isn't carefully and skillfully cut at the appropriate time it can be a permanent threat to the security of any adoption placement.

We Must Know Ourselves

And our energies might be spent better in looking at ourselves. Are we making full use of the professional knowledge and advice available to us? Are we training our workers to know the boundaries of normal development in children so that their observations can supplement and assist those of our consultants? Have we the courage to discharge the responsibility we have assumed? Or must we share our doubts and fears of the unknown as well as our knowledge of pertinent facts? Have we the courage to face squarely our inevitable areas of inadequacy? And can we derive from them the stimulation for increased efforts to widen and deepen our knowledge and for greater sharing of the results of our efforts?

I recognize that there always will be situations in which delays are inevitable. We shall always have the older child to place. That is another topic and a challenging one. But when we can, let us place the baby early. Let us by all means make use of every available tool to increase our knowledge and to guide the adjustment of child and family. Where justifiable doubts are present, let us have serial tests made.

But why can't these tests be done more often in the adoptive home, with adequate preparation and interpretation given to the parents? Why would it not be feasible some day to have psychological tests given to all babies as are physical examinations? Why cannot these tests be viewed as an early step toward vocational guidance rather than as a measurement of abstract adequacy? Do not healthy, well-adjusted parents want primarily the optimum development of their children within their capacities?

Science indicates that individually our maximum capacity for mental development is fixed at birth, but that our chances for achieving it are modified by our later environment. We now believe that even intelligence quotients can be raised, in an adequately supportive and stimulating climate. Those of us in adoption work have held front-row seats at many of these performances. We have evidence that emotional quotients have no such prenatal roots. Fortunately, high intelligence quotients and high emotional quotients are not mutually exclusive; but neither are they necessarily correlated. We in adoption work are today selecting the soil that will nourish many of tomorrow's emotional quotients. Here at once is the adoption worker's deepest responsibility and greatest challenge.

Placing the Second Child for Adoption

LYDIA T. HICKS

All parents undergo a maturing process through caring for, and learning to understand the differences in, each child who comes to them, whether through birth or adoption. How much the first child has endured the burden of parental learning is often not appreciated until after the arrival of the next baby. Then parents will often tell us that although they had thought they were perfectly comfortable with the first after the normal anxiety of the early weeks in their new role as parents had worn off, they now realize that there are varying degrees and different ways of being at ease as parents. Even in the midst of difficulty, although worried about the outcome, parents are apt to be less encumbered by the fear of failure to do the right thing. They have learned more of their own potentialities. To have become better acquainted with the core of the inner spirit is an enriching experience, and the second child reaps a generous harvest.

The first child usually benefits by having a brother or sister even though the emotional hurdle, at the beginning, may be hard to take. The coming of the second child increases the first child's maturity in the eyes of the parents. Sometimes, the increase is out of proportion and the first child suffers by being pushed out of his infancy too fast; but normally, it is just enough to inject a wholesome opportunity for some independent growing. By growing up together in the give and take of family life, both children may be expected to be better prepared for adult interpersonal relationship than if each had grown up as an "only" child.

What I have said is true for any child and his parents. In adoption, there are additional advantages. The first child and the adoptive parents can relive the placement process and thereby feel again at a deeper level, the meaning of adoption. The parents who have lived through the practical acceptance of adoption, and have had their complex feelings about adoption "tested out" by the first child, are able to help the second one accept adoption more naturally. Two or more adopted children growing up together in a family will find it easier to carry any feeling of being different, because they can share it.

By the time the second child is placed, adoptive parents are more sure of their relationship to the agency, and consequently less anxious or self-conscious, more "themselves." Not only does this enable the agency to arrive more confidently at the decision to accept their application for a second child, but the agency can select a particular family for a particular child with more sureness. The agency has more understanding of the subtle ways in which the parents function and therefore more understanding of how they may be suited to the child. With their greater acceptance of the agency, the parents are freer to recognize mistakes they made with their first child. This increases their capacity to meet the needs of two children.

Adoptive parents asking for a second child may not need the same experiences they sought with the first child, and so may be ideally suited to accept, love and help a child with special needs. If their experience has enabled them to provide a calmer, more relaxed atmosphere, they usually will not need from the child so much emotional response so quickly; thus there will be less pressure upon the child for achievement.

A Second Child Placement

Because her mother had great difficulty in surrendering her, Theresa was eight months old before she could be placed for adoption. From the first, she had been high-strung. She startled and cried easily. She continued to have feeding difficulties with some regurgitation at all meals. Allergy to common foods resulted in loose stools or skin rash, unless she was kept on a rigid diet. All tests had ruled out any disease or abnormality. What Theresa seemed to need was the permanency of warm, loving, relaxed family life.

The Bradley family was chosen for Theresa because of the way they had helped Jack, their first child:

The worker who had originally taken Jack under boarding care at eighteen months of age did not recognize him after the two and a half years that had elapsed. Then he had been a thin, frail, colorless, girlish-looking boy who retreated within himself when confronted with a strange face; on seeing a new toy he would draw his hand back as though fearful of making contact. Now Jack is strong, sturdy, confident, handsome and boyish looking, with sparkling eyes and a friendly grin.

His adoptive parents recalled how little by little Jack had relinquished his fears. The Bradleys had loved him just as he was, and had never tried to hurry him, even by a kindly "big boys are not afraid." The warm, accepting atmosphere which they created nourished this emotionally-starved little boy. As he was able to move out a little, they had no need to hold him back, nor to over-praise. Their giving was a sort of overflow of plenty.

The Bradleys are unusually well-endowed with a naturalness for living and loving. The adoptive father is a skilled workman whose self-respect extends to all people, and who enjoys the work he does and takes pride in it. He is well organized and relaxed. The adoptive mother has a sturdy spirit, and sensitivity as well as strength. The intuitive sort of communication between husband and wife proved to be a true indication that they would be of equal though complementary value to a child, without any hurt feelings or rivalry between them as they changed from a "couple" to a "family."

Jack resembled the adoptive father in physical appearance and ethnic background. At the time of placement we thought he was like the mother in personality, but by the age of four it was plain that identification with the father was influencing him to become like him in every way.

The agency believed that it would make a more balanced family if the Bradley's second child were a girl; this was in accord with the family's preference. Theresa resembles Mrs. Bradley not only in general appearance and coloring, but also in inner strength. We felt that Theresa was using this strength negatively, but that when freed for constructive use it could enable her to take advantage of what the Bradley family could give.

Theresa's parental background, in nationality, general education and achievement, was similar to Jack's and very much like the Bradleys'. In some second-child placements there is a vast difference in backgrounds, though the qualities of the children themselves are similar enough to eliminate unhappy comparisons. At our agency we have learned to think ahead, when the first child is placed, to the possibility of placing a second. This may modify the way in which we present the first child's background. For example, if the parents, grandparents, and close relatives all worked successfully in professional careers, instead of spelling this out with enthusiastic tone of voice, we might say in a matter-of-fact way that the parents were both engaged responsibly in professional work. Then, if later on a second child is to be placed who has promise although he comes from a less promising background, the adoptive parents will be less likely to question the wisdom of the choice.

Our agency centers confidence in the child's own potentiality more than in what he may inherit. But we make allowance for the fact that most adoptive parents, lacking the agency's experiences in this area, are apt to place more confidence in heredity.

Considering Ages of Both Children

At the time of Theresa's placement, Jack was four years old. Although they had begun to consider another child when Jack was three, the Bradleys wanted him to have his parents all to himself for this extra year, because he needed to consolidate his gains before being subjected to competition with a younger child.

Timing is important in planning the placement of a second child. Consideration should be given both to the children's ages and to the preparation of the first child and the adoptive parents for the second placement. While there are no cut-and-dried rules about children's ages at the time of placement, there are general guides. The first child will be less threatened by his mother's involvement with an infant if he has begun to establish some independence for himself in walking and eating. From then on his interests have a more outward pull. And as long as there is no dearth of homes for normal white infants with conventional backgrounds, it seems fairer to both children and parents that the first child be able to express himself verbally before having to share his parents with a newcomer. There can always be exceptions on the basis of need. If he has learned to talk in sentences he is still more able to cope with feelings of jealousy, since expressing hurt in words diminishes the need to express it with body blows.

But if the first child needs to hold on to babyhood longer even though chronologically he "ought" to be ready to move ahead, he should not be pushed by the placement of another child. His unreadiness may spring from his own early deprivations, rather than from his adoptive parents' need to keep him too dependent or to push him ahead too fast.

Sometimes our well-founded confidence in the adoptive parents' competence as parents, coupled with their eagerness to get their second child quickly, tends to make us lose sight of why we originally thought it better not to place a second child until their first has progressed a little further. Often the adoptive parents "plead through their first child" by saying such things as, "He asks in his prayers every night for a baby brother (or sister)," not understanding that children who do this are usually mirroring their parents' wish in order to get approval.

A little margin of age difference between children can preserve buoyancy for the adoptive mother which will bear dividends for the children. We are apt to forget that during the winter both children may be down at once with the communicable diseases, and if one baby is out of diapers the stresses and strains are diminished.

People may think they want to adopt a child who is older than their first. Such a plan can be worked out occasionally, but very few older children who come to an adoption agency could tolerate the strain of such a placement. It is too hard for a child as emotionally deprived as the majority of these children to have to step into a ready-made role of older and forbearing sibling to a securely established younger one, who will always be given more leeway because he is younger and realistically more dependent. Almost always, more will be expected of the older one than he is able to live up to, and he will have slight opportunity to regress in a normal way.

It is very important to allow time to prepare the first child and to create the proper atmosphere for receiving the second child. There is not any one thing parents should do to prepare the first child, but they need to be alert to how he may be affected by the coming of another child, and to strengthen his ego in preparation for it. Sometimes the simple advice to promote him from his crib to a bed in a larger room starts an adoptive parent on a whole new train of thought. One parent was amazed to find how proud it made the boy to feel he was recognized as old enough to make such a move.

An adoptive mother told us recently that in thinking about a second child she had begun to realize that her enjoyment of her son's babyhood had kept her from giving him enough opportunities to try to do things for himself. She saw the wisdom of waiting a little for a second child until both she and the boy had had more time to experiment in freedom—she in giving it, he in exercising it. We felt that this mother was growing responsibly through her insight into past mistakes.

Preparation of the Family

The Bradleys, though outstanding adoptive parents, had had considerable growing to do at the beginning, and they deepened their understanding of the meaning of adoption while helping Jack get ready for Theresa.

They were now well past their struggle to accept infertility. This had been fairly well handled at the time of their first application for adoption, but there were some remnants of feeling about it which were reactivated at the time of Jack's placement. This had made them a little reluctant, at the beginning of placement, to put into words for Jack anything they thought he might be feeling about his former life, including his boarding parents. They felt that if they said nothing, all would be forgotten, rationalizing that Jack, then almost two years old, was too young to understand. But with the worker's help they had been able to take the next step in their own growth, for Jack's sake.

Their relationship with the agency became firmer after they had come to terms with their own first reluctance to talk with Jack about his past. If the worker had not been able to get through to them about that topic, it is likely that this small rift would have developed into a larger one. Adoptive parents frequently project upon the agency their own reluctance to tell a child about adoption. The child may then begin to take on their attitude of fearing the agency and eventually blaming it for some vague error. This confuses the child and is apt to cause him to be ashamed of being adopted.

When the Bradleys had "swung round the circle" and consolidated the gains they had made in their own emotional development, they could think about Jack's natural parents in a more mature way. And Jack, a little older, was able to comprehend more. Hearing about his natural parents again shortly before the coming of the second child helped him to realize the loving care with which parents bring children into their life, and to feel the respect that his adoptive parents have for his first parents and for Theresa's first parents. Repetition is a vital factor in the learning process, provided it is not repetition by rote. In a new setting and at a different stage of development it can bring vision and inspiration.

About two weeks before Theresa's placement, the Bradleys visited the agency with Jack. Their emotional acceptance of adoption was affirmed and strengthened by reliving with him, at the agency, the story of how and where "we first saw you and knew you were the little boy we had been waiting for." The agency playroom had associational values for Jack. He asked thoughtful questions, which the Bradleys answered honestly and with respect for his past associations. Upon the return home, the Bradleys noted that Jack had become even surer of his relationship to them. Although Jack knew that there was to be a baby sister or brother sometime, he was not told specifically about Theresa until after his parents had seen her and made their decision. Because of Theresa's age and general anxiety, a two-day placement process was planned. This would also give Jack a chance to participate with his parents in beginning to relate to Theresa before she came into the home.

Child's First Meeting with Family

Adoptive parents often need help to understand why their child should not be with them for their first introduction to a new child. Many have thought it would prevent a child from being jealous if he could "pick out" his young sister or brother. But they lose sight of the basic truth that it is the parents, not the children, who are responsible for creating a family. Then, too, parents are not free to make a sound decision about the new child if they are constantly aware of needing to protect the first child from feeling left out. Even more important, if the child should prove to be not the right one for them, they might hesitate to make a negative decision because of the effect upon their child.

When the Bradleys were told about Theresa, they listened attentively and interjected comparative material about Jack.

They approached Theresa gently at the first meeting, waiting for her to show readiness to consider them. She surprised both worker and family by soon settling down comfortably on Mrs. Bradley's lap, with an air of well-being.

On the second day of placement, Jack was introduced to Theresa. His presence was a real help to her; a four-year-old can be of great interest to a baby.

Mr. and Mrs. Bradley gave Jack time to find himself and to move slowly toward Theresa. Gradually they incorporated his play activities with the baby's. Mrs. Bradley told the worker in Jack's presence that he had picked out a name for a sister, and that they would gradually introduce it after Theresa had become used to them, so that she would not be confused by losing her name while so many new things were coming at her all at once.

As the Bradleys moved warmly and competently into the relationship with the baby, they talked companionably with both children about what was happening, such as how they would put on Theresa's wraps, carry the bundles, drive the car.

Because they had constructively lived through Jack's various reactions as he struggled with his fears, the Bradleys were able to provide Theresa with a comfortable atmosphere, without pressing her for an early return of affection or other indications of growth. Theresa had found parents in whom we had more than ordinary confidence. As she is "settling in," all evidence points to a happy growing up.

A Handicapped Second Child

For Juanita, it was even more important to select parents well-known through agency experience.

Juanita, born with a hare lip and cleft pallet, was eight months old when she was placed for adoption. It was expected that she would need several plastic surgery operations. Even then, it was quite possible that she would have a speech defect and a facial scar for the rest of her life. Doctors believed that speech therapy would eliminate the difficulty, but when pressed, they could not be entirely reassuring.

Juanita had an endearing personality, and was so alert and responsive that everyone who came to know her minimized her physical defect. She continued to trust and enjoy people even though in her short life, she had undergone considerable pain and discomfort from two operations. Juanita also had a strong determination. It had served her well through early hardships, but it could cause much difficulty if she did not learn to channel it constructively.

The caseworker wanted a family who had already had at least one child. Juanita needed parents, who could face the uncertainty of the outcome of the prospective surgery without pitying her— either at present or if the surgery proved unsuccessful. She should not grow up expecting special consideration because of a handicap, or in any way feeling self-pity. She should not have to overcompensate with strident or driving behavior.

This seemed like a large order to expect adoptive parents to fill. But about the time that Juanita needed parents, the Smiths asked for another child who "just everybody wouldn't want." They were not trying to "get a foot in the door." Since they already had two children, they knew it would not be easy to get a third child. Besides, they did care about helping people.

Their two children, Janet and Howard, are twelve and nine. There is something special about this couple. Their integrity and warmth shine out; there is real communication between husband and wife, and unusual understanding of children. The children have always been given as much independence as they could handle. There has been unusual good judgment in this respect. Janet is comfortable within herself and well-accepted by her school friends. She is feminine in appearance as well as in interests. Although making only average grades in school, she excells in domestic arts. Harold's academic interests are equalled by his athletic ability. He reads books far beyond the fourth-grade level. He, too, is popular with his age group. The parents appreciate each child and value each for himself.

It was felt that this family constellation was right for Juanita: there was a big sister old enough so that there would be no grounds for comparison between the two children. There would be no comparison with the brother because of sex difference and age. In personality and intelligence Juanita was the equal of the other children. In coloring and general appearance she resembled Mr. Smith more than Mrs. Smith, and she looked very much like Janet.

We gave as much thought to how the personalities of the three children might act and interact as Juanita grew up as we would have had there been many homes from which to choose. But the determining factor in selecting this home for Juanita was the agency's experience with Mr. and Mrs. Smith as parents. Their approach to a child's differing needs, their warmth and integrity, their freedom from any need to pressure a child, even subtly, gave us confidence that Juanita's needs could be met, so that even if her physical handicap could not be removed she would have the chance to grow up free of an emotional handicap. This placement has worked out exceedingly well.

Sometimes when adoptive parents have successfully helped a first child with a serious handicap there is a strong temptation to place a second child with a similar problem. Whether or not to do so depends upon whether the first child has consolidated his gains sufficiently to relive his own problems through another child, with whom he is sharing his parents. It would depend, too, upon the readiness of the adoptive parents to go through this again. It might be safer to place an "easy to care for" child with such a couple.

Home Study for a Second Child

There is a danger that a homefinder may feel too sure of the second-child applicants because of the agency's basic knowledge and relationship with them during study and supervision of the first child's placement. The worker could have a sound basis for such a faith insofar as past experience goes. But the passing of one or two years can bring new factors that must be evaluated.

In different phases of development, children require a deepening of parental capacities. The different stages of a child's growth may reactivate old trouble spots in a parent's own "skipped stages" of emotional development. This is true for any parent, but the adoptive parent is not only learning to be a parent but is often, consciously or unconsciously, continuing to work on assimilating and accepting his or his spouse's inability to produce a child, as we saw in the Bradleys. Community attitudes and questions of relatives or friends may augment and precipitate anxiety. This can affect the adoptive parents' ability to help a child understand and accept his adopted status. It is normal for this struggle to be going on. Our concern is not with the struggle but the degree of struggle—whether it is being faced realistically, whether it is diminishing, and how much of it is still present at the time of the second-child application.

Perhaps the chief way in which the second-child application home study differs from the study for the first is that it involves evaluating the couple's feeling about their cumulative experience as parents to their child. It is also necessary to understand their child. It is vitally important to understand not only his relationship to his adoptive parents, but how he is meeting the demands of growth. We look for indications of his developing independence. Is it commensurate with his age, or is he being pushed beyond his ability or kept too protectingly close to parental care; or regardless of normal parental attitudes, is his emotional development retarded because of his early emotional deprivation? Is the child comfortable within himself, enjoying his relationships with others; or is he indiscriminately friendly or too shy and withdrawn? Continuity in a child's development should be stressed. He does not live in separate compartments but is influenced by every experience he has had.

The Family Constellation

In planning for the placement of a second child, we are reinterpreting the resolution of forces in the interpersonal relationships of a family of three, as they have grown and changed since our last contact with them. How will this balance be affected by the addition of another child? If the answer is positive, then what sort of child should be placed here?

Since sound marriage is fundamental to the well-being of children, it is important to find out how the marriage relationship has been affected by a child, and how the responsibilities of parenthood have been shared between husband and wife. If one parent is dominant, is it because of greater or less maturity? Does he need to compete with the partner or wish to prolong the child's infancy in order to relive his own life, or is his dominance due to a genuine understanding of the child, and a desire to help him and to support the partner? How has the child been affected by any of this?

With which parent is the child most comfortable? What is the other parent's reaction to this? If one parent is less successful, is it the one of the same sex as the child? Has this parent grown sufficiently to take on another hcild? If so, would it be better to place a child of the other sex?

At the time of the first home study, there were estimated strengths and weaknesses which were expected to affect the potentiality for parenthood, such as—ability to give of oneself, to admit mistakes, to use difficult experiences constructively, to accept things as they are, and such tendencies as the need to control, possessiveness, defensiveness. Have these tendencies materialized as the result of having a child?

Re-evaluating adoptive parents' acceptance of adoption at various levels of their experience need not be a formidable undertaking. It requires that we be alert for signs pointing to growth or lack of it in their accepting attitude. In the case of an older child, we note whether they are aware of a child's fumbling ways of trying to talk about his past, and can recognize when he is trying to find out if he is to stay with them permanently. He may be confused about his status and struggling to ask how babies are started and how this applies to him. If parents utilize the veiled opportunities children present to try to open a conversation and give true answers understandable to the child, then we know the parents are arriving, or perhaps have arrived, at an acceptance of adoption.

With younger children it is harder to discover what the adoptive parents' attitudes are. It is helpful to ask what they remember about the parents of their child, what they are telling the child now about how he came to be theirs, and what they have thought about the answers they may give to questions he will ask when he is older. If he is old enough to ask questions about birth, does he understand the difference between being a birth child and being an adopted child? How have they explained to their child the agency and the worker's visit? What is the adoptive parents' relationship to the agency?

Conclusion

It is reasonable to expect that more than 75 percent of the applications for second children could eventuate in placement. These applications offer a golden opportunity to the chlidren and to the agency because the adoptive applicants have been enriched by their experiences as parents, and because the agency has a basis in experience for knowing them better than it does couples making a first application.

In engineering, "feedback" is a frequently used term. This means a returning gain to all involved in a process. In second-child placements there is feedback for the children and for the adoptive parents who have the opportunity to reaffirm the gains they have made as parents and to accept their inability to bear a child. Last of all, there is gain for the agency in re-evaluating the first home study in terms of on-going parental experience. This is an opportunity for research, a chance to observe how early predictions have eventuated, which enables us to continue to deepen our understanding.

CHAPTER 15

Adoptive Placement of Infants Directly from the Hospital

ELIZABETH I. LYNCH and **ALICE E. MERTZ**

This paper deals with the placement of forty-five infants in their permanent adoptive homes directly from the hospitals in which they were born. The infants studied comprised twenty-one boys and twenty-four girls (including two sets of twins), who were placed at the ages of seven to twenty days by the Los Angeles County Bureau of Adoptions.[1]

These direct placements were made as a result of the general interest in "early" placements which has been increasingly reflected in the literature on adoption. The Los Angeles County Bureau of Adoptions, a public agency established in 1949, first attempted to make placements within three months whenever possible, and then, in many instances, within six weeks. Finally, spurred on by the satisfactory experience with these early placements, by the reports of a few direct hospital placements made elsewhere, and by firsthand knowledge of the real satisfaction evidenced by mothers who had arranged independent adoptions directly from the hospital, our agency began in 1952 to use the same plan in making some adoptive placements. Three such placements were made in 1952, eight in 1953, and thirty-four in

---

[1] The agency is indebted to Mrs. Juanita Nichols, supervisor of the caseworkers involved in work with natural parents, and to Dr. Judd Marmor, consulting psychiatrist, for their interest in and contributions to the success of this project.

1954, totaling forty-five children (including the twins), and forty-three mothers.

We have been exceedingly pleased with all of these direct placements; in not a single case has the placement been unsuccessful. Not only have the infants grown happily and wholesomely in their permanent adoptive homes, but we have found that it is much more satisfactory to the natural mothers to place their children directly with adoptive parents than to place them in temporary boarding homes. The placements have also pleased the adoptive parents, who have been especially glad to receive newborn babies.

There is as yet little literature on the subject of adoptive placements directly from the hospital. For a considerable period of time, however, psychiatric and social work writings either by implication or specifically have supported "the earliest possible" placements. The tremendous importance to infants of continuous loving care from birth has been emphasized repeatedly. Dr. Sibylle Escalona[2] has stated that a child's early experiences should have a loving "definite rhythm and sameness." Dr. Margaret A. Ribble[3] has shown that the human infant is born with undeveloped brain cells and that the oxygen needed for their development for physical and mental health must be secured through consistent "mothering" from birth onward. Social work literature has stressed that both the emotional and the intellectual development of the young child are best promoted by early placement in the permanent home, since the adoptive parents, in contrast to temporary parents, can give love freely without constantly risking the hurt to themselves in loving a child greatly and then losing him. Also, helpful standards have been outlined by Dr. Viola Bernard[4] and others for the selection of the child, the natural parents, and the adoptive parents in making early placements.

Study of Early Adoptive Placements

When we began to make our first direct placements late in 1952, the six criteria established for the selection of such cases closely resembled criteria for other early placements: (1) legal

---

[2] Sibylle Escalona, in discussion on "Problems of Infancy and Childhood," *Transactions of the Fourth Conference, March 6-7, 1950,* Milton J. E. Senn, M.D. (ed.), Josiah Macy, Jr., Foundation, New York, 1951.

[3] Margaret A. Ribble, M.D., *The Rights of Infants,* Columbia University Press, New York, 1943.

[4] Viola W. Bernard, M.D., "Application of Psychoanalytic Concepts to Adoption Agency Practice," in *Psychoanalysis and Social Work,* Marcel Heiman (ed.), International Universities Press, New York, 1953, pp. 169-209.

barriers to immediate adoption should be absent, since relinquishment cannot be taken when an impediment exists, and since adoptive placement should not ordinarily be made until relinquishment has been made; (2) the backgrounds of the natural parents must be good; (3) the natural parents must be consistent in their desire for adoption; (4) prenatal and delivery history should present no significant problem; (5) the health of the infant should be satisfactory; and (6) the adoptive parents should be eager and able to accept such a placement.

In 1952 all infants placed by the Bureau were given psychological examinations before placement. The eleven infants approved for direct placement in 1952 and 1953 were given such examinations. The results of these examinations became confirming, but not essential, evidence of the desirability of the placements. A second psychological examination was given approximately six months after adoptive placement, and the results showed that these children had not only sustained their original good ratings, but in most instances had improved upon them. The psychologist commented on the superior adjustment of these children, remarking that they showed ''signs of security which only genuine love could have developed.''

Encouraged by the success of these eleven placements, in 1954 we began making placements directly from the hospital on a larger scale. Psychological examinations were dispensed with, since by this time they were being used by the agency only when the need for them was particularly indicated by developmental problems.[5] Also, some placements were made in which the backgrounds were not above average, and in which the children showed some evidence of health problems. The thirty-four additional placements made in 1954 represented about 8 per cent of the total agency placements for that year and 15 per cent of placements exclusive of children with special needs, of which minority groups are a part. Direct placements covered none of the latter group, owing to the lack of adoptive homes.

In the total group of forty-five, three infants were placed in their adoptive homes in seven days or less; twenty-two between eight and fourteen days, and twenty between fifteen and twenty days. Nearly three-fourths of the infants had been born in maternity homes from which it was easier to make direct place-

[5] See articles by Mary Elizabeth Fairweather, "Early Placement in Adoption," *Child Welfare*, Vol. XXXI, No. 3 (1952) pp. 3-8, and by Kenneth Dick, "Toward Earlier Placement for Adoption," SOCIAL CASEWORK, Vol. XXXVI, No. 1 (1955), pp. 22-26, relative to the use of psychological tests for infants.

ments than from general hospitals, since infants could be kept there longer, allowing sufficient time for planning.

In order to evaluate the agency's experience with this group of children, the case records of parent, child, and adoptive parents were read. For the children placed and the adoptive parents selected, it might be considered that, in one sense, the 1952 and 1953 cases, which had a second psychological examination six months after placement, constituted a type of control study group.

As a further control or contrasting group for the natural parents, forty-four additional parent case records—a sample of the 1954 non-direct placements of the Bureau, exclusive of children with special needs—were reviewed. In these cases it was found that twenty-four mothers could not have signed the relinquishment sufficiently early for direct placement because of serious physical, legal, or other problems. In twenty cases, however, the criteria for direct placement could have been met. The reading of the two sets of parent records, the forty-three direct placements and these twenty later placements, comprised a valuable comparative study which enabled us to see more clearly the respective factors in those case situations in which the mothers relinquished their children early and those in which they relinquished them later. The following material is centered on a description of the outstanding characteristics of the forty-three mothers who participated in direct placement, together with a statement of the major factors differentiating them from the others.

The Natural Parents

The natural parents of the forty-five infants had come from varying social and economic backgrounds, although most were from the middle income group. They ranged from a farm girl whose life had been spent in the fields to a mother from a wealthy family, who faced a problem of alcoholism. They came from families of good repute and, by selection, from families of good backgrounds in health, with no known potentially inheritable diseases. Nearly two-thirds were 21 years old, or younger. In about one-fourth of the cases the mothers had been married, and several had had children. Two had had a previous child out of wedlock. Of the forty-five children only two were born in wedlock.

In many instances the mothers and fathers had known each other over a considerable period of time. There were only a few brief acquaintanceships, and in some cases a degree of devotion had existed and marriage had been planned. The natural fathers, however, did not play an active part in the adoption process, and except for three fathers, including the two married ones, we had no contact with them. Although it is agency policy to see the father when this seems indicated and the mother has given consent, it would have been difficult to reach the majority of them. More than half of the fathers were out of the county; some of them were in the armed forces. Moreover, in all but two instances, the mothers were discontinuing contact with them. Most of the mothers had told the fathers of the pregnancies and were greatly disillusioned by the lack of help offered. A small number of mothers had not told the fathers, and wanted no further relationship with them.

In general, these mothers were of good or average intelligence, many of them undoubtedly in a superior category. They had been successful in achievement in school (a fourth had had some college work), or had had success or satisfaction in their jobs, some of which were positions of considerable responsibility. The eleven student mothers were resuming their schooling and the remaining mothers were returning to employment, which consisted largely of office work.

These mothers, with some exceptions, showed considerable emotional maturity. They were able to use the worker constructively to help them work through their plans and, indeed, their ego strengths and their ability to plan were their most outstanding chacteristics. They were realistic in accepting responsibility for their present situation and for doing something about it. Many stressed that in this experience they had "changed," "grown up," "seen things they did not see before," and so on. Many said they had learned much about themselves and their relation with men. Many hoped to marry and have other children in the future.

The mothers were consistent in their lack of ambivalence and in their desire to place their children for adoption. Only three showed some wavering, immediately after birth, but these soon settled on adoption as the only possible plan for them.

In evaluating the meaning of relinquishment to these mothers, it could be said that, in general, some other psychological need was so compelling that relinquishment of the child became a necessity. These needs appeared to be of two kinds, either a self-interest apart from the child, or such a profound interest in the child that it became necessary to provide a normal home for him with two parents. Sometimes there was a combination of these two factors, each compelling in itself. In about nineteen of the cases, self-interest appeared greater and in sixteen, interest in the child greater, with the remainder showing about an equal interest in themselves and in the child.

Miss Fairweather has well said, "When a parent's own needs absorb all his energies . . . or when a child presents an impossible impediment to the attainment of more desired goals, the relinquishment of that child can offer a relief outweighing any conflicting feelings."[6] There may be added to this a most powerful need to give the child the increased social status and opportunity that adoption would bring. One mother said, "I see my child at four, and I cannot give him what he needs." Another said, "I see my son at ten and I cannot give him the father he should have." The other major needs or desires that absorbed the energies of this group included the desire for further schooling, the desire to protect their own or their relatives' reputation and social standing, the desire for a fuller life than unwed parenthood would bring, the desire for employment, and the need to reject or give up a child whose father was most unacceptable.

The Relationship of the Natural Mothers with the Agency

The material already given has reflected much of the nature of the relationship of the natural mothers with the agency. In addition, it should be said that good work appeared to have been done by the agency workers in strengthening them emotionally, so that they became free to discuss their situations and to work out their future plans.

Acceptance of the mother was immediately evident on the part of the caseworker and trust in the agency was the mothers' resultant response. These mothers knew that they were respected as individuals, and that the Bureau was supporting them through this very difficult experience. They also knew that it was their right to make the decision as to whether or not their children should be relinquished and that, if relinquished, their readiness determined when this would occur. The possibility of adoptive placement either directly from the hospital or at a later time was discussed and plans other than adoption were fully explored. These mothers, then, who participated in direct placement, gained considerable knowledge of the adoptive process. In addition, through the relationship with

---

[6] Mary Elizabeth Fairweather, *op. cit.*, p. 3.

the caseworker, many showed other gains in understanding themselves, in relating to others, and in working toward lives of wholesome satisfaction.

Of the number of mothers who showed substantial growth, the two mothers who themselves had been born out of wedlock were most outstanding. One of these was a 19-year-old, previously divorced girl, an entertainer with questionable activities. She had traveled in vaudeville as a child and loved its gaiety and constant movement. She was proud that, although she sometimes changed schools as often as weekly as a youngster, she had been "left behind" only twice. She was indeed a very bright person with a tremendous capacity for enjoying life and for assimilating experience. When she applied to the agency, she was using heavy make-up, swore loudly, and dressed in extremely poor taste. Through the casework relationship, reinforced by a positive experience in the maternity home, she began to use gentler language and to dress more appropriately. There were inner changes also. Most significantly she redefined for herself her relation to her own 2-year-old child who was living unhappily with a grandmother. This mother found that she wanted two things for the future—social opportunities that adoption could bring for the coming child, and immediate adoptive placement that would ensure that such opportunities had been begun; for the 2-year-old she wished to establish a stable second marriage where this child would be welcome. She proceeded with plans for a better vocation and for the new social relationships that she now desired.

This mother, like the other mothers participating in direct placement, made one gain that needs to be stressed. Not only did they attain a sense of contribution to their children in providing for adoption, but also they derived a sense of achievement from the decision to relinquish them as quickly as possible. One mother said, "Thank you for helping me to finish my part of the planning so that my child can have a permanent home." The parent records reveal that these mothers had gained some sense of being "good" mothers and of "giving to" their children both by planning for adoption itself and by the early placement that eliminated the use of a boarding home.

In the control group where relinquishment was delayed, the mothers appeared less frequently to have a sense of "giving to" the child. Their comments can be summed up as, "I now see that I must 'give up' my child." These mothers did not gain the positive feelings derived by those in the direct placement group through eliminating the temporary home and through being closer to the placement of the child with his adoptive family.

In retrospect it appears that in a number of cases in which direct placement resulted, the discussion of such placement was of great significance and precipitated much thought about the interests of the child, thus helping the mothers to decide when they wished to relinquish the children. The discussion of direct placement occurred with most of these mothers before birth, and with the remainder, shortly after birth. One-fourth of them requested such placement. Every one of them wished to have her child quickly settled in the adoptive home and to avoid the use of a temporary home. One wonders how large a part the desire to eliminate boarding-home placement may play in the decision of so many mothers to place their children independently rather than through an agency.

In contrast, in the control group there was no discussion of direct placement in most cases or a lack of sufficient interpretation of such placement in others. In ten of the control cases the mother was consistent about wanting adoption, or only slightly ambivalent. It is possible that if the worker had fully discussed direct placement with these mothers, some of them might have wished to participate in this plan. Of interest, too, is the part that such discussion might have played in the other ten cases where ambivalence about adoption was somewhat stronger, or the mother was otherwise upset emotionally. In many of the latter ten cases there was an additional factor present, however, in that the mother was continuing a relationship with the father.

Another difference seen between the two groups was that in the direct placement group the contact with the caseworker, while extending over a slightly shorter period, nevertheless averaged nearly the same number of interviews as in the control group. Thus, those in direct placement averaged six interviews as against six and one-half for the others. It is also of interest that in the direct placement group a much larger percentage of the mothers was able to have the same worker for the entire period of their relationship to the agency than was true for the control group.

The significance of the discussion of direct placement with the natural mother, together with other factors mentioned, emphasized the important role of the worker in the eventuation of a direct placement plan. The worker's own acceptance of such a program carries great meaning. Mature and experienced workers may feel more secure about knowing when a mother is ready for relinquishment and may, therefore, find the plan of direct placement more usable. In addition to the worker's acceptance and skill, other factors were found in both groups which had a part in determining whether direct placement was possible. Of great importance was the amount of time the worker had to give to such placement. Direct placements immediately after the birth of the child are indeed time-consuming because they involve taking relinquishment, pediatric examination, obtaining birth information, matching the child with adoptive parents, and actual placement, all within a few days. These activities require work with the natural parent, the child, and the adoptive parents. Also, the interest and co-operation of other agencies, including maternity homes and hospitals, are necessary in promoting such a program. Thus, if such a program were to be undertaken, much administrative planning, in-service training, and community interpretation would be required to the end that natural mothers who should participate in such a program would do so and, conversely, that those who were not ready would be given sufficient time to work out their plans in the way best for them.

The Adoptive Parents

In general, the adoptive parents of these forty-five children closely resembled other adoptive parents in the variations shown in age, length of marriage, positions held, and annual income, and the fact that some of them (ten in number) had had other children.

Practically all these couples had expressed a desire to have an infant, but were not rigid about it. In fact, they appeared to be flexible in all respects. A high percentage indicated a willingness to take a child with problems in his background or a child in whom some minor illness might be present or might develop. None of these parents appeared to have unreasonable goals for their children.

The Children

These children were, in general, well developed physically and had good mental potentialities. A full report about delivery and the condition at birth, a developmental history while in the hospital, and a complete physical examination immediately prior to placement were obtained for all of them. Most of them had very good beginnings, including satisfactory birth weight. Eight, however, who were placed in 1954, showed some physical limitations at birth, but four of these recovered before placement.

The four children with problems remaining at placement were as follows: In one breech birth extensive X-rays were taken before and after placement in regard to a possible hip injury which was finally ruled out. Three of the four twins had some difficulty—in one set one twin had a slight case of clubfoot, in the other set each had slight jaundice and, in addition, one had a slight tremor following a breech birth. The adoptive parents did an excellent job with these children, so that these problems were worked through satisfactorily before the final adoption.

Six of the children who were in good condition at the time of adoptive placement developed physical problems of some seriousness later. One developed a heart condition at five months which, after medical attention, was found to be such that she was expected to grow up normally. Two infants developed slight strabismus, one had a hernia operation, one vomited severely, and one had numerous "brown spots" (with varying diagnoses) that later disappeared. In all these cases the adoptive parents obtained medical care and followed through on recommendations without anxiety.

We have reported elsewhere on the results of psychological examinations given to the infants placed in 1952 and 1953. Although the children placed in 1954 did not have psychological examinations, these would have been possible had problems of any degree of seriousness become apparent.

Success of These Placements

These infants, before placement, were as planfully "matched" to the adoptive parents and to their children as those placed at an older age. Remarkably enough, even physically these children appeared to have been matched to their new families as well as children who had been placed at an older age, and the case records contain many comments by the adoptive parents and the caseworkers about the successful matchings that occurred. In all instances, the adoptive parents were exceedingly accepting of these children, although they also revealed a normal anxiety about assuming new responsibilities. Although the reality factors in each child's situation were explained, no suggestion was made that any special "risk" was involved in adopting newborn children. Not only was it felt these parents were ready for such risks, but from the adoptive home studies they had already learned that some element of risk exists in the rearing of all adoptive children as is true of all natural children. None of them showed any uncertainty about their ability to face possible future problems.

All these children obviously offered great satisfaction to the adoptive mothers and fathers as they watched them grow. The parents who had previously adopted children at older ages remarked that taking the child when he was newborn brought many additional satisfactions. Grandparents also found it easy to accept these children. Indeed it was felt that in these placements there was an early development of parental feelings that were unusually dynamic and vital.

These parents seemed to need no special help with these infants, and the few supervisory problems that appeared came several months after placement. In general, the progress of all these forty-five infants in their adoptive homes has been excellent. This progress has been confirmed by reports from their doctors, from the adoptive parents, and from the agency workers. The final adoptions of all those placed in 1952 and 1953 were approved, and a considerable percentage of the 1954 group has also had final approval. The range of the supervisory period has been the same as for other placements—from six months to somewhat over a year. Although the placements made in late 1954 had not, at the time of the study, reached the point of consideration for final court approval, not a single case of rejection by the adoptive parents or by the agency had occurred and none was expected.

Conclusions and Recommendations

We believe that these adoptive placements directly from the hospital have been very successful. We believe, too, that the natural mothers benefited by the very early relinquishments that permitted them to have an additional sense of ''giving to'' their children by helping to place them immediately in their permanent homes. Professional staff members of the three maternity homes in Los Angeles have reported that many of the mothers who place their own children independently do so to avoid an interim placement.

All these infants benefited by receiving loving care practically from birth. These placements were thought to be especially helpful for the children with physical problems; for them the alternative to direct placement might well have been months or even years of care in boarding homes as ''children with special needs.'' The adoptive parents were ready for newborn children and they benefited by being able to participate so early in the children's growth.

The study of these children raises the question of whether this plan of direct placement from the hospital can be extended to benefit other children, including those with physical difficulties, and to help other natural and adoptive parents. One wonders what would be the effect upon persons in the community if there were general knowledge of the possibility of such placement. It is recognized that any interpretation on this subject must always emphasize the right of the natural parents to make the decision as to whether an adoptive plan shall be made and, if made, what the timing of adoption is to be. However, some natural parents who avoid coming to an agency because they believe this leads to interim placement might use agency help if they knew that direct placement was a possibility. This interpretation may be one method by which the advantages of agency adoptions over independent adoptions can be stressed so that the protections and services of the former will be extended to more children and parents.

CHAPTER 16

Adoption for the Handicapped Child

ANITA COLVILLE

Today, for adoption planning, the term "handicapped child" is used to include the physically handicapped, the emotionally distressed child and the older child. The danger in the use of the term is that it may focus attention on the handicap without awareness of the whole child.

When we plan for physically handicapped infants, we must not eliminate them arbitrarily as candidates for adoption. Early recognition of the problem and prompt diagnostic work-up are essential to determine the full extent of the physical disability. This requires close cooperation with and interpretation to doctors and other specialists. Early diagnosis is frequently a preventive measure, especially in many orthopedic defects which are correctible while the child's bones are soft and manipulative. The agency, in planning for the child, is perhaps more actively involved with the medical prognosis and treatment. These factors will indicate the degree to which the child can accept normal family life. In evaluating the child's physical condition, we must visualize him not only as a health problem, but also as a developing personality in all areas.

Early Adoption of Handicapped Children

We may be in error when we continue a child in boarding care because of a long series of treatments or an eventual operation.

The emotional health of the child would be bolstered by the greater sense of security and support he would receive from adoptive parents. Perhaps the greatest benefit of a permanent family for a handicapped child, is the assistance he receives in acknowledging and accepting the limitations imposed by his incapacity.

The adoptive parents should not be denied caring for their child in infancy. Supporting and caring for the child through difficult experiences caused by his handicap develops their feelings of parenthood. For the child, having his parents as early as possible provides the best conditions for growth.

If we conclude that the handicapped infant will best be served by adoption placement, we as agencies are responsible for finding parents for him; parents who, knowing the elements of risk, are willing to accept them as part of their child. Early awareness of the child's needs would make adoptive placement for him more feasible than waiting until the child is older, when he may have partially outgrown the physical problem, but now may have the additional trauma of emotional uprooting.

Preparing the Older Child for Adoption

We are still hesitant and fearful in placing the older child. Theoretically we agree that age in itself shall not preclude adoption. What is the problem in placing the older child? The key to his successful placement is the child's readiness and capacity to form new parental ties. The success or non-success of many adoptive placements depends on preparing the child for separation from his natural or substitute family. The child cannot relinquish these ties and replace his loyalties without the understanding, support, and cooperation of the adults in his world. The supportive role of the caseworker can be of the utmost importance to him at this time.

The first step is to learn what the child's living experiences mean to him, to assist him in understanding who he is and what has happened to him. Again and again I have been impressed with the child's confusion over his own identity. So frequently we realize that much has been done to the child but that we have overlooked his right to participate to the extent of his capacity. In trying to over-protect the child, we do him a wrong by inhibiting his using his strength to participate in this new move.

Recently I reviewed two cases of older, physically handicapped children, both seven years of age at the time they came under agency care. One child was the victim of congenital glaucoma; the other suffered from the congenital absence of a left hand. Age and severe physical disabilities are sizeable detriments to placement, but the emotional difficulties of these severely traumatized children far outweighed these problems. In retrospect we see that adequate diagnostic work-up could have brought these children to our agency earlier when the primary placement problem would have been the physical handicap alone. Our ability to place the child with glaucoma and not the other was based on the difference in degree of emotional damage that had been inflicted upon the children.

The child we placed was able to make relationships and use the support offered by the caseworker and her own parent, who helped release the child to her new life. The other child had been so perniciously damaged, his sense of his own value so shattered, that he was unable to separate from his old ties. He had an unfinished emotional involvement in his past and could not free himself to invest in new meaningful relationships.

Sometimes indecisive natural parents delay older children's adoption, and the child is kept in "cold storage." Intensive casework to relieve the parents' guilt and help them relinquish the children would lessen the number of older children needing adoptive placement. We would avoid the tragedy of older children with the emotional disabilities that so often accompany a series of replacements; children who need permanency, but are too fearful to give of themselves or to accept the demands of a reciprocal relationship with an adoptive family.

Evaluating the Child's Needs

In placing these children for whom it is difficult to find a family, we must evaluate carefully the child's personality, his emotional and physical health, and his capacity to establish a relationship based on the faith in adults he still has. We must recognize the child's own feelings about his handicap and to what extent he sees it as an inadequacy on his part and as being responsible for his lack of a family. We must actively help the child understand his status and reconcile his feelings about separation from natural or foster parents. When we have achieved this, we can turn to our homefinders for adoptive parents.

The keystone to placement of these children is homefinding. This is the challenge! These children, who have so much to offer in satisfying a couple's desire for a child, cannot seek their own parents-to-be. This is the agency's responsibility. Paramount in fulfilling it is the worker's diagnostic skill in finding the couple with the unique capacity to foster one of these youngsters. There are families who can find happiness in meeting the challenge of these children, in developing their potentialities; and there are families who can be satisfied with what may be only a partial success, feeling that is better than none.

In a child-centered agency it may be easier for the worker to determine her fundamental responsibility, whether to the child or to the prospective parents. These two are not in conflict, for a successful placement depends on mutual satisfaction in the parent-child relationship. If the worker is divided in her conviction and feels that she is offering a "second class candidate" for adoption, she will not evaluate the true potentials of her applicants. The parents need freedom of decision about the risks they will take. Their motivation for taking a handicapped child must be evaluated. The request may be based on neurotic elements of the couple's personality, but it is the use and the degree of the neuroticism measured against their other qualities that determines whether the effect on the parent-child relationship will be constructive or detrimental.

Using Community Treatment Resources

The financial burden of medical or psychiatric care may make families hesitate to consider the handicapped child. Knowledge and understanding of community resources for meeting the specific needs of those with special handicaps may help the couple overcome this concern. Many programs, such as those for the blind and for crippled children, are available to all, and carry with them no traces of stigma or inability to provide adequately for the child. When no facilities exist, the agency may wish to consider ways to make available assistance that would supplement without intruding or destroying the family's feeling of adequacy and responsibility in caring for the child. An agency grant could be established to provide special care for the child if this is a barrier to his placement in a particular family.

As agencies united to find for every adoptable child a family of his own, we need to campaign intensively, to interpret and to educate prospective adoptive parents to the realistic needs of these children. We should cross the boundaries of our respective agencies and work together to create opportunities for children and adoptive families.

The eventual establishment of a national adoption exchange may help us to achieve our objectives. Seven states, one of them

New York, are now experimenting with this program. There is also a local exchange under the auspices of Adopt-A-Child to which member agencies submit information about children and families for whom placement has been delayed for some reason. Our experiences in developing these exchanges on a smaller scale and working out the intricacies in cooperative placements will be valuable as the program is enlarged on a national scale.

Summary

Our challenge today is to take the protective measures for children that are within our means: early comprehensive diagnostic study, early surrenders when there is no place for the child in his own family, early placements to avoid emotional disfigurations. We must act as spokesmen for children who need homes. Children can look appealing, children can look pathetic, but they can't speak for themselves. Even if they could, they couldn't say all the things that have to be told. Our challenge and our responsibility is to speak for them in order to act for them in finding homes.

•

Discussion

E. ELIZABETH GLOVER

Before discussing some ways in which agencies are trying, or might try, to meet the needs of certain children through adoption placement, it is important to enunciate a principle which may seem elementary, but is essential—that every child with no continuing relationship with his natural parents, who can benefit from living in a family should be provided an adoptive family. Unless agency administrators and staffs believe this strongly none of the methods or resources spoken of here are tried with much conviction or prove very effective.

In talking about special children we include children of minority groups, older children, physically handicapped children, sibling groups, children with emotional problems, and the "legally handicapped" child.

Finding Homes for Special Children

Planned recruitment programs are necessary to obtain families for children of certain races and for those with special conditions and needs. For some time, agencies have published stories about the need for adoptive families of Negro, Puerto Rican or Oriental ancestry. Some have spent great amounts of money and energy on radio, television, speaking engagements, and numerous other methods for broadcasting this need.

We have too often neglected to take into consideration the public's long-standing attitudes and misunderstandings regarding agencies' "ideal requirements" for adoptive families. These assumptions, based on some of our own publicity, make families unwilling to risk being turned down. We also often assume that the interpretative methods we have always used will be effective in recruiting for a special group of children. From my own observations and limited experience in trying to recruit adoptive homes for the Negro child, I am convinced that we have much to learn about interpretation. I have a notion that we have not made enough effort to get help and suggestions from the average Negro man and woman in our communities, but have relied too much on economic and social leaders. Until we know more about the kind of questions in the minds and hearts of average Negro parents, we will not be able to lead them into our agencies, because we will not know how to dispel some of the misunderstandings which must be dispelled before they will approach us. In the Maryland Children's Aid Society, we are making a small beginning toward closer communication with our average Negro community through several committees of Negro citizens on the Eastern Shore with whom we are working and our committee members are learning things that neither knew before.

In order to interpret a program and to recruit effectively one must have some general requirements and know how flexible one can be. I think we have been defeated at times by what the public has thought were our requirements, however ridiculous some of them may have sounded, and we have been defeated at other times by our own unrealistic qualifications. For a while we had a great many families asking for the limited number of babies agencies had for adoption. In order to handle this situation it was natural to ask for the maximum for a child in every way in which we could. We need not apologize for selecting parents for a child who have the most to offer—*when* we have a choice.

We should apologize when we deprive a child of an adequate family because we cannot accept the reality of the choices we have. One of our Eastern Shore Committees said to me last month,

"Agencies have to make up their minds. They must accept adoptive homes where the mother works, where the parents may be older than one would like, where there is no bathroom, or else choose to allow children to remain in boarding care." When we come to terms with our modifications, we will have to reeducate the public so that it will not be afraid of us, as it now is.

Children Who Are Not Legally Free

My next point concerns ways of helping the child who for a variety of reasons, usually the refusal of non-interested parents to relinquish, is not legally free for adoption placement. The first thing we must do is make up our minds whether we believe that parents' rights supersede what can be considered in judicial proceedings as "the best interests of a child." If we believe a child's "best interest" should be served first, we have made considerable progress. Next we should make the fullest use of the statutes in our respective states and not be afraid to petition the court even when a contest may ensue. I wonder if petition contrary to parents' wishes is used as much as it might be for some children in long-term foster care.

Sometimes there are ways of working within difficult laws and yet not being defeated by what appears hopeless in the beginning. For instance, in a given situation it is clear that the agency will never be granted legal or parental authority to place a certain child for adoption although the agency knows that if a family with whom the child had been living for a year would petition the court for adoption the Court would feel free to act "in the best interest" of the child and grant the adoption.

In such a case it would seem that the agency could find a family who would accept the child knowing that when the time came to petition the court, the parents might contest. This is not the way we wish to place children for adoption, but in given cases, is it not better, when planned responsibly, than boarding home care until adulthood?

It goes without saying that agencies, board and staff, have an obligation to work for changes in statutes relating to adoption and to termination of parental rights which will allow children's best interests to be served.

Another method used on occasion for placing children with problems such as incompletely diagnosed serious illness, is to make the placement with the understanding that adoption may or may not be an eventuality, but that if it becomes desirable and possible, the agency believes this particular family would make good parents.[1]

Financial Aid for Adoptive Parents

Agencies might obtain adoptive families for some children for whom no other way can be found by subsidizing the income of adoptive parents. I have no direct experience with this method except in a most limited way. I have participated in plans where the agency paid the legal fees of an adoptive family because of their financial circumstances, and where the agency provided a year's supply of clothing for a child in advance. This is a temporary method of assisting a family financially and is quite different from a clearly worked out arrangement whereby the agency commits itself indefinitely to financial aid. If we believe that no child should be denied his own family because of economic conditions, then it is equally right that he should not be denied adoptive parents. If a child is not placed for adoption because of the financial circumstances of a potentially good family, he will still have to be supported by some agency, private or public, until he is grown. Is it not better that he have that financial support in a family which will give him the additional care and protection inherent in good adoption placement?

If we accept the principle of subsidizing adoptive families in individual situations, we might find that there are other children in foster care who could be adopted. There are probably children who have been in their foster homes for some time who become free for adoption either legally or through their natural parents' disinterest, whose foster parents would like to adopt them but are unable to do so without continuing financial aid.

Agencies are now working toward another method—the development of state and national exchanges or clearing houses through which agencies within states and throughout the country may assist each other in obtaining adoptive families for special children. The Child Welfare League is working on a national plan and some State Child Welfare Bureaus are also considering practical means of implementing this idea.

This proposed method of agencies joining to help individual children has great merit and appears to offer real hope. It will not prove its potential value, however, unless agencies everywhere begin carrying individual responsibility for recruitment and reeducation in their local areas.

---

[1] Belle Wolkomir, "The Unadoptable Baby Achieves Adoption," *Bulletin*, CWLA, February 1947.

CHAPTER 17

Negro Adoptions—Challenge Accepted

MILDRED HAWKINS

This is the story of how one community has tried to deal with the problem of finding adoptive parents for Negro children. We have learned much and the results, although not dramatic, have been gratifying. We know that this same problem exists in hundreds of other communities, and that some of these communities are making a real effort to grapple with the problem. This paper is presented with the hope that other agencies may benefit by what we have learned, and go even further in finding ways to meet this ever-present problem of adoption agencies.

The problem of finding homes for children of any group is not a new one. It has not been so many years since adoption agencies had difficulty in finding homes for normal, healthy white children—children who are now in great demand by adoptive parents. Adoptions have doubled in popularity in the last fifteen years. Now we find ourselves with many more homes for white children than we have children free for adoption. Most white children under the age of twelve, even those with crippling defects, can be placed in adoptive homes, if efforts are made to locate the people who can and will accept the challenge of loving and raising such a child. The "slow" white child can also be placed without too much difficulty, especially if he is able to attend public school. These handicapped white children fall into the group of "hard-to-place" children and present a problem of their own. But it soon became apparent to us that the placement of children of minority groups had to be approached as a special problem, different and separate from the problems of hard-to-place children of other kinds.

The Citizens' Committee on Negro Adoptions came into existence in Lake County, Indiana, in March, 1953. It was instituted by the Placement Division of the Lake County Department of Public Welfare. Its goal was to find homes for the increasing number of Negro children available for adoption, and also to try to discover why Negro couples seemed reluctant, at best, to respond to previous recruitment endeavors. The process has been a slow one; new techniques had to be found, new ideas tested, "tried and true" standards remodeled as we became increasingly cognizant of the difficulties involved in meeting the somewhat different and always difficult problem of finding adoptive homes for Negro children. The program was started at a time when relatively little was being done in this area. There were no foundation grants to help with our experimental efforts; we started from grass roots and have continued to work entirely on our own and with our own resources.

The Community Setting

Lake County, Indiana, is in the northwest corner of Indiana (near Chicago) and has a population of 514,000. Of this number, approximately 20 percent are non-white. In addition to the growth of the non-white population, Mr. Joseph D. Perfetto, of the United States Immigration and Naturalization Service Office, recently estimated that there are more than 30,000 aliens in Indiana, 12,000 of whom reside in Lake County. These are people from approximately eighty-five nations of the world. Such figures will help you to understand why adoptive placements in Lake County are not easy.

The large concentration of the Negro, Mexican and Puerto Rican population is in the Indiana cities of Gary and East Chicago. Of Gary's 180,000 population, 36.1 percent is non-white, while that of East Chicago is over 20 percent non-white. East Chicago is called the King City of Steel, with 30,500 steel workers. The population of East Chicago at present is approximately 57,000, with no room for further growth. Workers have been imported from Mexico since the early 1920's, and during the last few years many have also come from Puerto Rico to try to better the conditions of their families. Many men have come to this region without their famliies, hoping to bring them at a later date—a fact which no doubt has contributed to the rise in the number of children born out of wedlock. Housing, which has not expanded with the influx of workers, has deteriorated, with the result that many of the established white families have moved to the suburbs, continuing their employment in the city.

The Increasing Need for Homes

It was in September, 1952 that the Lake County Department of Public Welfare made a study of the children available for adoption and the number of homes available for them. We found that we had about twenty homes for every healthy white child free for adoption. On the other hand, we had *no* Negro adoptive homes for more than half of the thirty-seven Negro children then free for adoption. We realized that more Negro children were being released for adoption each year, with no corresponding increase in the number of available homes. Two factors contributed to the increase in the number of children; More Negro children were being born out of wedlock, and more Negro mothers were releasing their children for adoption. It therefore became evident that more adoptive homes must be found or these children would live out their lives in foster homes or institutions. (On a national basis, the 1953 reports of the United States Children's Bureau estimates that among Negro infants alone, 30,000 to 50,000 need homes. Illegitimate babies comprise the largest percent of this number.)[1]

The Negroes in our community had not been too receptive to taking children into their homes for adoption. They had been busy making a living and attempting to improve their economic and social status, and had not considered taking on the additional burden of raising children who were not theirs by birth (despite the fact that we do not charge a fee for our adoption services). At least, this was the assumption of the agency.

We decided to take a new look at the situation. After all, the Negroes in our community had made great strides socially and economically, and much had been accomplished in the past few years in integrating the Negro into community life. Surely there were families in this area who had achieved to the point where they could consider a family through adoption. But how were they to be made aware of the need, and how stimulated to want to adopt and to take some positive action in that direc-

---

[1] United States Children's Bureau, *Adoption of Children,* 1951, Statistical Series No. 14, 1953.

tion? We decided the first problem was for us to start the ball rolling, but that real accomplishment must come from the Negroes themselves.

We had already begun to realize that the initiative and even demanding pressure which we had learned to expect from white adoptive parents was not to be forthcoming in the case of the Negro applicant. And, as Lois Pettit has pointed out in a recent article, "Essentially the difference between the Negro and white applicant is that the latter carries some reasonable expectation of acceptance of his application, while the Negro applicant consciously or unconsciously expects to be rejected."[2] He may have had previous negative experience with the law and public agencies, and he asks himself (and often the worker) if this is worth another rejection. We had to realize that "The potential adoptive parent's own desire to be a parent is the motivation we must seek, strengthen and mobilize. He (not the child) is our client at this point."[3]

Interpreting Adoption to the Community

Then, too, there was the tremendous problem of community interpretation. "Explaining adoption to the community is complicated by largely negative community attitudes toward dependency, certain types of behavior and social breakdown in general, especially when they appear in minority groups."[4] In our efforts to arouse community enthusiasm, or at least to try to overcome apathy, the attitudes of the social workers themselves were important. It was hard not to feel hostile and antagonistic toward the people who exhibited indifference or negativism toward their efforts and failed to provide homes for children who would otherwise be denied this opportunity. The worker must come to grips with his own feelings before he can convince people of a minority group that he accepts and understands them.

With all of this in mind, the director and the supervisor of the Placement Division of the agency sought out leaders of the Negro community and invited them to meet together on March 11, 1953. The response was enthusiastic, and from this meeting developed the Citizen's Committee on Negro Adoptions. This

[2] Lois Pettit, "Some Observations on the Negro Culture in the United States," *Journal of the National Association of Social Workers* (July, 1960), p. 107.

[3] Report, *Joint Recruitment Project for Minority Adoptive Homes*, March 1956 to June 1959, Marjorie L. Faraday, Director. Distributed by Children's Home Society of California, Los Angeles, Calif.

[4] Michael Schapiro, *A Study of Adoption Practice*, Vol. III, Child Welfare League of America, 1957, p. 49.

committee then expanded, with sub-committees, such as the Interpretation Committee and the Resource Committee. The committee consisted of a minister, several housewives, a doctor, a real estate man, an insurance man, a school teacher, the wife of a local newspaper editor, the head of the Urban League, and other representative people in the community. The insurance man saw a personal reason for wanting to serve on the committee. It would be an additional opportunity for him to sell life insurance if he could help find adoptive homes. After all, what was wrong with this motive? We had no fault to find with life insurance for people who could afford it and if, through his efforts, one home was found for a child without parents, then this insurance man would have been a valuable member of the committee—for a child had found parents!

Much time was spent on interpretation to the community and on recruitment of adoptive homes. From April until June of 1953, an intensive campaign was carried on to recruit Negro adoptive homes. A series of articles and pictures was published by local newspapers. Thirty-one spot announcements for radio transmission were written by members of the committee. These were used by two local radio stations at times when housewives would be listening while doing their housework. The announcements were kept simple and short. For example:

"You don't have to be a Joe Louis or a Jackie Robinson to adopt children. Many Negro children need kindly homes and loving parents *now*—and kindness and love are two things that really count at the Department of Public Welfare. Apply *now* for *your* little boy or girl. Call TU 2-9341 *today*, or stop at the office at 400 Broadway, the next time you go that way."

"The Negro man who works next to me at the mill told me that he and his wife would like to have children, but have had none in their ten years of married life. When I suggested they apply at the Welfare Department, he wondered if a man with a less than sixth grade education would be considered. Later he spoke to a welfare worker, who took his application and the home was studied. Now this couple has a five-year-old son of their very own. There are no real obstacles. Negro couples interested in children should explore their interest in adoption with the caseworker assigned to that job at the Lake County Department of Public Welfare, 400 Broadway, Gary, Indiana. For further information, call Mrs. ———————— at TU 2-9342 for an appointment."

The committee also wrote and put on a live fifteen-minute

radio skit called "According to Statistics—OR—It Ain't Necessarily So." The skit clearly portrayed the need for adoptive homes. A Speakers' Bureau, composed of members of the committee, also gave many speeches to various group meetings. Letters were sent to organizations, stating the problems and needs and offering the services of the bureau. The entire placement staff of the agency was briefed on material to use in making contacts with the public in regard to adoption. During the months of June and July, 1953, twenty-one applications were filed. Eight of these became approved homes after the social study was made. This may sound like a very small number, but we considered it tremendous. In 1953, seventeen Negro children were placed.

Due to staff shortage and lack of direction, the Citizen's Committee on Negro Adoptions was not reactivated until October 1954, during which period there was a lag in the number of Negro applications. Efforts were then increased, and mayors of the three largest cities in the county were persuaded to issue the following proclamation to the local newspapers:

City of ——————— (Gary, Hammond or E. Chicago)

OFFICE OF THE MAYOR

PROCLAMATION

WHEREAS, There is a large number of Negro boys and girls in Lake County who have been deprived of childhood's birthright—a permanent, happy home—through no fault of their own; and

WHEREAS, These children have been placed in child care institutions and foster family boarding homes and, while these child care facilities are beneficial, they cannot give the happiness and stability that can be derived from the permanent, happy home life that is part of legally belonging to a family just as other children who are living with their natural parents; and

WHEREAS, All children arc the real wealth of the nation, these children in need of adoptive homes should be given the same concern as other children of the community. Like all other children, they, too, are our hope for thc future; and

WHEREAS, It is therefore fitting that the needs of these unfortunate children in need of adoptive homes should have a week set aside for the purpose of calling the community's attention to their need for a happy home life; and

213

WHEREAS, The Citizen's Committee on the promotion of
Adoptive Homes for Negro Children in conjunction with the
Lake County Department of Public Welfare, has launched a
program, "Operation of Happiness," beginning the week of
November 14 to November 20, 1954, to obtain great interest
among our citizens in adopting Negro children who unfortunately are without a permanent family life,

Now, THEREFORE, I, —————————, Mayor of —————————,
City of Lake County do hereby designate the period from
November 14 to November 20 1954, as "NEGRO CHILDREN
ADOPTION WEEK."

Dated this 12th day of November, 1954.

Mayor, City of —————————

Work with the Applicants

During this campaign, thirty-five applications were received
and twenty-nine were approved after study. However, we found
it necessary to do much work with our applicants during the
study. Some would say, "I don't know if I am doing the right
thing or not, for I always thought that if God wanted me to
have children, he would have given them to me." Of course, we
emphasized the need of those children who did not have parents and the responsibility of the community to provide such
parents if possible. We talked of the joy children can bring into
a childless home, along with the responsibilities involved. We
found, too, that it was up to us to reach out to these applicants
and to show positive acceptance of them as people. It was discovered, too, that, although white applicants might see many
people during the course of an adoptive study it was helpful to
Negro applicants to have contact with, and develop a relationship with, only one caseworker. It was a matter of education,
both for us and for the applicants, and it took time before
couples gradually began to let themselves be interested in taking children into their homes on a permanent basis—something
some of them had wanted for a long time.

We also found that many Negro couples were very limiting
in the kind of child they desired. A prominent restriction was
that of color. "Some Negro mothers are outspoken in their
preference for the lighter-skinned child with 'good' hair (not
frizzy or woolly)."[5] They sometimes wanted only a child whose

[5] Case illustration included in Rose Cooper Thomas, *Mother-Daughter Relationships and
Social Behavior*, Social Work Series 21, The Catholic University of America Press, Washington, D.C., 1955, quoted in Lois Pettit, *op. cit.*, p. 108.

skin would not be darker than that of either parent. When the question of color arose, though, it provided a rare opportunity for the worker to offer understanding and to discuss more freely with the client his feelings about this subject. Sometimes, too, applicants wanted only a little girl or a child of a certain age. These barriers were often broken down when the situation of *one* particular child was presented to them.

There was again a lull in the activity of the committee; in 1956 they were called together again and have been constantly and consistently active since that time. On December 1, 1957, a Negro social worker with one year of graduate work in the field of social work was hired by the agency to work with the Citizen's Committee in Gary and to organize another such committee in another part of the county. He has kept the Gary Committee active and has organized a committee to serve Hammond and East Chicago. While most of the response has come from Gary, we have been able to place a few Negro children in other parts of the county, so the effort has been worthwhile.

Techniques for Stimulating Interest

The following techniques have been used to stimulate interest in adoption of Negro children and to inform the community of the increasing need for adoptive homes:

Letters have been sent to ministers of the community, asking that they talk about this need from the pulpit and give out brochures prepared by the agency or committee.

Letters and statements of requirements were mailed to pastors of churches with Negro congregations in other cities with large Negro populations (after writing to that local County Department and obtaining consent to take the applications and make the necessary studies).

The Speakers' Bureau continued to function as needed.

Posters were prepared and placed on buses. These were recently replaced with very attractive, commercially prepared posters which were purchased by the committee.

A film, *Eddie Gets A New Home,* has been procured twice, and is excellent for this purpose. It was shown to many groups of people.[6]

Posters were prepared for places of business and placed by members of the committee. One committee member insisted that a poster be placed in the Internal Revenue Office as a

[6] This film may be obtained from Michael Schapiro, now area supervisor of the Children's Home Society of California. Write to him at 897 Hyde Street, San Francisco, California. The rental fee is $15 for one week.

spot where people being interviewed would have to face it.

Thirty spot announcements were prepared, presented to local radio stations, and used freely at different times during the day.

Newspaper articles and pictures were prepared and used freely by the press.

Satisfied adoptive parents have written articles for the "Voice of the People" column of local daily papers, telling of their happy and satisfying experiences with their own adopted families.

One agency worker created a very effective window display, consisting of Negro dolls with appropriate posters, pleading for homes for these children who do not have parents who can care for them. This display has been used many times in prominent windows of downtown stores and has been shown at gatherings of Negro people and at meetings.

The committee has put on teas with an interesting program regarding adoption—usually followed by small group discussions.

The committee put on a style show at which clothes were modeled by adults and children, with the announcer working in such phrases as "This is a mother and daughter ensemble. If you do not have a daughter or wish another daughter, why don't you get in touch with Mrs. ———— at the Welfare Department and see if there is a child available for you? This poster will tell you where to go and whom to call."

A panel discussion was tried, with members of the committee, an adoptive couple, and an agency staff member participating. All heads of block units were invited by the Urban League.

Articles advertising our need for Negro homes have been published in Negro newspapers in Chicago.

Social studies are sent to the State Adoption Resource Exchange for children we are not able to place, and adoptive studies for couples whose specifications we cannot meet.

Couples who have previously adopted children and who are making good parents are contacted to see if they might be interested in an additional child. We do not always wait for them to come to us, although we certainly have not tried to overpersuade them to take other children if they are not interested.

The large percentage of Negro children placed are born out of wedlock. We realize that we are doing a "mopping up" job at the point of placement. The real problems of why children have to be placed and how they become available would constitute another paper. However, the children who are available for adoption have the right to an adequate substitute home if such can be found. As a placement division, we are doing our best to supply the best possible homes for these children.

More Negro girls and women are giving up their children for adoption with each passing year. This may in part, at least, be due to the fact that the Negro community has not previously been aware of the need to adopt. Now they find they cannot keep unrelated children in their homes without being questioned about the legality of such a situation. Too, they are not eligible for help from public agencies without a license to board children. In many situations where a child has been in a licensed home for several years, and where the foster parents saw no need to make any changes, agency workers have been able to interpret to them the need for permanent status of the child in their home, or the possibility that the child might be placed elsewhere if a suitable adoptive home could be found. Through such interpretation, the foster parents have realized the importance of making the child their own, legally, and have instituted adoptive proceedings with the approval and help of the agency.

The Question of Standards

The question of having more flexible standards for homes of minority groups always rears its head. This problem has already been given some attention in this paper, but at this point I should like to explain how—if and when different requirements seemed indicated—they were and are decided upon.

The decision to place a child in a particular home is made by an adoption committee. This committee is composed of the adoptive consultant, the supervisor of the Foster Home Division, the worker carrying the case of the child and her supervisor, and the Placement Division head. Each home is carefully studied and submitted to the Indiana State Department of Public Welfare for its approval. There is sometimes the decision of whether it is better for a child to be placed permanently in a somewhat "sub-standard" home or to live the rest of his life in a foster home—never legally belonging and never being entitled to Social Security or any inheritance in case of death of the foster parents.

We have never relaxed our standards to include adoptive parents who had nothing to give a child but a name, nor have we relaxed to the point of endangering the life or morals of a child.

We have tried to find warm, loving people who, though they may not have had much formal education nor much to give in a material way, have a place in their hearts for a lonely, unwanted child. If we had homes with higher standards (as sometimes we do) we could use them; but in the absence of such homes, we feel that it is better for a child to be loved and wanted by someone who can give some guidance than to grow up with no one really caring about him.

In view of the above, we do not necessarily require that a Negro couple be unable to have their own children. We will place more than two children in the same home if we feel the couple can handle and love that many children, and have the finances to support them and room in the home for them. (Incidentally, we have never placed more than four children in the same home.) We may place a young child or an infant with people who exceed the age at which babies are placed with white couples. We assess the ability of the couple to handle a little money, rather than emphasizing the need for what might be considered an adequate income. We do not insist that the mother figure give up her job and stay at home all of the time, if she can make adequate arrangements for the care of the child while she is out of the home.

There could be much argument about relaxing the above usual requirements, but when the choice is between having parents who are your very own or living in a foster home or institution the rest of your life, we feel justified in these decisions.

The Progress Made

The following adoptive placements of Negro children have been made by the Lake County Department of Public Welfare since the organization of the Citizens' Committee on Negro Adoptions: Seventeen placements were made in 1953 and in 1954, and twenty-one in 1955 and in 1956. In 1957, thirty-four placements were made, in 1958, thirty-five and in 1959 (the year of the steel strike), thirty-one. In 1960, from January to June, nineteen placements were made.

Thus we have a total of 195 Negro children placed in adoptive homes in the last seven and a half years. Of this number, two children have had to be removed from their adoptive homes because of lack of acceptance by the adoptive parents. Most of the children placed are under two years old. However, children from two to eight years often find homes. By placing our infants, the older group gradually diminishes. In other words, if more children are made free for adoption at an early age, we will have fewer children reaching the age of eight in foster homes.

While the above figures are encouraging and we feel that much has been accomplished in finding homes for these 195 Negro children, still we realize that we must never relax our efforts. Each year the number of Negro children available for adoption grows. At present we have in Lake County forty-four Negro children who are legally free for adoption, and forty-three more who will soon be legally free, making a total of eighty-seven children who will need homes as soon as possible.

Every effort must be put forth each year to increase community resources through interpretation and stimulation of interest. Children of minority groups must not be neglected and we cannot afford to give up on a single child until we have tried every possible resource. "We need to take a positive approach as we interpret adoption. If we really believe that adoption is a good thing for everyone involved, let's say so. If we really believe that adoptive parents are pretty wonderful people, let's let them know it."[7] *It can be done!*

---

[7] Marjorie L. Faraday, *op. cit.*, p. 58.

CHAPTER 18

Placing the Older Child in Adoption

ANNE LEATHERMAN

Today, the number-one challenge to child-placement agencies is to find new and improved ways of bringing together children with special needs and couples interested in being responsible adoptive parents to them. Older children—those between 6 and 14—who are without parents most certainly have special needs. However, progressive child-placement agencies and their board members are no longer saying older children cannot be placed for adoption, for many such children are being placed with considerable success. Social workers are giving more and more credence to the theory that any child who needs a family is adoptable if he can develop in a family setting and if a family can be found which will accept him. This presupposes that the child's own parents are unable or unwilling to keep him, and that the child is ready and has the capacity to accept new parents and to adjust to a new home.[1]

In Texas our experience has convinced us that older children can be successfully placed for adoption through competent agencies recruiting adoptive homes with special qualities.

In 1956, of 173 children placed through the 20 county child-welfare units in Texas, 45 were above the age of 6. Among these

[1] Citizens Committee on Adoption of Children in California, Los Angeles: A citizens committee looks at adoption of children in California. Final report. 1953.

220

were 27 Latin American children and 13 Negro children. Twenty-four of the children were placed along with at least one brother or a sister, sometimes with more. We have proceeded under the policy of gearing adoption intake to the needs of the children in the custody of the State Department of Public Welfare who are legally free for adoption and who are diagnosed as adoptable.

It is surprising how easy it has been to find homes for school-age children. In spite of the fact that we have about 10 children of this age group available for every couple interested in adopting them we have had considerable success.

One of the factors behind this success has been the State Adoption Resource Exchange, set up in 1949. The public child-welfare units are required to register with the Exchange children available for adoption and families seeking children. Invitation to participate on a voluntary basis, regularly or occasionally, has been extended to the 22 licensed private children's agencies in the State. A few out-of-State agencies have also participated.

We have developed a form known as the "profile on children" and one called the "profile on adoptive family." These forms, which list items such as religion, coloring, intellectual capacity, and health, are sent to the State office of the Public Welfare Department where a preliminary matching job is done. The unit or agency with the child is sent a copy of the profile of the family which seems best suited to the needs of the child. Records are then shared between the agencies or units involved and a decision reached. The couple usually goes to the locality where the child is living for final presentation and placement. Follow-up supervision of the placement is carried out by the agency which referred the family.

Though there are still some kinks in this procedure we have been more than satisfied with the results.

We know we are taking certain calculated risks in this program. However, for the sake of the children we feel we can allow adoptive parents to take these risks with us if they are willing to do so. Along with most adoption workers, we have been convinced by evidences of the effects of maternal deprivation that the earlier the placement the better the child's chances for successful adoption. Nevertheless, we also believe that the warmth and acceptance of the right adoptive parents in a community with favorable attitudes can heal many of the psychic wounds suffered by a school-age child.

The formula is simple—the right home plus the right community equals a happier school-age child who becomes a productive, happy, social adult. The definition of "right" presents the difficulty. Much remains to be learned about this. But since children cannot wait until all the gaps in our knowledge are filled and our skills are perfected, we are proceeding cautiously on the basis of what has already been learned and tested by ourselves and others.

Points To Remember

We will assume for the purposes of this paper that good casework help has been given the natural parents and that the release of the children with whom we are concerned has a valid legal and social casework basis. Under such circumstances we have found the fundamental points to remember in working with an older child to be:

1. *The influence of the past.* The child will have had experiences in the past which are exerting an influence on his behavior today. While the social worker cannot find out all about the past, she must learn as much as possible about it from all available sources and weigh its influence on the child's present thinking, feeling, and behavior. Some of this influence will be in the child's consciousness and so be accessible to the social worker, but a large part of it will be repressed into the unconscious storage compartment of his personality. Even so some of this can be defrosted by a skillful caseworker so that it will pour into the child's consciousness.

To be faced with a troubled youngster, conflicted in his loyalties to parental figures, expecting and needing help, is a great challenge. Since social casework is designed to help change attitude and behavior and to strengthen a person's grasp on reality, caseworkers are equipped to meet this challenge. They must, however, test, refine, and reshape their work by further experience and research. For this it is important to record experiences.

2. *The complexity of the older child.* The older he is the more complex is the child, the more problems he will have faced, and the more injuries he will have sustained. However, normal children generally have a great deal of resilience, adaptive powers, and ability to sustain equilibrium through hard times, pain, and difficulties. Generally, children are far more flexible than adults. Actually, inflexible adult caseworkers have sometimes blocked the chances for older children to have adoptive homes.

While the age at which the child sustained injury is of diagnostic importance, it is also important to remember that a child's personality is in a fluid state until he reaches adolescence. Any uprooting will bring problems and reactions but these may be only transitory and each child will react in a unique way. Some children will never be able to adapt to an adoptive home at all.

3. *The child's responsibilities and potentialities.* The problems facing the older child in need of placement belong not only to the adults concerned with him but also to himself. He must face them and take responsibility for his own internal feelings. He has within himself the potentialities for bringing about appropriate changes in his thinking, feeling, and behaving.

An important resource for caseworkers is a philosophy of life which can be called on in helping older children and young adults set goals and progress toward them. Facing reality is an important element of this.

Social workers cannot change unhappy pasts for children. However, a social worker can let a child know that she recognizes that "things are tough" for him; and help him to see that the past is irreversible and that the future can be brighter if he is willing to begin now to make it so. The social worker can help the child to see that, while some unhappy times are bound to come, the adoptive placement promises rewarding times for him also and that the mother- and father-to-be will be kind, understanding, loving, and permanent. She can also help him to understand that the use he makes of the placement as well as of her help will be up to him.

4. *The child's changing nature.* Every child is a continually changing constellation of potentialities without a fixed personality. Social workers can help to provide the environment and the emotional climate conducive to constructive change. Unless the social worker hopes and believes that under given circumstances the child will have a happier time, she is defeated from the start.

Children diagnosed as psychotic or psychopathic should not be placed in adoptive homes. They do not make good placement risks, for even loving parents have difficulty bearing with their behavior. I do not believe that a social caseworker is equipped to diagnose these conditions alone. When a child's behavior is extremely atypical for his stage of growth, it is always important for the social worker to consult with a psychiatrist after the child has been given projective tests by a psychologist.

Qualities of Adoptive Parents

Adoptive parents of older children need all the qualities that are usually deemed desirable in natural parents, with some important extras. Neville B. Weeks has described some of these in a pamphlet prepared for the Child Welfare League of America:[2]

> From the beginning of their contact with the adoption agency, the successful adoptive parents showed a genuine desire to help a child develop at his own pace and in his own way for the child's sake, not theirs.
>
> They were able to enjoy a child and to respect his individuality and independence without expecting him to show direct appreciation.
>
> They were people with inexhaustible stores of humor, fun, and resilience which helped them to survive the inevitable trials and tribulations of the first months of placement while the child tested their love for him.
>
> They seemed to have a deeply rooted spiritual faith or practical religion which gave them a comfortable philosophy of life and a basic confidence in human nature.
>
> The successful adoptive parents could accept the fact that a child who has suffered emotional deprivation as the result of a broken home experience may always bear the scars of this wound to some extent and may, therefore, never be able to change some aspects of his personality or behavior. Moreover, they had to be able to sustain any positive feelings that the older child might have about his former relationships and to permit him to talk freely about his past...

I would like to add that adoptive parents must recognize that they need to gain satisfaction in other areas than the parental role if they are to be the kind of parents their children can enjoy and want to emulate. Children should not be burdened with the full responsibility of providing the emotional support an adult needs to become well-integrated.

Diagnosis of Readiness

What then are the general criteria by which we can judge whether a school-age child can accept an adoptive placement, given the right help from his social worker and the kind of home which would meet his individual needs? In the Texas program we believe that the prognosis is good if:

---

[2] Weeks, Neville B.: Adoption for school-age children in institutions. New York: Child Welfare League of America, October 1953.

1. The child has been able to relate to his own parents or to another adult in a meaningful way, showing confidence, respect, and faith in others; if he shows potentiality for giving and receiving love and for identifying with a mother- or father-figure of his own sex; if he gets along with his peers and is not "a lone wolf"; if there is some depth to his inter-personal relationships. In questionable cases in the area of relationships, psychiatric consultation may be in order. Perhaps every child over 6 who is being considered for adoptive placement should have a psychological examination.

2. The child has accepted the fact that he cannot return to his own parents, and shows some ability to measure his own worth and have respect for himself. Such a child may still have some fears and anxiety about taking on new parents and need casework help to deal with them.

3. The child can say openly or indirectly that he wants an adoptive mother and an adoptive father and can respond to the social worker's efforts to get them.

4. The child takes some responsibility for himself, recognizing that he can gain more by trying to adjust to a new situation and new parents than by resisting adjustment. He gives evidence of having a healthy conscience. He shows ability to learn from his mistakes as well as his successes.

5. The child's mental and physical capacities are within normal range. (The child who is not producing up to his capacities may also be adoptable if the deviation is not too great. The services of a physician and a psychologist can help measure these potentialities.)

6. The social worker believes adoptive placement is right for the child. (If she does not, she will not be able to help the child or the adopting couple.)

These criteria need to be tested against carefully evaluated experience and used with wisdom and good judgment. They simply offer a start in identifying the qualities of growing personalities which seem most favorable for successful adoptive placement. Other points may be added and clarification made as to how the absence of one or more of these specific ingredients might be offset.

In addition to such criteria adoption workers need some general guides on the subject of how and when to separate brothers and sisters who for some reason cannot be placed together in the same adoptive home.

Treatment Goals and Processes

Because preparation of the child for placement is an individual process, the various possible approaches must be subject to adaptation, according to the needs of the child. Each child will react in his own way to separation and to new relationships.

We have, however, identified five treatment goals in working with older children being placed for adoption:

1. *To help the child see the reasons for placement and to handle his reactions to separation from his own home.*

This should be tackled as soon as possible in order to prevent pathological repressions and fixations. It can be accomplished only when a true casework relationship has been established with the child.

Experience has shown that with an older child who has a living parent it is better if the parent lets the child know he approves the plan for adoption. However, it is unusual for a parent to be able to do this. In very rare instances the child might sit in on interviews with the parent and social worker. This would be a way of letting the child know the social worker is acting in behalf of his parents for the child's best interest. It is not usually a wise plan, however, especially in cases where children have been so severely neglected that court action has been taken and where neither parent can accept responsibility for participating in the plan to release the child.

After the child is in the agency's custody he should be encouraged to talk frankly about his parents. If the child is to understand the reasons for separation and need for placement the caseworker too must talk about the parents but without passing judgment, spoken or implied, on them. Perhaps the caseworker can relate their inability to be parents to difficult childhood experiences—something the child can understand. Both the social worker and the child must realize that the child's loss of his parents is a painful fact that cannot be changed or altered and must be faced, understood and somehow philosophically accepted.

Children need help in living through an experience of this kind. They may have to play it out if they cannot talk about it. They will not be able to move on to the new until they assimilate the old and are able to leave it.

Not all children who remember their parents can be helped to accept the fact that their parents have given them up forever. However, the degree to which a child can accept this is dependent upon a combination of factors: the age and stage of development of the child at the time of separation; the demonstration of interest or lack of it on the part of the parent following the initial physical separation; and the type of circumstances—such as desertion, death, or imprisonment—bringing about the separation.

The degree of the child's reactions to loss of his parents may eventually be mitigated by the security and positive relationships provided by the new family.

Because separation under any circumstances means desertion to a child, the child who has been freed for adoption feels he is somehow not worthy of love and has secret fears that something must be wrong about himself. This is why he needs to experience a relationship he can trust before he can trust another. The social worker can help him experience this through the quality of her own relationship with him.

The child must sense through verbal and non-verbal communication that the social worker likes him and cares what happens to him and that she represents the agency which stands by always to assist him. Sometimes the social worker can help achieve this sense of trust through tangible gifts of candy, chewing gum or toys, and treats at the corner drug store. For many children a gift is a proof of love.

In order to be able to trust again the child who has suffered from disappointment at the hands of many adults needs to find someone with whom he feels free to be himself; who accepts him whether he is good or bad. The social worker must demonstrate to him that she does care about him and what happens to him; she must always keep all her promises to him. Somehow she must get across the fact that she can be trusted and that there are other adults who can also be counted upon.

2. *To prepare the child for placement in his adoptive home.*

The child needs to feel that the worker understands he has many different feelings about the adoption. The prospects of going to a strange home with unknown adults, a new school, and a new community and of making new friends are frightening. The social worker can let him know she understands his fear and can help him conquer it.

This can only be done gradually, a step at a time. The child can be told about the new home, the neighborhood, the school, what his room will be like, and what the boys and girls in the neighborhood are like. He can be assured that the new mother and father will know about him and will be interested in him and want him to like them. He must be told, too, that there will

227

be times, even after placement, when he will be unhappy but that he will be with people he can trust and that he can grow to be happy if he gives them a chance to love and care for him. He must also be told that the new parents will discipline him, but that this will be because they love him.

The social worker should make it clear to the child that she wants him to feel as comfortable as possible about going to live with his new family before final placement is made. In some instances, weekend visits with the adoptive family are possible and the child can discuss his reactions to them with the case-worker. Sometimes the family comes to the locality where the child is to spend a week or more before the final placement is made. In such instances, the child and parents-to-be should be given time to be alone together without the worker being present.

The key to the actual move will be the child's readiness for it. The child will usually be interested in the fact that those responsible for his care, such as his foster parents or institutional houseparents, approve the adoption plan. He should have a choice about retaining or changing his first name and be given some selection in what he will call his new mother and father.

3. *To prepare the adoptive parents for accepting the child.*

To fail in this is to borrow trouble. The caseworker can suggest that adoptive parents think over what they have observed in other children of the child's age. She must describe the child to be adopted, telling about his medical and social history, and his current medical needs, if any. She should emphasize the positives in the child's background and the effect they have had, or are likely to have, on the child.

The social worker should also try to give the adoptive parents a sympathetic understanding of why the child's biological parents cannot carry the parental responsibility. She should also help the adoptive parents to examine their own feelings about parents who are immature and inadequate and who have neglected their children, and to come to accept the negative factors present in the child's background. She should encourage them to allow the child to discuss his memories and, by remembering their own childhood feelings about separations, to learn not to react to his reminiscences with anxiety. She can also encourage them to remember their own childhood feelings when faced with new situations and separations.

The caseworker must help the adoptive couple understand that bringing up children is complicated; that there will be times when their patience is exhausted as there are with natural parents; that the child will sometimes regress in his behavior in ways that will not easily be understood; that he will need to test their love; and that seeking help from the social worker will not represent failure on their part but, on the contrary, will be an indication of good parenthood.

4. *To present the child to the couple in the most effective way.*

This requires careful thought. Experience has shown that an older child should be protected from the adoptive parents' reactions to the first sight of him. Arrangements might be made for them to see him across the counter at a toy shop, at the zoo, or in the agency office before an actual introduction is made. Thus the child will be protected from the force of his first impact on them and possibly from another experience of rejection.

Prospective adoptive parents carry an image of the child they want even though they may not be aware of this. They need to be helped to realize that no child is going to match this image and to be given a realistic view of what to anticipate. Some couples react quickly after seeing a child in making their decision about him, while others need more time. The caseworker should not push them into a quick decision nor allow it to drag on indefinitely.

The child should be made to look as attractive as possible for the first presentation as first impressions are lasting ones. The meeting should be as casual as possible.

A series of short visits to the adoptive home before placement can be particularly helpful to children over 12 years of age. However, a child of this age, or even younger, is apt to guess the reason for the visit. Perhaps it should be explained. After the visits, discussions need to be held with the child about whether the visit provided him any satisfactions and how he liked the people. Such visits should not take place until after the adoptive parents have reacted favorably to what they have been told about the child and to their first view of him.

The worker can also let the child and couple know some of the questions which will be directed to them by people in the community and can suggest answers to them.

5. *To give maximum casework help during the adjustment period.*

Problems around authority, behavior, and competition with peers crop out repeatedly in older children. The worker can help the family distinguish between what is normal behavior and what arises from placement or as a result of a deprived background and so needs special handling.

The school and the total community play a large part in the older child's adjustment to adoption. Every child-placement worker knows of evidence of peer cruelty from youngsters with impulses to control and dominate others. The formation of cliques with exclusion of other children is a normal phenomenon with preadolescent children. The caseworker can help adoptive parents help their children to handle these problems as well as problems associated with the physical and emotional changes that come with adoescence.

Adoptive parents of adolescents need to be able to accept the fact that their child is coming to them at an age where it is normal for children to begin to emancipate themselves from dependency on adults and to understand that the typical adolescent tends to rebel at the authority of parents and teachers.

Research Project

Time alone can tell how well the principles described here are serving the children for whom they are applied. In Texas we have great faith in the feasibility of adoption for older children who do not now have a normal family life. But we want to know more about how this can best be achieved for them.

Therefore the Texas State Department of Public Welfare is planning an exploratory research project on followup of older children placed in adoption by the child-welfare units. Special note will be made of children in sibling combinations. The research team will include our State psychologist, the director of field staff, and the supervisor of licensing who is the former consultant on foster-family care. We look forward to some interesting results from which we can draw evidence to improve our diagnosis of a child's readiness for placement as well as to determine the factors which make for success or failure in the adjustment of adopted children placed at 6 years of age or older.

That success, in varying degrees, is possible we are sure, and we are eager to sharpen our tools for achieving it to the maximum.

CHAPTER 19

Adoptive Placement of American Indian Children With Non-Indian Families

ARNOLD LYSLO

During the past decade there have been many programs designed to promote the adoption of all children who need it—the handicapped child, the child in the older age group, and children of minority racial groups both within the United States and from foreign lands. But the Indian child in need of adoption has remained the "forgotten child," left unloved and uncared for on the reservation, without a home or parents of his own.

The Bureau of Indian Affairs has long been concerned about the report from their welfare staff that many children who might have been firmly established in secure homes at an early age through adoption have been passed from family to family on a reservation, or have spent years at public expense in Federal boarding schools or in foster care. They have never had the security of family life to promote their development and assure their future. Largely because of a lack of facilities for finding families who would be interested, the adoption of homeless Indian children has not been widespread.

In September 1958, the Child Welfare League of America agreed to participate with the Bureau of Indian Affairs in a demonstration project to plan for Indian children needing adoption.[1] Through the project we propose to select, for purposes of adoption, from fifty to one hundred or more homeless Indian children from all parts of the country. Thus far thirty Indian children, ranging in age from a few days through six years, have now been placed through specialized adoption agencies, primarily with non-Indian families, and the adoptions of these children are being evaluated by qualified research personnel.

The overall result of these placements we believe, will be a permanent interstate plan for the placement of Indian children needing adoption. Equally important, however, those social agencies currently responsible for the planning for Indian children are being stimulated and encouraged to develop new, intensive programs for adoption of these children within their own states.

American Indians living on reservations number approximately 300,000; more than half are minors. Most of these Indians live in some one hundred and fifty-four identifiable tribal jurisdictions which come within the responsibility of fifty-one agency offices of the Bureau of Indian Affairs.

The number of out-of-wedlock births to Indian unmarried mothers has never been accurately determined, but reports by health, education, and social work personnel on the reservation indicate that the figure is high. Illegitimacy among Indian peoples is frequently acceptable, and the extended family is by no means extinct. The unwed mother may bring her child home to be cared for by herself, her family, or some relative, and he may be successfully absorbed by the tribe. However there are many situations where this is not the case. The Bureau of Indian Affairs has found that many of these children are left to run loose on the reservation without proper care or supervision, and a permanent plan is never made for them.

The Indian unwed mother seldom receives the assistance usually available to the non-Indian. Isolation and a general attitude that her situation is "natural" have precluded the counseling indicated to give her any choice in planning for herself and her child. Because the Bureau of Indian Affairs itself is not authorized to engage directly in the field of adoption, and because adoptive applicants have been so limited in number, very few unmarried mothers are ever given any choice but to keep their children.

[1] Special recognition should be given to Miss Aleta Brownlee, former national Child Welfare Consultant for the United States Bureau of Indian Affairs, for her role in setting up this project.

One of the first tasks which I undertook as project director was to make a thorough study of tribal laws and appropriate state laws. I also talked with Indian leaders on reservations and with the four national Indian organizations concerning the need for, and merit of, the adoption project. We learned that the problem of the dependent child is one of the major problems of Indian people today, and that by and large, they approved of the project for those children who had no opportunity for a home of their own on the reservation.

Certain tribes, such as the Shoshone, Navajo, Winnebago, and some of the Sioux tribes are known to have occasionally permitted off-reservation families to adopt their children. However members of some other tribes, such as the Apache and Mojave, have expressed opposition to the adoption of their children by white people. In a few states, including Kansas, New Mexico, Arizona, South Dakota and Washington, private adoption agencies have placed some nonreservation Indian children in white homes. These limited experiences have been for the most part successful. It is believed that with understanding and faith in the good will of adoption agencies, those tribes now opposed to the adoption of Indian children by white families will acquiesce. It is also believed that adoptive homes, particularly in nonwestern states where there is less prejudice against Indians, can be found.

Operation of the Project

Any Indian child of one-quarter or more degree of Indian blood, if he is considered adoptable physically and emotionally, may be referred to the Indian Adoption Project. While we have accepted a few off-reservation children already in the custody of some social agencies for adoption placement, and we feel some obligation to assist the agencies in planning for these children, our primary objective is to serve the Indian child whose residence is on the reservation, and as such, is the responsibility of the Bureau of Indian Affairs.

The Indian Adoption Project has concentrated on those areas where the needs of Indian children are the greatest. Currently, the project is operating in fourteen major reservation areas in six states—Arizona, Montana, Nevada, North Carolina, South Dakota and Wyoming. Criteria for selection of a reservation include the following: a qualified social worker on the reservation employed by the Bureau of Indian Affairs; permissive attitude on the part of the tribe; a public health facility, and cooperative attitude on the part of its staff; the interest and cooperation of state and county public welfare agencies and private agencies wherever possible.

Initially, two high-standard adoption agencies in the East were selected to participate in the project. The majority of our children have been placed through these two agencies—Louise Wise Services of New York City and the Children's Bureau of Delaware, Wilmington. More recently, other League member agencies have become affiliated with the project.[2] They have provided a service to the project either by placing an Indian child or by serving a family in their locality who expressed interest in adopting an Indian child.[3]

The contribution made to the Indian Adoption Project by the participating adoption agencies has been much more than merely placing an Indian child for adoption. Their enthusiasm in planning for Indian children, and the adoptive families which they have been able to find for them, has caused many social agencies in the child's home area to take a "new look" at the Indian child and his adoptability. Personal contacts between the agencies have proved invaluable. Workers and executives from the adoption agencies have visited reservation areas to see Indian children and learn something of the Indian way of life. The social workers from the Bureau of Indian Affairs and other social agencies have escorted Indian children east and learned about the programs of the adoption agencies here. These personal contacts have helped to ease the many tensions in making such long distance placements, and have developed a sense of trust between the agencies.

Representatives of the adoption agencies have also taken leadership roles in institutes on adoption sponsored by the Bureau of Indian Affairs. And last, but by no means least, the legal counsels of these agencies have given invaluable assistance in handling the many complications which may arise in interagency and interstate adoptions.

The Gains for Indian Children

We believe that the Indian Adoption Project has proved a real stimulus towards the improvement of all social services to Indian children and their families. Social workers from the

---

[2] Boston Children's Service Association, Boston, Massachusetts; The Spence-Chapin Adoption Service, New York City; the Children's Bureau of the Indianapolis Orphan Asylum, Indianapolis, Indiana; and The New York Foundling Hospital, New York City.
[3] The Project Director would welcome participation of other adoption agencies that may have adoptive resources for Indian children.

Bureau of Indian Affairs as well as from state welfare departments report that there is a new emphasis upon early permanent planning for Indian children, and that children are no longer allowed to remain in situations of severe neglect because no other plans are available for them.

At a recent Bureau of Indian Affairs Conference on Adoption held in South Dakota, Miss Margaret Lampe, Adoption Consultant for the South Dakota State Department of Public Welfare, reported that since the beginning of the Indian Adoption Project two and a half years ago, the number of Indian children referred to the welfare department for services has increased tenfold. She stated that since the late 1940's the number of Indian children referred to the welfare department for adoptive purposes has increased considerably, but because of the limited adoption resources within the state for Indian children, the social workers became very discouraged. Miss Lampe also said that as a result of their work together on the Indian Adoption Project, there has developed a new and better working relationship between the welfare department and the Bureau of Indian Affairs, with a mutual respect for each other's problems. Similar experiences have been reported in other states where the project is operating.

One of the responsibilities of the project director is to take back to the Indian people reports about those children who left their reservations for adoption through the Indian Adoption Project. These people have been pleased with the reception and quality of service which their children have received in the East, and they have been doubly pleased by the kinds of families which have adopted them. Indian people are coming to learn the advantages and safeguards of agency adoptions, and some tribes are moving towards effecting tribal regulations whereby all children needing adoption off the reservation would be planned for through licensed and approved adoption agencies. In the process, they are asking many intelligent questions about the whole area of adoption.

We have been fortunate in this undertaking to have received a grant from the Elizabeth McCormick Memorial Fund which has enabled us to incorporate a research component with the project. The objective of this research is to develop systematic knowledge about the characteristics of couples who have adopted American Indian children and thereby to learn more about the phenomenon of adoption across ethnic and racial lines. An equally important objective will be to develop a portrait of the adjustments of these couples for a period of one to two years after children have been placed in their homes. Factors in the backgrounds of these individuals which may have prepared them for this rather unique experience will be explored, with special emphasis upon value systems which tend to support an essentially nonconformist life adaptation. In addition to probing motives which stem from sociological factors in the couples' lives, more unique motives of individuals, including those of a potentially neurotic kind, will be scrutinized. Where possible and appropriate, comparisons will be made with other adoptive couples who have adopted children of their own ethnic background.

It is realized that a project like the Indian Adoption Project deals with the end result of many complex social problems. We feel that this project for helping a small segment of children is justified, for through it the League can become involved more deeply in basic problems in the care of Indian children, and can help improve the general conditions among Indians.

CHAPTER 20

Adoptive Families for "Unadoptable" Children

RUTH TAFT

Some of you may have attended the Adoption Workshop in New York in May 1951 and may even have been in the study group led by Callman Rawley. If so, I am sure you will remember the furor he created by challenging one of our basic concepts, namely that of matching adopting parents and children. Mr. Rawley asked why likeness should be taken into consideration in placing children for adoption. Needless to say, he got the expected answers: that a child wants to be like his parents, that parents can more easily identify with a child who resembles them, and that the fact of adoption should not be accentuated by placing a child with parents who are different from him. These are but a few of the answers based on sound practice which were given with great feeling, but Mr. Rawley persisted, asking if this need for likeness is really a need of the family and the child or the need of the adoption worker. I do not intend to go further into this discussion, but the tremendous amount of hostility that was aroused was indicative of our fear of even considering that perhaps there are children and families who can accept a great deal in the way of difference. Also that perhaps, we, as adoption workers, might be able to help prospective adopting parents further develop their own capacities for the acceptance of difference. Here I am not talking about the little differences like the color of eyes or hair or nationality, but big differences like the child whose natural parents are patients in a mental hospital and the child who is part white and part Negro. My use of the word "difference" in this connection may surprise you since children like these are usually referred to as children with "problems in their background." It is here I think we have been caught for the word "problem" connotes something to be worked out and the child becomes a problem to be placed rather than a child. Some of these problems cannot be worked out. We do not know the solutions, so is it not better to concentrate on prospective adoptive families, to develop skills in evaluating their strengths rather than getting caught in our fears that John, the son of mentally ill parents might some day become mentally ill, or on the one chance in who knows how many that Rob, a child by mixed marriage, might some day father a child with Negroid features?

Miss Mary Elizabeth Fairweather, in a paper* discussing the placement of babies under three months for adoption said:

> "Let us concentrate less on our fears of unknown factors in a child and try harder to develop greater ability to know our adoptive applicants and to realize what they can offer as healthy, nutritive soil in which a new life can develop.

> "Normal, well-adjusted adults, given the opportunity, can weigh the risks of reasonable unknowns, arrive at a decision, and find a healthy way to adjust to the results of their decision."

Does this not apply just as much to the children ordinarily denied adoption? Have we given our applicants the opportunity to weigh the risks for themselves or have we labeled a child unadoptable because of our own fears. Also, if we are completely honest, a child is usually denied adoption, not because adoption is a poor plan for him, but because the adoptive parents may get hurt. It is true, there are some children for whom we cannot find homes, but let us admit that. Should we leave the child to carry the burden of being "unadoptable"?

Placing the "Unadoptables"

I should like to tell you about our experience in selecting homes for two such "unadoptables," John and Rob. John was ten months old when he was referred for adoption placement. His parents were both patients in a mental hospital. He was an attractive, alert, lovable baby, but was tense and suffered from

---

* Child Welfare—March 1952.

eczema that appeared to be of emotional origin. The foster mother loved the baby, but was afraid no one would want to adopt him. The pediatrician was horrified that the agency would even consider him for adoption because of his parentage, the psychologist feared that the child already was showing signs of emotional disturbance at ten months.

John's history was given to three of the leading child psychiatrists in the country. One said, "It would be my own impression that such a combination of factors would weigh heavily for the possibility of this child becoming schizophrenic and I would certainly question the advisability of adoption except after a long period of observation preferably in the adoptive home and with the full knowledge of the adoptive parents."

The second opinion was: "It would appear that the family background is quite heavily loaded with psychopathy, but in spite of this I believe that it is reasonable to assume that under proper foster home care the patient would be expected to develop and progress normally. It is assumed that there is no organic brain disease and that his Intelligence Quotient is at least within the normal range. It is my impression that under these circumstances adopting parents would not be taking any undue risk. The problem in psychiatry often entails a question as to whether environment or constitutional factors play the major role in the development of the personality structure, but my own feeling is that the character of the emotional relationship to parents or to foster parents is the main keystone to the personality development of any individual."

The third specialist consulted was inclined to agree with the second opinion and said that the influence of hereditary factors in the development of mental illness is largely unknown and that even research on this specific subject may not be able to take into account the contributing factors which are environmental and not hereditary.

We did not know what the signs of disturbance in John meant. Inheritance? Maybe, but the child was growing up amid the fears of the foster mother, the disapproval of the pediatrician, and the question of the psychologist—not a healthy, relaxed atmosphere in which a child could develop. In the adoption department there was confusion and fear, too, until we gave up trying to figure out all the things that might happen and concentrated on what John needed in the way of a family.

In the first place, we felt he needed acceptance—acceptance without fear. We wanted him to have a family where there were other children so that all the hopes and expectation of the family would not center on him. We wanted easy, relaxed parents with conviction about adoption and confidence in their own ability to provide a good and satisfying life for a child. There were other factors that went into our thinking, too. John was a bright child and should be placed with parents who could offer him advantages. We felt also that more sophisticated people would not be as threatened by the mental illness in John's background.

When we knew what we were looking for, we found we already had such a family. I am sorry there is not space to give details about the Allens, but they met the above requirements even to having adopted two children from the agency. We told the Allens about John and gave them all the information we had including the reports from the three psychiatrists. They were not overwhelmed.. The fact that John's mother had become ill following marriage indicated to them that she was psychologically not ready for marriage. They mentioned friends and a relative who had had breakdowns following pressures or experiences for which they were unprepared. They felt that John, given a happy and secure growing up period, had every chance of developing into a well-adjusted, emotionally strong person.

However, whether he does or not, should he have been denied adoption? Should the Allens have been denied the opportunity to weigh the risks for themselves? For those of you who are worried, the eczema and tenseness have disappeared. The following is a quotation from another psychological test given when John was twenty months old and after he had been in his adoptive home ten months:

> "His general maturity level is close to twenty-four months and development is considered fully normal and shows signs of high average ability at this time. All the indications are that personality development and his present emotional status is good and favorable. This is considered a remarkable behavior picture in view of the history, and certainly this child should be treated in the future on his own very fine merits rather than to receive any coloring from his background. He is entirely accepted by his excellent adopted parents."

Finding a home for Rob was a different matter as we did not have one on hand, and it meant developing one that could meet his needs and accept him with his difference. Rob was fifteen months old. His mother was white and his father a light-complexioned Negro. Both parents were unusually intelligent and

Rob was a child with great depth, sensitivity and strength. In appearance, Rob was a white child and the physical anthropolgist who examined him supported our conviction that he should be placed as a white child. He gave the following statement:

"My examination of Rob leads me to the conclusion that whatever Negro ancestry he may have is very slight in its genetic effect. He might readily pass as a white child since at this stage of development he reveals no obvious Negroid traits. In my opinion he is not likely to become Negroid as he grows older and I would anticipate that any children he might have in the future, assuming he married a white woman, would not be any less white in appearance than he."

Preparing the Parents for the Adoption

At this time there was a home in study which seemed completely right for this little boy. The Potters were sophisticated, intelligent people, had many cultural interests, and had unusual sensitivity along with a delightful sense of humor. However, like most adopting applicants, they had been at different points in terms of readiness for adoption and the study had been moving slowly as the Potters, Mr. Potter in particular, worked through some of their feeling about inability to have their own children and fear of adoption. Mrs. Potter, at the time of application, had accepted the fact she could not have children but Mr. Potter was still clinging to a vague hope that such might be possible in spite of the discouraging medical report. Mr. Potter approached adoption in a very business-like way. On their first two trips to the office, he brought a folder containing correspondence with several agencies, medical reports, and life insurance policies. His questions were carefully thought out and his whole attitude was rational and scholarly. Mrs. Potter was well aware that her husband had to work this out in his own way and at no time did she push him or become annoyed even though she was completely ready for adoption. It soon became apparent both from what Mr. Potter told me about himself and the way in which he approached adoption, that he was a person who moved slowly and thoughtfully, but once his mind was made up, his conviction was unshakable. His own illustrations of this related to the fact that he had not settled on a job until he was 24 and had not married until he was 29. There was no question but that Mr. Potter needed help in arriving at the same kind of conviction about adoption and together we worked on his questions as he brought them in. Honesty was most appealing as he dared to risk rejection in order to clarify a point for himself.

241

For instance, during one interview I asked him how he could know that he could take on someone else's child and make it his own. His answer was, "How could I know I could take on my own child?"

At the time that Rob became available for adoption, Mr. Potter had worked through his questions, had expressed his confidence in the agency, and I had great confidence in what they would have to offer some child. However, I had done little with the Potters in terms of what they were hoping for in a youngster. Right along they had shown a good bit of flexibility as to what they could consider both in a child and his background but at this point both felt that the decision rested with the agency as to the kind of child they should have.

Phase two of the study began after a brief skirmish during which the Potters accepted that if they were ever to tell a child he was chosen, they would have to have some part in the choosing, they settled down to work on their hopes and expectations for a child. They decided they could accept either a boy or a girl up to a year of age or perhaps a little older. They would hope for a child with the capacity for college but would not be too disappointed if such were not possible. They expressed particular interest in a youngster with some creative ability recognizing their own part in helping to develop whatever talent there might be. Nationality did not matter in the least as long as there was some physical resemblance to them. A long line of mental illness would worry them but physical or social problems in the background would not concern them unduly. They felt they could be happy with a shy, quiet child or an active, vigorous one and would love a child for his own unique quality rather than for a possible extension of themselves.

At this point we had conviction that the Potters would have a great deal to offer Rob and that he would have a great deal to offer them but the question was whether they could accept the amount of difference this child presented. With this in mind, we went back over the record to see what the indications were. The following are excerpts from the record:

1. "He (Mr. Potter) felt that they are reasonable people, that they are inclined to be easy going, flexible and can take things pretty much in their stride. This enters into the fact that they could be quite flexible in what they could consider in a youngster except that a child with too much temperament would not be too much like them. I (the worker) felt the Potters were genuinely extremely flexible

242

about what they could consider in nationality extraction providing the child was not too dark or a red head.''

2. ''They have a large circle of friends, and talked with considerable zest about their house. It is a very modern houseboat and their friends who have Colonial taste are somewhat amazed at it.''

3. ''Mr. Potter is one of a family of three children and his parents live in Georgia where he was brought up. However, his father came originally from upper New England and is one of a large family of old Yankees.''

4. ''Mr. and Mrs. Potter described themselves as being very different, and there was a nice kind of banter back and forth regarding these differences. Mr. Potter is intellectual. He is thoughtful and quiet. He loves music, plays the violin, enjoys his records, paints pictures that never get shown, and generally leads a sort of quiet life. Mrs. Potter, in contrast to her husband is an animated, vivacious person who likes people and sociability. She enjoys modern dancing and has studied it. The Potters have been married for eight years and each seems able to stand on his own difference and yet come to terms with the other.''

Here were definite indications that the Potters were secure people within themselves, were comfortable in their difference from others as evidenced in their way of living (the houseboat) and might have the capacity to take on Rob and his difference. So we told them that occasionally the agency has a child who is part white and part Negro, but who, to all intents and purposes is white. Their first reaction was surprise that the agency would know it and then admiration that the agency would be honest about it. It was their feeling at that point that if the agency had determined, insofar as possible, that this was a white child, they would have no question. We agreed however, there were many other aspects that would need to be considered and they expressed definite interest in continuing this discussion.

The next time the Potters came to the office with their questions and their convictions. They knew it was an old wives tale that there might be a throwback, that is, a Negro child appearing in a future generation, but they wondered if there was anything scientific on this. We quoted from some books on genetics that the chances of such occurring were extremely remote but at the same time told them we doubted that a positive statement could be made that such could not happen. The question came up, of course, as to whether the child should know of his Negro

243

ancestry. The Potters felt it was unnecessary to tell the child, and that this was something they could carry. We spent a good deal of time talking about the meaning to them of bearing this knowledge through life, how they would feel when the child was engaged, married, expecting a baby. Mr. and Mrs. Potter said they could carry this.

Eventually, we wrote them a note telling them we had a youngster in whom we thought they might be interested, that there were complicating factors in the situation, but if they would like to hear about this child, we should be glad to talk with them. When they came to the office, they said accusingly, "You didn't say whether it was a boy or a girl." They knew what the complicating factor was. We gave them all the information on Rob and his background. Everything about the child appealed to them and we assured them that his background was unusually good.

After they had seen Rob, we asked the Potters what they would do if, someday, by chance, Rob found out about his ancestry. Mr. Potter's answer was, and I quote exactly, "It will be up to us to raise him strong, to meet whatever life has to offer." He went on to say that they have no race prejudice and he knew they would be able to handle the matter with him in an unemotional way.

After completion of the adoption, the following letter was received from Mr. and Mrs. Potter:

"The birth certificate was very welcome, for it was a milestone on a long and happy road. We are very grateful to you for your gracious assistance, and the results of our collaboration, as summed up in Rob, bring us new delights daily. We look forward to seeing you soon on another such mission."

The selection and development of adoptive families is within the power of the agency. Absolute knowledge of how an individual child will turn out is not. If we can be wise in selecting the family for the child with a high degree of difference, and courageous in working with the family toward a greater acceptance of difference, there will be fewer children denied adoption. To repeat what Miss Fairweather said:

"Normal, well-adjusted adults, given the opportunity, can weigh the risks of reasonable unknowns, arrive at a decision, and find a healthy way to adjust to the results of their decision."

Let us be sure to give them the opportunity.

CHAPTER 21

Adoption for School-Age Children in Institutions

NEVILLE B. WEEKS

A three-year experiment in the adoptive placement of school-age children from orphanages and institutions recently completed in North Carolina shows that it can be done and to the satisfaction of the children and the parents. This experiment was made possible in 1950 by a special grant from the Duke Endowment to the Children's Home Society of North Carolina, a private, statewide adoption agency. It was a cooperative project in which the major participants were the Children's Home Society, seven private child-caring institutions, and a number of county public welfare departments throughout the state.

The original purpose of the project was twofold: to determine whether there were children in institutions who could be released for adoption, if they needed it, and could benefit by adoptive placement, and whether suitable adoptive homes could be found for such children. By the end of its third year, the project had grown into a full-scale program and had won wholehearted acceptance from the North Carolina Orphanage Conference, an organization which included all of the 32 licensed child-caring institutions in the state. Additional funds were raised to provide for an expanded service in adoption for older children as a regular part of the program of the Children's Home Society.

Developing Cooperative Service with Institutions

The private institutions in North Carolina had nearly 4,000 children under care in 1950 according to published surveys, and there were still long waiting lists for admission to several of the large church-sponsored orphanages. None of these institutions was licensed to place children for adoption but some of them had small foster home programs. Only a few had social service departments or casework staff of their own. And only a few could give casework services to parents, relatives, or foster parents over and above that involved in planning the admission of children and helping the children while under care.

Some children were remaining in these institutions for an average of five years or more, and some from the time they were five years of age until they were 18. Institutional superintendents and child welfare workers alike were becoming increasingly concerned about the numbers of children who stayed for long periods. They were especially concerned about those children whose ties with their relatives and native communities seemed to have deteriorated beyond repair and who would, therefore, approach young adulthood with no roots outside the institution. Could adoptive placement be a desirable alternative to institutional placement for some of these children? If children whose homes could be rehabilitated through casework service were returned to their own relatives, or if those whose parents would consent to permanent family placement could be released for adoption, would it be possible for orphanages to give more effective service on a short-time basis to additional children?

In a joint search for answers to some of these questions, child welfare leaders in various parts of the state agreed to work through the Children's Home Society on a demonstration project for at least three years. The project was conceived as a cooperative one because it was recognized that the specialized services and skills of an adoption agency were needed in safeguarding the basic rights of the children and their parents and in evaluating the social and legal factors. Some institutions asked the Children's Home Society to come in on a consultative basis to help them identify children who might be considered for adoptive placement; others referred specific children who they felt needed adoption.

It was right, therefore, that the first step was to find out whether the relatives could offer each child a satisfactory home. During the period of the study, under our guidance, the family and guardianship status of some 200 children in seven orphanages was carefully reviewed by the institutional staffs concerned. The children's individual situations and personalities were thoroughly studied and evaluated and numerous visits were made to their relatives and guardians. Thus, with the cooperation of the local agencies where the relatives resided, occasionally, plans were worked out for children to be returned to their own families.

When it was definitely established that there was no prospect of a child returning to his relatives, and it appeared that he could benefit by adoptive placement, the Children's Home Society took on the casework job of securing voluntary legal surrender from the parents or guardians and of finding prospective adoptive parents. During this period, the child remained under the institution's care. The Children's Home Society assumed full responsibility for the placement and supervision of the child in the adoptive home. However, written agreements were worked out with each institution to provide for further joint planning in case the placement failed.

Eighty of these children were selected as possible "candidates" for adoptive placement. Of this group, 20 children, all between five and 12 years of age, were actually placed for adoption within the period. Ten of the children have been legally adopted. In seven other cases, adoption is well on the way to satisfactory completion. Only three of the children placed so far proved unable to adjust to adoptive homes.

Thirteen of the original 80 children studied were able to return to their own relatives. For 21 children, neither adoption nor placement with relatives proved feasible. However, some of these children were transferred to foster homes or to other institutions better able to meet their special needs. When the project period ended in December 1952, 26 children from the original group were still under consideration for adoption, although still in their respective institutions.

Interesting By-Products

The experiment in North Carolina has no doubt been duplicated in other parts of the country, and others may have recognized as we have, that there has been a tendency to rely too much on existing facilities in child welfare. This often leads us to select only those children and those families who could use the resources we already have. By pooling resources and services, these institutions and agencies found that horizons for the institutional child could be greatly widened. For example, several of the institutions began to use the services of the adoption agency consultant in some of their conferences regarding the admission of children. They were considering accepting more children on a temporary basis with a constructive discharge plan in view. For children who appeared to need long-time care, they wanted to clarify the possibility of adoption right from the start. One institution which functioned primarily as a diagnostic and treatment home for children with special problems, enlarged its program to admit (for an evaluative study) school-age children being considered for adoption.

Sometimes the children, too, expressed their satisfaction by recommending our service to others. For example:

Nine-year-old Billy made a friendly visit back to the orphanage six months after he had gone to live in his adoptive home and talked with us quite seriously about several other little boys in his former cottage there "who ought to have new mothers and daddies like mine." A few months later, Billy happened to turn on a television program when the president of our Board of Directors was speaking about the older children's project. Excitedly, he called his adoptive father in to hear the program and said, "This man is right, Daddy. He's telling people how wonderful it is for kids like me from an orphanage to find a new home. It's just like he says!"

Need for Expanded Services

Despite the best efforts by all our child welfare programs to preserve the child's own home for him whenever possible, and to gear our institutional and boarding home services increasingly toward "temporary care," there still are a substantial number of school-age children who can never live with their own parents, and some who continue to move from one temporary situation to another, under some form of agency care. Some relatives, having been persuaded that our professional services could lead to a better chance of happiness and security, have in all good faith entrusted their children to our care. Moreover, the fact that their children seemed unable to adjust may have discouraged some parents' efforts to take their children home.

And what of the frustration and disillusionment for the children themselves? Sally was such a child. She had strong feeling that she was "not worth loving" after long years of change and insecurity. A highly sensitive and intelligent little girl of eight, she summed up the hopelessness she felt about her situation when she told her caseworker at the institution that she had been

"thrown away by her mother because she wasn't any good, picked up by a welfare lady and taken from home to home until she finally came to an orphanage where she would probably have to remain for the rest of her life."

Sometimes sentimental resistance to permanent separation of children from their blood relatives has stood in the way of our acting in the child's best interests. Often we clung tenaciously to the hope that the parent could eventually give parental care effectively. With emphasis on the needs of the child, we have found that some parents, when unable to provide a home, can be helped through skilled casework to accept a voluntary plan of adoptive placement for their child, and to find ultimate satisfaction in having enriched their child's life through this opportunity.

On the basis of the experiences of the past three years, we have concluded that adoption agencies do have a special obligation to broaden their services to include some of these detached older children. Although older children are being placed for adoption in increasing numbers*, it is still safe to say that too many in the adoption field have been so occupied with the refinement of psychological, medical, and social techniques for minimizing the risks involved in infant placement that we have underestimated the possibilities of adoption for the school-age child.

The Older Child Has Older Problems

The children we were asked to serve in institutions presented a wide variety of personality and behavior difficulties for most of them had already experienced long periods of separation from their natural parents. There were all sorts of anxieties, temper tantrums, speech defects, bed-wetting, allergies, poor grades in school and a host of other symptoms of insecurity and damaged egos. The evaluation of their adoptability was based on a dynamic weighting of all their characteristics—mental, physical and emotional—in relation to their heritage, past experiences, and present relationships. Depending on the situation, a series of medical, psychological, and sometimes psychiatric examinations were a part of the study of each child. When we could understand how his difficulties had developed

---

* *Adoption Practices, Procedures and Problems,* Child Welfare League, 1952. Two-thirds of the agencies which answered the 1950 questionnaire accept older children for adoption.

and what purpose they served for the child we found that they were not necessarily a barrier to adoptive placement, providing that the child possessed the capacity to form meaningful relationships with other people.

Often a child who had been labelled a "special problem" in the institution was able to respond more quickly than we had dared to hope when he received the warmth and affection he needed in his new home. The radical changes in emotional climate plus the new factor of permanency, and identification by name with the adoptive parents, often brought out unknown strengths and inner resources in the child which no one suspected. Even in the best boarding homes or institutions where caseworkers, teachers, housemothers, boarding parents or others in group care programs gave warmth and acceptance to the child, they were unable to reach his utmost depth of feeling and response because they could not completely satisfy his craving to belong in a very personal way. Adoption seems to give some older children the incentive they have been lacking to make full use of their native capacities. George was a poignant example of this process:

> George was referred to us by his institution at eight years of age. He was a noisy, stubborn little boy who was making very little progress in school and who was still in the first grade bceause of all the changes he had experienced before coming to the institution. He was referred with an intelligence quotient far below average, but with a diagnosis of "emotional retardation due to trauma and rejection." Two years of repeated medical, psychological and neurological examinations, plus special tutoring in school and play therapy on the part of his institution and a nearby child guidance clinic were required to assure us that George was ready for adoptive placement.

> Whenever I visited George at the institution, he would ask me, "Are you going to find me a home or aren't you?" As time wore on, he began to compromise with us by saying, "If you can't find me a new mother and father, how about getting me some nice grandparents to live with?" He had become very fond of his housemother who was a grandmother herself and who had found "some love deep within George" which others had not seen because of George's negative behavior. Several possible adoptive homes had turned him down because he was so far behind in school.

It took an appealing story in a newspaper to find a home for George.

Out of 60 responses to this appeal, we received only 22 applications from would-be adoptive parents. Only three of these families stayed with us through the Home Study and were approved. Fortunately, one family was right for George.

He was ten years old by the time he met this couple, a skilled laborer and his wife who lived in the country and had plenty of space and lots of pets. After his first visit to their home, George returned to the institution to pack up his few personal belongings and say "goodbye" to his pals. He announced that he liked this home and wanted to go to live with these people next week because, "She let me bake a biscuit and He gave me a shave!"

These were the homey acts of love and acceptance which had impressed George most even though he had enjoyed many new experiences on his preliminary visits with his prospective parents.

During his first summer in the adoptive home, George tried "everything in the book" on his new mother and father. By fall he settled down, realizing that his actions were not going to throw his adoptive parents off balance because they really wanted him. He began to show his feeling for them in more positive ways. He also achieved all A's in school for the first time in his life, including conduct in the classroom. His adoptive parents said that they felt "so lucky to have won George as our son."

Children Must Be Prepared for the Change

Frequently, institutional children express their fear of change by reacting at first quite negatively to the very word "adoption." Some of them felt that an adopted child had probably been unwanted all along and was "put out" of the orphanage because he did not get along well with other people. For example, nine-year-old Joey had been told by his cottage-mates that adoptive parents "pretend to love you at first, then they grow to hate you, and later on they kill you somehow." Joey wanted a home badly, but he needed a lot of reassurance because he had lost both his parents when he was a baby and was unable to recall what it was like to have a family. He had built up so many fantasies about "dream parents" that his first adoptive home failed for him within a few weeks after placement. He returned to the orphanage where he was able to review the whole situation with his caseworker and began to think more in terms of "real mothers and daddies." Eventually, plans were set in motion for a second adoptive placement. This time Joey knew what to expect of parents and the home is working out very well for him.

Preparation for adoption of the older child was focused on helping him to gain a real understanding of his own family situation and a comfortable acceptance of the fact that his relatives are unable to care for him, and are, therefore, willing to have him become a part of another family if he wants to do so. Since, in most cases, older children are well aware of their original family identity (and if not, they should be given full opportunity to understand their past relationships before placement), they can and do channel their loyalties and personal feelings for their former relatives and associates into positive and constructive relationships with their new adoptive families.

This can be very reassuring to adoptive parents who express anxiety about the degree or extent to which the school-age child may be able to sever his ties with the past, even though there is always the possibility that he can be recognized by former associates. Of course, the rate at which the older child could take on new parents varies with the degree to which he had been rejected or neglected in the past. We found the child whose home had been broken by divorce or desertion superficially more eager for adoption, but taking longer in the end to achieve deep and satisfying relationships with adoptive parents. Children who had lost their parents through death or permanent physical disability moved more cautiously, but more realistically into adoption and established firm loyalties and mutual trust in their new family relationships much sooner after placement.

The case of Dorothy, age 12, will illustrate this:

A full orphan, Dorothy had been old enough when her parents died to remember their love for her. "I don't think I want to be 'dopted out as far as I know now," she said when we first consulted her about plans for the future. But she added, wistfully, "Do you have any homes in mind?" Several weeks later she announced that she definitely was not going to be adopted, "that is, by strangers," she said this time, leaving herself a convenient loophole.

We let her share step by step in the process of determining whether any of her elderly aunts and uncles could possibly provide a home for her. When she was fully convinced that they could not but assured that she could keep in touch with them herself, she began to question our home-finding procedures quite specifically.

"How do you know whether adoptive parents are good Christians who do not drink too much and who will not die right off because of poor health? They might look all right on the surface," she pointed out, "but can you really tell what they are like on the inside?"

We showed Dorothy how we went about our home studies of the families who applied to the Children's Home Society to adopt a child. She put all of us "through our casework paces" for the next few weeks, testing things out for herself, even to the extent of running away from the orphanage, walking barefooted to another city where a girl friend was living "just to see what someone else's home was like."

When Dorothy finally let us know that she was ready to meet some prospective parents whom we thought she might like, she took the initial meeting in her stride with remarkable poise and self-confidence. After getting acquainted with the family through a series of visits to their home, she decided that she had found the new parents she wanted for her very own. She has signed her own legal consent to adoption to be filed with her parents' court petitions, as well as a "Brother-and-Sister Agreement" with her newly acquired foster brother who refers to these documents as "Legal Ownership Papers." He is mighty proud to have a "blonde" in the family whom he can show off to the other fellows in high school, and he has already delighted Dorothy by advising his mother not to force her to take piano lessons if she doesn't want them, but "for goodness sake, let her take dancing lessons so she'll be popular when she grows up."

Selecting Adoptive Parents

The search for adoptive parents for these older children necessitated an intensive recruiting of families of various social, educational, and economic status. The advantages to babies and adoptive parents of starting life together as early as possible has been so widely publicized that people have become discouraged about applying for an older child. Many mature families had been ruled out as adoptive parents in previous years because they were "too old for babies." Now we needed to assert our faith in the flexibility and potentialities of the school-age child who truly wanted to become a member of a family by adoption, as well as in a family's capacity to make him their own.

We enlisted the cooperation of newspapers and radio stations. We printed a booklet about our service to institutional children, gave numerous talks before civic clubs and church groups, and interviewed community leaders all over the state telling of the need for adoptive homes for school-age children.

During the three-year period, as a result of these concentrated efforts, we received over 200 inquiries from families who were interested in the possibility of adopting an older child. These were carefully screened through correspondence and personal interviews, and a total of 95 applications was accepted for more thorough study. As might be expected, only a small proportion could be approved and used for the institutional children.

Of the 19 homes we used during the project period, 14 worked out well. Three of these adoptive families were successful with pairs of brothers and sisters, six were able to fit a school-age child in very happily with their own or previously adopted children, and five took a single child as their first experience in parenthood. Unfortunately, the five other homes studied did not work out well, and the children had to be removed after the first few weeks of placement. In two of these cases, however, it was possible to make a satisfactory second placement for the children involved.

Qualities Required of Adoptive Parents of Older Children

The successes as well as the failures have pointed to some of the characteristics which we believe to be essential guides in the selection of adoptive parents for older children. The basic requirements are the same, of course, as those we seek in adoptive parents for infants: fundamentally happy and satisfied people, well-balanced family relationships, and sensitivity to human needs with capacity for warmth, understanding and affection in accepting a child not born to them. In addition to these qualities, the people who prove successful as adoptive parents for older children had some special attributes:

From the beginning of their contact with the adoption agency, the successful adoptive parents showed a genuine desire to help a child develop at his own pace and in his own way for the child's sake, not their's.

They were able to enjoy a child and to respect his individuality and independence without expecting him to show direct appreciation.

They were people with inexhaustible stores of humor, fun and resilience which helped them to survive the inevitable trials and tribulations of the first months of placement while the child tested their love for them.

They seemed to have a deeply rooted spiritual faith or practical religion which gave them a comfortable philosophy of life and a basic confidence in human nature.

The successful adoptive parents could accept the fact that a child who has suffered emotional deprivation as the result of a broken home experience may always bear the scars of this wound to some extent and may, therefore, never be able to change some aspects of his personality or behavior. Moreover, they had to be able to sustain any positive feelings that the older child might have about his former relationships and to permit him to talk freely about his past. Many adoptive parents soon learned that there was real security for them in the fact that these older children knew more about themselves and the reasons why they had been placed and that they had participated actively in choosing this new way of life for themselves.

Throughout the Home Study process, the adoptive parents were given plenty of time to build and experience trust in the adoption agency and to use their relationship with the caseworker constructively in evaluating themselves and their expectations of a child in their home. Before adoptive parents and an older child were brought together for their first meeting, a mutual feeling of confidence had been established so that there was firm conviction on the part of both agency and family that this plan had a good chance of succeeding. The adoptive parents recognized that they could not "try a child on for size" and let it go at that. They were prepared to get acquainted with the child gradually until they knew that they wanted each other enough to live together and to work toward a real basis for love and understanding. In other words, as some of our adoptive parents have put it, they were willing to regard the adoption like marriage—"for better or worse, for richer or poorer, in sickness and in health. . . ."

Conclusions

Our experiment in inter-agency service has shown that adoption can be a satisfactory alternative for some children in institutions who have no other homes and that often suitable adoptive parents can be found for them. When we began our work on this demonstration project we determined that a quality rather than a quantity job was essential. We had the assistance of many child welfare specialists throughout the state, but we found few guideposts in professional literature by which to steer our course. We used the trial and error method from the start, proceeding cautiously for at least six months to lay the groundwork before we placed a single child. A very large proportion of our casework service consisted of consultation and interpretation with staff members at the various institutions which were interested in participating, and with the relatives and friends and former professional associates of the children who needed a home.

The basic rights of both parents and children in this delicate process needed constant emphasis in every phase. The school-age child's full understanding and participation at each step in the process was essential if placement was to succeed. It is important that the plan should be not only for the child but of and by the child.

As a result of these experiences, we have a deep conviction that no child is too old for adoption as long as he wants and needs parents.

ADOPTION SERVICES AS RELATED TO ADOPTIVE FAMILIES

Adoption Services As Related To
Adoptive Families

Introduction

The reasons adoptive parents have for adopting a child are
many. But whatever the motive, these parents usually believe
that they will find satisfaction from taking a child into their
home. The majority have wanted and tried to have a child of
their own.

Adoption exists in almost every society in the world. Normally childless couples want a child to complete their family
and this prompts their effort to adopt a child. As Joshua Liebman says in *Peace of Mind,* "Men and women desire children
out of their marriage and that very desire in the human heart
is the best proof of an overflowing quality of generosity that
is inherent in human nature. The parent is driven by the irre-
sistible desire to add something to life, no longer to receive
something from life."[1]

Since families wanting to adopt a child so often have had
difficulty in obtaining one through an agency, many families
turn to other sources. Sometimes they pay large sums of money
to persons who commercialize placements of children.

Families obtaining children from agencies have safeguards
in several ways which create advantages for them over taking
children independently. The parents were protected from hasty
decisions and the child was not deprived of his own parents
unnecessarily. The natural parents' rights were terminated
through relinquishment or court action and there is no question that the child is legally free for adoption. The agency
knows through its evaluation that the child is adoptable, both
physically and mentally. The agency shares with the adoptive
family pertinent information about the child's family and background. The natural parents will not know where the child is
being placed. The agency is ready to help the adoptive parents
and share in responsibility for the child for a year after placement or until both family and agency agree that the final legal
steps should be taken.

Good procedures do not involve unnecessary hardships and
difficulties for any of the parties involved in adoption. The

---

[1] Joshua Liebman: Peace of Mind, p. 71.

slowness in obtaining children from adoption agencies resulted from the fact that approximately 10 families applied for every child legally relinquished to agencies by the natural parents. This situation existed in all sections of the country. Because of this disproportionate demand for children, a large number of adoptive applicants were unable to obtain a child even though they had the qualities which would make them excellent parents.

Many adoptive applicants limit their opportunities by requesting babies. Although the number of applicants for white infants exceeds the number available, this is not true for Negro infants, older children, children of mixed racial ancestry, and handicapped children. For these children the number of families applying is insufficient to meet the needs.

Because agencies know that they cannot meet the requests of all families and their staffs are limited, they are not always able to interview personally all applicants to explain some of the problems. The placement agency exists primarily to serve the child regardless of which adoptive home is used or if no adoptive home is used. The adoptive home is a facility for the use of the agency in service to the child although the needs of families desiring children are met too. Service given to adoptive parents coincides with the agency's primary purpose of serving the child's need for a suitable home. Misunderstandings arise when the agency's primary purpose is not understood by prospective adoptive parents.

Agencies are troubled by their failure to meet adequately all the needs of their communities and are making valiant efforts to improve or expand their adoption services. However, adoptions will always be limited by the number of children available for permanent placement. Obviously too when an agency has several hundred inquiries a year and places in the course of a year about one hundred children, the agency does not have a large enough staff to have an individual interview with all persons inquiring about adoption.

In addition to individual personal interviews, other devices enable agencies to give better service to adoptive applicants, such as sending out leaflets with information about agency procedures, form letters, using telephone interviews both to give and to obtain factual information, meeting with groups of adoptive applicants to consider policies, procedures and how the agency will work with them, and limiting the time an application will be continued on an active basis.

Some agencies have a policy of placing only one child in a

home, others not more than two, while still others have no fixed maximum. When restrictions are established, it is usually on the basis of expediency and because there are so many applicants that the agencies think the children should be divided among more families. This practice is not necessarily in the best interests of all children.

A number of agencies now place family groups which include several brothers and sisters. When such family groups are so large the children cannot be placed with one adoptive family, homes are found which accept the need for children to keep in touch with each other through visits after adoption.

Most agencies have a definite policy with regard to an upper age limit for adoptive parents. This policy rests upon the belief that the best age interval between the child and his adoptive parents is one that is normal between children and their natural parents. In general forty to forty-five years is the maximum age limit set for parents adopting an infant. Older adoptive parents may secure older children. Individual circumstances of the family and child merit exceptions.

In general adoption agencies, voluntary or governmental, place children within the state in which they are located and licensed to operate. Exceptions to this practice occur in the placement of difficult-to-place children, and also in large urban areas where parts of other states are closely connected to a metropolitan area. In such cases adequate safeguards for the home study, placement, supervision, and completion of adoption should be assured with consideration of all jurisdictional questions.

Since the agency which has the child for placement usually has the guardianship of the child, the procedure of adoption becomes more complicated in out-of-state placements that require services of other agencies. In instances in which out-of-state placements are made, the procedure generally requires requesting agencies in other states to make the evaluation of the adoptive home, supervise the child after placement, and complete the legal adoption after the trial period in the home required by the adoption law. A number of voluntary agencies, including those making placements in nearby states, send staff members across state lines to make their own home studies and provide their own supervision. As a rule this requires an agreement about interstate placements with the state welfare departments of the states in which children are to be placed.

Customarily children of a given religious faith are placed in adoptive homes of the same religious faith within the larger groupings of Jewish, Catholic and Protestant religions. This is not usually the case in relation to various denominations of the Protestant faith. A number of states have made provisions in their laws requiring consideration of religious affiliations in placing children; in some states regulations established for licensed child-placing agencies require this. Even when it is not required, child-placing agencies tend to follow this procedure.

Children are placed in homes of similar religious backgrounds because it is the preference of natural parents to have their child reared in their own religious faith. While some parents are not active members of a church at the time of relinquishing the child, they have usually been reared in a particular faith and consider themselves affiliated with a specific religion. Both church groups and child-placing agencies agree that it is desirable. Many agencies question the soundness of this policy if it means a child will be prevented from having adoptive parents. When such is the case they consider it in the best interest of the child to deviate from the policy.

The practice of placements within the same religious faith is not consistent in independent placements. In cases in which a child has been placed independently in a home of a different religious faith and has remained there for some time so that a deep emotional tie exists between the parents and the child, courts do not usually deny the completion of adoption purely on the basis of religious difference. In such cases the traditional policy of the court is to consider the total well-being of the child. In recent years, however, some cases have not been decided in accordance with this traditional policy.

What life in a home is like under the surface is of the greatest importance to a child since his future happiness and attitudes are largely determined by his early experiences. Therefore, in evaluating the prospective adoptive family, the agency needs to know whether the adoptive parents are mature adults capable of easy and loving relationships, secure enough in their marriage to share their love with a child of other parents, to face life's difficulties courageously, and to take the risks involved in adoptive parenthood willingly.

The purpose of the adoptive home study is not just to evaluate the applicants and their potentialities for growth and parenthood, but also to help prepare them for what is coming and the inevitable changes which will occur when a child enters the family. Sometimes adoptive applicants have not thought through what it will mean to them to share their life with a child.

The agency needs to assure itself that this couple really desire the responsibility of being parents, that they have tried medical services to have their own child, and that they have made a satisfactory adjustment to their own infertility. Adoptive applicants should not be rejected if the cause of infertility cannot be determined but each case should be considered individually in relation to other factors.

Often couples begin with unrealistic expectations in regard to the child they want. If they can adapt their wish for a child to the kind of children who are available and need adoption, they show a capacity for growth and change. They may be able to use the agency's help constructively in arriving at readiness for the kind of children available.

Adoption is not the answer for all childless couples. It is the agency's responsibility during the course of the home study to help the applicants decide if adoption will make them happy. Although the agency-wide focus is on the child and his welfare, the agency worker needs to focus on the adoptive applicants and their happiness while working with them.

Families with limited incomes are as eligible to receive a child through adoption as are those with higher incomes. Far more important than the actual amount earned is the stability of employment of the adoptive applicants, how the family spends their income, and whether they are able to manage and live within it. The family is expected to have, however, sufficient income to assure acceptable standards of living with some surplus for unforeseen emergencies.

The physical and mental health of the adoptive applicants is important to ensure a child parents with reasonable life expectancy, the ability to care for him, and the security of having parents until he reaches maturity.

Most important of all in determining suitability of adoptive applicants are their personal characteristics, the warmth and affection they can offer a child, and their ability to accept him as an individual with rights of his own.

One of the most difficult services in adoption work is that of informing applicants when they are rejected by the agency as unsuitable adoptive parents. In the past little consideration was given this service. While there is now agreement that the family needs to know the decision, there is not agreement on what and how to tell them. More attention needs to be given to the best methods of handling this difficult problem.

Rarely does a single reason make a family unacceptable. If possible the explanation given them by the agency must leave them with as much self-respect as when they came to the agency. The reasons given them should be truthful and acceptable to them so as not to increase further their frustration and conflict, their immaturity, or the tensions between the couple. If no reason is given, the applicants will certanly try for a child elsewhere or resort to a private placement and miss the advantages of social services for themselves as well as jeopardize the child they receive.

Good practice in child adoption procedure requires knowledge both of the qualities of the home of prospective parents and of the potentialities of the child. The history of the child serves to evaluate a child's suitability for adoption, and to help adoptive parents know whether they want to assume responsibility for this child and accept him as theirs.

After the agency has selected a home for a child on the basis of information about the adoptive family and the child, it gives the family the essential social and medical history of the child.

Agency information shared with the family also includes the facts on which a decision of adoptability is based. From the medical history come the facts about the child's health or handicaps. Educational and occupational history enrich the general background knowledge. If there are negative factors undesirable to give and if these were eliminated in evaluating the suitability of the child for adoption, these need not be told.

In giving history to adoptive parents so that they may meet some of the child's questions gradually as he grows up, discrimination is necessary. Some things are not important to give and are better omitted even though they are part of the record.

The information given by the agency depends in some ways on what the adoptive parents can accept. They may not get the impact of all the information at one time but think things over and may return with questions, i.e. between the time they first see the child and take him. It is necessary to know adoptive parents well enough to estimate how accepting they will be of certain information and what will cause undue anxiety for them.

There are facts adoptive parents should know when they are taking a risk that one cannot insure against completely from a medical viewpoint, such as arrested tuberculosis or congenital syphilis which has been treated and apparently cured. They need to know the situation and prepare to take the risk.

In matching physical appearance of the child with adoptive applicants, agencies are trying not to overemphasize the fact that the child is not their own even though they know that the parents accept the child as adopted. However, physical appearance as a factor in the integration of a family may be unduly stressed. In natural families the husband or wife accepts the fact that a child may not look like him or her. The color of hair or eyes seems relatively unimportant. Stature and build might be given consideration although that is not too significant if they are within the normal range. Appearances are unimportant when compared to personalities and how they relate to each other.

In the matter of matching nationality backgrounds other questions arise. The intermingling of nationalities both in the child's ancestry and in the adoptive parents' ancestry often make it impossible to determine the dominant nationality in either background. Certain nationalities have distinct personality traits and these need to be considered in a placement. A few adoptive parents have decided feelings about certain nationalities in the background of a child which should always be considered.

In its contacts with adoptive parents, the agency tries to give them a sympathetic understanding of how the child came to be available for adoption, how the mother or both parents felt about giving him away, and the circumstances of their lives that led to the difficulty. This interpretation helps adoptive parents understand the natural parents so that in the future they can give the child a constructive, acceptable understanding of them.

An adoption agency usually asks the adoptive parents to keep the child's history confidential. Relatives and friends do not need this information any more than they need to know complete information about children born to their friends. Although friends and relatives may be curious, it is better for them not to know so they will not judge the child adversely on the basis of his history as he is growing up.

If the family is satisfied with the history, the agency then arranges for the family and child to become acquainted. The initial contact is usually in the agency office. In the case of older children the prospective adoptive parents may take the child out alone for a ride or shopping expedition if the child is ready for this. Later, the child may visit in the adoptive home. When the child shows by his readiness that he has some acceptance of his new parents, he is placed in the adoptive home.

Occasionally a family may decide after seeing a child that there is something about the child's personality that they cannot accept fully. Such a possibility should be discussed with them in advance of the placement. Then they will feel free to discuss their doubts with the agency worker and feel assured that refusal of a particular child will not automatically cause their home to be rejected for further consideration. Naturally the agency should be sure that they are not rejecting the idea of any child. But every adult is not immediately drawn to every child he sees even though he truly loves children.

The adoption laws of the individual states usually require that the child remain in the adoptive home from six months to one year before the adoptive parents may petition the court for legal adoption. This provision assures the integration of the child into the family and his full acceptance by them before any legal step which may be irrevocable.

During this period prior to the legal adoption, the agency worker visits the adoptive home regularly to help the adoptive parents understand the child, to give additional information about the child if needed, and to find out whether the family—and the child if he is an older child—wish to proceed with legal steps.

In the beginning adoptive parents often need help in relating to the child. To facilitate the integration of the child into a new family, the transition from the original family must be made. The agency needs to share with adoptive parents its information about the child and help them understand the total situation from which the child comes. During these visits the worker watches the child adjust and determines if he is well cared for and gaining security in the family.

If the child is the first and only child, adoptive parents need help with the tensions characteristic of this situation. With a second child parents, natural or adoptive, are more relaxed and not as exacting.

With an older child the integration process is more difficult. The parents need help in realizing that separation from a child's past life does not mean completely giving up his past. The adoptive parents must understand that the older child needs a family who will let him talk about his past experiences and live with his past memories for awhile as needed. The child's readiness to discuss his past with his new parents is often a sign of growing security. Only as a child's past and present are consolidated can he begin to make a good adjustment with his new parents.

Adoptive parents may have negative behavior and even hostility to meet from the child. He may "test" his new family in many ways to discover if he is really wanted regardless of his behavior. Adoptive parents need to be prepared for these possibilities so that they will not feel they are failing with the child.

Another area in which adoptive parents need help is in explaining adoption to the child and answering his questions. While an agency cannot put words into the mouths of adoptive parents or give all-embracing specific information, it can give help of a general nature.

The child should learn who he is from those he loves and trusts—his adoptive parents. If he is told by them and not by some outsider who desires to make him unhappy, he must be told when he is still very young. He ought, as a matter of fact, to grow up knowing who he is—or it will come to him as a great shock, which may seriously affect his relationship to his adoptive parents and friends. He ought then to be told before he will understand the full significance of what it means. It is not a good plan to stage a revelation of his identity. He should be told incidentally and casually, but simply and sincerely, so he will know what he is being told is true but that it does not alter his position in his relation to his new parents.

At a later date he is going to wonder who his own parents are, why they gave him up to others, and where they are. These questions will have to be answered or he may spend unhappy hours brooding about the whole situation. If adoption has been the careful, thoughtful process that it should be, the agency will have anticipated these problems with the adoptive parents and they will be able to give truthful answers.

When a child asks, "Why did my family give me up?" his age should be considered in the answer given. At any age the child should be given the conviction that his parents loved him but could not keep him. The circumstances of his birth should not be highlighted. When a child is ready by chronological and emotional age to talk about birth out of wedlock, if that is pertinent to his background, he may be given the facts of his birth.

266

Several devices have been used by adoptive parents to recall for the child how he came to live in their home—such as motion pictures, photograph and record books.

Adoption services as related to adoptive families inevitably raise the question of cost since professional service is expensive and funds of most agencies are limited. For many years adoption agencies charged adoptive parents no fees for the agency's services. More recently, however, some adoption agencies are charging fees based on the services given and on the ability of the adoptive applicants to pay for this service. The number of agencies charging such fees is still relatively small in relation to the total number of agencies placing children for adoption.

The trend toward the charging of fees developed because agencies did not receive sufficient financial support from communities to meet requests for service received from parents of children. The number of children agencies can accept for care depends on their income.

In some places community funds have suggested that agencies make a charge since they are unable to support the work and its necessary expansion. Payments of adoptive parents are interpreted as a means of sharing the cost of services and in this way stretching contributions to serve more children. Almost no agencies charge the full cost of the service provided.

While agencies and workers are not in unanimous agreement on whether fees should be charged, they do agree that funds should not be solicited as a condition for placement of a child; that the fees charged should be clearly defined at the time of the initial application for service; and that such fees should be based on sharing the cost of service.

Fees charged are usually graduated in accordance with the ability of the family to pay rather than the cost of the care provided the child placed. The care of one child may be very costly because of essential medical expenses, such as correction of a congenital hip dislocation, and for another child relatively inexpensive. The home most suitable for the individual child is not necessarily the one most able financially to reimburse the agency for expenses.

Studies of fee charging are needed. Agencies now charging fees need to make detailed studies of the procedure including community implications, changes in contributions to the agency, changes in the group of adoptive parents making application, and what adoptive applicants and parents really think about the practice. Studies are also needed, and some have recently been completed, to determine unit costs of the parts of foster home placement programs, including adoptive placements. These are helpful in giving a more accurate measure of costs to be considered.

The following papers deal with recent developments in the application process; factors involved in the selection of adoptive families; the role of the social worker in helping families after placement; and the practice of charging fees for agency services to adoptive families.

CHAPTER 22

Some Casework Implications in Adoptive Home Intake Procedures

RITA DUKETTE

Complaints of the public about the adoption agencies have rung loud and long for all to hear. Common accusations are that agencies hoard children as a miser hoards his gold; that applications from families are accepted begrudgingly, if at all; that the agencies attempt a meticulous matching job which puts nature to shame; and that the applications which are accepted are studied suspiciously, as if the applicants were guilty of being poor risks until proved otherwise. Happily, many of these complaints are fading in the light of more thoughtful work by adoption agencies. They are still common enough, however, to behoove us to look at our practices to see if they can command the support of the community, and also our own professional respect, by meeting the following requirements of good adoption:

1. Families are chosen who give promise of being able to provide the requirements for the healthy development of the children who need them.

2. Homefinding is begun promptly, so that the children can be placed when they are very young.

3. Placement is accomplished as constructively for the adoptive applicant as possible.

4. The adoption placement is preceded by careful work with the natural parent so that the decision to place the child in adoption represents the best plan for him.

In any scrutiny of practices involved in the handling of adoption applications such questions must be answered as:

1. Are the applicants chosen for study those who are most likely to be adequate parents for the children for whom the agency is planning?

2. Are families made available in time so that children are placed as soon as they are ready?

3. Are homefinding methods time-saving?

4. Are families dealt with constructively so that adoption application does not engender self-doubt or resentment?

Keeping Perspective Was Difficult

In seeking the answers to these questions it is important to be aware of the many pressures besetting the adoption worker. In few casework settings has there been so much difficulty keeping the primary responsibility foremost. One of the greatest pressures contributing to this difficulty is the great longing of the adoptive applicants for a child. Motivated by a wish to ease this longing, the caseworker often accepted applications more from her wish to give the applicants a child than because of their capacities to be good parents for any of the children the agency had responsibility to place. She frequently found herself retreating from the far-reaching implications of her responsibility to choose parents for a child and unconsciously sought refuge in procrastinating devices like waiting lists and rigid entrance requirements for adoptive parents. Some of her responsibility she passed on to the adoptive parents by sharing with them every worrisome detail of the child's history that there could be no doubt that they knew what they were getting. Sometimes she was beset by confusion about her responsibilities, feeling people had "a right to be studied as adoptive parents." She found it hard to see clearly that her responsbiility was to serve the children under the agency's care and that what served them well would also serve the adoptive applicants and the community.

A great deal has been learned about the qualities of parents which cause maladjustments in their children, but until recently, the qualities of good parents have received much less attention. Consequently, some of the uncertainty of the adoption caseworker came from the fact that the qualities which she should be seeking in applicants were not clarified. Even if she succeeded in defining these qualities, an even more difficult problem was to identify them in the childless couples who came to her. Conflicted in her judgment that some applicants would not make good parents by her wish to be "accepting," and by her unconscious attitudes toward parent people, she found it hard to turn people away. This meant she was again caught in the confusion which so often seems basic in slowing down the adoption process—accepting, even by implication, the responsibility of seeking children for families instead of families for children, or in a form once removed, assuming therapeutic responsibility for the personality problems of the applicants. The caseworker found herself torn in her wish to meet the needs of all families applying, and her responsibility to find the most suitable homes she could for the children under care. Sometimes she herself was not well placed in a preventive program and her tendency to wish to treat the applicants arose out of her real wish to be engaged in therapy.

Purpose of Program Redefined

There are many evidences that the adoption agencies are growing up, taking responsibility which is rightly theirs and developing insight into the meaning of specific practices, modifying these when that is indicated. It was in an attempt to assume such responsibility that the Illinois Children's Home and Aid Society tried to look clearly at its adoption program. Out of an examination of its intake practice with adoptive homes, the administrative procedures which will be described were developed.

The Illinois Children's Home and Aid Society is a nonsectarian child placement agency giving both foster and adoptive care. It is the purpose of this agency's program to place each child wisely as early in life as possible. A wise placement is believed to be one which gives promise of providing a loving and protecting relationship with mature parents who have enough in common with the child's heritage and characteristics to offer him an opportunity for a sense of identification with them. These parents should also be able to accept the fact of his adoption and help to integrate it. It is not presumed that ideal placements will be provided. The chance that next year a home with more advantages might be found is accepted as part of the child's and the agency's reality so that the agency has come to live comfortably with the goal of an adequate home for each child. The development of the agency's intake practices was built on the conviction that, to acheve the purpose of the program, procedures should be developed soundly and administered as constructively as possible for the adoptive parents, within an aware and sympathetic relationship.

Using the Telephone Interview

The first step in the application process is a telephone conversation between the applicant and an experienced caseworker who is well informed about the agency's specific needs for adoptive families. The proportion of applications to placements usually is about 15 to 1. The children cared for vary greatly in background and characteristics with a sizable proportion of Negro children and, regularly, a few Oriental children. The telephone conversation with the applicant is for the purpose of determining, as economically as possible, whether there is some likelihood that the agency would be well advised to pursue the application. The conversation is also used to interpret the agency's way of working and to give information about the general adoption picture. These conversations are leisurely; time is taken to ask about the applicant's medical situation in relation to infertility history, religion, nationality, general physical characteristics, age, length of marriage, employment, housing and general health. Specific wishes in relation to a child are also discussed. This material is evaluated first from the standpoint of its implications for the applicant's general maturity and readiness for adoptive parenthood and, secondly, in terms of its relationship to the needs of the children for whom the agency is seeking homes. It is recognized that such an evaluation is necessarily gross. Depending on the circumstances of his situation and the agency's needs, the applicant is told either that there is no likelihood of being able to pursue the application, or else that the application will be considered in terms of both the children for whom the agency will be planning and other families under study. As sympathetically as possible, it is made clear that consideration will be in terms of the children for whom the agency is planning, and that choices of families are not based on isolated details but on evaluation of all the factors involved. If it is possible to pursue his application, the applicant will be given an appointment for an interview within a short specified time, presently four weeks. If he does not hear from the agency within that time, he will know that the agency was not able to proceed with his application. The fact that the applicant's problem is a common one is given general interpretation in an attempt to depersonalize his feelings about his childlessness and about the agency's inability to help him with it through adoption.

Though he is given permission to do so if he asks, the applicant is not encouraged to reapply, since this really constitutes a waiting list, and the agency's situation at a given time is fairly typical. The reasons, in terms of economy of time and service, for proceeding by considering the applications currently available instead of going back to old lists are explained and related to the agency's awareness of its responsibility to the children needing homes. For similar reasons of economy of community service, applicants are requested not to apply to the agency if they have made application elsewhere.

Service Has Been Expedited

When a waiting list was used, families felt it necessary to call often to reiterate their eagerness. With the present way of working there are few return calls and this fact, as well as the lack of apparent hostility when the agency finds itself unable to proceed, seems to strengthen the conviction that this procedure offers the applicant acceptable and positive consideration. The applicants themselves endorse the practice of making a definite decision early, even though the decision may be a negative one for them. Again and again we hear applicants say, "Well, at least it's good to know where we stand," or "We appreciate a definite answer." If an appointment is given it is explained that this is purely for further exploration and that the agency cannot assure the family that it will continue with them to actual placement. In case a study is begun, the application will be reviewed in terms of needs after the first interview and as the study proceeds.

The telephone interview has many proved values. One is the opportunity it gives the agency to spend its time studying the families most likely to be suitable for the children for whom homes are being sought. Another major value lies in the opportunity it gives the applicant to present his request verbally to a sympathetic listener, when he is ready to make it. Thus the psychological readiness of the family to participate in adoption is utilized. Understanding that individuals seek adjustments to accommodate the realities they face, we recognize that the individual who applies to adopt a child must somehow handle his readiness to do so either by proceeding with adoption at the agency, if that is possible, or by seeking other solutions. It is important that he be given a sympathetic answer about the chances of the agency's being able to help him, if he is to proceed to develop other solutions and to do this with no loss of self-confidence. This is "his right"—to have help which will enable him to use his energies positively in seeking a solution to his problem. He should not be encouraged to hope indefinitely, as a long-postponed adoption application sometimes permits, only to have his hopes dashed later. It is important, too, that his request be acted upon before he has modified his own situation to accommodate his childlessness.

Another reason for deciding soon after the application is made whether or not it can be studied is the practical fact that the applicant seldom remains unchanged over any appreciable period of time. In the past when waiting lists were kept, by the time the agency became ready to make the studies, often the family was no longer in a position to adopt.

The first interview, which is held with prospective parents in the agency office, is used to clarify further the general circumstances which had been discussed over the telephone, but particularly to explore in more detail the way the family had attempted to cope with the fact that they could not have their own child. This is diagnostically significant because the individual's reaction to any reality as important as this is revealing of his usual way of meeting difficulties. It also throws a great deal of light on the significance to him of having an adopted child instead of his own. The other areas of exploration such as housing, friends, interests, health, also reveal the applicant's general maturity and readiness for adoptive parenthood. Awareness of special characteristics, appearance, special strengths for caring for children or special needs on the applicant's part in relation to a child, help to indicate the suitability of the family for a specific child.

During this interview, some of the specific considerations relative to adoption such as differences in background are suggested in order to help the family begin to explore their feelings about these questions and to think about handling them later with a child. The methods involved in the adoption process—the study, the placement process and the supervision period—are clearly defined and responsibility is placed on the applicant for deciding if he wishes to try to participate productively in each of these processes. It is understood that his continuing with his application implies such assumption of responsibility.

At the end of the interview the family is told as in the telephone conversation either that the agency will not be able to pursue their application or that the application will be considered in the light of the needs of the children and the available families. If, on the basis of these, it is possible to study the application, an application blank will be mailed within the month. The family is asked thoughtfully to consider their willingness to work with the agency before returning it.

Therapy to Adoptive Applicants Avoided

When it is clear in the interview that it would be unwise to pursue the application, the reason for this is shared with the applicant if it is one he can understand without self-doubt or hostility, and one he can use to improve his situation. Otherwise, the inability to consider the application is related to the general problem of individual placement needs. To help the applicant therapeutically to understand how to remove the defects in his adjustment which constitute the obstacles to acceptance as an adoptive parent is not seen as the responsibility of the adoption department. Applicants who need and want help with their own problems are referred to the proper resource. It is acknowledged that the major responsibility for the maladjusted adoptive applicant necessarily rests with agencies established to help troubled adults.

An important consideration in a positive handling of the application is its realistic consideration in relation to placement needs and not primarily as an evaluation of the applicant's capacity to be a good parent to any child. This is real for the agency staff who attempt to relate individual needs of children to individual capacities of parents, and it is important for the applicant because it preserves self-esteem which could easily be undermined by a more total and isolated judgment.

Decisions Based Solely on Children's Needs

It has been interestingly apparent in practice that this realistic approach to the acceptance or rejection of applicants in terms of needs has left the caseworkers much more free of the old conflict of accepting or rejecting applicants as people. Decisions about applications have been related in general to the children available and the caseworker has been better able to share this with the applicant than when decisions were made without specific relation to needs. Her greater comfort with a more tolerable responsibility has affected her relationships so that when rejections are made this is done earlier and more supportively.

An important part of the intake caseworker's task is the interpretation to individuals in the community of the agency's ability or inability to study an application in which they are interested. Here the most understandable interpretation relates to the needs of the children under care. The point must be made that the agency necessarily bears the responsibility for deciding which applications are most appropriately studied for the children available and that the content of the information which leads to such decisions cannot be shared without violating the confidence of the applicants. If the agency's practice is consistent with its interpretation of its intake policy and its practices accomplish their purpose of wise early placements, it should not be hard for the policies to be understood and accepted. To presume that they will be well understood and well accepted by everyone would be to deny our knowledge of the effect on such understanding of individual interests and concerns. At least if they are developed thoughtfully and interpreted with care they will have as good a chance of being understood as we can presently provide.

Thoughtful adoption practice requires careful examination of all the procedures which are involved in it from the standpoint of their usefulness in achieving its purpose and their implications for the adoptive applicants whom they concern. This examination of practice properly begins at their first inquiry and applies not only to families accepted for study but also to those whom the agency cannot accept. The primary responsibility of an adoption agency is to place its children wisely. The agency carries an equal obligation to the adults who come seeking a child to respond to them in ways which safeguard their self-respect and their capacity to find an acceptable solution to their childlessness. The adoption agency has an obligation to evaluate all of its procedures in the light of these responsibilities and to modify them if necessary to advance these goals. When the agency is clear about its responsibilities, aware of the implications of its practices, and has established procedures which do advance its purpose, that purpose is seldom defeated by the old conflicts and confusions. Responsibilities fall into their rightful places, children become clearly the agency's first charge, and one consideration becomes its lodestar, the placement of its children with adoptive parents who can give them opportunity for healthy, happy living.

CHAPTER 23

A Plan for Improved Service to the Adoptive Applicant

SARABELLE McCLEERY

For all of us there are times when well known objects are seen in a new light, when old problems take on new meaning. Familiarity sometimes dulls perception and a shift in focus can be helpful. In 1950, The Boys and Girls Aid Society of Oregon put into effect a method of handling adoptive applications which eliminated the long waiting list. This solved some immediate practical problems, but, almost more important, it brought with it a change in perspective and showed a way to give better service to the applicant without losing sight of the agency's responsibility to the child.

The Society, a state-wide, child-placing and child-care agency, is sixty-seven years old. Since 1945, a major emphasis has been given to adoption, but the agency remains a multiple-function agency that offers maternity service to the unmarried mother, whatever may be her plan for the child, in addition to programs of foster boarding home care and service to children in their own homes. About 120 children a year are placed in adoption. For most of the infants needing placement there may be ten or more applications, but for older children, family groups of children, children of mixed racial background, or in other complicated situations it is often necessary to recruit applications actively. To control volume, the Society had tried closing intake to applicants, but this proved unsatisfactory because considerable time was required to deal with inquiries on an acceptable basis and because of the difficulties encountered in locating homes for children with special needs.

The standard procedure with adoptive applicants had been to maintain open intake, to give each couple a preliminary interview promptly, to study enough applications to place all the children, and to handle the excess number on an individual basis. The majority of applications remained on a waiting list. Community relationships seemed reasonably good and the public in many ways looked to the Society for leadership in the field. However, the long waiting list presented a problem because it provided no prompt or definite answer to the applications of the majority of would-be parents. Applicants and their friends became restless and critical. Although work with disappointed individuals took considerable time, no one felt that the well-being of these childless couples was materially advanced.

A major cause of difficulty lay in the fact that the long waiting list seemed to accent rather than reduce the elements of dependency in the relationship between the applicant and the agency. Dependency is present in some degree whenever an individual is forced to request an important service from another. It is increased when he must seek it as a privilege and not as a right. The more basically meaningful the service, the more danger that this dependency will develop unhealthy aspects, especially when the individual does not know how his request will be treated. The ability to give or withhold children places great power and authority in the hands of an agency and tends to place the applicant in the role of supplicant. Even though the counselors may try to counteract the dependency in individual interviews, the unavoidable delays, uncertainties, and frustrations of a long waiting list work against a couple's ability to handle their relationship with the agency in a mature and strong fashion. Some may become openly hostile or aggressively dependent, and tensions can carry over into other aspects of their personal life. Some may feel more inferior than before, some more distrustful, some more angry at the marriage partner for making it impossible to have a normal pregnancy. If a couple is told that no child will be placed, there may be additional problems. The pressure of accumulated frustration means that rarely do applicants permit the agency to select the most appropriate time to say "No." In their urgency they usually ask for reasons, and these reasons, when given in a personalized fashion, often have appeared to leave them with weakened defenses and less able to handle tensions already in existence.

The Proposed Change

Procedures first developed by the Adoption Institute in Los Angeles County, California, provided the basis for a proposed change in our agency. They were designed primarily to reduce the period of waiting for the majority of applicants and to keep each couple informed at all times as to what they could expect, but they also provided a less personalized way of telling families, when necessary, that no child could be placed with them. The change provided for a periodic check which would keep the waiting list proportionate to the number of children to be placed. All families would know within three months after they applied whether or not their application could be continued and they would learn within six months to a year whether or not a child could be placed with them.

Although there were many obvious advantages to eliminating the long waiting list, there also were drawbacks that had to be considered. The most serious of these was that when we received applications we could continue to hold open only those most suitable for the particular children we would be placing within a reasonable period of time. If there were many more applications for a certain kind of child than there were such children available or expected to become available for adoption, only the number needed for the children could be kept active. Good families would have to be disappointed. Although this was a real disadvantage, it is apparent that the same number of suitable families have to be disappointed under any system as long as there are more such applicants than children. Under the proposed plan, families at least would know promptly what they could expect. If their applications were not continued, they would be able to apply to another agency. They would also be able to reapply to the Society if they wished to do so.

Making the Change.

Before the change was put into effect there was extensive advance study and preparation. Because of the Society's special place in the community, few of its actions go unobserved, and reactions usually are direct and vigorous. Therefore, nine months' intensive work was done in preparation. Community reaction was secured in numerous individual conferences with families interested in adoption and with other interested persons. The plan was studied by the Board of Trustees of the

Society, was discussed with representatives of the State Public Welfare Commission, with other agencies, and with the Council of Social Agencies.

As the study of the proposed plan progressed, our confidence in it increased and by January, 1950, we were ready to test public reaction on a larger scale. Particularly, we wanted to know the feelings of a large number of applicants. A series of three letters was sent, the first on January 6, the second on March 23, and the third on May 23. The story also was given space in the leading newspapers. The letters were sent to families having an active application on file, and copies were sent to members of the Society, to families who had earlier received a child, and to any others who had shown an interest; they were sent to a total of 1,740 people. In the first letter, the problems involved in keeping a long waiting list were discussed, the proposed change was described, and suggestions were invited. While the letter did not require an answer, many families did reply, and only three did not favor a change. Typical reactions were as follows:

> As one of the applicants, I would like to express my approval of the proposed plan. My husband and I still would like very much to adopt a child but . . . if we are disappointed we'll just make the best of it, knowing that perhaps there are many others who will be disappointed too.

> A fairly rapid turnover in applications would seem to be to the advantage of both applicants and the Society, even though it means that some families are going to be disappointed sooner rather than later.

> It has taken a lot of long, hard thought and soul-searching to be able to answer the question concerning cutting down your lists. It is hard to be rational about this matter because there is always the horrible possibility that one's own name would be among those to be dropped. However, we agree that with the present discrepancy between numbers of applicants and numbers of babies, the situation is an impossible one. It is a hard thing to cut off hope for so many couples who are eager to adopt a child, but in the long run certainly a far kinder and wiser thing to do than to allow them to hope falsely. From your point of view, we can't see how you can hope to function otherwise.

In the second letter we tabulated the responses and quoted from them; the effect that eliminating the waiting list would have on the current list of applicants was brought out clearly and families were invited to think about the fairest method for present applicants to reapply under new procedures.

Not many answered this letter and as general reactions still seemed favorable it was decided to make the change as proposed. The third letter described the plan that was to go into effect July 1, 1950. To make sure that children would continue to be placed during the period of adjustment and to avoid the necessity of drawing against new applications before the plan was fully in operation, a sufficient number of families was carried over without the necessity of reapplying. For the others, the reapplication process was simple. They had merely to let us know by card or telephone if they wished to apply under the new procedures. On June 30, 535 applications were closed; 121 of these reapplied in July and 52 came back to us at some time in the succeeding eleven months. Although we do not know the individual situations of those who did not get in touch with us, there have been no negative community reverberations.

How the Plan Operates

The plan that was adopted provides the framework for a systematic handling of all applications. Persons interested in adoption are encouraged to attend a group meeting as the first step in the application process. This meeting is defined as the family's opportunity to get acquainted with the Society. It is not part of the Society's individual study of the family. About ten couples meet with one staff member. Full discussion is encouraged, and although usually a large range of subjects related to adoption is brought up, the leader tries to make sure that the families understand what will happen if they apply to adopt and the reasons back of these actions.

If, after learning about the program, a couple decides to file an application, they arrange for a personal interview with a member of the professional staff. When their application is completed, they are notified in writing and are told that they will hear from the Society, by a specified date three months in advance, whether or not their application can be continued for study.

On the date promised each family receives one of two types of letters from the agency. One letter states that the application has been accepted for full study and gives the date that the family can expect interviews to begin. The other letter lets the family know that their application is being closed, and that they may reapply after six months if they wish. The decision as to which families can be carried forward for the full study is based on the need of the Society for homes. The preliminary period permits a study of trends regarding the number and kind of children becoming available for adoption and the number and kind of applications for such children.

The nature of the study was not changed. The families, however, are better prepared for their participation and they know the date by which they can expect the study to begin. Each family is notified in writing when the study is completed.

No decision regarding the use of a family is made immediately upon the completion of study. Instead, there follows a three-month period during which every studied application can be compared with other studied applications in relationship to children becoming available for adoption. If a child becomes available and there are no applications for that kind of child already on the approved list, a placement may be arranged before the three months have elapsed. However, this post-study period is used to make possible the selection of applications most suitable for the children. At the end of the three months, unless placement already has been made, each family is again notified of what can be expected. One letter lets the family know that "We regret to inform you that your application is not being continued beyond this time." The other letter states: "We are very glad to inform you that your application to adopt a child through the Society has been selected for placement on our approved list."

The applications approved for placement are varied so as to provide the broad range needed for a good selection of homes for children. The list is kept short and is highly selective, since it is expected that all families reaching this point will receive a child within a few months. A high degree of certainty is possible because at the end of the preliminary period a balance is established in number and variety, and after the study there is a thorough review of the situation before selections are made.

Effect of the Plan

The plan was developed to provide a framework within which the large volume of adoptive applications could be handled with economy of time and energy. Also, it was important to develop a method whereby families not needed for the children could be notified of this as promptly and constructively as possible. Quickly it became apparent that these purposes had been achieved. The favorable first reaction continued, and work with the dissatisfied has been reduced to the point that it is no longer felt to be burdensome. In addition, we found that our entire relationship with applicants was thrown into new perspective. Probably the most significant change was a lessening of the destructive elements of dependency in the relationship between applicant and agency. The full procedures are known to the applicants, and the agency is bound to adhere to them as long as they remain in effect. If the agency fails to live up to its promises, the applicants know they have the right to demand better service. This removes many uncertainties, and the applicant need not feel he has to beg for consideration. To hold the agency subject to rules that are known and open to evaluation by those dependent on it tends to reduce the authoritarian aspects to proportions that can be better handled.

In another way, also, the new procedures have a direct effect on some of the destructive elements involved when couples have to turn to a social agency for children. From the beginning, applicants are actively helped to prepare themselves for possible disappointment. They are given the statistics on applications and children available for adoption. In the group meeting they look about them and see that the other people interested in adoption also make a good appearance and also have an urgent wish for children. Emphasis is placed on the Society's duty to "screen in" enough suitable applications to find homes for all the children. "Screening out" is not a rejection but an unavoidable necessity. The families are told the kind of things that will affect their chances of getting a child. Some of these are personal to the couple; others are directly related to the needs of individual children and the current situation of the agency. The importance of factors such as age, health, personality, income, and living arrangements is not underrated but it is emphasized that these must be taken as a part of the total picture which will include the whole life of the family, the needs of the children, the volume of applications. Since families are applying for a child, not for a diagnostic evaluation of their family life, the agency has a responsibility, if no placement can be made, to notify them as promptly as possible, but the findings of the study will not be given. Although people vary in their ability to understand these interpretations in the original explanation, most families seem better able—if the philosophy is maintained in subsequent work—to mobilize their own strengths to meet disappointment than when more personalized and oversimplified reasons were given for certain families' not receiving children.

The above interpretations have had value in public relations also. Previously, the implication had usually been that if a family did not receive a child from an agency there must be something wrong with the family. This feeling existed even though it is well understood in adoption agencies, and probably is fairly well known in the general community, that adoptive applications greatly outnumber children available. Not only is the implication inaccurate and a source of unnecessary damage to the self-esteem of the applicant, but it also often caused the public to rise to the defense of families who were considered to be unjustly evaluated. Within the agency it is known that because of the number of families applying, selection must be made and the basis of selection will vary according to needs that shift as different children become available for adoption. Unless the number of children needing homes justifies the expense, most applications will not even be fully studied, and after study the decision to use or not use a home is reached only after reviewing complex and interrelated facts.

In addition to providing a more constructive framework for the service to the adoptive applicant and an intellectually defensible basis of interpretation to the community, the plan has had a direct effect on the attitudes of the staff members themselves. It has provided a structure within which genuine friendliness and interest would not imply that there was unlimited time to spend or that a child certainly would be forthcoming. Our earlier experience had shown that adoptive applicants are able to exert considerable pressure, both in and out of the interview situation, and when there is no workable method of handling this, the persons on the receiving end sometimes react with mixed feelings, which frequently can have an adverse effect on the applicant. The staff has been enthusiastic about the plan and looks back almost with disbelief to the days when a feeling of apprehension had to be overcome before many interviews lest the applicant as well as the application be rejected.

It seems clear that the plan has resulted in a more basic acceptance of the adoptive applicant, his right to apply, his right to fair and impartial consideration, his right to participate in the planning. By providing a workable solution for some of the gross and overwhelming problems rising out of volume, it has paved the way to improving the quality of service. With this foundation laid, it is hoped that more effective work can be done in the future.

CHAPTER 24

When a Couple Plans to Adopt a Baby

BEATRICE PRUSKI

Couples that apply to an adoption agency for a child often have very little idea of how the agency goes about getting children for adoption or of how it decides which applicants are to receive children. They are likely to feel that the process is mysterious and that the agency makes its decisions arbitrarily. When a couple does not receive a child for adoption they often resent this and feel that the agency must consider them in some way inferior.

Agencies use different methods of meeting this problem. One agency that uses a group technique in working with the applicants is the Los Angeles Adoption Institute, a non-profit, fee-supported agency. This agency serves not only couples who apply for a child, but the child's natural parents. And its first interest is the welfare of the child himself.

In the interest of the child, the agency wishes to make clear to all applicants just what its purposes are, how it proceeds, and what it requires of couples wishing to adopt a child. It has found that an effective way to do this is by means of a group meeting, not as a substitute for separate, individual interviews, but as a preparation for them.

Couples Face Same Problems

The group meeting gives the couples their first opportunity to talk with professional staff members of the agency. Before that, they have had only a brief conversation with a receptionist, who has checked their eligibility with regard to age, residence, citizenship, and length of marriage. The receptionist has noted also some additional information on race, religion, and number of children, has assured them of the agency's desire to be of service, and has explained that all general questions would be discussed at a meeting to be attended by a number of other couples who also were applying for a child.

The meeting is held in the evening; usually about 10 couples attend. Joining with other applicants brings home to each couple that they are not alone with their problem. Also, group discussion can modify the extremely personal point of view of an individual family's situation. Each couple is part of a group in which all have faced the question of sterility and are now taking the same chances of disappointment in trying to adopt a child. They feel that all will be treated alike.

The group meeting helps to set the tone for all later individual relations with the agency workers. At the time of this first contact there are 20 clients to 1 professional worker. The couples have the support of a group of other couples who hope to become adoptive parents. Their problems are immediately identified to some extent with the problems of the agency, and they are asked to join in trying to solve them. Through questions that other couples ask, which might not have occurred to them, they see the whole situation in broader terms. Also, people who do not easily formulate in words the things that concern them, or who are shy about asking, benefit through the verbal facility of others. The dominance of the professional worker is reduced to a minimum; and a more mature, a more cooperative, and a more nearly equal relationship is established at the outset.

When the Meeting Begins

The method of handling the meeting varies somewhat with the worker who acts as leader. Since people begin arriving at least 20 minutes early, this time needs to be used in some way other than having them sit around self-consciously. At first, couples were asked to write down their ideas about their adoption plans, but later a more flexible plan was followed. The leader gives out paper and suggests that the people jot down questions they wish to ask, but she also carries on conversation with those who prefer to talk. The discussion starts not later than 10 minutes after the designated time.

Discussion may start directly with the questions uppermost in the minds of the couples, and gradually may be shaped into a general outline; or the leader may follow an outline, allowing time for discussion of each point. Whichever method is followed, a number of fundamental questions always emerge, although the content differs somewhat at different meetings.

All groups ask about the origin of the agency, who is behind it, and how it is financed. Since the Institute is fee-supported, the leader explains this type of financing, as well as the method of paying the fees. This leads up to the agency's procedure for applicants; this is discussed and then a written statement of it is distributed for the group members to take home. Under this procedure, which aims to solve the problem of long lists of applicants and an indefinite waiting period, each couple's application moves according to definite time intervals, and the applicants always know where they stand.

Each group is asked whether they can think of a better plan. Although it is a long time since anyone has made a new suggestion, the discussion helps the applicants to realize that the agency is doing everything in its power to show them consideration.

Agency's Procedure Explained

Every group is interested in where we get our children, what we know about the child himself at the time of placement, and what we know about his background. The leader explains that the agency tells the adoptive parents all it knows about the child's background and makes clear that it would never place a child with a family that would be uneasy about any specific fact in his history. The role of heredity is discussed from the point of view of helping the applicants to clarify their own beliefs before the individual interview that each couple will have with a staff member. Only two definite points are made: (1) That we have no conclusive evidence on what is hereditary; (2) that many characteristics run in families, but that this does not necessarily mean that any particular characteristic, other than physical ones, is transmitted by heredity rather than by environment.

The applicants always ask, and are frankly told, what the agency is looking for in homes for the children. It is most gratifying to see how simply and spontaneously this discussion focuses on the needs of the child, rather than on the needs of the applicants.

The leader begins with the question, "Suppose that you had

to surrender a child of your own to be reared by strangers, what things would you want to be sure were present in that home and what things would you want to be sure were not there?"

All groups spontaneously place personality and emotional traits first. Experience has shown that it is best to keep this discussion in general terms. Too much detail in this field, particularly if illustrated by examples, tends to make some people uneasy and self-conscious in the individual interviews that are to come. Properly handled, however, this discussion makes for greater ease and frankness later. The mere fact that the applicants gain some idea of what the agency is looking for, instead of depending on rumor about agency standards, gives them much more assurance.

The agency is able to make the point that it does not bar people because of any specific experience of their own, such as a broken home in their childhood, or a divorce. It is interested only in what these experiences have done to them; and the final result may be favorable, since people who have met and solved problems are stronger than those who have not.

The group knows the agency does not consider itself infallible in evaluating their situation and that it needs their help. The worker explains fully the agency's attitudes on finances, living space, health, and life expectancy, and it has never met with anything but complete approval of these. Each couple sees, as a result of discussion, that the agency's standards are not artificial values of its own.

Every Adoption Involves Risks

It is well known that personal anxiety is often relieved through group discussion. People are able to ask questions that might be difficult for them in an individual interview.

For example, "If the child develops a handicap, will the agency take him back before the final adoption?" Couples usually ask this because they fear they might lose a child after they have become attached to him, but sometimes the question is whether they can return a child who is unsatisfactory to them, and what will be done about the fee in that case. They want to know what risks they take in regard to the child himself. The agency does not minimize these risks, especially since it believes in placing babies early in life.

Every group contains some people who are concerned about these risks, and some who dismiss the whole question on the ground that you take even greater risks with a child of your own. In the discussion, the group performs its own therapy for extreme attitudes of either type. Many couples have told the worker later that they felt she was overstressing these risks, and so the agency now tells the groups how very few real problems it has encountered regarding the children placed.

Major anxieties seem to concern the question of the applicants' own qualifications and the reputed strictness and artificiality of agency practices in general. Here too the group sets its own standards and performs its own therapy. Sometimes, although rarely, this discussion arouses such anxiety that a couple decides not to proceed with the application. Most people, however, feel enough security in their marriage, and at this point have enough faith in the agency's fairness, to go ahead in a much more relaxed frame of mind after the group discussion.

Interesting emotional reactions are often noticed during the meeting. Couples often move physically closer together and frequently hold each other's hands. Naturally they feel an implied challenge in the discussion of qualifications; and in the face of it, surrounded by other people experiencing the same challenge, a couple will become more conscious of their unity and of how much they mean to each other. One can sense their decision to stand by each other. The expression of their faith in each other seems to help them go through the rest of the procedure with greater frankness and courage.

Couples have frequently told the workers, and also have mentioned to outsiders, how much more information they have given than they had originally intended to give. When they are asked why, they usually answer, "Because we felt from the beginning that you cared what happened to us and would do the best you could for us." The agency feels that the close emotional unity of the group meeting has a great deal to do with setting this tone.

One of the chief ways in which the group meeting saves time later is that it stimulates the applicants to visualize themselves as possible parents before the individual interviews. Conscious effort is made to have them do this to prepare themselves to cooperate later in their interviews.

The agency is now trying to formulate the best content for group meetings in relation to the interviews. At the time of the individual interviews applicants are asked for comments on the group meeting. On specific points the comments are often constructively critical, and on the subject in general they are usually enthusiastic. People often tell the agency they have thought considerably about certain points afterward or have discussed them with friends.

Group Meeting Has Several Values

One value of the group meeting is the contribution it makes to the agency's own thinking and to clarification of policy. On a question that hinges on how people in general feel, an agency will gain more by bringing it up in a group meeting than by having the staff debate it among themselves. One such question is that of placement of a child with handicapped parents—whether or not such a child would be injured by community attitudes. This is a sensitive area today and one which no one can dismiss lightly in view of the number of men who returned handicapped from the war.

By the time the Institute set its policy on this, it had behind it the thinking and feeling of a number of the applicants, who certainly represent a broader sample of the community than does any agency staff. The couples talked very frankly on this point, with some differences of opinion but much fundamental agreement. It was evident that most of them felt that to preclude placement of a child in a home there must be some reason beyond the physical fact of a parent's handicap itself. They gave example after example of people they knew who were in this situation and of the neighborhood attitude and apparent effect on the children.

In group meetings, discussions of problems are kept general, but many couples remain to ask questions later about their personal situation. This also saves much time for everyone concerned, since special problems can be clarified before the couple makes another special trip for an interview. Through the discussion they become aware of problems that might otherwise not emerge until later in a personal interview.

As already noted, preparation for rejection of applications is achieved in the group meeting as it never could be through any number of individual interviews. The applicants know that only a few of the couples who are sitting there with them can possibly be given a child, because there are not enough children to go around. They know that all these people are sensitive about sterility, and that this condition is one of the main reasons why they are at the meeting.

The agency explains that the applicants will be notified of rejection simply by a form letter and tells why no reasons will be given at the time. The couples know that they will be told during the interview about tangible reasons such as finances or health or about anything they could change without getting involved in problems of psychotherapy.

When the couples are first asked if they would like to have reasons given, the answer is almost universally yes. However, the leader points out what it might do to a marriage if the reasons for rejection were focused solely on one person and not the other. Again, she shows that attempting such explanations would add to the size of the fee. She makes clear that if the explanations were given briefly and not followed up by help in solving the problems, the result would be at least nonconstructive and might be injurious. When the applicants stop to think of all these factors most of them come to agree with the agency practice. People with any degree of imagination or insight realize that in applying for a child they are not asking for discussion of deep emotional problems to which they may have already worked out some sort of adjustment, or which may not even exist.

The agency stresses that when it has nothing constructive to offer it has no desire to convince the couples that its decision is right, and there is always the possibility that its workers are mistaken. Although the agency must abide by its own best judgment in doing its job, no one is infallible in evaluating emotional traits and estimating their effect upon a child who is not yet there. It would be unfortunate if anxieties were aroused that might not even be based upon reality and that the agency is not prepared to work out with the applicants.

Not Enough Babies for All

There is no doubt that not giving reasons for a rejection can arouse great anxiety. However, it is made clear that because of the surplus of applicants, standards for acceptance are high, and therefore reasons for rejection are not necessarily serious.

It is true that, in spite of this preparation, some applicants do request reasons at the time of rejection, but the number is very small and the request is usually prefixed by the statement, "We know that this is contrary to your policy, but we hoped in this case . . ." Usually a restatement of the agency's position is sufficient to close the matter without great resentment, although the agency sees its share of people whose only desire is to strike out irrationally at something. However, for most reasonably well-adjusted people, and these make up the vast majority of couples who apply for babies to adopt, a good preparation for the rejection is found in the group meeting.

The group technique has proved so successful that the agency's director is now considering extending it in two other possible ways. One would be to have small groups of accepted applicants come together prior to receiving their child for a discussion of child care. The other would be for small groups of couples ready for final adoption to discuss the court procedure and questions of later child development.

CHAPTER 25

Competence and Conscience in Homefinding

DOROTHY HUTCHINSON

The source of this title has nothing to do with homefinding. I borrowed it from an article entitled "Conscience and the Undergraduate" in the April, 1955, issue of *The Atlantic Monthly,* written by President John Sloan Dickey of Dartmouth. This article is addressed, not to homefinders, but to the parents of the modern undergraduate in the "free-wheeling" liberal arts college, and it deals reassuringly with the old conflict between science and religion. It seemed to me the article conveyed an arresting idea which, when it is removed from its context, can be applied aptly to homefinding. President Dickey says that, in the liberal arts college, "neither competence nor conscience is taken straight. . . . it is the mixture that counts. . . . it is the human interplay between these two poles . . . that brings to a man those liberating and civilizing qualities men never quite define nor ever quite deny."

It was of interest to me to apply this idea about competence to homefinding and to see how competence on the job is affected by the conscience of the person doing the job. I have been struck by the relation of these two factors to each other in practice; how the mature, flexible conscience of the homefinder results in a voluntary opening up on the part of the foster parent; how, on the other hand, a too rigid conscience closes the door to the very relationship that enables a homefinder to evaluate a home accurately and to liberate it for use.

Competence in homefinding can be taught and thus learned. Knowledge of what to look for in foster parents—standards of living and of family relationships, methods of child care, and so on; in other words, knowledge of "what it takes" to be a foster parent—is essential to competence in homefinding. No amount of knowledge by itself, however, produces foster homes. It is the conscience of the worker which, in the enduring sense, determines whether or not his competence can be put to productive use.

Lack of Flexibility

Experience shows that it is in adoption studies that the homefinder's conscience is likely to tighten up. Here there is less flexibility. This is understandable. In adoption the homefinder's decision has lifelong results for the child and the adopting parents. Therefore, the responsibility of the worker lends itself to the demands of a more exacting conscience, with the result that the home studies show less flexibility and perspective on his part. I remember recently reading an adoptive study in which it was noted that the would-be adoptive mother, following a hysterectomy, had suffered a temporary mild depression. A nice young woman, happily married to a mature and understanding husband, she was reacting to every woman's most basic threat—not to be able to have a baby of her own, and not to be able to give a loved husband nature's greatest gift, a baby. After three months of living with this unwelcome fact, after three months of patient understanding on the part of her husband, she lifted herself out of her depression and went into sublimated action. She found a job with young children in a church-connected service. Thus she found creative satisfaction in her womanhood and some substitute fulfilment for her thwarted motherhood. She did not remain in her self-indulgent depression but liberated herself from it. She was moving psychologically in the direction of health. Her application to adopt a baby was part and parcel of the same healthy design. The point of this story is the overconscientious conscience of the homefinder, to whom the fact of a depression, per se, was a danger signal not to be taken lightly, and correctly so. However, the homefinder's responsibility to accept or to deny this application influenced her conscience to a point of seeing only the depression, not how the applicant had resolved this. In other words, the fact of depression stood alone without evaluation of its nature, its connection with a real event, and its healthy solution. An overburdened conscience rearranged the evaluation picture, putting undue weighting on a false pathology. What seemed a depression was really a period of normal mourning.

The above story suggests a social work conscience superimposed upon a personal conscience. By the former I mean specifically a conscience that has absorbed indiscriminately the culture, the standards, the values deeply imbedded in years of social work practice in general, and of adoption practice in particular. One might call this a pseudo-professional conscience —one which, in this case, adheres fixedly to set standards of healthy personality for all adoptive applicants. The point overlooked is that many healthy people who wish to adopt a baby have lived through unhealthy experiences. The crux of the matter is not necessarily the unhealthy experience itself, but what the person has done with his life in spite of this experience: whether he now enjoys release from its traumatic effects or whether he is still chained by its power over him; whether the problem has evaporated or whether its infection is still a source of psychic irritation and suffering.

I would be the last person to deny that we must have standards for all foster and adoptive homes. Surely, without these we fail in our responsibility to children. On the other hand, there is such a thing as applying a particular standard in a wholesale fashion without regard to individual factors. There is also such a thing as preferred behavior projected by us onto those who wish to take children into their homes. Many times I have read in adoptive studies that during the study itself the parents have been discouraged from buying baby equipment (such as a crib or a carriage) ahead of time, meaning before the study is complete and the home has received a stamp of official approval. The parents' action is frequently looked upon with a certain amount of hidden fear on the part of the homefinder. He sees the parents as persons who unwittingly deny the worker's evaluative responsibility; who take the situation into their own hands and, by so doing, fail to acknowledge dependency on the agency. To me, looking unfavorably on such behavior is a little ridiculous. After all, if a couple want a baby enough to prepare ahead as they would for their own, what is wrong with this, even if they buy something more expensive than a crib. If a couple have confidence in their being accepted before the homefinder is ready to say so, what is wrong with this? Wherein lies the danger? In little and big situations like this our professional doubts in regard to potential adoptive couples have to be checked against a knowledge of healthy behavior for all couples having babies, not against standards arising from overactive consciences. Such consciences frequently are derived from a social work culture so weighted in pathology that we tend to overlook health and normality. Real competence in homefinding means the unlocking of pertinent data necessary to the making of a sound judgment and the objective examination of these data unencumbered by the temptation to use face-saving clichés and so-called official standards.

Competence in homefinding emphasizes bringing the adoptive parents in on the process itself. We want them to participate in what is happening to them. We say we want the study to be a mutual living event of a positive character rather than a stereotyped investigation, as the study is so often conceived of by the applicants themselves. The theory that the would-be adoptive parent should share in all the steps taken by the homefinder in the process of approving his home would seem open to doubt. How many applicants are really interested in this process? In my opinion, the prevalent idea held by adoptive applicants— that the home study is "red tape"—comes from our need to make it unmistakably a professional experience for ourselves, and this, in turn, comes from our own insecurity in this greatest of all social work responsibilities.

I see nothing wrong about making the home study both professional in quality and educational to the applicants, but the crux of the matter would lie in how this is done. If we overemphasize the process, we play up to our own need, not to theirs. The applicants are likely to respond with annoyance and hostility if our interviewing and our interpretations seem unnatural to them; that is, if our words, questions, and manner are strange and not in accord with their life experiences and values. The most truly professional interviewing always feels natural to the person interviewed, and adoptive applicants are no exception. If a woman is having her own baby she wants to see her doctor regularly because she knows his knowledge and skill mean safety for herself and her baby. The adoptive mother is also getting a baby. She wants to feel safe, too. She wants the acceptance of the homefinder. She wants his knowledge and skill to bring about a safe placement; she has not counted on a mysterious analysis of her personal qualities. The own mother knows that her doctor is not concerned with her goodness or her badness as a person, but only with her pregnancy. But the adoptive parent, whose heart is set on a baby, is threatened by the homefinder's evaluation of her personality and of her family relationships. In other words, goodness and badness, not her need, now seem to her to take precedence. Herein lies the tremendous dilemma in homefinding. How to meet need and, at the same time, to say yes or no to this need, is the rub. How to satisfy the desire for a baby and eventually to approve or to disapprove of this desire is, in essence, the inherent conflict in the homefinder's responsibility. It is this that makes him take refuge in both personal and professional defenses. The answers to these questions are not easy, but there are answers.

Freeing the Conscience

In the *Atlantic Monthly* article originally referred to, President Dickey speaks of the twin and dual purpose of the American liberal arts college, that is, "to see men made whole in both competence and conscience." He says further, "There is almost no form or field of learning that does not multiply a man's power economically, socially, politically, or physically" (and, we could add, psychologically). He adds, "The creation of competence at every level of education is commonplace," but "it is the job of the college to keep competence civilized." In referring to the liberal arts college he writes, "the cause of liberal education will not be overrun by vocationalism if the college holds to its birthright and remains committed as a matter of purpose to serious concern with the issues of conscience. A concern for the choice of good and the rejection of evil in an institution of liberal learning quickens all humanistic studies and prevents our increasing reliance on the physical and social sciences from smothering those intuitive insights which both produce and spring from goodness in a man. . . . To create the power of competence without creating a corresponding sense of moral direction to guide the use of that power is bad education," and finally he adds, " 'The doubting mind always seemed to me a part of the believing mind.' The understanding of such paradox is the fruit of full maturity."

Applying the above thoughts to the work and responsibility of the homefinder, it would seem that real competence cannot be dissociated from the affairs of the conscience; in other words, the homefinder, to be competent, needs to be freed to a reasonably healthy degree from those infantile conflicts that affect his ability to evaluate accurately, objectively, and generously. I am

297

thinking of such conflicts as those connected with authority, dependency, and sex. As a liberated person the homefinder is able to take on the evaluative responsibility without too much wear and tear on himself. His superego is easy and non-exacting because it is no longer bound by the forgotten problems of childhood. His ego does not have to be mollified by a childish "bad" conscience. Thus, he is able to use his competent knowledge of behavior to diagnose and to evaluate more accurately. He can like and say no at the same time because he is "for" the applicants, good or bad. His acceptance of them is felt by them. His interviewing seems pertinent and natural and within the culture and experience of the adoptive parent.

All this is to say that maturity in homefinding means the worker can doubt and believe in the applicants at the same time. He may have doubts about the wisdom of their plans, about their capacity for parenthood, about their happiness in this venture, but such doubts are an integral part of his acceptance of them as people and of their need, whatever this may be. His acceptance of and belief in them as people enable him to doubt in their behalf and for their best interest. Belief and doubt are opposite sides of the same coin; they cannot be integrated without a positive transference won by the homefinder. His doubt also acts as a safety device against his need to find the perfect home, the perfect marriage, and the perfect child for the perfect family. Surely, the responsibility of the homefinder is psychologically a keenly demanding one.

The homefinder is faced with many variables in the lives of many people. In all home studies he weaves his way through to a decision, using a knowledge of people and of behavior which is tempered with a kind of generous understanding that we call acceptance. His competence and his conscience are familiar with the fact that healthy and unhealthy behavior are quite close together, like the blood relations they really are. For example, there are many quite normal people who have masochistic or sadistic elements in their personality. Some masochistically inclined women will do wonders for handicapped babies. With them they will have uncommon patience and understanding; they will defend the child who needs defending, and out of love for him and identification with him will attack aggressively those who pity the child. Such a woman can render great service if our professional conscience will allow her to do so.

To me it is of great interest that we classify foster and

adoptive parents as "approved," "rejected," "refused," and so on, when actually we *always* approve, in the sense of acceptance, and we *never* reject applicants as people. Such classifications suggest appeasement and hostility when neither should be present. Perhaps we seize on these terms to appease a troublesome conscience.

Competence and conscience go hand in hand. As President Dickey suggests, conscience is what civilizes or humanizes our competence. By this he means (I am sure) a generous, flexible conscience, one that likes itself and can live with itself without conflict and the need to project. The homefinder integrates conscience with competence. He can doubt and "believe in" at the same time. His doubt is mature because it is without suspicion. His acceptance is not conditional. His conscience is generous to all people, but especially to his own self, as it should be.

CHAPTER 26

Casework Considerations in Rejecting the Adoption Application

RUTH MICHAELS

The primary purpose of an adoption agency is to find the best homes possible for the children entrusted to its care. In the course of accomplishing this end, the agency meets the requests of an equivalent number of families wishing to adopt children. But the service is geared to the needs of children rather than those of families; if it is occasionally necessary to choose between a possible injustice to a family and a possible injustice to a child, the agency must, by virtue of its essential responsibility, protect the child.

There are always some applicants unsuitable as prospective parents because of their inability to provide adequate maintenance, or their inability to function physically or psychologically as parents. Even after eliminating these families, however, the agency is forced, by the extreme disproportion between the number of children available for adoption and the number of families wanting to adopt, to refuse children to many who would probably do at least as good a job with a child as the majority of biological parents in the community, and who would qualify if the problem were that of finding adequate homes for large numbers of homeless children.

Almost all the couples wishing to adopt feel that a child is important to their happiness and that they are able to provide adequately for a child. At the present time, however, many adoption agencies are finding that they have only one tenth the number of children requested. In the difficult selective job, the agency naturally chooses those families who seem most likely to provide a setting where a child can grow freely, according to his own needs and capacities.

The Selective Process

A small proportion of applicants can be ruled out without an interview. These are couples ineligible because they do not meet certain requirements of the agency; for example, persons living outside the geographic area the agency serves; single persons; couples past the age limit; couples with children of their own, or with two or more adopted children.

A careful casework interview is held with all other families. The purpose of this initial interview is to give the prospective parents the opportunity to discuss their interest in adoption, what they have to offer the prospective child, and how they hope a child will meet their needs; it enables them to learn the facts of adoption—its risks, protections, and waiting time. This first interview helps the applicants determine their own readiness to file an application in the face of these realities and enables the agency to sift requests sharply, selecting those homes that convey the initial impression of being able to offer a rich, wholesome, emotional life to a child. Ordinarily this intake process consists of one joint interview, although a second interview with either prospective adoptive parent or both may be held if the worker feels it is necessary.

Obviously, an agency cannot take the responsibility for permanent placement of a child on the basis of one or two interviews. Before the definite decision can be reached, the agency must know a great deal more about a family, with material gathered from a succession of interviews with both applicants, separately and together, in their home and in the office. The home study consists of such interviews with the applicants and, if they seem acceptable, of physical examinations and use of references as well. Finally, if the home is approved, there remains the process of selecting a particular child, suitable for this family in general appearance, background, health history, temperament, and expectation of intellectual development.

Intake as the Major Sifting Ground

Because of the disproportion between requests and available children, it seems advisable to set controls on the number of

301

families placed on the waiting list. Even with controls, a family usually must wait two years before a home study is begun, and sometimes even longer. In this time, while waiting hopefully and fearfully, they develop a tremendous stake in approval of their home. When they are then engaged in full and intimate discussion of their vital relationships, so that their probable way of handling the new, untested relationship of parenthood can be evaluated, rejection must carry the implication that somewhere in this self-revelation they have betrayed their unfitness for parenthood.

As part, then, of our essential responsibility to the family, it would seem fairer and kinder to do the bulk of sifting at intake, accepting only a limited number of applications for the waiting list, and letting all other families know that their applications cannot be accepted. It seems better to make a decision on the basis of known limits and make this decision known to the families who will not be able to receive a child from the agency than to encourage them to build up false hopes.

Aim of the Selective Process

In selecting the families who may file applications, we recognize that although we are in a position to set high standards, no family is ever perfect as long as families are composed of human beings. We realize that all living has its risks, and that we cannot foresee all the risks and potential problems that may arise. We do try to select families who will not add to these unpredictable risks additional serious hazards inherent in their essential rigidities or lack of warmth, or in their wish to have a child meet their own neurotic needs or maintain or change the marital balance. Our ultimate aim is to select parents who have a mutually satisfying marriage and who are sufficiently mature so that a child will not be thrown into a competitive situation with one parent for the other's love and attention. It is important that the man be an adequate father-image and the woman an adequate mother-image; that both have accepted the fact that their children will not be biologically their own and can take on an adopted child with a real sense of parenthood; and that both be free from the kind of general free-floating anxiety that impairs the capacity to relate to the needs of others.[1]

The intake process eliminates not only the families who show

---

[1] For further discussion of casework criteria for adoptive parents, *see* "The Selection of Adoptive Parents: A Casework Responsibility," by Ruth F. Brenner, Child Welfare League of America *Bulletin*, December, 1946, p. 1.

gross incapacity to meet these psychological criteria but also those who raise doubt of their ability to meet such standards; if there were several times as many children, it would be appropriate to explore the nature and extent of the actual risk in the patterns and attitudes the latter group present because they often have many positive things to offer a child.

The Adoptive Applicant

In this curious reversal of normal social agency practice—being placed in the position of refusing the service requested to about 85 to 90 per cent of the persons applying—we have an obligation to understand the emotional pressure that pervades an adoptive application and what happens to the person in the process of our "sifting."

Adoptive applicants are couples who, for some reason not of their own choosing, have been unable to have their own child. They vary widely in the strength of their initial impulse to have a child and in the length of time that they have been trying; but even those who have been least sure that they wanted to have children have always assumed that the choice was theirs. Usually, they have had a long series of medical examinations. Sometimes the cause and definiteness of sterility have been determined quickly and definitely, and they know, for instance, that the man has a complete absence of live sperm cells. More often, there has been a long series of diagnostic tests and therapeutic procedures, and sometimes several attempts at artificial insemination, disturbing both to the husband and to the wife. During this time, the couple's sexual life has been focused on the attempt to conceive, with times and positions for intercourse determined by medical prescription in the effort to have a child, rather than by spontaneous affectional impulse, to a degree often detrimental to the enjoyment of their sexual relationship. And increasingly, as the attempts and the treatments were not productive, has come the unanswerable and disturbing question, "What is wrong with me?"

When people are reasonably mature and secure in themselves and in their marriage, this is an experience which, although unpleasant and to some degree disturbing to everyone, can be incorporated without basic damage to their capacity to function in their personal relationships. However, for many people, the knowledge of their sterility is another blow to an already shaken and damaged sense of their own masculinity or femininity. Often they do not have the support that comes with the knowledge that they are satisfying and satisfied marriage partners. Infertility therefore represents a second major failure in the essential function of being a man or a woman.

At the time of application, then, many adoptive parents are feeling a deep anxiety about themselves and their own worth and a real uncertainty about their capacity to be good and acceptable parents. Often, too, they have an unspoken concern about whether their partners continue to want them or are regretting the marriage. And because persons who are burdened with anxiety and a need for reassurance are often least free to relate to a child's needs, they are frequently those to whom, in view of its own need to limit and select, the agency must deal a second denial of their impulse to parenthood, creating for them another crucial failure.

Rejection of the request to adopt, therefore, almost always comes after at least one blow to the person's sense of personal worth and sexual adequacy, and it always carries with it the further negative experience of having the essential control of the planning of family life taken out of one's hands.

The agency, in rejecting, is placed in the position of administering this blow. There is no softness that can remove entirely the sting of being denied parenthood for the second time—first by life, and then by society. There is small comfort for the applicants in the knowledge that it is a stringent selective process that necessitates the denial; for there always is an awareness that others have been chosen for parenthood, and they have not. Perhaps for those whose own insecurities have made sterility itself an unbearable threat to their integrity as men and women, refusal necessarily carries with it the weight of further trauma.

It is part of the adoption agency's responsibility, however, to minimize the destructiveness of rejection as much as possible for each applicant. The person wanting to adopt brings his concern and his need to the agency, and his experience with the agency has important emotional connotations. He is not an inanimate object, to be graded and sifted, accepted or tossed aside. He is a person who, in his very coming, is living through a deep-rooted emotional crisis. He is as much the agency's client as is the child to be placed. We have a responsibility to use our psychological knowledge to understand what he is going through, and to apply all our understanding and skill toward helping him through that crisis with a minimum of damage.

304

Helping Withdraw the Application

The most helpful service the intake worker can give to the adoptive parents who must be refused is to help them withdraw their request to adopt, thus avoiding altogether the traumatic implications of refusal.

If it is possible for people to participate in the decision that they will not adopt a child, their childlessness is no longer something that a depriving life and a depriving society have forced upon them, but represents a choice they have made themselves. It is sometimes possible to help applicants who have conflict and indecision about adoption to recognize their ambivalence or unrealistic motives, so that they make their own withdrawal.

> Mr. and Mrs. Black came in four months after losing a 3-year-old son suddenly, and three months after Mrs. B bore a still-born premature baby. They blamed the doctor for not coming at once when they reported their boy's early symptoms, and it became evident that they also blamed themselves for not calling another doctor or using an emergency hospital. The worker said that although this was natural, certainly they had a right to trust the judgment of the physician whose province this was, and they evidently did everything possible to make the situation clear to him and to put pressure on him to come. If he, with his medical knowledge, could not realize the seriousness of the sudden illness, how could they expect it of themselves?
>
> It developed that they wanted to adopt because of their fear of what happened to their own children, and their hope that this could be a quick and ready-made way to bypass the risks of having their own. The worker helped them to see that adoption, with its waiting time and risk of elimination because of the shortage of babies, was no easy answer; that living with any growing child carried risks of pain and loss; and that the real question was whether, after an experience like theirs, they could bear to take those risks again with any child, own or adopted. They themselves saw that adoptive parenthood, like biological parenthood, carried uncertainties they were not sure they could bear; and that if they really could face the anxieties of parenthood, they might perhaps as well take a chance on their own child as on adoption. They decided to withdraw their request to adopt until they had settled this for themselves, reserving the right to return if they decided that adoption was

the risk they wanted to try. They did not again communicate with us.

Sometimes, when the husband and wife differ in their readiness to consider adoption, the intake interview can be used to help them see their own unreadiness to go through with the process:

Mr. and Mrs. Weiss came about the adoption of an infant. It had not been absolutely determined that they could not have their own child, although the chances were slim; and Mrs. W felt that she did not want to wait any longer for a child. Mr. W brought out many questions about the effects of heredity on a child and how adopted children turn out. The worker, recognizing his fear, helped them see that they had some difference in their readiness for adoption; and Mr. W could say that he would still prefer to have his own child. Both felt that Mr. W was the sort of person who needed to examine the risks and possibilities of an important new venture thoroughly before entering into it. The worker agreed that certainly adoption was important, and that people should be sure they wanted to take the risks involved before attempting it.

The worker commented that evidently Mr. W was not sure he could feel comfortable about being a parent to a child strangers had borne. He enlarged on his own question and fear. The worker told them about the shortage of children, and the need of the agency to limit applications drastically, saying that one of the things the agency needed to know in deciding which families to add to the long waiting lists was which were most likely to feel like parents to children placed with them, and that it would be hard for us to know this when the Weisses did not yet know it themselves. The worker suggested that perhaps this was something they needed to settle for themselves first.

Mr. W seemed very relieved, and Mrs. W agreed that they should withdraw their request for the present, and explore the possibilities of having their own baby. They could then decide whether, if they absolutely could not have their own, they preferred to accept the risks Mr. W feared in adoption or the possibility of a childless marriage.

If the conflict is of such proportions that it would in itself be a cause for rejecting the request, a skilful interview often can help applicants to decide upon such withdrawals, which provide

306

the soundest, most constructive way out for the clients when they themselves are conflicted about adoption or parenthood.

The Worker's Attitude as Help

The application of the social worker's professional knowledge of personality and of diagnostic skills in the selection of adoptive parents is comparatively new. In adapting casework knowledge to this group of clients, it is important to set up criteria for adoptive parents based on what we know of personality and family relationships, and diagnostic techniques to help us determine whether a family can meet these criteria. In the pressure of setting up criteria, we have sometimes lost sight of the client's place within the casework process, and the ways in which we can make the interviewing experience a constructive and helpful one for him.

In the face of the deep significance to the client of rejection for adoptive parenthood and the large number who must realistically be refused, it seems at first glance paradoxical to speak of "help" to the client we are refusing. And yet, as we review our experience, we find that there are many ways of saying "no," and that although we cannot entirely remove the pain of rejection, we can be sensitive to the risk of making it worse. An unsympathetic or critical attitude that devaluates the person or the importance of the decision makes it harder for the client to live with the fact of rejection. Conversely, whatever we can do to convey to the client our essential respect for him and recognition of what he has to offer a child helps to reduce his sense of failure and to bolster his confidence in his adequacy, even though he does not get a child.

The most important single factor the worker can introduce to make rejection bearable is honest respect for the client who must be refused. It would be an easy and fatal error, because of the need for extreme selectivity, to assume that if we look hard enough, we shall find among the clients coming a few perfect couples whom we can accept, and that therefore any immaturity revealed by the client should be disqualifying. In a matter of such importance, the worker owes it to each family to evaluate carefully the relationship-patterns and attitudes they bring to adoption, and the degree to which their individual patterns and attitudes constitute a serious hazard to an adopted child. Although the shortage of children results in very high standards for prospective adoptive families, rejection, far from being arbitrary, must be based on cause—on the inability of each family to meet the standards set. Rejection must be based on sound diagnostic skills, or it is quixotic and irresponsible.

Mr. and Mrs. Stone exemplify a family whose application was refused because of the psychological risk to a child, although it was recognized that they had much to give to a child.

Mr. and Mrs. S were in their early 30's, and had been married for seven years. They both had lowered fertility, and their doctor had advised them that they probably could not have a child of their own. They had some experience with children and enjoyed those in their families. It quickly became clear, in their attitudes and discussion, that Mr. S adored Mrs. S, who was very beautiful, who came from a family more secure in their economic and social positions than his own, and who, he said, had always seemed a kind of fairy-tale princess to him.

They wanted a baby; and Mrs. S said she would consider only a little girl. It seemed they would not be concerned about illegitimacy and had no rigid specifications about a child's background. However, Mrs. S stressed that it was essential that the child be pretty. She herself, she said, was the daughter of a beautiful and talented mother; she knew how a child compared herself, under such circumstances, with her mother; and she felt a child who was not pretty would suffer by the comparison, and would have a serious psychological problem in growing up.

There is a narcissistic element in all parenthood which operates to further the parental attachment. If Mrs. S had a daughter of her own who did not turn out to be beautiful, she might still be able to identify positively with this child, who was "flesh of her flesh and bone of her bone," and accept her fully. However, in setting such a standard as beauty for an adopted child, Mrs. S already displayed elements of rejection; if a baby, pretty in infancy, failed to meet her standards of beauty as she grew up, Mrs. S might have difficulty in identifying with her and accepting her fully. It also seemed that Mrs. S, who even in thinking about a child saw the possible competition between mother and daughter as a risk for the child, might find herself in a serious and mutually destructive rivalry situation with a growing daughter, younger than herself and also pretty, who might eventually threaten her position as Mr. S's fairy-tale princess.

The worker explained the adoption situation, the long waiting lists, and the agency's decision to let families know immediately if there was no chance of including them, rather than giving them false hopes; and said that final decision was made by a reviewing committee, who went over all the reports of couples our intake workers thought would be good parents. A report would of course be submitted about the S's. It would say that they were young, attractive, intelligent, and well educated; that they seemed to have a really good marriage; that they had many friends and a variety of interests; that they could provide a comfortable livelihood for their family and would unquestionably do their very best for a child.

Yet it was only fair to warn them that even though we knew all these things and considered them good for a child, it was likely that the committee would not accept an application from them. Intake was being kept open chiefly so that we could ourselves explain to families the critical adoption situation and the fact that we were being forced to turn down even very fine families because of the shortage of children. The token number of applications being issued were usually going to families who would really be suitable for the sort of child we had fewest families waiting for. About 85 per cent of the families waiting, like Mr. and Mrs. S, wanted a girl; and most of them, also like the S's, were pretty alert people, with whom we would place only a child with good expectation of intellectual development. Half of our children, on the other hand, were boys; and only a small percentage gave clear indication in infancy of really good intellectual expectancy. Families needing the kind of child they had in mind, therefore, had very little chance of filing application, even when we were so favorably impressed with what they could give a child.

Preparation for Rejection

All the techniques for helping a client to accept the agency's refusal of his request should be based upon the assumption that everyone who applies has at least an impulse to have a child and to care for it, the intention of doing a good job, and something to give some child. This is so even though he may need to demand too much from a child in return, and even though what he has to give may not be sufficient to create an atmosphere of growth.

Therefore, the worker, during the intake interview, must be alert to opportunities to convey to every client a warm acceptance of him, and a respect for the qualities in his home which would be good for a child of his. When his request is to be refused, however, it is important to let him know that unfortunately, even with all he has to bring to parenthood, there is a strong possibility that he may be refused at this point. As far as possible, the onus of failure to obtain a child should be placed on the external adoption situation beyond his control and the agency's.

Thus it will help the client whose request is rejected to know clearly the realities of adoption. He should be told how few children there are in comparison with the demand for them, and why this is so in a world where so many children lack the emotional and economic necessities of living. He should know that of all the families who want children and would be good parents, the agency can select only a certain per cent (10 per cent in our agency). He needs to know that whatever his own need for a child, the agency is responsible for selecting homes geared to the needs of the children in its care; that not every "good" family is good for every child, and not every child can make every family happy; and that the agency has to take the ultimate responsibility for the choice and the decision.

He should be told of the tangible factors in his situation less threatening as a basis for rejection than his own speculations of inadequacy that militate against his application. A couple close to the agency's age limit can know that one of the considerations in the final decision is age, and that in so necessarily stringent a selective process, all things being equal, preference is given to people who are young and will still be young with a growing and adolescent child. Where the family to be refused still have a good possibility of having their own child, they should be told that when so many must be denied, preference is given to those who know definitely that they can have no other chance for parenthood.

In every way possible, throughout the interview, it is important to convey the sense that though we may need to reject, it is the application we are rejecting and not the applicant.

In our own agency we have felt that the worker should prepare the family for this rejection so that it will not come as an incomprehensible blow; the final rejection, however, is sent in written form, after a brief interval, to give the family an additional sense of having been fairly and seriously considered. Because we realize the importance of the kind of letter the family receives, we have given much thought to the composition of a letter (worked out and contributed to by the whole staff) which is used, with variations to suit the family's individual situation, so that we can all be sure that each letter, though sent by different workers, conveys the personal attitudes and factual explanation we feel to be most helpful to the family.

Protection of the Client's Defenses

The client coming to an adoption agency, unlike the clients of many other social agencies, usually comes as a person who is functioning acceptably to himself, with his defenses threatened by the painful knowledge of his sterility and its implications for him, but by and large still in good working order. The problems that we see because of our own training and skill are usually problems that he has no intention of sharing with us, and often things he does not know or want to know himself. Certainly, if we feel that his inner problem is such that he cannot provide the opportunity for growth and free development for a child for whom we are responsible, we cannot place a child with him, however intense his belief that a child and only a child can meet his personal needs. But even when we feel that he is neurotic or involved in personal or marital difficulty or has an unhealthy need for a child, we can only rarely refer him for casework or psychiatric help. To question his own solution (unless he has his own question about it which can be brought out) by offering him therapy instead of a child, with or without the promise that he might if treated be accepted as an adoptive applicant, directly attacks the defenses by which he lives, and intensifies the sense of having been weighed and found wanting. Because people cannot have their own child and have, therefore, come to us to see if they can get one through adoption, this gives us no right to stir up discomfort with their own capacity to function, and to add to the anxiety about themselves that may be created by their lives, personalities, and inability to become parents biologically or through adoption. A man may show many compulsive traits, for example, and yet be efficient on his job and a good husband to his wife. We would not want to place a child under the pressure of his compulsive standards, but neither should we imply that we think the standards he lives by are excessively high and that he requires treatment.

Conclusion

The adoption agency has an essential responsibility for maintaining the defenses of the people it cannot help, for supporting their functioning at the level existing when they come, and for seeing that the experience of making application does not make it harder for them to live with themselves and each other.

The caseworker doing adoptive intake can be caught between the impulse to give and the need to deny to so many the service requested; yet this kind of interviewing, like all casework interviewing, can in itself be a helpful service, and one challenging the worker's creativity and skill. A worker who can help a person being refused parenthood to go through the experience without further damage to his personality is giving real, highly skilled help. Only as we sharpen and amplify our techniques with the objective of giving such help to all people coming to us —though we may be able to give children to only a comparative few—are we meeting the full responsibility of the adoption agency to its community.

CHAPTER 27

The Adoptive Foster Parent

CONSTANCE RATHBUN

In an adoptive home study, the trained worker must recognize not only the agency limitations and her own subjective error but the unconscious drives and conflicts motivating the decision of applicants who wish to adopt, as well as their consciously expressed needs and preferences. The surprisingly small amount of literature on adoptions has so far concerned itself only slightly with the mixed feelings associated with the all important desire for a child. Only as we are aware of this ambivalence, of wanting and not wanting, and of the anxieties often indirectly expressed but stemming from such divided feelings, can we judge with some accuracy and skill who will be suitable parents for a given child. Our responsibility is to recognize when common fears or uncertainties, normal in a given context, become translated into something more neurotic that might play havoc with the child's future security.

Emotional Needs of Worker Affecting Evaluation

Before discussing some of the problems involved in the evaluation of adoptive parents, I should like to mention briefly the needs of the worker which are met in this particular profession. The choice of vocation in the child welfare field is often determined by an overidentification with the child. Especially in the field of adoption one finds such motivation. Unsolved emotional conflicts of childhood may lead the worker into this branch of child welfare where accepted power and authority are satisfying to her, or where legitimate concern with the child can play into her repressed maternal needs. Unsatisfactory relations with her own parents may send her on a will o' the wisp hunt for perfect adoptive parents. Because her conception of ideal parent figures has no counterpart in reality, and because she has so much anxiety about this subject, it may be very difficult for her to arrive at any final decision about the qualifications for parenthood of the applicants whom she is interviewing. If she wants very much to have a child of her own but is unable to, she is in a most difficult position to judge rationally when it is wise to refuse the requests of applicants experiencing a similar frustration. Thus before initiating any home study she must know with some clarity what subjective factors will inevitably weight her own conclusions.

Anxieties of Applicant

It probably requires a fair amount of "screwing up of courage" for many people to come to a social agency for help with this tremendously important and very personal problem. Most initial interviews, regardless of the content, are characterized by tension, self-consciousness, and uncertainty as to what the agency wants in the way of information and what its criteria are for good parents. In this first contact with the worker some expression of anxiety by the applicant is inevitable and normal. Where, for example, there has been the recent loss of an only child or perhaps repeated miscarriages, it is not uncommon for self control to crack, as this subject, fraught with so much feeling is touched upon. Even those who have not had to adjust to such experiences may be apprehensive when facing a professionally trained worker. They may have odd ideas of this species gathered from reading *Lily Crackle* or from third hand tales of someone who went to a welfare agency for financial help. A note of resentment creeps into their tone as they say theirs "is just another application filed away alphabetically with myriads of others." They may, at the end of an interview, say rather naively that this hasn't been as bad as they expected, which makes one wonder how grim was the anticipation. Another common anxiety is caused by the inevitable element of competition between applicants. They realize that there are not nearly enough children to go around, that in a sense they are bidding against other applicants, and so they want to create as favorable an impression as possible on the worker. Some can express directly their insecurity about this by asking what things we feel to be most important in judging families, and how we decide between the many on our lists. Most, however, assuming we want to know the more obvious points of age, religion, income, etc., are willing to talk freely about these but remain perplexed as to what subtler factors we may consider even more significant in evaluating them as prospective parents. The attitude of judging by the worker and the feeling of being judged by the applicant cannot be disguised by the label "adoptive home study" and, alas, we have no Dun and Bradstreet rating emotional stability, to which we can refer with ease and accuracy.

Attitude Regarding Childlessness

After sorting out adoption applications according to the more obvious categories of age, religion and economic status, concerning which each agency has its own policies, the worker faces early in the interviewing process the question of why a child is wanted. Most of the people seen are for one reason or another unable to have a child of their own. Sterility and the attitude of the client toward it must be considered. Dr. Florence Clothier writes that "failure in this all important biological function is in itself a source of the deepest anxiety and insecurity."[1] Some do express directly their feelings of helplessness and anger at a vindictive fate. One applicant labeled bitterly her inability to conceive as "a slap in the face." Many resent the apparent injustice in the denial of children to those who want them most and the ease of reproduction by those who do not seem to care. They resent the shortage of children available for adoption. They would frankly welcome, they sometimes say, a rise in the illegitimacy rate, unaware of the social and psychological implications of such a statement. Not long ago a husband who was obviously a conservative solid citizen, discouraged by long waiting lists, said that it would be almost worthwhile to pay some girl to get herself illegitimately pregnant, a point of view surely inconsistent with the rest of his moral code. His concern was much less with pure logic than with finding a way to meet his own deep emotional need.

Attitude Toward Medical Study

Social workers should be better informed on current concepts concerning the causes of sterility. Research in this field has

[1] Clothier, Florence. *Adoption Procedure and the Community.* Mental Hygiene xxv: 2, p. 200.

advanced markedly in the past fifteen years. In the past the family physician commonly told his patient that an infantile uterus was the reason she could never become pregnant. Now it is recognized that sterility is a relative term and may have multiple causation. In a hundred sterility cases studied, the average number of factors per case was 4.81, with about one-third on the male side and the remaining two-thirds on that of the female.[2] Most cases, however, showed a division of responsibility between the two sexes. At the present time there seems to be less resistance on the part of the man to submit to a complete sterility study, and less inclination to allocate to his wife all blame for lack of children. Conversely though, there is the wife who has been told there is no reason why she can not become pregnant so far as her own health is concerned, but who is overprotective of her husband's inertia here. She seems content to rest her case with the adoption agency on some such statement that the mumps her husband had in childhood made him sterile, though she has no clinical verification of this opinion. The attitude of such couples toward further medical study is worth exploration by the social worker and may be indicative of their deeper feeling about having a child. Reluctance to accept such a suggestion always raises the question why. Assuming for purposes of argument that a way can be devised for most couples to find this sort of medical attention, in spite of difficulties in obtaining medical services, what about those who could but who will not make any further effort in this direction? My feeling is that in such instances this unwillingness may be the expression of a deeply ambivalent attitude toward having a child, and that it is in effect almost an unconscious wish to have the agency recognize the part of them that does not want a child and so perhaps refuse their application.

Functional Sterility

Relevant to this is the controversial question of functional sterility. As defined by Dr. Robert Knight it includes those cases in which "the generative organs seem to be normal, but conception does not occur, even though no contraceptive measures are used."[3] When a person who has been unable to conceive adopts a child and then becomes pregnant, Dr. Knight assumes that an unconscious opposition to childbearing might have been responsible for this earlier functional sterility. The

---

[2] Meaker, Samuel. *Human Sterility.* Williams & Wilkins. Baltimore, 1934. p. 73.
[3] Knight, Robert. *Some Problems Involved in Selecting and Rearing Adopted Children.* Bulletin of the Menninger Clinic. Vol. 5. No. 3.

mechanism of this is still a matter of hypothesis and as such outside the scope of the adoption worker. However, since most people prefer to have their own children if at all possible, it is our concern that everything reasonable to accomplish this end should be tried before adoption. In some instances it may be possible through case work to help resistant individuals accept a more accurate diagnosis and possible treatment, and so pave the way to having their own child. When strong negative feelings about children are revealed, the agency should, as Dr. Knight points out, exclude such individuals as acceptable foster parents. The inequalities of supply and demand tend to weight the adoption applications in favor of those whose sterility is definitely established, and who would otherwise be denied the experience of parenthood. The hazards of adjustment in that family constellation of own and adopted child should make most workers rather wary of placing a child with a couple who may later be able to have their own. Not that the applicant is going to see eye to eye with the worker on this point, for invariably in such cases she will assure her that both children would be treated equally. It is the perspective supplied by follow-up studies in adoption and by an analysis of child guidance clinic cases with such a family set-up that shows how well-adjusted and emotionally mature parents must be to give adequate security and affection without detrimental discrimination to two children who entered the family by such diverse routes.

Emotional Relationship of Applicants

Many who apply to an agency to solve the problems created by their sterility do so only after several years of marriage. When hope of pregnancy is gone there follows a relatively long period of gradual adjustment to the idea of accepting someone else's child as their own. The sensitive worker should listen for clues to determine what sort of masculine-feminine roles have crystallized between husband and wife since they have lived together. The question is more than that of a mutually satisfactory sex relationship. If either has married a partner who is primarily like a parent, with whom he has continued comfortably in the role of a child, the subsequent displacement by an adopted child will introduce a note of competition. The rivalry that then takes place can precipitate such tension that the emotional health of the whole family suffers and the prognosis for successful adoption is poor. Dr. Frederick Allen in his book entitled, "Psychotherapy with Children," discusses this in relation to the advent of an own child which he says brings inevitably

317

"a realignment of sentiments of the two adult members of the group. Their roles as husband and wife assume different direction and significance in the new status of father and mother."

The somewhat older age of most adoptive parents may make them even less flexible to meet this change in status. Therefore the adoption worker must be able to decide whether a pattern has been too well entrenched for them to give up former satisfactions for the newer ones of parenthood.

Specifications About Child's Background

A subject which commonly arouses some anxiety in prospective parents is the background of the adoptive child. Some request that all decisions in this area be entirely the business of the agency. Others request explicit qualifications of ancestry, appearance and intellectual capacity. Most are willing to accept some of the unknowns and risks inherent in the adoption process. When unusual attitudes are encountered, the case worker must not reject the client immediately because of over-rigidity or indifference, but discover if she can the source of these feelings in his previous experiences. The person who prefers to know nothing at all of the adoptive child's true parents may be overfearful of the day when her child will question her on this subject, and use that lack of knowledge as a protection against unpleasantness. Perhaps this attitude comes from a deeper inability to accept emotionally the fact that the adopted child actually does have a biological and often cultural heritage separate from the adoptive parents, and may turn out to be a radically different member of their family group. From the point of view of the child, the earlier his placement with suitable adoptive parents, the deeper his identification with his new family and the less his need to turn in phantasy or actuality to his own parents. But the adoptive parents must be able to meet any later requests from the child for information with honesty, tempered by a sense of timing as to what is appropriate to discuss at a given stage of psychological development. Such a problem of course arises long after the probationary period, except when older children are placed, so that if any professional help is given, it will probably be through the child guidance clinic rather than the original placing agency.

When the request for a child is framed by a meticulous and detailed list of specifications, we should know that the applicant has anxieties from which he is protecting himself, knowingly or unknowingly. The case worker must not let herself be maneuvered into an academic discussion of heredity vs. environment at this point, since even the most fluent comprehensive citation of authoritative sources is not what the client is really asking for. The strictly intellectual approach to an emotional conflict of this sort just does not work. The better method is to look for the source of such anxieties. It might be in the applicant's observation of an ill advised unfortunate adoption in her own family circle. If so, does this in turn simply give weight to whatever unconscious conflicts she may have, and so provide a convenient rationalization of such feelings. The negative side of her wishes can then come out in a perfectly acceptable manner by saying that she does not wish to consider any child whose heredity includes alcoholism, feeblemindedness, insanity, emotional instability, criminality or other specific qualities of nationality or physical condition. Virtually this seems almost to be saying that she does not want a child, since neither one's own nor an adopted child has such a blameless escutcheon. At the same time we must never lose sight of reality factors. The applicants who belong to the professional group, whose relatives and ancestors have been outstanding members of their communities, whose nieces and nephews are lifted beyond the average child, are not being either unreasonable or neurotic in requesting a child whose intelligence is in the superior group and whose background does not read like a story of William Faulkner's. Even if they assure the worker as they occasionally do that they would be quite contented with a potential truck driver, the chances of happiness of the latter in such a family would be very slight.

Preferences Regarding Sex

Where a decided preference is shown for one sex it is worthwhile to elucidate what this means to the applicant. The blond blue-eyed cherub is described with amazing frequency. This could be the dream daughter the mother has always cherished, whom she can dress up, exhibit to her friends, who will always be loving and responsive, conforming, and who would have no more opportunity to grow up into a real adult than Little Orphan Annie. The wish for a daughter on the woman's part might be motivated basically by a desire to duplicate with the next generation a deeply satisfying dependency relationship with her own mother. The request for a boy generally comes from the husband, this being quite consistent with the traditional cultural role of the male in our civilization. In spite of the closeness of the father-daughter relationship, there is something primitively satisfying to a man to be able to say "this is my son" even when adoption takes the place of biological continuity. When an absolute refusal to consider a child of the sex opposite to that specified is made, it would be quite important before placement to discuss pretty thoroughly the reason for that ultimatum, since it would light up the client's attitude toward his own masculinity or femininity and his feelings of adequacy or inadequacy in these areas.

Fear of "Bad Habits"

A commonly expressed fear of applicants is that of bad habits which will have to be "trained out" of a child when he goes into their home. For this reason they often request a baby as young as the agency permits, not merely because they want as complete as possible an experience of parenthood, usually motherhood, but also because they wish the child to conform in all important respects to their social cultural pattern. The younger the child, the easier it is for them to attain this goal, and the greater the sense of belonging there is for both. It is true that frequent replacements in foster homes set up undesirable habits and distortions of personality that even the wisest of adoptive parents may not be able to eradicate. But the baby who has spent his first six months with an affectionate and reasonably capable foster mother is not headed very far down the path of misbehavior, even though he will show some reactions to being given new parents. If applicants seem unduly apprehensive about bad habits they think may have been already established, one might suspect something amiss in their own conceptions of babyhood, its rights, privileges and pleasures. A supersensitive attitude toward a baby's bad habits on the part of an applicant may correlate with an overemphasis on order and cleanliness, a drive for early toilet training, a fear of masturbation, and the whole symptom picture that represents deep anxiety in the face of demands for instinctual gratification. This is not to say that *ipso facto* all people with obsessional or compulsive traits should be excluded from adoption waiting lists. Rather in our foster home studies we must think *diagnostically* and evaluate to what degree such neurotic traits, when found, are capable of modification. The probationary period can then be a time for case work help so that the new mother can modify her need for too great conformity, and both she and her child enjoy an experience that would otherwise be characterized by irritation, frustration and fear.

Personal History Indicative of Capacity for Parenthood

The orientation of the adoptive home study is in the present but with implied commitments for the future. Because it is of necessity a "short term" contact there is no time for a leisurely exploration of psychological history from the prenatal to the present. But this restriction does not give the worker the right to ignore the major stresses and strains or the particular satisfactions and values individuals have experienced in the process of growing up with their own families, and which they in turn may either react from or seek to repeat with the new family which they hope to create. We must not try to extract history as such from slightly reluctant clients, but rather we must try to see patterns of responses already established that will be clues in their new role as parents.

Homes with Fathers in Service

The impact of world conflict superimposes new problems on staff and clients that can only be touched upon briefly in a paper of this sort. The dilemma of to place or not to place when the husband has gone or is about to go into service faces all of us now. On the affirmative is the conviction that we should parallel the normal community set-up in which families are being increasingly disrupted by war. On the negative is the inescapable fact that adoption is without exception an artificial institution. Because we have had no opportunity to judge the long time effect of such family dislocations on children, we can only argue from analogy of England's experiences and from our theoretical knowledge of psychological development. Before a permanent plan has been made for the adoptable child he has suffered the loss of his own mother and generally at least of one or more foster mothers. These experiences must cut deeply into his psychic structure. Then to place him deliberately in an adoptive home where for some time he will know only one parent is to put obstacles in the way of a normal childhood and perhaps adolescence. Most agencies feel that only in exceptional instances should the single person adopt. While the situation of the broken family is not identical some of the same reasoning applies. As long as we still have a back log of intact families to draw from, including the 4F's and the over 38, and as long as they meet our requirements in other respects, the child's best welfare would seem to me to lie with them.

If at the time of application the husband is already in service, and stationed in another part of the country or abroad so that he is unable to participate in the home study or the selection of a child, it would certainly be a gamble to accept such an application no matter how glowing the reports of him from relatives and friends. If he is about to go into the service and the agency still wishes to consider the application, here are some of the points that ought to be explored. How does the wife react to her husband's departure? She may be mature and stable enough to reorganize her life and to find substitute satisfactions that will to some extent balance her deprivations and loss. But she may be the sort who is dependent on her husband in all major decisions, who enjoys being protected and dominated, and who will then muddle through any new responsibilities. The more adequate person can meet the anxiety and depression of separation with fortitude and imagination. She certainly is the better adoption risk in that her motive is not simply a selfish one of filling in her own loneliness or of creating in the child an unhealthy overdependence, attaching to him the emotions that really belong to her husband. If she has common sense as well as agency advice, she would supply compensating masculine influences following her husband's departure, as uncles, friends, teachers or even a good co-educational school if the child is old enough. This would mitigate to some extent the dangers of a practically matriarchal family.

Absence of Father in Relation to Age and Sex of Child

The age at which the agency would place a child in such a situation is important, since in early infancy and during the ages of 6-12, a father is less important to a child than at any other time. Whereas a brother and sister might feel with equal keenness the absence of a father from their home, from what we know of the need for a father as a model, the boy's psychological development will be more seriously impeded than that of his sister. With his father away, it becomes difficult for him to adopt masculine parental standards and to develop mature self-discipline. His little sister would be exposed to the same danger of overdependence on her mother with its implications for adolescence, but not to the lack of a pattern on which she may model her femininity.

While other problems arising from the war situation add new difficulties to the ones we have always had to meet in selecting adoptive parents, our basic problem as case workers still remains that of knowing so well the personality patterns of our applicants that whether it be war or peace we can assure our adoptive children stable and happy parents.

CHAPTER 28

Supervision After Adoptive Placement

LOIS R. BEEMER

The supervisory period in the adoption process has been somewhat neglected in so far as concentrated study of it is concerned. Over a year ago the California State Department of Social Welfare reduced the minimum time required for supervision following an adoptive placement from one year to six months. The staff members in my own agency reacted to this change with some interest and sense of challenge. Would we be able to carry out our full protective responsibility in that length of time? Would we have to lower our casework standards? How could we organize staff time to permit us to work within this new time period? As we began to function under this new regulation we were stimulated to study more closely the supervisory phase of the adoption process.

The staff expressed conviction about the importance of the caseworker's role in supervision, being mindful of the intensive and helpful service that had been given to numerous families after adoptive placement. At the same time we realized that many well-prepared, mature, and adequate couples had needed little help, although they had shared their feelings with us freely during the period of supervision. We decided to review our cases in order to determine the basic goals and purposes of

323

supervision, what aspects of timing and procedure were important, and what specific or general services were given.

Many questions were raised when we began the study. Is the supervisory phase of adoption separate from the rest of the process, or is it so integral a part of the whole that it is seen primarily as a continuation of the casework process in adoption? Do we become too protective or authoritative because of an overidentification with the child, and forget that we should give equal service to the adults who already have the child and who will have full responsibility for him after our service is terminated? Should not this phase of service in adoption be as individualized as any other casework service? Should we not permit the caseworker and client the freedom to determine the duration, intensity, and type of help required in each instance? Even with individualized service, are there nevertheless certain similar aspects in post-placement contacts? Finally, which is more important—the duration of the supervisory period or the quality and pertinence of the help given during it?

In order to arrive at answers to these questions, we began to examine the extent to which we viewed the entire adoption process as a totality that included the supervisory period.

Home Study Sets the Tone for Supervision Period

During the home study process we have worked with adoptive applicants in relation to their motivation for adoption, their reaction to infertility and its effect on the marital relationship, their feelings of security in becoming adoptive parents, their general adjustment to marriage, their self-confidence and maturity, their acceptance of a child's need and right to understand and accept his adoption, and their ability to relate to the social worker and the agency in a trusting, co-operative manner. As applicants are helped to come to grips with these basic areas of their lives, they are prepared for adoptive parenthood. Exploration of these areas is a continuing process which does not end with the home study, but remains an important part of casework service throughout the placement process and the post-placement supervisory period.

From our experience we have become convinced that the effectiveness of our work during the period of supervision is determined ultimately by the completeness of what has been done by and for the client during the home study.

The B family illustrates how significant material, brought

sharply into focus by the placement of a child, was used in the later period.

Mr. B, age 34, an engineer, was a calm, relaxed-appearing person who took pride in his self-control and even disposition. Mrs. B, age 31, was a sensitive and thoughtful person with some college training. She had been adopted at the age of two by a family of social prominence. The B's were an intense and serious couple. Mrs. B was the infertile partner.

Linda was placed in this home at the age of two months. The B's kept in close touch with the worker, often asked for advice. Mrs. B had some need to do what she thought was expected of her and was most conscientious. On the third visit to the home, three months after placement, we learned that Mrs. B was worried about her irritation over the baby's crying. She finally admitted that she was afraid that, if she could not learn to control her own feelings, she might treat Linda as her adoptive mother had treated her. As a child Mrs. B had been subjected to rather severe punishment and inconsistent handling.

We had several interviews with her in an effort to be helpful. At one point she spoke of her wish to have many children and of the opportunities available for independent adoption. Certain diagnostic material now became clearer. In spite of the fact that Mrs. B expressed gratitude for our service, she had negative feelings toward the agency, which were obviously related to her own unsuccessful placement. She feared that since she had not been well placed, perhaps Linda was not. She needed to prove that she could be a better mother than her own adoptive mother. Mrs. B's need to conform seemed to be related to her own mother's inflexible handling of her as a child. More deep-seated conflicts around her own adoption emerged now than during the home study.

Mr. B moved along comfortably in his relation to the child and seemed to have some sense of Mrs. B's reactions. Linda showed every indication of being a happy child and of receiving love and security.

We had several contacts with Mrs. B in which her own adoption was thoroughly discussed. During this period her mother visited her and Mrs. B was helped with her apprehension about the visit. Eventually she was able to regard

325

her mother with some compassion and understanding. In general she developed considerable insight into her feelings and finally expressed her conclusion that she had just gone through an exceedingly helpful experience, very important to her personally and in relation to her role as a mother. We were sufficiently comfortable about this family to consider a a second application with them a year later.

When we examine the home study in this case, we find that Mrs. B had talked a great deal about her adoption and her relation to her parents. She had also expressed good intellectual awareness and sensitivity in regard to the emotional needs of children. It was not until she was faced with the reality of the responsibility for her own adopted child that she could bear to reveal freely the anxiety surrounding her own early experience and could ask for help.

Mrs. B had been helped to understand some things about her own adoption during the home study; but the placement of a child stimulated her, with the caseworker's help, to understand herself as an adoptive mother. While this is not a "typical" case, it does illustrate how the building up and eventual integration of a family by adoption were achieved through consistent movement begun at intake and continuing throughout the post-placement period.

Placement Sets the Stage for Supervisory Content

The actual placement is in many ways a culmination for both the child and the family. It is so packed with significant experiences for everyone concerned that it cannot be isolated from the responsibilities that are a part of the agency's supervision. The family members approach placement with apprehension, but also with a sustaining sense of what they and the agency have put into it. The decision to select this family for placement of a child has already been made. Hopefully, the social worker has moved confidently through this phase so that the clients feel reassured of the agency's trust in them as the right parents for this child.

The mutual trust of the agency and the clients provides the basis for free and enthusiastic sharing as we move into the contacts following placement. If, from the beginning, we have given these persons a sense of our belief in their capacity to become good adoptive parents, they will share with us both their enthusiasm and their concerns. Adoptive parents are vulnerable to criticism, and they must know that we are not critical of their early ambivalent feelings, but that we understand and support them. At placement the couple's anxieties about being accepted and about the type of child they will receive are ended. Now the reality of adoption strikes them. Our knowledge of them is brought sharply into focus, and significant new material and understanding are added. For some couples the reality of their infertility is experienced for the first time. Their concern over barrenness may be settled or suddenly may be stirred up again with renewed vigor and with feelings of guilt and inferiority. Since a comfortable resolution of the conflict over the inability to be biological parents is one of the most basic factors in successful adoption, clients frequently need to be offered help in this area. Just as the home study sets the tone, the actual placement sets the immediate stage for the content to be dealt with in post-placement contacts.

The Protective Aspect

Next in our study we examine our practice in relation to the protective role we play in the supervisory period. Legally we have this responsibility to the child who is placed. One of the most difficult tasks for many child welfare workers is to transfer their primary identification with the child to one with the adults who have, by virtue of a placement, become the principle clients in the adoption process. We need to begin at the point of intake, either in the group orientation meeting or in the intake interview, to show our trust in these adoptive applicants, even when we may not be placing a child in their home. We should not overplay the protective function. It is true that in a small number of cases we have to remove a child from an adoptive home. Even then it should be done with the full participation of the couple and with our continued acceptance of them.

The applicants should sense from our attitudes and work with them that there is a mutual sharing of responsibility by agency and family in the experience of adoption. We should never represent a threat to them. Although we must be concerned with the child's development, we can encourage them to share with us their own concerns and reactions through our obvious trust in them. As in any casework treatment relationship, we shall be more effective in our service when they keep in touch with us through mutual confidence rather than through fear.

The Content in Supervision

Although the post-placement casework service is an individualized activity, our study highlighted the fact that certain specific content appears in many cases during the supervisory phase. Couples who adopt an infant seem to go through a typical cycle during this period. At first they are tense and preoccupied with the physical care of the child and the sudden readjustment of their own activities and relationships. During our early contacts with them (following the telephone calls reporting "how we survived the first twenty-four hours") we listen to many details of the child's physical and emotional adjustment. We learn something about the shifting family relationships, the reactions of relatives and intimate friends, and how the child is responding to all these new experiences. We are interested in ascertaining the degree to which the parents are relating to the child on the basis of his needs rather than their own. We look for signs of healthy narcissistic identification with the child as they begin to make him actually their own.

Since so much happens for everyone involved in these first few days following placement, it is vital that an early home visit be made, probably within ten days, when both the mother and father are present. On this first visit, the couple will have a need for the agency's approval of their efforts to be good parents—a need that will never again be so great.

During this post-placement phase, the adoptive couple achieve real acceptance of the child as theirs and self-confidence and comfortableness about their adequacy as parents. This new security permits them to discuss freely the child's adjustment problems and, later, to consider how to deal with giving the child information about his background and the facts of his adoption. Finally, they achieve such a sense of adequacy that they no longer need our help.

As supervision proceeds, the parents are likely to ask a variety of questions, both general and specific, in regard to the social and emotional development of children. It is neither sound nor practicable to teach a couple how to rear a child. Since he will inevitably take on the attitude and the way of life of the family, we must guard against too much teaching of formulas for care and training. However, since we do possess a considerable body of knowledge about child development and parent-child relationships, clients will continue to use us as a source of information as they have during the study and placement phases. The information we give should be related to the particular child and family. Fundamentally we want to give support to the parents in following their natural feelings in handling the child.

328

In the adoptive placement and the adjustment of the older child, the problems are more complicated. With him, there is also a common pattern or cycle in the post-placement phase. Usually he will exhibit a "honeymoon" phase, a period of testing, and finally the assurance of acceptance and permanence. In these cases, the success of our work in supervision will be conditioned first by the careful selection of the right family and second by our thoroughness in preparing the child for placement. Assuming that these phases of our work have been done properly, we shall help him most by becoming identified primarily with his new parents as we proceed in supervision.

Another important area of discussion in the post-placement period concerns the child's background and how the information about it will be handled by the adoptive parents as the child grows older. We have found that it is helpful to introduce discussion of this subject in the first contact with adoptive couples, which in our case is during the group meeting in the orientation period. The couple will already have had some discussion with the social worker about the child's history and background prior to their first meeting with the child. After the child is in the home and the adoptive parents begin concentrating on him as a person, they tend to forget or to want to forget that he has a natural family.

Usually they are not ready to return to this subject until we move toward the end of this period. We realize that the adoptive family needs to accept this child fully and wholly for himself and that the information regarding his heredity may or may not be difficult for them to accept. We want, however, to be sure that they have full information about his background so that they can use it wisely and so that the child may use it in his own identification with his background. Experience shows that adoptive placements are sounder if the couple can become positively identified with the natural parents. It is important to discuss with the adoptive parents their reactions toward the child and his appearance at the time they first met him, and to elicit their feelings about how he differs from them in appearance and background. We should present the positive aspects of the natural parents' decision to give their child for adoption. The quality of the child's identification with his natural parents and his feelings about himself will be based almost entirely upon the attitude of the adoptive parents toward his background and toward adoption in general.

During the home study, suggestions are given about how to help a child absorb and integrate the fact that he has been adopted. We recommend that the term "adoption" be used from the beginning, associating it with expressions of love, but not overemphasizing it to the point that the child feels "different." In discussions of the child's background and the meaning of adoption to him, we must also consider the feelings of the adoptive parents.

Some maturing of the adoptive parents inevitably occurs after placement, and our efforts toward helping couples in the process of self-examination before and after placement contribute to their growth. To quote from some final interviews with adoptive couples:

> The L's feel we have known each other for a long time and many things have happened as we have talked together which they felt were difficult at the time, but which have been helpful to them.

> The M couple's growth following placement has been much greater than is usual. They both have become much more mature individuals and, at the same time, freer in expressing their feelings. We used the final interview to review the year of supervision and to look forward to the future with some brief discussion about how they would be handling the matter of adoption with Kevin as he grows older.

Are we learning some significant things about the length of the supervision period? We cannot minimize the importance of what transpires in the process of consummating an adoption. Does the recent trend toward shortening the minimum time required for supervision mean that we shall render less service? Or shall we be improving our service because of our more frequent contacts with clients? In our agency we have found that more effective service is being given in the shorter period of six months than when it was extended over a whole year. In the long run, the number of social work man-hours has not been too different. Shortening the time of agency activity reaffirms our purpose of making a family independent of us, emphasizes to the couple the fact that the child is really theirs, and shows our wholehearted confidence in their capacity to function as adoptive parents. If there are gross factors which do appear in these early months, or if we are placing older children, the agency will necessarily continue to supervise over a longer period and will work more intensively. Usually, however, only a limited number of telephone contacts and possibly a few additional interviews are necessary.

In conclusion, we believe that the needs of the case as seen by the client, the agency, and the social worker, rather than pressures or arbitrary time limits should determine the duration as well as the quantity of service given in the post-placement period. In our efforts to extend and improve adoptive service to larger numbers of children, we need to explore further the content of this important phase of adoption—the supervisory period. As casework techniques, knowledge, and skills improve, we shall be able to give even more effective service during all steps in the adoption process so that those who wish to adopt a child will choose a professional service to help them in this serious undertaking.

CHAPTER 29

Supervision of the Child in the Adoptive Home

FLORENCE G. BROWN

The supervisory period is undoubtedly the most neglected aspect of adoptive placement. Often, when agencies are under great pressure, contacts are curtailed after the child has been placed. In the placement of children in temporary boarding homes, agencies plan very regular supervisory visits and few agencies would place children in boarding homes without provision for adequate supervision. In adoptive placement, the agency must give its approval to the legal adoption knowing the permanence of the decision and that there is no later recourse as there is in boarding care.

Is Supervision Worthwhile?

Adoption agencies, as well as most other social agencies, work under great pressure and have insufficient staff, but is this reason enough to curtail this part of our job? Is it due to a lack of clarity of what is involved in supervision, or perhaps a lack of conviction about the importance of our role during the supervisory period? Might it also be due in part to a feeling that if we have selected our adoptive homes carefully we do not need to be closely involved after the placement? If so, this concept should be challenged, as even the most careful study by the most skillful caseworker cannot possibly foresee all that

332

may develop in the future. Our studies help us predict, but we cannot assume that our predictions are always correct. Some things cannot possibly be predicted and can be seen only after placement, and, therefore, we can only know how valid our predictions were, by observing the child in the adoptive home. The adoptive parents and the child need our help to grow into a family unit. No pressures should be permitted to determine the quality of supervision. It is no reflection on a worker nor on an agency to find that there are problems after placement and that help is needed. We are subject to criticism only if we are not aware of what is happening or are so afraid to face the fact that our selection was not a good one that we just close our eyes to the problems that occur after placement.

The director of the agency and the Board must have enough conviction about the importance of supervision to include this in estimating staff needs as they do the number of children to be placed during the year. To agree that supervision is important is not enough unless we make it realistically possible.

The caseworker's personal adjustment and life situation enter into her attitudes toward families and adoption itself. In some cases this may be shown by the worker's over-identification with certain families, and in other situations, it appears in a more subtle form. Selecting parents for a child must have a psychological effect on the worker and this role can bring anxiety as well as satisfaction. This is true of the worker's role in supervision as well as in the other steps of the process, and may be the reason for certain blind spots during this period. The worker may on the one hand need to feel that the placement must be a good one because of her earlier study, but may also have an unconscious fear of learning that perhaps she has made a mistake. She may be reluctant to see too much because of the anxiety it might provoke in herself. Another factor in the situation is the desire on the part of the adoptive parents to be an independent family as soon as possible and, therefore, the supervisory period can appear as a threat to their desire for independence. Their feelings about this can affect the worker, and she might feel like an intruder. The desire for independence is healthy and we need to respect this, nevertheless we still have the responsibility for the child.

Purpose of Supervision

Supervision should be thought of in relation to our initial study and the placement itself and not as a separate part of the process. The selection of the adoptive home is the first step in guaranteeing a sound placement, and the initial introduction of the child to the family and the entire placement process are part of our study and selection. The reality of adoption is the child living with his new family and their adjustment to each other. Our goal in supervision is, therefore, the successful integration of the child in the family. It is a fallacy to assume that all the answers lie only in the selection of the home—adoptive placement is a continuing relationship, beginning with the couple's first letter to the agency, and not ending until legal adoption is completed.

The term "supervision" does not adequately describe our role during the period after adoptive placement. "Supervision" has many authoritative implications and reflects only the child-protective aspect of our work. We retain custody of the child and, therefore, our role must be somewhat authoritative. However, since our aim is to see the family established and to help them toward getting along without us, our approach must be positive and helping, rather than only authoritative. The family should have adequate interpretation regarding the purpose of supervision to lessen the anxiety which could be created and help them to see us as a source of security rather than as a threat.

Our role during the supervisory period is therefore twofold:

1. A protective role toward the child; and

2. To give help specifically related to the adoption situation. In the first we have a responsibility to the child to observe his progress and development before we give our consent to the legal adoption. It is here that our role can be authoritative to the point of removal of the child from the adoptive home, if the problem is sufficiently serious. We would consider removal after placement, and before legal adoption only for reasons such as a mental breakdown, death, serious incapacitating illness or separation of the adoptive parents. Even in such cases, we should examine each individually to determine whether or not the child should remain. Before considering removal, we need to offer every possible help to the family.

The second purpose of supervision, helping the child and parents to form an integrated family, is of utmost importance. Regardless of the extent to which the adoptive parents and we feel that the parents have come to terms with their inability to have their own child, their conflicts may be stirred up again.

The study and selective process are the beginning of helping the family toward a better understanding of adoption and some of the problems they will have to face, including such experiences as telling about their adoption in the community and eventually explaining his adoptive status to the child. Although these are discussed at the time of the study, it is important to discuss this again after the placement. The "telling of adoption" is often a troublesome area and, when the time approaches most couples probably wish that they did not have to tell. That there is some conflict about this matter should not worry us, if we select couples who will be accessible to help. Even during the supervisory period some of our discussion may still be theoretical as far as infants are concerned. Some agencies have therefore considered the advisability of holding group meetings for adoptive parents after legal adoption is completed and when the children are several years old. Such meetings would undoubtedly prove helpful in supplementing our earlier service to the family.

Integration Is Goal

At Louise Wise Services, the agency's role in supervision has been discussed at several seminar sessions with Dr. Viola Bernard, our Chief Psychiatric Consultant. At one of the seminars Dr. Bernard said: "The more skillful we become the more we can play the integrative role, reducing the need for authoritative action to a minimum." Spotting trouble during the placement process and dealing with it then, is not so threatening to the family as an authoritative action at a later date. On the basis of our experience that very few situations have arisen where we have felt that a child should be removed, it seems that we are right to interpret our role to the adoptive parents as one of helping the parents and their child to integrate as a family. Certain problems will arise that we and the family did not anticipate but these are usually part of normal family living and fall well within our helping function. Periodically we will be confronted with a serious problem and here we must be conservative in deciding how to carry out our responsibility. We cannot apply the same criteria at this point as at the selective stage. If our remedial efforts fail, we must then, in these extreme situations, remove the child and bear the consequences of the painful step. Our agreement form and the understanding which families have of our responsibility give us the right to do this without our explicitly emphasizing this possibility with all families at the outset of supervision.

The following is a case in which the agency seriously considered removing a child during the supervisory period but was able to avert this because of the family's readiness to use help from the agency:

The J.'s, a couple in their early thirties, applied to the agency after they had been married about six years. The medical reports indicated that it was impossible for them to have their own child.

At the initial joint interview, there was some evidence that Mrs. J. was a tense, anxious person, and it was the worker's impression that she was not completely reconciled to her husband's infertility. In the individual interviews that followed, it was felt that the J.'s had a good marital relationship and considerable warmth and sensitivity. Because of the many positives, the agency decided to continue with the study. Recognizing that the J.'s might need some help in moving into adoption, the agency planned more than the usual number of interviews. 15 months after their initial contact with the agency the J.'s were approved and Amy, a five-month-old little girl, was placed with them. Mr. J. became ill the day before they were to see the baby, and on the day of the "showing," while the worker was telling the J.'s about Amy, Mr. J. had to leave the room several times, saying that he had a stomach disorder. The J.'s immediately responded to Amy indicating that she was "their baby" and took her home two days later.

The worker spoke with Mrs. J. on the telephone a few days after the placement, and although Mrs. J. praised Amy and said that she was a wonderful happy baby, she stated that she herself was not well. She thought she had contracted whatever Mr. J. had at the time of the "showing," and commented that she became so tired when she handled Amy that they had to engage a maid to help her.

The first visit very shortly after placement indicated that there were obvious difficulties. It was apparent that the J.'s needed to work out some problems in their marital relationship and around the infertility. The reality of having a child in the home brought things to a head. Intellectually Mrs. J. wanted to be a mother, and yet she was struggling against it. She still had a great deal of feeling in relation to the whole sterility question and thereby to the acceptance of adoption. Mr. J. could recognize the psychological aspects in Mrs. J.'s illness, as well as his own at the time of the "showing." Mrs. J., however, had little insight regarding her own role and projected the problem on her husband and to the agency.

There were no outward symptoms of Amy's being affected by Mr. and Mrs. J.'s problems, but the agency was concerned about the ultimate effect on her. During the first three months after placement, the worker had very regular contact with the J.'s including home visits and office interviews.

In discussing this case with our psychiatric consultant, serious consideration was given to removing of Amy. However, it was decided to postpone the decision and to further explore what potential the J.'s might have and whether the agency could be of help to them. The worker told the J.'s how the agency viewed this, and that it could not disregard their problems. Although the J.'s reacted with some anxiety, they both agreed that they wanted to work closely with the worker.

The worker continued to see Mr. and Mrs. J. on a regular basis and helped them both to gain greater insight into their situation. She saw them together, and individually, and also visited in the home to see Amy and to observe the "climate" between the parents and the child. The positive changes became more and more evident. The tensions were diminishing and this was becoming an integrated family unit. The agency gave approval to the J.'s to proceed with legal adoption, and the final adoption took place about fifteen months after Amy was placed with the J.'s.

This situation points up the need to see the family study, the placement, and the supervisory period as a continuing helping process, with our goal being the integration of the family. Throughout our contact, diagnosis and treatment are inseparable, even though our emphasis differs in each step, and after placement the diagnostic aspect becomes subordinate to treatment.

Flexibility Is Required

In reviewing the J. case, it is apparent that an important clue was missed when Mr. J. became ill, and this was something that should have been explored further, rather than proceeding with the "showing" and placement. In an article on the first sight of the child by prospective parents* Dr. Viola Bernard states:

> When adoptive parents first meet the child offered by an agency, they face more fully the actuality of parenthood. This sometimes arouses latent conflicts, with marked anxiety and rejection of the baby, in contrast to previous manifest attitudes. Help based on psychodynamic understanding is needed as the couple and agency re-evaluate the adoption.
>
> Case studies of this group illustrate common patterns and significant differences in conflicts and methods of handling them. When deep-seated opposition predominates, adoption is dropped; with help others work through the crisis successfully. Such measures at this stage may prevent later maladjustment for the adoptive family.

In the case of the J.'s, in spite of a very careful study, some of the real problems did not appear until the reality of adoption was imminent. Obviously, we should have stopped then, and it is possible that we could have helped them at that point. If not, we would have rejected them. After placement, the situation was quite different. Before considering removal of the child we had a greater responsibility to try to help the family with their problems. If we could not have helped them, we would have had no choice but to remove the child.

The J. case also shows the need for agency flexibility in deciding the length of supervision, and the number of contacts during this period. The ruling of the state department of welfare in each state must be followed in determining the minimum requirements, but these should always be seen as "minimum" and not what is necessary for good casework practice. Although an agency does need to develop uniform practice, this can also lead to superficiality. Ideally, supervision should be for as long as it is needed in a given case, and the number of contacts, as well as their content, should also be individually determined. Just as in our studies of prospective adoptive parents the total number of interviews varies, this same concept should apply to supervision.

---

* Bernard, Viola J., M.D., "First Sight of the Child by Prospective Parents as a Crucial Phase in Adoption," *American Journal of Orthopsychiatry*, April, 1945, Vol. XV, No. 2, p. 230.

The timing of our supervisory visits is also of importance, and it is sound to plan the first visit very shortly after placement, so that if there are any problems, we can immediately offer our help. In the case of the J.'s, the worker became aware that there was trouble when she telephoned a few days after placement. However, in many cases this might not be revealed on the telephone, nor should we wait to let the parents take the initiative in letting us know that there is a problem. In some agencies, extra time is spent in supervision on "special cases," however, we cannot select the "special cases" unless we know what is happening in all of our placements.

When the Child Does Not Develop Normally

One type of situation that can be troubling to an agency during the supervisory period is that of the child who is not developing according to expectations. In such a situation, as described in the following case, there is always the question of the role and responsibility of the agency:

Ruth was placed with the K.'s when she was six weeks old. The K.'s were both college graduates and were a very bright young couple. They were warm and flexible, with many fine potentials for parenthood, and it was felt that they would be able to meet the additional risks of an earlier placement, which at our agency is under three months of age. Although, at the time of placement, Ruth was a healthy, well-developed child, when she was three months old the worker noticed a kind of sluggishness and questioned her motor development. The three-month psychological test showed that her development was inconsistent even though her score was quite high. At six months, and also at a year, Ruth tested in the dull normal group. It was noted that she was a very passive baby, needing strong physical stimulation before responses were elicited. The K.'s spoke of Ruth as being "lazy" and not doing things as rapidly as other children, but showed little concern about it. There was an exceedingly good adjustment between the child and the parents, and the K.'s proved to be the mature and understanding parents that we had expected.

It was felt that during the supervisory period it would be important to determine the meaning that Ruth's development had for the parents, and their reaction to it. In order to observe the child's development as well as the parents' reactions, the worker visited quite frequently. After Ruth had been with the K.'s for almost a year, they asked about going ahead with legal adoption. They said that having Ruth had been a wonderful experience and that they were extremely happy with her. Before agreeing to legal adoption, the worker pursued the discussion regarding Ruth's development, as she wanted to be completely sure that the K.'s were facing the real situation, and that they recognized that Ruth might always be slower than other children.

Further discussion revealed that the K.'s were aware that Ruth was a slow child and that this might continue into adulthood. They did not deny that it troubled them a little but insisted that that made no difference in their feeling toward her. They said that they were Ruth's parents, and they loved her. They felt that their own awareness of the situation was important and that understanding Ruth's potentialities would help them in working with her. With this knowledge they would not push Ruth and would understand that if she did not do certain things it was not because she did not want to, but because she needed more time. Their attitude was that they took their child for what she was, and not for what other people expected of her.

In the K. case, the worker's observations of the child were extremely important, and this situation points up the need for adoption workers to have a knowledge of the development of infants and to be able to recognize whether a child is functioning normally.

It was obvious that regardless of Ruth's slow development, this was a very good placement, that the K.'s accepted the child and loved her. In reading the record, one might wonder whether the worker herself became too anxious about Ruth's progress, and yet it was helpful and necessary for the K.'s to have been brought face to face with the situation before proceeding with legal adoption.

In such situations we must be careful not to project our own prejudices and need to check on our objectivity. If the worker feels that the child is not developing normally, it is advisable to have the agency's psychologist and pediatrician participate in further observations of the child. If the child is adjusting well and is happy in the home, and if the family wants to keep the child in spite of any unanticipated physical or mental problems that may develop, our responsibility is to help them to become aware of the implications so that they can handle the problem most constructively.

The Older Child

The integration process is more difficult in the placement of older children, and as a report of the Child Welfare League states:*

> "Older children and troubled children do not settle into the hearts and home of a new family with the comparative speed and ease with which a baby does."

In placing older children, the agency must be prepared to give a great deal more in terms of time and effort than is usually needed in the placement of babies. The child's preparation for placement and the entire placement process has to be worked out very carefully, with the child actively participating in all steps.

Placements of older children are initially extremely difficult for the child and also for the adoptive parents. The older child who is placed for adoption usually has had many negative experiences, often including severe rejection by parents and sometimes foster parents. Often he has been severely traumatized before referral for placement. Regardless of how much help the child has been given before going into adoptive placement, the placement itself often reactivates many of his own problems, and creates a feeling of anxiety. He may have expressed that he "wants adoptive parents forever" but yet he is afraid. He cannot trust parents until he really feels secure with them and he has to "test" them out in many ways. At the same time he wants their love and the security of their home, he may do everything to threaten it. It is only when he can feel within himself that he is really wanted, that the parents "want him forever" regardless of his behavior, that he can lose some of his anxiety and begin to feel that he "belongs." During this early period, he may need to hang on to much of the past regardless of how negative it may have been. This may take the form of frequent telephone calls to the former foster family, or of telling the adoptive parents that everything in his former home was "better."

While this is going on with the child, the adoptive parents

---

* *Adoption Practices, Procedures and Problems: Report of Second Workshop under auspices of Child Welfare League of America.* New York, March 1952.

are also going through a difficult period. They wanted a child very badly, and may have a great deal to give. Before they have had the opportunity to develop a solid relationship with the child, they may have to cope with the child's negative behavior and hostility. Therefore, in selecting adoptive parents for older children, this aspect must be very carefully considered with the parents. They need help in realizing that "separation" from a child's past life does not mean completely giving up his past, and that the child's need to hang on to his past does not necessarily mean that he is unhappy in his new home. On the contrary, the child's readiness to discuss his past with his new parents is often a sign of growing security, and it is only when the child's past and present can be more or less consolidated that he can begin to make a truly good adjustment with his new parents.

The adoptive parents need help in understanding the meaning of the child's behavior as he struggles through this early period, and even though we may have felt from our study that they should make good parents for an older child, we cannot assume that they are prepared to handle some of the problems that are innate in the adoptive placement of most older children. Our help to them, as well as to the child, must come before the placement, during the placement, and all through the supervisory period. As is true in the case of the younger children, the length of supervision should depend on the individual case and it should end only when the need for it ends. The decision to end the supervision and go on with legal adoption should be decided upon by the agency, the parents and the child.

CHAPTER 30

The History-Giving Interview in Adoption Procedures

LELA B. COSTIN

"History-giving" is a term often used in adoption agencies to describe that part of the placement process in which prospective parents are given selected information about the child whom they are soon to see and consider for adoption. This giving of information about the child and his family background is often one of the less well thought-out aspects of the adoptive process.

One reason for the lack of clarity about this particular interview is that history-giving is an area in which we have little real knowledge on which to base our practice. We lack objective data in regard to what adopting parents have wanted to know about the background of their adopted children and what children have wanted to know from their adoptive parents about their adoption and their natural parents. We have formulated opinions based on some of the cases we have known. We know something about the highly successful placements, and we are familiar with the less successful ones when problems later emerge in child guidance clinics. But we lack data about success or failure in the in-between group. Such data might be gained from careful follow-up studies with groups of adoptive parents or of adopted children or of both.

Legal adoption in the United States, although it began in 1851 when Massachusetts enacted the first adoption law, is still relatively new as a field in which the professional social casework method is applied.

Adoption has been rooted in the tradition that adoptive parents afford a resource for the care of the dependent child deprived of natural family ties. The adoptive family, in consequence, was not thought of as applying to the adoption agency; but rather was offering to take a child into their home and assume complete responsibility for him. Unlike other clients of social agencies who were seen as people with problems, complex motivations, and mixed feelings, having their own difficulty in applying for help other families managed adequately without, adoptive applicants were not approached as clients at all. Rather, in the beginnings of adoption work, the approach of the adoption worker was very much like that of the lay community seeing only the generosity and responsibility of the adoptive families, and the financial, social, and cultural opportunities they could afford a child.[1]

In recent years, however, adoption agencies, while still maintaining that the child is the principal focus of responsibility, have come to recognize three sets of clients—the natural parents, the child, and the adoptive applicants. With this recognition, new techniques and new principles have developed rapidly.

The sharing of background information with adopting parents is one of the aspects of adoption about which there are many differences of opinion. Workers would surely agree that a family should receive whatever information the agency possesses which is pertinent to the child's future development, but how much more to tell an adoptive family is controversial. Why should we give the adopting parents any family background information beyond the fact that the agency believes, on the basis of its best professional judgment, that this child and this set of parents are suitable for each other? The first purpose of doing so is to help prospective parents to make a decision about a particular child and to help them form a secure relationship with the child. A second purpose concerns the child's possible future wish to know about his natural family and the adoptive family's capacity to give such information in as con-

---

[1] *A Follow-up Study of Adoptive Families,* Child Adoption Research Committee, New York, March, 1951, p. 134.

structive a manner as possible. In short, information is given to strengthen the placement, and this goal should guide the worker in selecting the kinds of information to give to a particular couple.

Principles in Giving Background Information

A number of principles should be kept in mind if the history-giving interview is to be constructive. One of these is the necessity for *individualization* both in the choice of material to be shared and in the way in which it is presented to the new parents. There is no set pattern or outline to follow at this stage of the adoptive process, but it is easy to fall into a routine way of approaching this step in the placement—a pattern that may or may not be appropriate to the particular child and his prospective parents.

Workers probably find it easier to individualize that part of the interview that concerns a discussion of the baby himself. This is what the parents want to hear about. They are freer in their questions and the worker also may feel an enthusiasm for this part of the interview, particularly if he knows the baby well and is eager to have him go to his permanent home. But he will do well to temper his enthusiasm for the baby and keep descriptions close to the facts—those facts observable to anyone who is seeing the baby for the first time. A baby whom one person describes as "pretty," "cute," and "appealing" may appear quite different to someone else; and although it is desirable to convey warmth and acceptance of a baby in talking about him to his prospective new parents, too much enthusiasm and approval on the part of the worker may not leave the parents free to express unexpected conflicting feelings and concerns when they first see the child.

In other situations, in an effort to prepare new parents for the child "just as he is," workers are overly conscientious in their descriptions of "unattractive" characteristics such as "a big nose," "protruding ears," or "dark skin." Such descriptions are reflections of how the worker perceives the child, and the new parents, if allowed to see the child without such a forehand description, may perceive and describe these same features in positive terms.

Viola W. Bernard writes of a child for adoption whom one worker described as follows: " . . . Jimmy has a slight convergent squint which is barely noticeable and an open bite which is noticeable but rather cute." Another worker describing the child at about the same time stated that "the open bite detracts from his appearance to some extent." Dr. Bernard then says:

This neatly illustrates the factor of worker's subjectivity in appraising physical defects. Although very minor in this instance it can assume importance. Thus workers often worry about the negative effect on prospective adoptive parents of telling them about a child's defect lest this will cause the couple to reject the child. Sometimes these workers fail to realize how much their own subjective negative attitude toward a certain attribute may tip the scales for the clients, nor how the subjectivity of the latter, if left free of influence by the worker, may actually value or ignore the so-called defect. Furthermore, the negative or positive value placed on such a specific physical attribute of the child by worker or prospective adoptive parent may vary with other less conscious feelings of like or dislike toward the child of which the judgment about his appearance is a displacement.[2]

Prospective parents will want to hear about the baby's progress in the hospital nursery, his feeding experiences, his sleeping pattern, his reactions to people as seen in the boarding home or in his visits to the doctor. Accounts of these experiences can help the parents to know the child they are about to see and are less likely to build up mental images that may obstruct their freedom to relate to the child than are specific descriptions of features, coloring, or body build.

If the child to be placed for adoption is no longer an infant, considerable information about his earlier experience should be given the adopting parents so that they will be able to understand his behavior during the early phases of their adjustment together. If the child's experiences have been such as to forecast significant problems of adjustment in his new home, the new parents should be given a careful interpretation of these experiences so that they can meet problems with calmness and understanding. If his experiences have been such that he has learned excessive fears, the new parents will need to know the background of these fears and how the child acts out his tension if they are to be of maximum help in leading him to greater security.

[2] Viola W. Bernard, M.D., "Application of Psychoanalytic Concepts to Adoption Agency Practice," *Psychoanalysis and Social Work,* Marcel Heiman, M.D. (ed.), International Universities Press, New York, 1953, pp. 185-186.

The Need for Individualization

When we come to that part of the interview in which we give information about family background, the need for individualization in the choice of material is sometimes overlooked. Unless there are unusual circumstances of heredity the worker may be inclined to give a more or less routine presentation of the same kind of material as has been given for preceding placements, with not enough thought to what kind of information may have meaning in a specific situation.

Generally speaking, we should begin with what the parents want to know, and then give whatever additional information will help the adopting parents to identify with the child. The latter can be done during the same interview, after the parents have seen the child, or during the period of supervised placement, as the need and opportunity arise.

It is important to individualize the way in which information is given about the marital status of the child's parents and the reasons why they decided to place the child for adoption. Some couples' attitudes about illegitimacy are well thought out, and they have a rather clear understanding of the social forces that complicate the rearing of an illegitimate child by his natural mother. With such couples a statement to the effect that the child's mother was unmarried and felt unable to provide the kind of home she wanted her child to have may be sufficient. Another couple may have mixed feelings about illegitimacy and about mothers who give up their children. (Probably too often we consider illegitimacy from a social worker's point of view and fail to appreciate the deep-rooted emotional connotations it has for most persons in our culture, even those who become good adopting parents.) In such instances the worker may need to give more specific information about the circumstances that brought about the mother's decision, about the mother as a person and her wish that her child have a permanent, secure home. In other words, the second couple may need more opportunity to relate to the natural mother as a person in order to arrive at a sympathetic understanding of why this child is available for adoption.

Since infants surrendered for adoption most frequently are born to unmarried mothers, couples usually will have been helped during the study process to examine their attitudes toward illegitimacy and the unmarried mother's surrender of her child for adoption. Adoptive applicants may, however, have

347

quite different attitudes about married parents who surrender a baby for adoption. When this is a circumstance in the background of the child offered them, one or both of the adopting parents may have conflicting feelings as to whether the baby should have left his own home. In such situations the worker must be prepared to give considerable help to the new parents in handling their feelings. It is important for adoptive parents to be comfortable with the knowledge of why their child's natural parents gave him up if they are later to help him accept adoption as right for him.

Frequently natural parents have had previous marriages; or there is a present marriage, but not to each other. There often are siblings or half-siblings. If such information is given, the worker should consider carefully why and how he is giving it.

Fathers of infants placed for adoption frequently play a smaller part in the information given adopting couples. If the alleged father has been concerned for the welfare of the natural mother, has helped her during the pregnancy, or has been willing to be interviewed for the purpose of furnishing information about himself, this can be used with some adopting parents to further a positive orientation to the child's background.

Giving background information about the natural parents in terms of occupation, nationality, education, and appearance sometimes appears routine to the worker, but here again it is important to individualize the material and to examine it for accuracy, pertinence, and the meaning it has to a particular adopting couple. Many times *how* the information is given is more important than the facts themselves.

Adopting couples often show interest in the nationality background of the child. Even when they do not, workers sometimes assume that this information should be given routinely, without examination of why this is included or how accurate their statements about it may be. If the natural parents come from closely knit nationality groups such as exist in metropolitan centers, or from families where parents or grandparents emigrated to this country, nationality background usually can be reported with some degree of accuracy. In such instances nationality background may be of interest to adopting parents and may be a factor in their relating to the child, particularly when they see this background as somewhat comparable to their own.

In many instances, however, the worker has asked the natural mother about her nationality background only for the purpose of filling in the case record face sheet. The mother, who may have little knowledge of or interest in her nationality background, has then cast about for a reply, and the worker has recorded "Swedish," or "French-German," or "Irish," depending upon what the mother's mental associations have yielded. Many times the mother knows nothing of the father's nationality background, or the worker does not ask about it, forgetting for the moment that the father contributes half of a child's nationality background.

In many instances the true situation is that nationality background has been lost sight of through several generations of living in this country, and the nationality labels on the face sheet mean nothing except as they take on meaning to the worker or adopting parents. Perhaps social workers need to re-examine their own feelings about nationality background, and to re-assess in each individual case the degree to which nationality background of a child is important and the purpose for which the information is to be used.

Educational background of natural parents is often of interest to the adopting family. It then becomes important to have a clear understanding of the meaning of educational achievement to the adopting parents. This cannot be assessed simply by noting how far they went in school and what they say are their ambitions for a child. An adoptive family of limited education may have high educational expectations for a child and may find it harder to accept the knowledge that a child's natural parents left school early than would another couple who themselves had received advanced degrees and were perhaps employed in an academic setting.

When we know that the natural mother or father left school early, we may also know that there were such circumstances as pressing economic need, lack of interest and encouragement from parents, or emotional needs which went unsatisfied and which sent the person along paths other than school. Conveying an understanding of these forces can help to make the fact that the natural parent left school early acceptable to adopting parents who might otherwise have wished for higher academic achievement in the child's background.

Sometimes in giving background information we allow ourselves to overemphasize the fact that one or both of the natural parents were college graduates. By overevaluating this circumstance in the child's background, we reveal our own subjectivity about the value of education, and fail to individualize the meaning this fact has to the child's new parents and the degree of emphasis it should receive in the total picture presented.

Parents may inquire about the appearance of the natural parents, perhaps seeking a basis for expecting the child to resemble themselves. Or the worker may believe that a somewhat detailed description should be given in the event that the child eventually asks what his natural parents looked like. We need to keep in mind that what adopting parents are seeking (and probably the child too if he asks what his natural parents looked like) is the reassurance that the important family members in the child's background are not unlike the new parents in appearance. If we can convey the knowledge that in general the child's natural parents were similar in many ways to the adopting parents, we shall have done more to further an acceptance of the child's background by both the adopting parents and the child, than by giving a detailed description of how the worker visualizes the natural parents.

Obviously, the worker should be alert to any unspoken anxieties about background and be prepared to help the adopting parents with such concerns by providing pertinent material and discussing it with them. Sometimes it is the lack of information which is the problem, as, for example, in those instances in which we have no information, or very little, about the father of the child for adoption. The worker cannot assume that the new parents are comfortable about this lack of information. Even those who say they would just as soon not be told anything about the child's natural parents do not mean that it is unimportant for the agency to have such knowledge. In such situations the agency must first be careful to select adopting parents who can be expected to accept this absence of information without undue anxiety. But even when such parents have been selected, opportunity must still be given to discuss their feelings about the lack of information.

The Principle of Participation

A second principle to guide the worker in the interview in which background information is given is the importance of engaging the family's *participation*. Participation is important not only because of the diagnostic significance of questions and comments but also because participation results in greater understanding and integration of the material presented.

Sometimes the casework principle of client participation is ignored in this history-giving interview. One reason for this is undoubtedly to be found in the reluctance that adopting couples sometimes evince in sharing their feelings. A discussion of the natural parents of the child whom the man and woman hope to take into their family points up for them again that they are unable to have their own children and are taking someone else's child for their own. Then, too, after months of preparation they have arrived at a crucial phase in their attempts to adopt and they have a stake in withholding from the worker feelings or reactions that they think might endanger the realization of their hopes.

A second reason for the lack of client participation in this interview may well lie in the worker's reluctance to become too much involved with this part of the adoptive process. If the worker feels that the background material at hand is too limited, or "not good enough" for this set of parents, or if he is inhibited by the realization that there are many unknowns and difference of opinion as to what information should be given, unconsciously he may prevent active participation on the part of the adopting couple. Perhaps he has allowed his own identification with the adopting parents to go so far that he, too, finds it easier to give an undiscriminating recital of facts. Or if he has missed the underlying meaning of earlier statements on the part of adopting parents about a child's background, he has overlooked important cues, which could be used as a basis for directing the history-giving interview.

If there has not been effective client participation throughout the course of the adoptive study, it is unlikely to occur at this stage of the placement. If there has not been genuine two-way communication between the worker and the adopting couple but rather a simple gathering of facts about a situation, then each succeeding interview may only reinforce the withholding of feeling on the part of the client. When this has been the basis of the study, then the history-giving interview usually consists of a recital of facts by the worker, an indication from the parents that it sounds all right and they have no questions, and a moving on by the worker to plans for the next step, which is probably that of their seeing the child. In such situations it is very difficult for the worker to assess the true feelings and reactions

351

of the family to the information given, which may have created questions or anxieties for them. When these reactions go undiscussed, the questions may arise later and complicate the first meeting with the child.

Dealing with Hereditary Pathology

A third principle in sharing background information with adopting parents is related to *agency responsibility when there is pathology in the child's background*. It is difficult, of course, to determine exactly what constitutes hereditary pathology. Before we can use the label "hereditary pathology" we must have specific information subjected to whatever medical, psychological, psychiatric, neurological, or endocrinological consultation is required in determining the hereditary implications for future development.

If, after such scrutiny of the pertinent factors in the individual case, it seems evident that the "pathological" background has no significance for the child's future development, the information in question should not be shared with the adopting family. Adopting parents look to the agency for responsible decisions about the probable future development of the child who is offered to them. To share inappropriate information about "abnormalities" is to weight that information with undue significance. We must remember that there is a certain amount of anxiety present in every parent-child relationship and, by discussing irrelevant "pathological" factors in the background of the child, we may heighten unduly the otherwise normal tensions in the relationship.

When the significance of the pathological background for the future development of the child cannot be determined after appropriate consultation, the agency must decide on an individual basis how and what information should be given to the family, using as effectively as possible all understanding of the situation and its meaning to the parents.

There will be instances, however, in which the information we have about the child's background justifies the conclusion that certain hereditary factors may influence the child's development or that of his offspring. The first step in such cases is to select parents who have shown qualities that lead us to believe that they are able to accept a child for whom the future holds more than the usual risk. They must be able to live with the possibility of future appearance of disease, with the constant uncertainty that this entails. They must be able to examine critically and honestly their feelings at being offered a child with such heredity and their true attitudes toward the disease in question. This means being able to separate, for the time being, their strong pull toward having a child from wanting this particular child with this particular background. They must also be able to assume responsibility for possible medical care which might be extensive.

The worker has certain responsibilities in these instances beyond a factual presentation of the material. He must first take a critical look at his own subjective feelings about such heredity. If he cannot sort out these feelings adequately, he may be unable to create the atmosphere that supports and encourages the prospective parents at the same time that it leaves them free to accept or reject the child whom the agency is offering them. The worker must realize that the family may lack the scientific knowledge that would enable them to evaluate the hereditary background in question. In such instances this information should be supplied, and time given to discuss and assimilate this new knowledge. The worker has the difficult task of determining, in so far as such predictions can be made accurately, that this set of parents can or cannot accept this child and the possibility of handicap in his development without too severely impairing their ability to functon as parents.

Above all it must be remembered that the agency carries the primary responsibility for determining the implications of a child's heredity for his future development. This calls for appropriate professional consultation combined with a conviction about the power of environmental influences on a child in a happy, secure home. Undoubtedly in the past social workers, perhaps through their hesitancy about asking adopting parents to experience risk, or through their own reluctance to take responsibility for decisions about a pathological background, have drawn conclusions where geneticists are still feeling their way. We must remember that the kind of background information frequently given by natural mothers does not lend itself to scientific appraisal. We need to keep abreast of developments in the field of genetics and improve our skills in collecting information about a child's background when there is indication of pathology.

The Child's Wish to Know His Background

Another purpose for which background information is shared with adopting parents concerns the child's possible future wish to know about his natural family and the capacity of the adopting parents to handle the situation constructively.

A variety of forces operates in the individual's development and crystallization of "the self." Much of the struggle for a realization of the identity of self emerges at adolescence, as the child continues his attempts to relate himself to his world and becomes concerned with what he appears to be in the eyes of others as compared with what he feels he is. For the adopted child, the development of an inner identity may include an additional force—his attempt to understand his adoption and to identify with a second set of parents, the biological ones. His problem then is to integrate this understanding with all the other identifications gained through his childhood experiences.

Whether the identification with natural parents will be a positive one and whether the child will emerge from his attempts to understand and accept his adoption with minimal conflict depend in large part on the quality of the adoptive parent-child relationship and the attitudes of the adoptive parents toward his background. It is the adoptive parents who are in the key position to give their child a sense of basic worth in relation to his origins. This may involve giving the child little or considerable specific information about his natural parents, depending upon many factors in the individual situation. But one factor is of prime importance as the adopted child seeks to understand his adopted status and perhaps seeks specific information about his natural family: the feelings of the adoptive parents toward adoption and their adopted child, and their degree of respect for his family background.

Thus the social worker conducting the history-giving interviews has both an opportunity and a responsibility to help in the situation that may arise years later when the child brings questions about his background to his adoptive parents. This does not imply that we are able to give adopting parents specific answers to their child's future questions. In our attempts to help adoptive parents with this aspect of adoption we are faced with the fact that there is no large body of experience growing out of social work or psychotherapy with adults who were adopted as children. We do not *know* that large numbers of adopted children have wanted to know their natural parents' age, appearance, nationality, occupation, or education. Perhaps they have wanted to know quite different things. Perhaps we have sometimes failed to acknowledge this problem with adopt-

354

ing parents, and instead have given them the feeling that we believe there are ready answers to the questions their child will bring to them about his adoption. But even when we cannot give adopting parents specific guidance in anticipating their child's questions in future years, we can help in laying the groundwork for this part of the adoptive parent-child relationship.

Conclusion

The way in which we conduct history-giving interviews at the time of placement may set the stage, so to speak, for the future. Our aim should be to help the parents recognize several things: (1) Even when they have no conclusive answers, it is important for them to enable their children to bring out their questions in an atmosphere of understanding. (2) Their child will need a satisfying image of his natural parents if he is to attain the stage of emotional maturity which they want for him. (3) The identification with natural parents which he incorporates into his "self" will depend, in large part, not on the facts of his background as such, but upon the adoptive parents' feelings and attitudes toward his background and his questions.

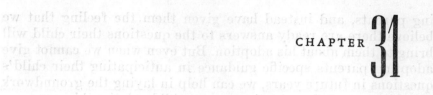

The Adoptive Applicants See A Child!

MORRIS H. PRICE

Many of us hold the opinion that adoption work is basically generic case work. At times in the kaleidoscopic shift of adoption work this conviction gets shaken; but upon further examination I have reaffirmed for myself that inexperience rather than basic differences explains phenomena that at first startle and baffle one. At one stage above all others the reactions of some applicants seem so unexpected and puzzling that we wonder whether our usual case-work skills and criteria suffice, whether these are not totally different situations and our usual knowledge inapplicable.

All case workers who have had contact with applicants for adoption know the drive and the anxiety with which applicants press for a baby as soon as possible. All our skill barely suffices to temper their importance in the face of our short supply. They endure stoically our requirements regarding what we need to know before we can even say we can consider them. We do a careful, complete study and decide that this is an excellent couple, mature, fully ready to accept a child not their own. We think they have worked through their feelings about the unknowns in adoption and that they have trust in the agency and its procedures. Feeling completely assured, we discuss a specific child, one which in our estimation any family would want,

356

and plan to have them see the child. At that point out come doubt and vacillation—is this a good baby, is it normal, is the agency sharing fully, how about the risky background, is it not too large or bald or too small? Faced with such responses it is a rare worker who is not thrown, who does not question whether the study was as sound as he thought, and whether our judgments were not unsound. This "startle" reaction on the part of the worker is most likely to occur in agencies where, having only a small adoption program, the workers do not have a chance to build up a body of tested experience as a background for these unexpected reactions.

Can our generic case-work knowledge throw light on this? Do such reactions indicate an invalid study? Does such behavior mean that not only this baby but, in fact, not any baby should be given to this family? We might well add another question: Does the opposite reaction of complete acceptance and lack of question always indicate that our study and judgments are completely sound?

An adoption study, carefully and skilfully done though it may be, remains to a large degree an intellectual process. Our discussions of adoption can only be at this point a fantasy rather than a real experience.

Adoption applicants come to an agency consciously or unconsciously on the defensive. They know that they must sell themselves, put their best foot forward if they are to get a baby—which is their concrete request from us. By using our conviction that they are not simply being "judged" in a unilateral process, we try to make the study a mutual experience in which agency and applicant explore together what they want and whether the agency can meet their request. Our degree of success may vary, but we know that, like applicants for jobs, these people come with all their defenses up in order to sell themselves to us. Even in the areas in which we are most successful in gaining their confidence, we know that many of their responses, though of truthful intent, are rarely based on the knowledge which comes only from experience.

An experienced supervisor once commented that she had been in the profession of case work for many years before she *really* understood the concept of ambivalence. She could give lectures on it—in fact, had; but only when she went into her own personal analysis did she feel for the first time that she *really* understood ambivalence. Our concept of training case workers through field work is grounded in the same concept of the need for the actual experience rather than merely intellectual discussion; we recognize that students need several years to make real the intellectual theories they can quote so well.

Another basic tenet in case work is that we pose hypotheses based on best available knowledge at specific times; that as hypotheses they must be tested as the relationship progresses. We have to be ready to modify, even abandon, our earlier formulation if client reactions and behavior contradict the soundness of our initial thinking. I recently encountered an anecdote regarding Dr. Freud, who when a person commented that after all what could you know about people unless you had analyzed them replied, "And what do you know then?"

Our experiences seem to indicate once again that the reaction of applicants to seeing a particular child must be evaluated on an individual basis against the background of our full study. Given the reaction, we can try to understand how and why these reactions fit into the hypothesis of our study. The reactions may indicate premature or unsound evaluation on our part, may indicate need for further exploration, or may fit perfectly into our findings. Although the reactions may startle us, we may see that they are actually a normal reaction to the impact of facing in actuality what has been previously only fantasied. Instead of their fantasied and ideal child, the applicants face the reality, and some shock is to be expected. If the last is the explanation and the people are given time, they can, with supportive help, come back to a balance.

A couple were being offered a child in adoption. The study had raised some question, but on the whole the agency felt comfortable in taking this action, since, in our opinion, the child was fully adoptable. Their own pediatrician however, raised questions about the child's rate of development and commented that he would advise against their taking it. The wife wept and voiced her indecision—a normal reaction. The husband blustered and came out with his conviction that he could remake the child. His attitude raised questions which resulted in further exploration. In conclusion, we felt that this couple could not serve as adoptive parents.

In another instance a young couple whom we considered excellent prospects met a baby. In the interview in which the baby is described, for the first time they began to reveal their distrust of the agency and their fear of "background" of agency babies.

(All this had, of course, been discussed earlier.) When they saw the baby, their doubts crystallized into open dislike of the baby, which they had to find "Mongoloid" in order to justify their panic reactions. This child had been thoroughly checked by experts and was a perfectly normal child.

As we reviewed our material, we found clues which we had missed as to the wife's rivalry with her mother and other indications that this couple had not as yet fully accepted being adoptive parents. We decided to explore the situation again with further interviews in order to assess these. Now the wife was able to verbalize her disappointment in seeing a real baby of a certain type as opposed to her fantasy. She was able to discuss some of her distrust of the agency on the basis of her work experience as an untrained worker in a public relief agency. Further study convinced us that this couple, although good prospects, would turn down any first baby presented to them. The reality of the experience of actually seeing a baby permitted them to face and come to grips for the first time with their doubts and hesitation. These seemed not to be available for discussion until the actual confrontation brought them into consciousness. With further exploration, we reaffirmed our original evaluation and felt that this couple were now ready to adopt a child. We offered them a second child. Their response was careful and thoughtful; there was no panic, but there was a basic difference in their reaction to the process because now they had really worked out their fantasies and could really face starting to be parents to a real child.

In another case, a family was offered a baby about whom the worker was markedly enthusiastic. Out of her over-identification, she reacted negatively to normal questions from the couple. In turn, they reacted to her hostility with suspicion and hostility. When they saw the baby, they were, to the worker's open anger, lukewarm. With supervisory help the worker saw that the couple's reaction was normal, especially in view of the worker's overidentification with the baby. Basically, the worker resented failure of the couple to become as strongly attached to the baby in one contact as she had become through several months of seeing the baby frequently. With this focus the situation could be re-evaluated with positive outcome. The family was helped to verbalize their just resentment of the worker's attitude, and the process started of placing this baby with the ultimately delighted parents.

As a final situation I will give in more detail a situation where, starting with the "startle response," after re-evaluating the total situation there was thorough working-out into a successful pre-adoptive placement.

This family, a young couple, had been co-operative throughout the period of waiting. The study indicated a couple of flexibility and maturity. The worker was assigned when professional decision agreed that this family should be approached to take this most desirable baby. In verbal presentation they accepted warmly the situation yet were quite free to ask questions about the baby. Their impatience showed by pressing for speeding up the timetable: When could they file adoption papers?

The worker, partly in reaction to their pressure, made plans for them to meet the baby in two days, two days later to have their pediatrician see the child, and then to take the baby home from the pediatrician's office. Their "trust" in the agency was boundless. The worker tried to temper their ebullience—she warned of the probability of the child's lack of response to seeing them at first. All such possibilities were brushed aside as to be expected and no barrier.

The day came. "They stood off and looked at him asking if this were he." Immediately the ambivalence begins to trickle through: he has hardly any hair; he is very, very big. The worker noted increasing urgency in their mutual attempts to get a personal response from the infant. "They were playful but more restrained than was to be expected with their exuberant spirits." They expressed their "surprise" but responded to the worker's attempt to elaborate only in terms of plans for seeing him again, purchasing his clothes, etc. The next day the worker called to ask if they had talked about the baby. "They had been doing little else. They had had an unsatisfactory tryout . . . you cannot love a child right off. This is a great step, and they would adjust if given time. . . . It has been quite a shock to find a child so big." The worker finally helped the husband to expand on his apprehensiveness and suggested his doubts. He formulated his opinion that they needed a "trial period" of a few weeks before they could know whether they wanted this child. He projected all the reasons for this doubt on the unsatisfactory experience of seeing the baby in the office setting. Against this he protested considerably. He still wanted to go ahead with the original plan—to see the pediatrician, etc. The worker, however, indicated that we could not engage in a trial-period arrangement. She was firm in conveying our feeling that there needed to be more time and thought before proceeding with our original plan. Another interview was arranged, and the next step of taking the baby to their pediatrician was postponed.

In the interview the couple voiced their relief over "blowing off" at the worker and the agency over the telephone. They were able to elaborate; they felt that they had been rushed, had not been allowed time to weigh the pros and cons, had been presented a concrete plan and allowed no time for indecision. Again the worker helped them to express their fears and helped them to bring out the anxiety which had been precipitated by direct contact with the child. They were now able to bring out their feeling that they were not sure they could trust our agency's pediatrician's opinion that this was a normal child.

Despite their doubts, the couple continued to press for sticking to the original plan with the addition of a few weeks' "trial period." The worker was firm in saying that we felt there would have to be further delay in order to give them a chance to know more definitely their feeling about this child before we proceeded.

A plan was made whereby the child would be brought to their home for a period of an hour or so. When the worker arrived with the baby, the family had made all sorts of preparations. They had borrowed a teeter-totter, a high chair, a playpen. The record gives the worker's description of the gradually increasing response of the parents to the child and the child to the parents. There was real response which indicated that these three people were relating to one another. At the end of the visit the worker and the couple arranged for a visit with the baby two days later.

When the baby came the second time, the family did not any longer feel the need of toys and other props to amuse the baby. Their immediate response was quite warm. The worker suggested that she had another call to make and would leave them alone with the child and come back in about an hour. They were most pleased by this suggestion. When the worker came back, the record gives the impression of a family group who had known each other for some time. The response of the couple was markedly enthusiastic. This was the child for them, and they wanted to go ahead as fast as possible.

The family now was perfectly sure that they wanted this child—subject, of course, to the usual agency probation period

361

of one year. A few days later the couple met the worker and the baby at their pediatrician's office. In contrast to his earlier comments, the husband proudly quoted that the pediatrician had said that the good size of this baby indicates that he had had especially good care in the infant home where he had been living.

The reaction of applicants to an actual presentation usually has great diagnostic and prognostic significance. But the particular significance must be carefully evaluated in the light of our full knowledge about the couple and of our knowledge that good adoption placements depend on cementing abruptly relationships that grow slowly and naturally with own children. These reactions should not be casually labeled either as normal or abnormal, for the same behavior may stem from entirely different sources of circumstances in individual situations. We must continue to be alert to the individual situation of *this* family with *this* child. Our alertness should include a willingness to evaluate critically too eager acceptance of a child; since we know that in varying degrees all applicants have fantasies which the reality contradicts, lack of hesitation can be a danger signal.

CHAPTER 32

Adoptive Parents Need Help, Too

ARTHUR L. RAUTMAN, Ph.D.

It is the lot of most adopted children to lack information regarding their ancestry. There are times in the lives of these children, however, when this lack of knowledge of their family background is most questioned and most troublesome. During these periods, of course, the child turns with his questions to the only parents he knows; and in a great many cases, what he finds is that they, too, are distressed—not only by their own lack of information regarding him, but also by their inability to help him with his problem.

No one feels the need for preparation more than does the substitute parent when he is confronted by his adopted child earnestly asking for information that he—with all his love, alas —cannot give and in all probability desires even more than does the child himself. Forewarned is half-prepared, however; and if adoptive parents are aware of the significance of these periods of questioning, they will be able to supply the missing words, as it were, during these times, so that much discomfort and needless groping on their own part, as well as on that of their adopted child may easily be avoided. If the adoptive parents have a clear understanding of the naturalness of this questioning and can prepare themselves factually and emotionally for such questions well in advance, neither they nor the child need find this recurring cross-examination seriously disturbing.

The first period of questioning usually comes when the child meets people outside his own immediate family circle, either children or adults. By this time he should, of course, have an acquaintance with the term "adopted" and also a fairly adequate understanding of its meaning. We have no choice but to give the adopted child accurate knowledge of his adoption before others can give him this information through disparaging hints and innuendoes. He needs to have a matter-of-fact understanding of his situation, so that when he is told by other children that he is "adopted," he may know what the term means.

Even a child as young as three or four years of age can understand a straightforward explanation of the simple fact that once upon a time his mother and father wanted a baby to live with them and so they found him and took him home with them to be their child. With the help, perhaps, of a picture book describing their search (the home-made scrap-book type will be especially appreciated) and with repeated telling of this story, along with his favorite tales, he will accept the idea of his adoption as a matter of course.

It is easy, in fact, to make a young child proud that he has been adopted. He can be made to feel that he has been especially selected and that being adopted gives him a special distinction, that it is an honor visited only upon a chosen few. It sets him off from the common run of pre-school children; and if he feels secure in his own relationship with his foster parents, he will be pleased at the knowledge that he is adopted, that he holds a secure place in the hearts of those who have *chosen* him to be their child—not for what he can do, or even for what he can become, but because of *who* he is.

Inevitably, however, there come times in the lives of even the most secure of children when the affairs of the day have not gone to their liking and problems weigh heavily upon young shoulders. There are disappointments, deprivations, and punishments for wrongdoing. At such times all children, adopted or not, will question the sincerity and affection of their parents. Children in all ages have created and re-lived the Cinderella myth whenever they have felt themselves abused. Own children, as well as adopted youngsters, turn upon their parents in anger and scream, "You are *not* my mama! I hate you!" Own children, too, go out into the street and tell the interested passer-by that

364

their parents don't love them any more and that they have decided to run away and never, never come back. And if he is an own child, and if the neighbors who overhear this little family scene are well aware of this fact, both they and the parents smile sympathetically at the childish outbreak, wait until all is calm once more, and start over.

If the youngster is an adopted child, however, an underlying insecurity or feeling of uncertainty on the part both of the child and of his parents may cause emotional repercussions that do not die so quickly. The adoptive parent, in all probability, will be deeply hurt at these times by the angry accusations and will review her own relations with the child with misgivings, seeking to find some point at which she has erred. She will strive to make restitution for imagined mistakes, and in so doing she will tend to overcompensate or to overdo, to shower excessive attention and affection upon her adopted child, in order to prove to the child, to the entire world in fact, but mainly to herself, that she has been a good parent and that she does not deserve the child's hate. Often at these times her behavior will offset the disciplinary program that she had carefully planned in more rational moments, and the feelings of uncertainty aroused by the incident may remain to haunt both the adopted child and his parents for weeks to come.

Early adolescence or the junior-high-school age is likely to initiate a period of thoughtful reexamination of the meaning and significance of being an adopted child. Now, as a rule, the individual becomes aware of the biologic link of the generations and begins to visualize himself as part of the chain that stretches from the present into the most remote past. Since at this stage he is of a more than usually romantic and idealistic nature, he may find disturbing the exclusion of his beloved, but in this sense alien, foster parents.

Other questions, too, arise for him: What will he hand on to future generations? How will his future mate look upon this break in the chain? When he was younger, the knowledge that he was an adopted child had set him off from the group in an interesting way, and being adopted was, therefore, considered a mark of distinction. The adolescent, however wants above all else to be *like* the others, so now the knowledge that he is different sets him off from his group with an uncomfortable feeling of being "left out."

As a rule, however, the young adolescent's questioning is

casual. The problem is not pressing; and since the youngster at this age tends to accept both himself and others on a superficial basis, the matter is usually soon lost in other interests. Being able to wear the correct sweater and to use the latest slang often gives him sufficient identification with his own group so that he is able to feel that he "belongs," and he will usually be acceptable to his crowd on these terms.

During late adolescence, this old question is frequently revived, and this time in a more serious form than heretofore. The pre-engagement period may bring this desire for specific information to a surprising intensity. Individuals who seemingly have always lived happily with the knowledge of their adoption and had, we thought, accepted the fact in all its aspects, now may unexpectedly turn accusingly upon their adoptive parents, begging for more and yet more information. The problem is now pressing. Time has become short. They desire specific knowledge, for they need to visualize in concrete and definite terms the biological link that uses them to connect an unknown past to an unpredictable future.

Even in the minds of the adoptive parents themselves, this interest in the biological aspect of inheritance and the emphasis placed upon this single phase of the individual's life may crowd out the well-known fact that *social* inheritance, too, is extremely important. In their anxiety they overlook the fact that the attitudes, skills, and many of the behavior patterns that make for successful living are reactions that are not determined by biological background, be it good or bad, but are *learned* from those with whom the child grows up.

Many of the characteristics of an individual that were formerlybelieved to be rather rigidly determined by his biological heredity are now recognized as capable of being modified, sometimes to a surprising extent, by the people and conditions that influence him as he is passing through his early years of life. No biological inheritance, however good, is adequate by itself to supply all that is necessary for successful marriage and parenthood. It is the social pattern in which the individual grows up that tends to set the pattern for his future life. Barring those occasional accidents of development against which even the best biological background can provide no guarantee, the importance of handing on to future generations a desirable social inheritance may well rival the significance of the biological heredity.

The marriage of the adopted youngster may precipitate an

366

even more difficult problem, both for the young husband and wife and for the adoptive parents, who still watch from the side lines with deep concern. Even under the best of circumstances, marriage and the establishment of a family present problems. If one of the marital members was an adopted child whose own biological family background is unknown, certain additional difficulties may well be anticipated. Whenever the development of one of the children born to this couple does not conform to some preconceived expectation, the mother or father who was adopted as a child may again revive the old problem of questioning his biological antecedents.

His child's physical features may differ from his own or from those of his wife or from the dream ideal that they have held for themselves. The rate at which the youngster is developing, the speed with which he learns to sit up or walk or talk, or the school difficulties that he encounters may not be in keeping with the developmental pattern of either parent or of any known biological ancestor; and this discrepancy may arouse a new wave of doubts in all concerned.

Forgotten will be the fact that both the process of child development itself and also the way in which characteristics are inherited are always too complex to be entirely comprehensible in our present state of knowledge. Forgotten, too, is the fact that even if all the biological antecedents of a particular individual are known, they are not really understood.

The adopted individual who lacks specific knowledge of his own ancestry is, *by that very fact,* cut off from the basic and most convincing explanation of these perplexing differences. Normally, any family group includes examples of wide variation in the pattern and the rate of development, as well as instances of striking individual differences at all ages. In the ordinary family, these antecedents are known; and many of these relatives are still present as part of the larger family group. In these cases, therefore, the family background not only gives evidence of these deviations from the "average" course of development, but it also provides knowledge of the ultimate results of these variations. Living persons whom the anxious parents know personally provide information and real-life illustrations as to how such individuals may finally turn out.

A child, for example, may resemble a specific member of her family in that she learns to walk or to talk later than is considered "average." Parents who know those in their biological background are reassured regarding their child's development when they realize that a grandfather and an aunt, or other members of the family, were "just like that" and nevertheless later were able to hold their own in the world of affairs.

Knowledge of this kind, however, is a comfort denied those parents who are ignorant of their *own* parentage. For their child, little is known of the developmental pattern of many of his antecedents, or of their ultimate achievements; and, therefore, even small deviations from an expected norm of behavior assume an exaggerated significance and may be seized upon by the overanxious parent as seemingly justifiable cause for deep concern.

A final yearning for knowledge denied may come when the individual who was adopted as a child faces old age. A desire to know and to visualize his own parents in old age may be developed; this information, he feels, might make his own position more peaceful. As a rule, however, the individual who has been able to solve the problems of his adoption up to this point finds this final questioning merely an idle curiosity, the lingering shadow of a search that somehow has lost its significance. Some are able to find consolation in the religious hope that this answer to life's bitter mystery will soon be found and that along with the stilling of all other vain strivings, this too, will find a happy ending.

What, then, can adoptive parents do to make this ever-recurring, lifelong problem of adjustment easier both for their adopted child and for themselves? Most of all, it is important to realize that the child takes almost all of his cues that lead to adjustment or to non-adjustment to reality from his parents, and that for this reason it is the *parents* themselves who stand in need of reassurance at every turn.

It is the parents—particularly the mother—that determine the emotional climate of any home. Children are amazingly alert in sensing the tensions, attitudes, and beliefs of their adult guides; the unspoken fears or doubts of fathers and mothers are detected probably quite as accurately as those that are openly expressed.

Fortunately, the positive attitudes of affection, satisfaction, and confidence are communicated to the youngster just as inevitably. The atmosphere of the home mirrors the feelings and the beliefs of the parents faithfully, whether these attitudes are harmful or constructive in their influence upon the child. There is, therefore, no better way for parents to help their adopted child find the security that he so greatly needs than through developing their own inner confidence and serenity.

Adoptive parents must also understand that the threat of the unknown is omnipresent; over all parents hangs a cloud of questions that are frightening primarily because they can never be completely answered. Adoptive parents particularly must realize that "the heart of another is *always* a dark forest," whether the youngster is an own child or an adopted one. They must understand that any mother or father facing his "own" child meets a great many of these identical problems; and that, after all, whenever any parent is confronted with the difficulties and strivings of an individual, growing personality, the barrier separating the generations is much the same, regardless of the biological relationship.

A realization by adoptive parents that there will be these definite periods when questioning of this sort is intensified can do much to forestall emotional disturbances. This is a recurring problem that will present itself in intensified form from time to time. Its reappearance does not mean that the adoptive parents have failed in their responsibility to the child. These repeated reexaminations represent a puzzle that can never be solved once and for all. At each age their child necessarily has his own questions; and at each age he seeks the answers to these questions on his own level, in terms that he is able to comprehend in the light of his experience.

Parents must know without question, too, that it is never possible to avoid these problems for their adopted child by protecting him. Hence they must prepare the youngster so that he will be able to withstand the idle questioning of others and —what is more important—they must help him achieve sufficient understanding so that he will be able to tolerate his own far more disturbing self-questionings. It is the responsibility of adoptive parents to teach their child how to answer the curious and to give the youngster ready-made phrases to use before the other individual gains the advantage. They must develop in their adopted child a high "frustration tolerance" for this particular question. They must help him develop the ability to meet this inevitable and repeated question with equanimity and poise.

Even more than other children, the adopted child needs to develop a realistic appreciation of the world as it is and a willingness to accept it as a place in which to live. He must learn to accept other people's place in it without self-pity and without demanding special favors. He should never be led to believe that because he is "different," he can expect special consideration.

In the final analysis, the basic needs of man are universal; and the needs of the adopted child are the identical needs of all: a feeling of security; a sense of being wanted in a world that is not of our own choosing; and confidence of being adequate to the demands that are made on us by a society whose rules and laws we did not help formulate.

For even the most secure and best-favored of us, a willingness to face reality is needed to enable us to meet the rigorous demands of day-to-day living. For the adopted child, the ability to meet such a world and its many exacting demands with equanimity requires a sturdy and realistic self-reliance; and he can learn this attitude nowhere so well as from his adoptive parents.

CHAPTER 33

Fee Charging for Adoption Service

EILENE F. CROSIER

The increasing knowledge of the meaning of money to people and its effect on their behavior and attitudes has brought about changes in casework practice which are of paramount significance, and this, among other factors, has been responsible for the development of fee charging systems in both the family and children's fields.

Historical Influences

By looking briefly into the history of social work, it is evident that several developments have contributed to changing a variety of activities which, together, once constituted an organized charitable function into a developing and expanding social service. Foremost among these factors have been:

(1) The contributions of psychiatry, which brought about a new and deeper understanding of the motivation for human behavior; (2) the aftermath of World War I, which particularly contributed to the beginning of the mental hygiene movement; (3) the passage, as a result of the great depression of the 1930's, of the Social Security Act, which, by establishing a broad, governmentally sponsored program, enabled and freed voluntary agencies to devote more

time and attention to experimentation in the field of meeting human needs through casework services; (4) the increase during and after World War II of non-economic problems among a large proportion of the population, which brought about an intensified awareness that people are often confronted with social problems unrelated to economic need and that social problems are not limited to any class or segment of our society.

In regard to this point, Mr. Leonard W. Mayo has aptly said[1]:

As a result of this knowledge which has been accumulating for the last fifty years, we now recognize the ultimate necessity for making social services available to all people in all economic groups. We now see that if the contributions of social work are worth anything, they are of value to all, not merely to one segment of the community.

This growing awareness began to be felt in the field of family casework and it is in this field particularly that sound bases and precedents were laid for the establishment of fee charging systems for social casework services.

Some of the clientele of family casework agencies were becoming aware of the fact that they were receiving professional help and they began to express a desire to pay something for the services they were receiving. The staffs of agencies believed, too, that they had valuable services to offer to a larger group in the community than they had been serving, and the consensus was that it was the responsibility of the agencies to make their services known and available to all who might benefit by them. Parallel with this, community leaders also believed that family agencies had valuable services to offer to a larger segment of the populace than they had previously been accustomed to serve. The problem then to be solved was how these services could be made acceptable to those who were financially independent and accustomed to paying for personal services, when the services had long been thought of as being needed by and available only to recipients of charity. Further, the unfortunate fact that charity still carried a stigma had to be overcome. The conclusion reached was that if individuals were given the opportunity to pay for services they received, such services might be more acceptable to and thus more widely used by those who needed them.

---

[1] Mayo, Leonard W., "The Future for Social Work," *National Conference of Social Work Proceedings* (New York: Columbia University Press, 1944), p. 28.

Precedents for Fee Charging

Precedents for the charging of fees for certain services already existed in child guidance clinics, day nurseries and in foster care programs of many children's agencies. Almost from the beginning child guidance clinics have charged fees for services rendered. Day nurseries have also charged fees, but these have usually been for partial payment of the actual cost of physical care of the child; as a rule, administrative costs and costs of professional services have not been included in computation of the fee charged. It is of interest to note in this connection, however, that in the day nursery field there is growing conviction that parents can make better use of the services of the agency by participating in and sharing the cost of the total function of the agency. Consequently, day nurseries have been experimenting with including the cost of professional services in the fees charged.[2]

General practice in children's agencies had long been that parents shared in paying the cost of board for their children in foster homes or institutions, but again no other costs have been included in the fees. The practice of parents' paying for clothing and medical care for the child varies from agency to agency. In all such agencies the fee has been related to the ability of the person to pay and the general practice has been to give the needed service regardless of the person's inability to pay.

As family agencies began to experiment and establish fee charging systems the fee was thought of as a means of the client's participating and sharing in the cost of service. In developing the philosophy and methods of fee charging, family agencies have become sensitive to the constructive use that can be made of the fee as a tool for the worker in the diagnosis and treatment process in casework.[3] The fee was not thought of as a means of increasing revenue or as full payment for services received.

Analysis by some agencies of the effect of fee charging has established in large measure the validity of the original assumption that paying for services they receive has facilitated the

---

[2] Bush, Dorothy W., "Fee Setting in a Day Nursery," *Highlights,* IV-V (November, 1944), pp. 112-112a.

[3] Berkowitz, Sidney J., "Use of Fees in Diagnosis and Treatment," *Fee Charging in a Family Agency,* Family Welfare Association of America, New York: (1944), pp. 6-14.

acceptance of these services by those financially independent and, in some instances, by those financially dependent.[4]

Simultaneously with the developments in the family casework field and in other fields, the experience gained in practice in the adoption field was bringing about a modification of the concept of the adoption service by social agencies, and this change in concept prepared the way for the acceptance by adoption agencies of the principles of fee charging.

When social agencies first began to offer adoption service the focus of concern was the needs of the children served, adoptive parents being considered primarily as a resource for homeless children. Slowly this limited concept of adoption as a single service gave way to a broader conception of it as a dual service to the parents and child on the one hand and a separate, equally needed, and important service to adoptive parents[5] on the other. It became increasingly clear that in meeting the needs of one group, financially dependent, adoptive services offered by agencies were meeting also the needs of a second group, financially independent. During this process the conception of adoption as a purely charitable act on the part of adoptive parents was in large measure abandoned. Thus, some of the false sentiment connected with adoption having been removed, the way was cleared for facing and solving the problem of adequately financing the adoption program and at the same time for meeting the needs of the two economic groups served by the programs of adoption agencies.

Findings of the study are based, therefore, on the replies of 46 of the 89 agencies which were listed in the Child Welfare League Directory of 1948, as offering adoption service. As of July, 1948, 15 of these agencies were charging fees for adoption services and 31 had considered or were considering the initiation of fee systems.

PRACTICES IN FEE CHARGING

Reaction to Fee Systems

The thoroughness with which the agencies approached and planned for the initiation of fee systems paid dividends in terms of acceptance by the staffs of the agencies themselves and by

---

[4] Penn, Sonia E., "Fee Charging in Actual Practice," *Fee Charging in a Family Agency,* Family Welfare Association of America, New York: (1944), pp. 15-24.

[5] For the purpose of this study, the term prospective adoptive parent has been selected to cover all terms used in referring to adoptive couples, since there are various terms in usage, such as adoptive applicant, adoptive parent, etc.

representatives of other community planning agencies of the establishment of the policy providing for the charging of fees. This is indicated by the fact that each of the 15 agencies reported that their staffs were in agreement with the plan. Moreover, of the 15 agencies, 11 reported the attitude of other community agencies such as community chests and welfare councils regarding the plan to charge fees for adoption. Only one agency reported an unfavorable attitude.

As the following table indicates, a considerable number of the agencies either did not know or failed to report their knowledge of attitudes of such groups as members of the legal and medical professions, volunteers, personnel of other casework agencies, and others.

TABLE 1.—ATTITUDE OF SOCIAL AGENCIES AND COMMUNITY GROUPS TOWARD ESTABLISHMENT OF FEE SYSTEMS AS REPORTED BY 15 ADOPTION AGENCIES CHARGING FEES, JULY, 1948

Community agencies or groups	Total agencies	Reaction known				Reaction unknown	Reaction unreported
		Total	Favorable	Unfavorable	Undecided		
Agency staff	15	15	15	—	—	—	—
Community chest or council of social agencies	15	11	10	1	—	—	4
Volunteers of agency..	15	8	8	—	—	4	3
Courts	15	7	5	1	1	4	4
Legal profession	15	6	6	—	—	5	4
Medical profession ...	15	4	4	—	—	7	4
Agency clients other than prospective adoptive parents ...	15	5	5	—	—	6	4
Other casework agencies	15	10	9	1	—	1	4

The attitudes of agency staffs, other casework agencies, personnel of fund raising and community planning agencies and volunteers of the agencies were best known. It is significant that where the attitudes of these groups had been determined, they were reported to be favorable in all but 3 instances.

Types of Adoption Service for Which Fee Is Charged

The types of adoption services for which agencies could conceivably charge fees are manifold, but, in general, all can be classified under two broad categories: (1) those services rendered by the agency when it is not itself the placing agency and does not control the placement and (2) those services given when the agency is itself the placing agency and maintains control throughout the entire placement process.

For the purposes of this study, agencies were asked to indicate whether fees were charged under any of the following circumstances which were classified under the first category: home studies or investigations made at the request of courts or other agencies, services given in connection with out-of-town inquiries, and services given to prospective adoptive parents who request some service from the agency after they have effected or are in the process of effecting a placement. Any services rendered by the agency directly to prospective parents when the agency participated from the beginning of the placement process, and regardless of the extent or character of the services given, were classified under the second category. Specifically, agencies were requested to indicate whether fees were charged under any of the following circumstances: if one or more interviews are held with prospective adoptive parents but they are not accepted by the agency for an adoptive home study, if an adoptive home study is made and the home is disapproved or rejected, if an adoptive home study is made and the home is approved for placement, or only if a child is placed in the home by the agency.

Since, in replying to the questionnaire, none of the 15 agencies reported circumstances under which fees were charged other than those noted above, it is assumed that the various circumstances included on the schedules adequately covered those under which fees would be charged.

The extent to which the 15 agencies participating in the study charged for services rendered when the agencies were not themselves the placing agency, and did not control the placement, varied considerably. In general, however, the tendency toward rendering the services requested without charge appeared to be more marked than the reverse.

The circumstances under which the agencies charged fees when they themselves were the placing agencies and controlled the entire adoptive process suggest the lack of common philosophical and practical bases for charging fees. Eight, or more than half, of the 15 agencies charged fees only if the adoptive process ended successfully in the placement of a child.

None of the 15 agencies charged for services involved in interviewing prospective adoptive parents whose applications were rejected after one or two interviews. Less than half, 6, of the agencies charged for making studies of the adoptive homes when such studies resulted in rejection of the application; 7 of 15 agencies charged for services when studies of adoptive homes culminated in approval of the home for placement. It is assumed that charging fees was not contingent upon actual placement.

The variation in the policies of these agencies regarding the services for which fees were charged suggests a lack of agreement, regarding whether agencies should charge for services given in connection with the adoption process, regardless of its outcome, or whether fees should be charged only when the adoption process ends in the placement of a child. This lack of agreement, strongly suggested at this point, is confirmed, as will be pointed out, by similar variation in agency policies concerning other aspects of fee systems.

Computation of the Fee

There was little uniformity among the agencies in the bases for the computation of the fees charged, but in general the fees charged seemed to fall into two broad categories, those based on some objective criteria and those whose bases were somewhat arbitrary.

There were 8 agencies which seemed to have used some objective criteria in computing the fee. In general 5 of these agencies based their computation on factors related to the cost to the agency of some part of the adoptive service, 2 relating the cost to service given to the child and 3 to service given to prospective adoptive parents. Of the 3 remaining agencies having objective criteria, 1 reported their fee was set at a figure equal to what might be the lying-in costs of prospective adoptive parents; another indicated it based its schedule of fees on the incomes of prospective adoptive parents and the third agency reported that it adopted as its fee the amount being charged by other community agencies.

Basis of computation	Number of agencies	Fee charged
Objective criteria	8	—
Agency cost	5	—
One-half per capita cost*	1	$150
One-half estimated cost of study and supervision	1	150
One-half estimated cost	1	100
3 months' board for child	1	150
6 months' board for child plus administrative costs	1	200 to 700
Other bases	3	—
Scale based on income of prospective adoptive parents	1	50 to 500
Equal to lying-in costs	1	200
Same as other community agencies	1	200
Arbitrarily set by agency	7	25 to 150

* Not including boarding care.

There was great variation in the responses given as to how the fees to be charged were determined by the 7 agencies whose bases for computing fees were arbitrary. For instance 1 agency merely reported that it seemed "wise to start with a small fee" while the fee in a second agency was based on the belief that it "should not be too high to preclude people of modest means, nor too low to be of value"; a third agency said the fee was designed to give the applicant the privilege of participating in the actual cost of making the study of the home. Four of the 7 agencies did not answer the question regarding how the fee was computed; since, however, the amounts of the fees charged were reported, it was assumed that the bases of their computations were arbitrary.

Services included in fee charged.—In an effort to arrive at some conception of what services were included in fees charged by the agencies the following question and classification of services were included in the questionnaire:

What services are included in the charge?

    a. health examination of the prospective adoptive parents

        (1) seriology

        (2) chest x-ray

b. attorney fees

c. court costs

d. costs directly related to the child prior to placement
    (1) board
    (2) clothing
    (3) medical
    (4) travel
    (5) psychological tests

e. other (specify)

Amount of the fee.—The study showed that the amount of the fee charged varied greatly from agency to agency with the majority, or 13 agencies, using a fixed fee system and 2 agencies using a sliding scale. Among agencies having a fixed fee plan the fees charged ranged from $25 to $200. As indicated in the following table these 13 agencies arrived at only 6 different figures in their efforts to determine what the fee charged should be:

Amount charged	Number of agencies
$25.00	1
50.00	3
60.00	2
100.00	1
150.00	4
200.00	2

Of the 2 agencies having a sliding scale fee plan, 1 had a minimum of $50.00 and a maximum of $500.00, while the other started the fee scale at $200.00 and had a maximum of $700.00.

TABLE 3.—POINTS IN THE ADOPTIVE PROCESS AT WHICH PAYMENT WAS REQUIRED EITHER IN LUMP SUM OR BY INSTALLMENT BY 15 ADOPTION AGENCIES CHARGING FEES, JULY, 1948

Lump sum payment plan:

Placement of baby 3*

Completion of adoption 2

After satisfactory medical examination of prospective adoptive parents 1

Installment payment plan:

Placement, adoption 3

Study, placement, adoption 2

Application, adoption 2

Study, adoption 1

Placement and each 3 months thereafter until fee is paid 1

* Includes two agencies which indicated they would accept installment paying but gave only one time of payment.

Services included	Fee	Computation
All costs related to child,[1] except clothing	$100	One-half estimated cost
Health examination of prospective adoptive parents, attorney fees, court costs	150	One-half agency's per capita cost[2]
Court costs, psychological re-test after placement	150	One-half estimated cost of study and supervision
All costs related to child, administrative costs covering home study	200 to 700	6 months' care and administrative cost
All costs related to child, except travel	150	3 months' board
All costs related to child, all professional services for preparing home	50 to 500	Income prospective parents
All costs related to child, except travel and psychological and court costs	200	Same as other community agencies
All costs related to child	200	Equal to lying-in costs
All costs related to child, attorney fees, court costs	50	Arbitrarily set
Psychological testing, court costs	150	Arbitrarily set
All costs related to child, except psychological testing	60	Arbitrarily set
Part of cost of home study	25	Arbitrarily set
Part of cost of home study	50	Arbitrarily set
Part of cost of home study and supervision	60	Arbitrarily set
Part of cost of home study and supervision, attorney fees, court costs, change of birth certificate	50	Arbitrarily set

[1] "All costs related to child" include board, clothing, medical examination and care, travel and psychological testing.

[2] In relation to bases of computation of fees this agency stated "only such services as related to adoptive placement are included, not boarding care." Hence the combination in this table seems contradictory.

Reaction of Prospective Adoptive Parents to the Fee System

It appeared from the limited data available that in general the fee system was universally accepted by the prospective adoptive parents.[6] Five agencies indicated that prospective adoptive parents were unanimously favorable to the fee system, and with one exception the other agencies reporting indicated high percentages of favorable response as shown in the following table:

Percentage	Number of agencies
100	5
99.5	1
99.0	3
96.0	1
95.0	1
74.0	1
Unknown	3

[6] The data are not very accurate because the base or number of prospective adoptive parents involved per agency from which the percentages were computed was not known.

Only 5 agencies indicated specifically that prospective adoptive parents objected to payment of fees. Three of these agencies reported that 1 percent of the prospective adoptive parents objected; 1 agency reported objection from 2 percent of the prospective adoptive parents and 1 agency reported that one quarter of 1 percent of the prospective adoptive parents objected to payment of the fee.

In only 3 agencies were the objections strong enough to result in withdrawal by the prospective adoptive parents of their applications. One agency showed a withdrawal rate of one-quarter of 1 percent, another 2 percent and the third agency's rate of withdrawal was 25 percent. This latter agency stated that objection to the fee as a reason for withdrawing was never openly expressed by the prospective adoptive parents.

One agency reported that 1 percent of the prospective adoptive parents accepted the fee system but later showed resistance.

Prospective adoptive parents in 3 agencies considered the fee the same as buying a baby while another agency reported that prospective adoptive parents believed adoption was an act of charity and should not be paid for. Two agencies attributed the objections to lack of financial ability on the part of the prospective adoptive parents and in another agency the objection registered was due to the fact that the fee had not been in effect at the time the child was placed.

The promptness with which and the extent to which prospective adoptive parents adhered to the plan agreed upon for payment provided tangible evidence of their favorable attitudes toward the fee systems. Not a single agency reported that any prospective adoptive parents failed to pay the fee charged. In fact 7 agencies found that 100 percent of the prospective adoptive parents paid promptly while in 5 agencies the percentage of prompt payments was from 90 to 100 percent. Only a few agencies showed that a small percentage of prospective adoptive parents paid slowly.

In addition to the generally favorable response of prospective adoptive parents to the fee system and their promptness in paying the fee some prospective adoptive parents offered to pay more than the fees charged by 11 of the 15 agencies. Seven agencies accepted these offers while 4 agencies did not accept the offers. Although the basis for this action on the part of prospective adoptive parents and agencies is not clear, the payment by prospective adoptive parents of more than the fee and the acceptance by agencies of such payments raise some questions in regard to the function and use of the fee. Does it mean that prospective adoptive parents do not feel that the fee is realistic and that they are not satisfied to pay merely a token fee? Do prospective adoptive parents feel that it is customary or expected of them to give something in addition to the fee? Is the fee being used as a casework technique as fully as it could be to help prospective adoptive parents work through their feelings about adoption?

Evaluation by Agencies of the Present Fee Systems

All but one of the agencies were in agreement that the fee systems in operation were successful. This latter agency stated that it believed its present fee plan was not successful because, "the amount of the fee should be increased in order to strengthen the adoption program."

Although 14 agencies stated that the current fee system in the agency was successful, 3 of the agencies gave no bases for their statement. The agencies making statements expressed them in a variety of ways but they revolved with one exception around 3 points: the favorable attitude of prospective adoptive parents and others; the fact that the fee policy was a sound casework practice and the fee system provided additional income for the agency. It is obvious that some of the reasons given for considering the fee plan successful are related to the factor or factors that motivated the agency to establish a fee system in the first place. The one agency differing from the general picture considered the current fee plan successful because it enabled better service to be given to unmarried mothers without charging them.

Of the 11 agencies giving a basis for their judgment, 5 gave a single reason and the other 6 gave a combination of reasons. The single reasons given by agencies were: (1) prospective adoptive parents prefer the plan and appreciate sharing the cost; (2) everyone satisfied with the fee plan; (3) agency can give better service to unmarried mothers without charge to them; (4) prospective adoptive parents were favorable to the fee; (5) actual practice demonstrates the fee system to be a sound casework practice.

The combination of reasons given by 6 agencies were: (1) a source of added income to the agency, it enabled the adoptive process to be a sharing process; and it helped prospective adoptive parents realize the responsibility they were undertaking and their role in working with the agency; (2) prospective parents as well as the community chest were favorable and the fee system provided an added source of income for the agency; (3) it was accepted by prospective adoptive parents, community agencies and lay people and was an added source of income although not large; (4) prospective adoptive parents were favorable and the agency considered it a sound casework practice; (5) prospective adoptive parents and staff liked the plan and it was sound from the casework point of view; (6) placed services on professional basis and increased the acceptance of babies, thereby combating the "black market."

The reaction of representatives of fund raising and community planning agencies to proposals to charge for adoption services was generally favorable and varied only in the extent to which the dominantly favorable attitude was qualified. Only 6 of the 21 agencies which had already consulted representatives of fund raising and community planning agencies had received from them unqualified approval of plans to initiate fee systems. In one of these instances the fund raising agency itself had requested that the adoptive agencies establish a fee system as a means of increasing income. Tentative approval by representatives of fund raising and community planning agencies who were consulted was reported by an additional 9 agencies.

The tentativeness of the approval was expressed in various ways. For example, 1 agency reported that the local council of social agencies had made no definite response, having left the decision regarding the establishment of a fee system to the adoptive agencies, but that the general budget committee of the fund raising agency had voted approval of the plan. The response of personnel of the fund raising and community planning agencies to the proposal by another adoptive agency to establish a fee system had been that public relations would be jeopardized by the establishment of a policy to charge fees. However in this instance approval to proceed to develop and submit a plan for charging fees had been obtained as the result of a joint meeting of the subcommittee of the adoption agency and the board of the fund raising agency. Other responses were accompanied by either expressions of interest in the results of study or specific requests by representatives of the fund raising and community planning agencies that further study be made before final decisions regarding establishment of fee systems were reached.

CONTRIBUTION

OF OTHER

PROFESSIONS

Contribution of Other Professions

Introduction

The social services of adoption assure a child a home that will offer him opportunities for desirable physical, mental, spiritual, and emotional development. Because of these social aspects, placement for adoption is the function of social agencies with trained workers.

The complex process of adoption has distinct legal, social and judicial parts that should dovetail into one forward moving plan of action that transfers a child from his natural family to a new family that becomes his in every sense of the word.

But these three professional disciplines—legal, judicial and social—are not the only ones that have specific contributions to make to adoption. Medicine, psychiatry and psychology contribute significantly during many steps in the adoption process. However, these fields do not carry primary and separate responsibilities for any part of the adoption process as the other disciplines do. The medical service to the mother during prenatal, delivery and postpartum care is, of course, the primary responsibility of the medical profession but that is not a part of the defined adoption process. Similarly treatment and examination services for individuals under care of medical, psychiatric and psychological practitioners are distinct from adoption per se.

First let us focus on the relationships and contributions of medicine, psychiatry and psychology as they strengthen the social service functions in adoption. Then we can identify the legal and judicial functions and their relationships to social service and to one another.

The term *placement* embraces a complicated process including study prior to separation of the child from his parents, the determination of how to achieve that separation once it has been decided upon as the best or inevitable attempt to solve the existing problems, the transition experience from the child's own home to what may be temporary living arrangements and relationships, the continued transition to the adoptive home, guidance and support during the new family's adjustments to one another, and termination of social service upon the completion of the legal and judicial steps that make a family a unit and the adoption an accomplished fact.

Responsibility for this placement process rests with the child-welfare agency but skills and knowledge beyond those inherent in social work contribute to its achievement. Social workers rely on the help of other professions—the doctor, the hospital worker, the psychiatrist, the psychologist. They rely also upon help of attorneys, court officials and judges who carry specific responsibilities in their own fields for steps in the adoption process.

As the skills and knowledge of medicine, psychology and psychiatry are used in adoptions, they must relate to the primary social-service function or confusion in responsibility and service to the child, natural parents and adoptive parents results. For purposes of adoption, these professions serve social service and do not carry primary responsibilities apart from that social-service function. Their role is that of the consultant and related resource that permits more competent social service, but does not interfere with the orderly adoption process.

In helping a child find a permanent home, the adoption agency must obtain from many sources factual information about the child's history and development. When this knowledge has been brought together and evaluated, the agency has the responsibility for making a decision, based on all the information available about the child, his adoptability, and the type of home situation that will help him make the best adjustment and enable him to reach his optimum personality development.

Many professions recognize the mental health aspects of adoption as do both the United Nations and the World Health Organization. These organizations have cooperated in meetings and in the issuance of reports to clarify the interrelationship of medical, psychiatric, and social work aspects in the placement of children for adoption.

Adoption agencies increasingly use psychologists and psychiatrists to add to their knowledge of the child and his development, the natural parents and the adoptive parents. These professions contribute to adoption work their insight into concepts of personality development, understanding of the unmarried mother as well as parents unable to assume their parental responsibilities, and greater awareness of the meaning of attitudes, conflicts, unconscious motives, and infertility in adoptive parents.

The medical and sociological factors involved in adoption have been studied for a long time but the psychiatric aspects of adoption work have received major attention only in recent years. Social agencies began using psychiatric consultants for other services in their programs before they perceived the many problems in adoption in which psychiatrists could give counsel and guidance. As in other areas of social work, the application of psychiatric concepts changed the approach to many problems of adoption.

From psychiatry, caseworkers have learned facts and theories about personality, the nature of man's inner needs, and the problems he faces as he tries to achieve gratification of his needs in his social milieu. They know better what tends to contribute to mental health or illness. They have learned the importance of information about the individual's emotional make-up—how he gets along with people, how great are his anxiety, guilt, hostility or seclusiveness, and other complex qualities of personal and social adjustment.

The psychiatric consultant in an adoption agency helps the worker arrive at a deeper and more comprehensive understanding of the adoptive applicants who apply for a child, the child who needs adoption and the natural parents of the child. He also helps social workers understand their own motivations, both conscious and unconscious, as they relate to working with people.

In adoption the lives of several people are crucially affected—not only the lives and future destinies of the children involved, but also those of the natural parents and adoptive parents. It is important, therefore, for every worker in this field to try to understand himself as well as possible, and become aware of some of the attitudes which interfere with his capacity to deal objectively with individuals. For example, in our American culture economic success is commonly considered one criterion of adequacy; or there may be a bias in favor of higher education. Yet neither money nor educational achievements in themselves are necessarily required to provide a successful adoptive home. The caseworker must learn how to discount his personal reactions to a given situation.

In studying adoptive applicants' personality development, we consider the nature of their behavior, motivations, inner conflicts, psychological defenses, and qualities of their relationships. The psychiatric consultant helps caseworkers analyze concepts of behavior and weigh specific factors in evaluating the emotional stability, security and warmth of the adoptive

387

applicants. This analysis calls for a high level of casework skill and depth of understanding of human behavior.

A few agencies have experimented with the use of Rorschach and other tests as aids in determining the capacities of adoptive applicants for parenthood. Currently, however, the consensus of opinion is that these tests are not too valuable in adoption and that agencies should be cautious in using any standardized tests. Contacts with adoptive applicants are too brief to solve some of the problems that may arise and results are not conclusive enough to serve as objective guides for decision.

Insecurity, anxiety, rigidity, and immaturity are present to a certain extent in most parents. It is the degree to which these exist which makes an individual undesirable as a parent. In appraising the capacity of applicants as potential parents, the caseworker needs to evaluate the individual's emotional qualities, his ability to control and re-direct some of his drives, and the degree of his acceptance of his strengths and limitations. His pattern of meeting his own needs and his flexibility in doing so indicate something of his ability to accept others as they are.

One can readily understand how invaluable is the knowledge of human behavior that psychiatry brings to the social-work agency. There need be neither confusion nor professional competition as psychiatry enhances social service in carrying out its responsibility. For psychiatry this is but a secondary contribution to its primary and direct one of therapy. A comparable relationship exists between psychology and social work in adoptions.

Agencies in the past depended heavily on the results of psychological tests in evaluating a child's potentialities and the kind of adoptive home needed for his maximum development. Frequently they held babies until after two years of age and sometimes had three tests given at intervals.

Psychologists themselves have raised questions about placing too much confidence in infant testing and predicting a child's future intelligence on the basis of a test in infancy. Because of these questions agencies became more discriminating in their use of tests and more willing to place infants at an earlier age, giving weight to the child's background and the broader implications of the history as well as to the psychological test. In many instances agencies place young infants without psychological testing.

Dr. John Bowlby has pointed out that "The failure of infant

388

tests to predict the future does not of course rob them of their value as an index of present development, a value which may be compared to that of the weight-chart which, irrespective of any predictive value it may have for the infant's future physique, remains a valuable guide to his physical progress during infancy."[1]

In planning adoption for older children the psychological test assists in selecting the home in which the child can make the best adjustment. Here, too, however, agencies must realize that various factors such as emotional insecurity, medical complications, congenital factors, and behavior problems affect the relationship with the psychologist so that the results may not be a true test of the child's abilities.

"It becomes evident that the intellectual growth of any given child is a resultant of varied and complex factors. These will include his inherent capacities for growth, both in amount and in rate of progress. They will include the emotional climate in which he grows: whether he is encouraged or discouraged, whether his drive (or ego-involvement) is strong in intellectual thought processes, or is directed toward other aspects of his life-field. And they will include the material environment in which he grows: the opportunities for experience and for learning, and the extent to which these opportunities are continuously geared to his capacity to respond and to make use of them."[2]

The relationship between the social agency carrying the adoption function and the medical profession is more complicated than that with psychiatry and psychology. Traditional practices and attitudes that precede the development of professional child-placing affect current practices. Medicine also has a direct function in the physical care of mothers and the delivery process that brings the doctor in contact with them at a significant time in the sequence of a potential placement for adoption.

On the one hand, the medical profession is a source of information for the social agency and provides necessary consultation on the medical and health histories of the individuals as their histories affect the evaluation for adoption. Agencies have always obtained medical and health histories for children considered for adoption but they have come to seek and use such

---

[1] John Bowlby: Maternal Care and Mental Health, p. 103.

[2] Nancy Bayley: On the Growth of Intelligence, in The American Psychologist, December 1955, p. 813.

information more effectively. The medical profession interprets the medical data, their pertinence and significance to the adoption plan. In this area the medical practitioner assumes a secondary function to his primary treatment role and becomes a consultant to the social agency as it fulfills its primary responsibility of placement.

On the other hand, confusion and misunderstandings arise when the responsibilities of these two fields are not distinct in the placement function. Much misunderstanding still exists between doctors and approved adoption agencies. Many physicians do not refer their patients needing adoption or other related services to social agencies.

Doctors offer the criticisms that there is too much red tape in agency adoptions, that the long waits are not valid, that investigation is too detailed, that requirements of agencies are arbitrary and unreasonable, and that capricious and unwarranted decisions are made. Because of these attitudes many of them participate in private arrangements in an effort to help not only the unmarried mother who is their patient but couples interested in adoption who may also be their patients.

The unmarried mother is interested in independent adoption placements of this kind because it offers quick service, "confidential" handling, a feeling of approval for praise on making the "best" plan for her child, a quick return to normal living, financial assistance which she often needs to meet expenses, and no record to jeopardize the secrecy of the whole procedure.

On the other hand the social agency giving service to the unmarried mother emphasizes her need for protection and time, gives casework help which can reduce the damaging effects on her personality and helps her develop self-pride and confidence so essential to mature living. Such casework help should also decrease the probability of the mother having another child out of wedlock. It protects the baby by determining whether the adoptive home is one into which a child should be placed and also whether this is the home for this particular child.

In speaking of such independently arranged placements, whether by a doctor, nurse, attorney, minister or other interested intermediary Dr. Viola Bernard has commented, "Many of these manifestly benevolent intermediaries sadly, if sincerely, underestimate the complexity of their task and overestimate their own fitness for it with sometimes lucky, often tragic results. Many act on an 'ignorance is bliss' approach whereby, for instance, an unconscious omnipotence fantasy may be gratified, all too often at the expense of the actual long-term welfare of the apparent immediate beneficiaries, the principal parties to the adoption."[1] Fortunately the trend in several areas indicates that agency placements are increasing.

Just as social workers object to doctors acting outside their field of competence by participating in placements of children, so doctors object to social agencies interfering with medical plans between doctors and patients.

For example, some doctors think that they lose their patients when they are referred to a social agency. Social agencies often lack adequate funds and for this reason do not continue to include the patient's private physician in plans made with her. A few agencies are trying to meet this problem by providing not only casework service and shelter care to unmarried mothers when needed, but private medical and hospital care with a plan that enables the mother to receive the services of a private physician of her own selection.

Infertility of parents is another medical area that touches the adoption program. Parents applying to adopt children may not have sought medical advice and help in correcting their infertility. The social agency has a responsibility to refer them to their own physician to explore this problem.

Members of the medical profession have stated that approximately one in every 8 couples is childless involuntarily, and that medical science now may achieve success in treating infertility in an estimated 25 to 50 percent of these cases.[2] In view of this hope, the medical profession needs to make such information more widely known to the public, to conduct further studies in medical research on infertility, and to provide more medical and psychiatric help which might benefit many childless couples whose needs cannot be met by adoption agencies.

As with medicine so with education, the social agency may secure helpful consultation from educators in instances of older children, and in developing plans that consider school needs of children being placed for adoption. Clarity of functions of the separate professions permits harmonious working together with benefit for the professions as well as the individuals served.

---

[1] Viola W. Bernard: Application of Psychoanalytic Concepts to Adoption Agency Practice, in Psychoanalysis and Social Work, edited by Marcel Heiman, p. 170.

[2] Adoption of Children in California, Citizens Committee on Adoption of Children in California, 1953, pp 62, p. 18.

The social service relationship to legal and judicial agencies is somewhat different, as pointed out above, from this consultant relationship social work has with medicine, psychology, psychiatry, and education. There are definite functions within the adoption process that require legal and judicial action. Harmonious and effective relationships can exist only if it is clear that these different functions in the adoption process supplement but do not overlap or threaten one another.

Although state laws usually prohibit individuals from placing children unless licensed as a child-placing agency, attorneys are responsible for many independent placements. These may appear to be direct placements by the parents (a step which is possible and legal), but actually in placements in which the attorney acts as intermediary the parents rarely know the identity of the family to whom the child goes, and the details of the placement are arranged and carried out by the intermediary, not the mother or parents.

The social worker cannot execute the legal instruments, nor should the attorney perform the placement function. Neither the lawyer nor the social worker can terminate parents' rights or establish new ones. The court in turn cannot be a judicious body if it works in a vacuum without the social and legal aids.

Unfortunately, social agencies have not established as close cooperative relationships as are desirable with the legal and judicial professions. The services of attorneys, judges, and courts are necessary to establish the status of adoption legally and safeguard the child's permanent rights in his new relationships. Working alone, the social agency cannot assure a child and his adoptive parents that he will not be removed from his new home.

Furthermore, the role of the court in abandonment proceedings is vital. It may mean the opportunity for a child to have an adoptive home with a permanent family; or, if the court action fails, it may mean long-time boarding care for the remainder of the child's minority, with the possibilty of several changes in boarding homes and life-long maladjustment for him. In cases in which the parent withholds his presence, love, care, and affection and neglects to support the child, the court bears a heavy responsibility. Many children needing adoptive homes are not legally available for placement by an agency until there has been court adjudication of rights and responsibilities of all parties. Too often in the past the court decision has tended to protect the parents' rights of possession rather than the rights of the child for his best welfare and future happiness.

In addition to its responsibility for legal advice to individuals and the execution of legal instruments, the legal profession assists in promoting the enactment of state legislation which will place legal restrictions on placement practices, afford protection from baby-selling rackets, protect parental rights at the point of relinquishment of a child, and those of adoptive parents at the time placement is made by natural parents, agencies, or others, and later when the adoption is completed.

It should be noted that continuing efforts are being made by many social agencies to establish more cooperative relationships with the legal and judicial professions as well as with the medical profession. These agencies have provided leadership in establishing community-wide committees to work jointly with the bar and medical associations toward a closer understanding of mutual problems. Largely as a result of such efforts the American Bar Association has an Adoption Committee as a part of its Family Law Section, the American Academy of Pediatrics has a Committee on Adoptions, and the American College of Obstetricians and Gynecologists has a Committee on Infant Adoption.

The social worker in an adoption agency must work closely with all these professions and can learn much from them. The social worker can also contribute to other professions from his knowledge of the social needs of the child and his general background of children and their problems. In these inter-professional relationships the social worker needs to be clear about the functions of the agency he represents and about his own role and responsibility in carrying out these functions. Otherwise he may place responsibility for casework decisions, which are properly his, on a person of another profession; or he may attempt to perform duties that properly belong to others. Then confusion and friction result for all.

The social worker needs an understanding of and proper respect for the knowledge, skills and responsibilities of the other professions as well as the limitations as their knowledge is applied to the social work program. The growth of mutual understanding and trust is often slow and the worker needs patience to accept this fact while he is learning through experience in these interdisciplinary relationships.

We all need to recognize and separate out the specific contribution of each profession giving service in adoption. All of these groups should pull together toward better adoption practices. If medicine, psychiatry, psychology, law, hospital administration and social work will each concentrate on improving its own part in adoption, and relating it to the whole, the goal of better adoption practice will be achieved.

Within the social work profession the need for research in adoption is great. Since successful placements must be based to a large extent on predictions of the agency in certain areas the bases for these predictions should be constantly tested and improved. There is not agreement among agencies and workers on a number of factors, such as the most desirable age for adoptive placement, the effect of boarding home placements prior to adoption, the use of fees, etc. More research in such areas should lead to greater agreement with respect to the most desirable practices. It should also serve to lessen the gap between what social workers think is good practice and what the community is ready to accept.

Selected papers which discuss some of the anthropological, legal, medical, psychiatric, psychological, and research aspects of adoption are included here. The contribution of these professions to the social agencies responsible for placement of children for adoption is invaluable in their tremendous responsibility of setting the course of the whole life of a child when he is too young to make for himself the momentous decision of choosing a new father and mother.

CHAPTER 34

Application of Psychoanalytic Concepts
to Adoption Agency Practice*

VIOLA W. BERNARD, M.D.

Adoption, as an ingenious psychosocial invention can offer
one of the finest and happiest adaptive solutions to the desperately frustrated needs of parentless children, childless parents,
and those who cannot be parents to the children they have borne.
Such are the human intricacies of this process of family formation on the basis of nurture rather than nature that sometimes
participants fail rather than fulfill each other and themselves.
Adoption agencies represent the community's stake in providing skilled professional services toward implementing and safeguarding this remarkable human experience. Ways and means
of carrying out such services logically evolve in relation to the
growth of understanding of the clients served. As psychoanalytic
concepts have enlarged and deepened general understanding of
human nature, they naturally are of special significance to a
field so closely concerned with areas specifically related to
major psychoanalytic contributions, such as child development,
psychosexual conflicts, dynamics of family relationships and the
role of unconscious motivation and emotions in behavior and
symptom formation.

* Reprinted by permission from PSYCHOANALYSIS AND SOCIAL WORK, Copyright, 1953, International Universities Press, Inc.

For purposes of this discussion the potential application of psychoanalytic concepts to adoption practice may be viewed from two main standpoints, i.e., the more general and the more specific. As to the first certain psychological principles, originally derived from psychoanalysis, have become the general property of modern thought and are integrated into all social welfare and social case work theory. In this way they influence all adoption practice despite the great unevenness prevailing in this field throughout the country. One instance of the more general relatedness of modern psychological insight to current practice concerns the struggle to replace independent adoption by qualified professional adoptive agency service. The greatest number of adoptions annually in this country are still those arranged outside of authorized agencies—the so-called independent adoptions (30). As is well known, there are two main types of non-agency adoption; the first, baby selling, or the "black market" type, exploits human need and suffering for financial profit. On an immediate level, at least, elimination of this evil seems more a matter for legislation and enforcement than psychoanalytically oriented agency practice. The other type of independent adoptions are those placements arranged for by well-intentioned intermediaries—most often friends, doctors, lawyers, relatives or nurses. Many of these manifestly benevolent intermediaries sadly, if sincerely, underestimate the complexity of their task and overestimate their own fitness for it with sometimes lucky, often tragic results. Many act on an "ignorance is bliss" approach whereby, for instance, an unconscious omnipotence fantasy may be gratified, all too often at the expense of the actual long-term welfare of the apparent immediate beneficiaries, the principal parties to the adoption. Although the methods of changing the present community acceptance of this well-meant independent adoption practice lie outside the province of the agencies' main service functions, the psychodynamic insights developed by professional adoptive workers provide impetus and clinically tested rationale for the necessary educational, legislative and community organizational programs. Furthermore, to succeed at all, or even justify success, such reforms must be supported by the professional adoption field in the form of constant improvement of services that actually carry out the best of what is known so far. Instances of destructive personally biased judgmental attitudes by professional personnel, or inflexible agency procedures detrimental to the needs of the clients may violate the current body of relevant knowledge as much or more than some of the non-agency adoptions, and thus handicap the desirable efforts toward professionalizing this work.

When approaching some of the more specific and detailed applications of psychoanalytic principles to case work in adoption, the existent unevenness of quality and diversity of method, already referred to, make it difficult to present material of uniform applicability. There is a high degree of variation in almost every aspect of agency structure and function in adoption, from state to state, within sections of the same state, and even within the same community. Detailed considerations of psychoanalytic application in adoption agencies cannot be undertaken without due recognition of these differences, and had best be directed to certain broad areas of function and types of case work regardless of the many particular ways agencies limit or structure their specific areas of responsibility. Naturally, many of these variations affect the nature, extent and feasibility of attempts to integrate psychoanalytic concepts. Among such variables may be included: qualifications of case workers in terms of professional training, experience and personality attributes; size of case loads per worker; quality and quantity of supervision; availability and orientation of psychiatric and psychological consultation; existence and nature of in-service training programs; degree of lay control over professional practice, and the social philosophy of those in control of general policy.

In general, social work participates in adoption by serving children to be adopted, both infants and older children, natural parents, and prospective adoptive couples, whether or not this is all undertaken by a single agency or divided among several whose quality of interagency collaboration is of the greatest importance to effective service. Although all these sets of clients will be considered separately for purposes of discussion, and are often served by separate agencies—children's agencies, unmarried mothers' shelters, etc.—it is well to keep remembering how enmeshed these different clients' emotional needs are with each other, and how the professional worker has an over-all responsibility of balancing the sometimes conflicting psychological needs and interests of all three, rather than overidentifying with any one at too great expense of another. This case work task of balancing clients' needs will be referred to again, but it is obvious that unobjective attitudes of "pro-unmarried motherism and anti-adoptive couplehood," or the reverse, while frequently operative in independent adoption, can lead to psychologically destructive outcomes. Resolution of the sometimes terrible difficulties inherent in this balancing task is helped by the generally accepted priority to the children's needs in case of otherwise deadlocked conflict of interest. Another general principle for all the clients is that adoption is experienced progressively through a series of gradual stages, rather than as any single event, such as the signing of papers and physical relinquishment by natural parents, or the moment of the child's actual entrance into an adoptive home. Accordingly, our focus will center on certain crucial steps along the way in this process by the participants, and on the twofold clinical functions—diagnostic and therapeutic — whereby professional services strive to safeguard and promote the maximum emotional well being of all concerned. Assuming, then, a general working knowledge of agency practices on the part of the reader, let us turn to some psychodynamic considerations in the course of work with each of these clients.

Services to children for adoption include: provision of temporary care between legal relinquishment by natural parents and adoptive placement; use of the temporary care interval to prepare the children for placement and to help some of them overcome bad effects of experiences prior to admission by the agency; as complete a diagnostic evaluation as possible in order to plan most appropriately; selection of an adoptive home; placement of the child with his new parents; periodic supervision of the new family until legal adoption is consummated six months to a year after placement.

The adoptive situation differs in so many ways for the infant and older child that it seems necessary to discuss some aspects separately. The infant, much more frequently sought by prospective adoptive couples, profits by the resulting greater selectivity the agency can exercise on his behalf in choosing his family. Once legally relinquished by his natural parents, the infant depends on the agency for temporary care until he is placed for adoption, and during this interval he is studied as totally as possible to confirm his adoptability, in general, and to assess his special attributes in particular, in order to place him at the optimum time in the optimum adoptive home. A child's adoptability (and this refers to older children as well as infants) is reduced by the degree and kind of physical, mental and emotional pathology he may present, as well as by the amount and nature of pathology in his family background, and sometimes by the composition of his racial heredity. Although

diagnostic study may conclude that a particular child is "able
to contribute to and benefit from family life"—as Miss Hallinan (13) defines adoptability—the term often denotes a social
reality rather than a clinical condition since it depends so
largely on the placeability which in turn is caused by many factors extrinsic to the child, i.e., the desires, capacities and fears
of adoptive parents and the home-finding zeal and skill of the
agency. A salutary trend is under way toward reducing the
numbers of children considered unadoptable by agencies. More
children who need it can thus benefit by family life and fewer of
these will be driven into risky black market or private adoption.
Growing experience (32) is validating the success of placements
that agencies formerly feared making. Many progressive agencies no longer rule out a child as unadoptable on the basis of
pathologically hereditary background alone, but decide the
question on the basis of the child himself, sometimes prolonging the period of his observation under care. Better selectivity
and case work with adoptive parents probably help account for
these improved results.

Diagnostic, prophylactic and therapeutic responsibilities of
the agency come into play during this period of temporary
care between surrender and adoptive placement. Of the infants,
some are newborns, straight from the hospital; others are a
few weeks or a few months older, some of whom have experienced a traumatizing succession of being shifted about between
different places and people, or other forms of stress, before
coming to the agency. The care they receive represents a
vital contribution to their future psychological development,
according to psychoanalytic assumptions and corroborating research. It simultaneously provides an opportunity for continuous clinical observation of each baby's behavior as the principal
diagnostic method, to be supplemented by psychological and
pediatric examinations and, in some selected instances, by
psychiatric examination as well. Because of the importance to
infant development of warm, relaxed human contact and adequate stimulation, temporary foster care seems far preferable
to group care. Considerable attention should be given to selecting and working with the foster mothers, and it follows, from
what has already been said, that the criteria of their selection
should be heavily weighted in the direction of personal attributes that can fulfill "the rights of infants" (26) by affectionate flexible mothering. Experience by the worker with the
maturational sequences of infancy and her insight into the

behavioral language of infancy helps her differentiate normal individual reactions from signals of disturbance calling for remedial action. Such action might take the form of helping the foster mother change some of her ways of handling the baby or even changing foster mothers. Fluctuations and aberrations in feeding behavior, for instance, are recognized as delicate barometers of the infant's condition. Anna Freud (12) has recently added to the sizable psychoanalytic literature around this topic by a theoretical contribution in which she differentiates three main ways in which the function of eating is open to disturbance: organic feeding disturbances, nonorganic disturbances of the instinctive process itself, and neurotic feeding disturbances.

There is a promising trend in psychoanalytic studies of child development toward combining more data from direct observation of infants and children with the information gained from analytic therapy of adults by reconstructions of their childhood in the context of their full life history. Direct observations have obvious methodological advantages for studying the preverbal period of the first year of life and from such investigations by Ribble, Fries, Spitz, Anna Freud, and others, adoption agencies may hope to gain much needed data of specific relevance in meeting their responsibilities and growth-promoting opportunities around temporary preadoptive foster home care and permanent adoptive placement. Thus, Fries (19), investigating factors in psychic development in a group of children she studied from birth to adolescence, offers supporting evidence—elaborated in detail—for the interacting influential roles of constitution, habit training and parental emotional stability on the personality outcome of her original infant group. In his researches into "Psychogenic Diseases in Infancy" Spitz (29) seeks to classify certain damaging consequences to infants during their first year according to causally insufficient or emotionally unhealthy forms of mothering. Correspondences between the types of disturbances and types of mothering are differentiated as to course and outcome in relation to chronological phases of ego development within the first year of life. In the light of these and many other studies, adoption for parentless infants by "good" parents seems even more than ever the most logical preventive therapy for what can be most devastating psychogenic illnesses, i.e., maternal deprivation and "mal-mothering" of infancy.

Rich potentialities for research on child development are

inherent in adoption agency work because of such favorable features as an unusual degree of control over environmental conditions, access to subjects and to history data, etc. Adoption agencies in turn urgently need the findings from such research and are in a special position to apply them toward the furtherance of mental health. A psychological investigation by Leitch and Escalona (18) illustrates the research possibilities of the adoption agency setting. In response to a "felt need to integrate our basic theoretical concepts with observable aspects of infantile experience," Leitch and Escalona studied reactions to stress of 112 infants under the temporary boarding home care of a Kansas adoption agency by psychological testing, observational procedures, interviews with boarding mothers and agency staff. Tension level changes were studied by observing changes in posture, motility, amount of activity, readiness to startle, respiration, circulation, purposive use of objectives, social responsiveness and attention span. "Extraordinary variability in the kind of situation which aroused tension in different infants was noted."

Predictions play such a vital role in the agency's selective decisions that lead to the merging into a family of a particular child and of a particular couple that the bases of predictions must be constantly tested and improved. Many questions as yet far from settled beset the adoptive worker daily. What influences on the infant's future development may be expected from familial incidence of psychosis in his background? What sort of character development can be expected of him later in the light of what kind of early experiences—especially as to parents and parent substitutes, physical health and habit training? How may his scores on infant psychological tests reflect his ultimate intelligence and how will this be affected by the kind of adoptive placement chosen for him?

Follow-ups of carefully studied placements are greatly needed for the validation of assumptions underlying practice that bear on these and many other questions. One attempt in this direction by Ruth Brenner and Ruth Hartley (4), in consultation with Dr. David M. Levy, evaluated the placement outcome of fifty children who were tested psychologically before and after placement. Agency predictions were compared with case work evaluation of the degree of success in family formation. This will be referred to again when we discuss agency work with adoptive couples. The psychological data "suggests that the value of infant psychological tests for prediction at three months, and even at fifteen or sixteen months, has been grossly overestimated by social workers. In order to obtain a test score which would in any individual case make accurate prediction of intellectual expectancy possible, it would be necessary to wait for testing until the child is four years of age.''

This leads us into an important question in which the adoption workers are showing considerable current interest and experimentation, i.e., how long after relinquishment should agencies keep babies under care before placing in adoptive homes, or put another way, at how young an age is it sound practice to place infants for adoption. There is a growing tendency toward revising previous policies in the direction of earlier placements which is indeed in keeping with psychoanalytic principles.

Escalona's study (10) of the use of infant tests for predictive purposes suggests promising possibilities that bear on this question. Seventy-two infants under the care of child placement agencies, including adoption agencies, were tested and retested after intervals varying from six months to several years. She stresses a shift in aim of infant testing corresponding to a changed view of intelligence from that of an already present potential awaiting realization during the maturation process to that of ''a fluctuating function, a delicate interaction of many forces and structural conditions—as one among many functions of variables.'' She points out that the test response ''is not something located within the infant organism and the immediate environment, i.e., the testing situation.'' Therefore, ''to the extent that the test scores obtained in infancy are regarded as predicting intelligence in later life as measured by subsequent intelligence tests—to that extent we are making a prediction not only about the subject but also about some aspects of the subject's environment at a later time.'' This coincides with the concepts that shaped the design of the Brenner-Hartley study in which the predictions of the subject's environment at a later time were made in respect to methods and criteria in choosing the infant's adoptive parents and assisting them in the early placement period. As stressed by Brenner, this newer view justifies and requires modification from the more traditional and almost exclusive emphasis on the adoptable child to dynamically oriented case work with prospective adoptive parents, even though the child remains the agency's primary client. Escalona's results lead her to expect that the validity of infant testing can be improved during the first half year of life by using the test situation as a framework for more comprehensive diagnosis of the infant's total functioning.

Another kind of data is germane to this question of the most desirable age for adoptive placement of infants. According to Spitz (27, 28) in several articles describing his psychoanalytic researches by direct observations of infants, most babies under six months are not yet capable of relating to the mother figure as a specific individual. Vital as the mothering experience is for the infant in the first half year, Spitz finds that its emerging ego development and capacity for object love has not advanced beyond its reacting to the maternal figure in terms of the satisfying or unsatisfying situation of which she is the central part. Her exact individuality therefore cannot be affectively perceived as such, so she is interchangeable as a person as far as the infant is concerned, just so that the mothering experience retains continuity and need satisfaction. After six months or so the baby's ability perceptively to discriminate has progressed so that his mother as a specific individual becomes all important to him. She serves in fact as a sort of external ego for him in view of his own helplessness and he may experience separation anxiety and even mourning reactions if he loses her. Strangers, recognized as such, are now reacted to with a certain degre of anxiety. To the extent that these observations by Spitz accurately reflect the timing of events in psychic development during the first year they would strongly support the desirability of adoptive placement before six months of age so that the mother-child relationship can be established with the permanent mother, and separation from the boarding mother effected while these are still essentially interchangeable for him emotionally.

The principle of balancing the interwoven needs and interests of natural parents, adoptive parents and adoptive children, mentioned earlier, is central to decisions around adoptive placements early in infancy. The Brenner-Hartley report reviews some of the thinking of this writer on the subject as of 1946 (4, p. 131). Selectivity as to such placements and some of the criteria to be considered were stressed. These included the natural parents' capacity and timing in reaching a final decision about surrender; the completeness of available family history for the baby and its degree of freedom from hereditary pathology; the prenatal obstetrical and birth history of the infant and its physical health as established by medical examinations; the capacity of adoptive parents knowingly to assume some added risks in terms of the child's development, as well as the natural parents' possible change of plan. The great advantages to adoptive parents and babies of very early placement and the growing body of successful experience with such placements since 1946 warrant our making them in greater numbers. As Fairweather (11) points out in "Early Placement and Adoption" agencies may well have overstressed the protection they could offer prospective adoptive couples against the development of physical or mental abnormalities beyond the predictive accuracy of medical and psychological procedures in infancy, since to give complete assurance of normal development "we should have to place adults, not children." (One might add that the process of holding the children for later testing under conditions of parental deprivation adversely influences the very attributes to be tested.)

Fairweather suggests instead that the case work services provided by the agencies constitute their main advantage over independent adoption from the standpoint of protection. Thus, those natural parents who are helped by case work are less likely to reverse their final decisions than those who feel that they were forced into signing or surrender by inner or outer pressure. The length of time the natural parent may need to reach a final decision to surrender and her capacity consistently to maintain the decision, once made, depends on many factors but among these the level of her emotional maturity, degree of ambivalence about surrender, and the quality of case work service available to her, and her accessibility to it are most important in considering the early adoptive placement of their infants. Oman reports (22) a study of one hundred mothers who had applied to the State Charities Aid Association for adoptive placement of their infants from the standpoint of their use of time before actually signing surrenders. Although ninety-six were certain they wanted adoption when they applied for it, over half of them—over 60 percent—changed their plans entirely or wavered. About one half of these finally did decide on adoption, the majority reaching that decision between the fourth and sixth month after the baby's birth. The 40 mothers who maintained their initial decision were thought to have derived emotional benefit from the waiting period between their seeking adoptive placement for their child and the actual surrender. Since Oman omits details, however, about the case work use of the interval between the baby's birth and surrender, it is not possible to evaluate whether equally sound final decisions might have been reachable sooner by more intensive or skillful case work help to these mothers. Fairweather reports on the successful adoptive outcome of seventy-one babies placed by her agency at three months or younger; twenty-one such placements made in one year (1947) were evaluated four years later by psychologists and case workers. The adjustment of all the children seemed healthy. When these were compared with a group of children placed at six months to two years, the adjustments for children and adoptive parents of these older placements were found to be slower and more difficult. Fairweather's conclusion that this difference in adjustment was due to the time of placement is somewhat open to question in view of the innumerable determinants of adjustment not taken into account by her study.

As to the prospective adoptive parents, it is true we seek for early adoption those who can best handle the added risks and who desire a parental experience with an infant who resembles a newborn of their own as closely as possible; yet these couples gain by the reduction of risks of another sort. I refer to the arousal of parental responsiveness, especially maternal, to the very young, totally dependent infant. Emotional risks to the adoptive placement from the parental side of the equation may stem from anxieties, inhibitions and conflicts in assuming the parental role frequently intensified for this group by their inner reactions to their long-standing incapacity for childbearing. Actual satisfying experience with their baby as near its beginning as possible can be of great protective value for the future child-parent relationship. In view of the potential advantages of early placement, when not contraindicated clinically, it is evident that agency procedures should work toward eliminating delays due to administrative rather than clinical reasons. Understanding what is at stake psychologically can give impetus to correcting the detention of babies in preadoptive boarding homes, for instance, because of staff delays in completing adoptive home studies.

In the adoptive placement of older children, the child must be planned with and not just planned for, as in the case of infants. Naturally, case work must cover a very wide range in meeting the needs of these children so differing in age, past experiences and current level of their total functioning. In general the work falls into the two broad categories of toddlers and older children. Because so many adoptive applicants prefer infants, suitable homes are harder to find. This difficulty is aggravated by the relatively higher incidence of some degree of disturbance in many of these children, particularly the older group, reflective of earlier deprivation and mishandling. These disturbances may be expressed in reduced ability to relate in appealing fashion to prospective adoptive applicants, so that the results of rejection bring about further rejection or, the child may require considerable case work help while in the agency's foster home before he can utilize the emotional nourishment offered him by permanent parents. Parallel to the direct case work preparation of the child for adoption—sometimes aided by psychiatric consultation—careful and sensitive interpretation of his behavior and needs to adoptive applicants, in advance of the first meeting, and thereafter throughout the gradualized steps of placement may be decisive for his placeability and the ongoing happiness of the newly formed family. Hallinan (14) describes some of the psychosocial implications of adoptions of older children, emphasizes the obligations of agencies to effect these, and reports successful outcomes for them.

All the social case work techniques and theoretical concepts underlying them of high quality child placement practice apply to this aspect of adoption work and need not be reviewed here. In addition, however, certain distinctive elements in adoptive placement need special consideration, notably the finality and permanence sought in adoption and its "real" rather than substitutive family membership which differs qualitatively from temporary foster placement. Establishment of a positive relationship between the child and case worker provides the most potent means of helping him in his truly great undertaking—the letting go of his immediate familiar world and the moving into acceptance of a new life with a "mommy and daddy for always." By this relationship the worker serves the child as a firm supportive bridge during his frightening and confusing transitions. She provides continuity between the shifting relationships he is losing and gaining, and on the foundation of the trust she can engender and the anxieties she can relieve, the child can tolerate those immediate painful feelings she may need to stimulate for the sake of his ultimate welfare. Specifically, the case worker must help the preadoptive child clarify, in ways compatible with his age level and individuality, his understanding and feelings about his past, present and future. What does he remember of his natural parents (or parent substitutes), and how does he understand their nonavailability to him now? Disregarding and disallowing his memories and feelings on that score can incapacitate him from moving ahead emotionally through a partial loss of his sense of self, and by burdening him with excessive unresolved frustrated longings, fears, resentments, and guilt. For instance, does he feel deserted and betrayed and, as Wires (31) has suggested, does he feel himself guilty of desertion and disloyalty to his earlier ties if he yields to the temptation of giving himself to the new adoptive family? The child needs help too with his comprehension and feelings about the necessity to leave his immediately preadoptive environment. McCleery (20) states, "He needs to know this definitely or he can feel, in a sense, kidnapped. . . . The worker must have the courage to face the truth with him without evasion, even if it involves pain" throughout the whole process to "free a child from the clinging hands of the past, and to equip him to go on to a more constructive happy future." Rainer (24) emphasizing the same principle of helping the child towards an understanding of previous separations as prerequisite to his acceptance of adoption writes, "Reaching this understanding often comes as a painful experience for the child. He may have feelings of personal worthlessness or questions about rejective experiences. He may be having difficulty in facing reality factors. . . . As these are brought out and the worker accepts his feelings and then helps him to clarify these in relation to his own worth as a person, he can move into new experiences." She adds that the difficulty of such tasks for children old enough consciously to experience the loss of their own parents should stimulate the preventive effort of helping parents reach as early a decision as clinically feasible regarding adoptive placement for their children.

The social worker's task may be seen as helping the preadoptive child survive an undue succession of prematurely ruptured attachments to parental figures with minimum hardship and psychological damage while repairing, conserving and fostering his capacity for healthy attachment to new parents. Appropriate reassurance based on understanding the child's language, behavioral and symptomatic as well as verbal, entails repetition, consistency and honesty by the worker. Enlisting and permitting maximum participation by the child in the adoptive planning and placement is generally recognized as a most desirable reassurance against his anxiety-laden sense of helplessness as a passive pawn at the mercy of all-powerful unpredictable grownups. Sensitive timing of the various stages of adoption attuned to the particular child's inner pace is a vital ingredient of reassurance; destructive anxiety can mount when certain steps of the process are too prolonged, such as between a child's relating to prospective parents and his actual placement with them; by the same token, however, panic may stem from feeling rushed and stampeded so that a more graduated spacing and slowing down is the most effective reassurance. Another general principle along this line with preadoptive children consists of consolidating each step along the way of new environments and new relationships by converting a previous unknown into a positively experienced known which can then furnish continuity as the next unfamiliar element is introduced.

Psychodynamic insight and concepts of personality development underly these principles and procedures for direct work with children for adoption so that theoretical substantiation in general may be found abundantly in the literature. It may be of some interest to single out, however, one ingredient of personality recently discussed by Erikson (9) because of its particular applicability to our topic. Erikson regards the inner institution of "ego identity" as crucial to healthy personality and defines it as "a sense of identity, continuity and distinctiveness. . . . a sense of who one is, of knowing where one belongs, of knowing what one wants to do . . . a sense accrued throughout the stages of childhood that there is continuity and sameness and meaning to one's life history." Ego identity, as something both conscious and unconscious, is normally established at the end of adolescence, according to Erikson, and sufferers from impaired or insufficient ego identity cannot "integrate all the various steps of their previous ego development, nor achieve a sense of belonging from their status in their society." By contrast, healthy ego identity entails "feeling that his past has a meaning in terms of his future but also from the feeling that the future has a meaning in terms of his past." It is obvious that the typical life history of a child adopted later than infancy, with its lack of continuity between successive, unrelated experiences and relationships—natural parents, institutions, foster homes and adoptive homes—is especially inconducive to healthy establishment of ego identity in Erikson's sense. Such a series of changing worlds for the young child opposes his accrual of feeling identical with himself. Correspondingly, however, this specific impairment may be greatly minimized and corrected by the case worker's therapeutic opportunities as discussed above, particularly as to continuity, meaningful relatedness to past and future, and the restoration of trust.

In the same paper Erikson relates the earliest stages of identity development to the young infant's gradually established sense of trust through repeated reassuring experiences of inner need satisfaction by an outer human world whose warmth and love can be believed in. Erikson views "a sense of basic trust in existence" as the earliest criterion of healthy infant personality. He regards the trust-mistrust conflict as the first nuclear conflict whose outcome depends a great deal on the very early child care and training. To support his view of trust formation as "a basic problem of social interaction," Erikson cites the "continuous retesting of the alternation of basic trust and basic mistrust" in regressive psychopathological conditions. This alternation pattern is extremely familiar to those working with children for adoption. The preadoptive vicissitudes so often experienced by these children are indeed inimical to this basic sense of trust and much of the adoptive case worker's skill and patience is directed toward its maximum repair and belated building. Whatever the case worker can accomplish and initiate along these lines before placement can hopefully be greatly extended and strengthened for the child after he becomes part of his adoptive family. Finding the kind of parents with whom this can take place, therefore, and giving them enabling support and direction constitutes the crucial indirect help to the child for which the direct preplacement work with him is a prerequisite.

The writer's main experience with adoption has been gained as psychiatric consultant to the Free Synagogue Child Adoption Committee so that the following case example illustrating some of the foregoing is selected from that agency with due recognition, as already noted, of the many prevailing differences in practice among agencies.

Jimmy was two years eleven months old when he started with us and he was placed in his adoptive home eight months later at three years seven months. Let us look more closely at some of what happened to him, in him and with him during those eight months of intensive and decisive experience.

Jimmy had been placed as a foundling of three months in an infant's institution where he remained for a year. He was admitted there in good physical condition and his health was essentially good throughout his stay. At sixteen months he was

409

transferred to a foster home agency and placed in a three-baby temporary foster home. Adoption plans could not be considered pending clarification of the child's parenthood by the Department of Welfare. Jimmy remained in the foster home until his transfer at almost three years to the adoption agency's foster home. When referred to the Child Adoption Committee available history from the two previous agencies indicated that his adjustment at the infant's institution was felt to be very good. The foster home had not fully met his needs with the result that "he is quite fearful of strangers, although he responds to the affection of people he knows and tends to demand excessive attention and to react with temper outbursts overreadily when frustrated. Intellectually Jimmy seems to be developing normally although when he was nearly two the psychologist could not administer a standard test because he was so upset and showed so much resistance. Motor development is good but language is retarded. Jimmy has a slight convergent squint which is barely noticeable and an open bite which is noticeable but rather cute." As an interesting sidelight, a different worker describing the child's appearance around the same time states that "the open bite detracts from his appearance to some extent." (This neatly illustrates the factor of worker's subjectivity in appraising physical defects. Although very minor in this instance it can assume importance. Thus workers often worry about the negative effect on prospective adoptive parents of telling them about a child's defect lest this will cause the couple to reject the child. Sometimes these workers fail to realize how much their own subjective negative attitude toward a certain attribute may tip the scales for the clients, nor how the subjectivity of the latter, if left free of influence by the worker, may actually value or ignore the so-called defect. Furthermore, the negative or positive value placed on such a specific physical attribute of the child by worker or prospective adoptive parent may vary with other less conscious feelings of like or dislike toward the child of which the judgment about his appearance is a displacement. It may not be irrevelant, for instance, that the worker describing Jimmy's overbite as unattractive at her first meeting had undergone an extremely trying session with him at the doctor's office where he had screamed in fear and anger from the moment of entering the building, ignoring her overtures. On the other hand, I overheard the worker who finally consummated Jimmy's adoptive placement in a general glow of mutual affection, refer to this same overbite many months later as "very cute and attractive.")

In outline, the casework with Jimmy proceeded as follows: Seven weeks after his first meeting with Mrs. K. at the Child Adoption Committee's office, brought by Miss P., his worker at the foster home agency, Jimmy left the foster home where he had lived for the past year and a half of his three-year-old life and was taken by Mrs. K. to a CAC foster home. This occurred at their fourth meeting. The objectives of this first four-session phase of case work included the separation from his foster mother whom he called "mommy" and preparation for the new foster mother and her family, referred to by Mrs. K. as "Aunt Marie" to help him better distinguish the difference in relationship between his temporary foster mother and a real "mommy", a term to be reserved for the adoptive mother. During this first phase a shift was accomplished whereby his initial clinging to Miss P., his former worker, and fear of Mrs. K., the stranger, was very gradually reversed so that he could increasingly let go of Miss P. and relate positively to Mrs. K. He was given repeated opportunities to test out and find out what Mrs. K. was like. In fact, he dramatized this by minutely exploring her face with his hands, a reaction he was to repeat with new foster parents and at the first meeting with his adoptive parents. His advances were encouraged and his retreatings respected. Through blocks and a doll house he was told about Aunt Marie's family and details of her house, such as just where he would sleep, etc. His smashing of blocks and avoidance of listening about Aunt Marie were recognized and accepted as his protest against the change, but after reassurance, candy, enjoyable play, cuddling and obvious acceptance of him and his feelings, the theme would be reopened with diminishing protest and increasing interest. At the next to the last session before the actual transfer, the child was obviously relieved by reassurance he would go back home that day and only next time to Aunt Marie's. The respite of "more time" can often avert trauma. On the day of transfer he cried on leaving Miss P. and was not cheered by the new clothes he had previously welcomed. Diagnostically this may be taken as a favorable indication of capacity to relate; the pain was mitigated by his ability to accept comforting from Mrs. K. on the basis of the rapport previously established. He wet his pants en route which was well handled by Mrs. K. and by Aunt Marie on arrival through Mrs. K.'s help. Symptomatic enuresis recurred from time to time during the eight months under CAC care, almost always specifically traceable either to separation anxiety and resultant hostility or to testing out the tolerance of new parent figures after an initial period of "good" behavior.

The second case work phase occupied the next five months and included ten visits by the case worker, as well as many additional telephone contacts between case worker and foster mother. The objectives were multiple. Jimmy and his new foster family took to each other extremely well. The worker's first task was to reestablish her positive relationship with Jimmy in view of his greater ambivalence for fear her visits might mean her taking him away again from his new found family with Aunt Marie. Thus, he was enuretic in the home for the first time the night before her expected visit and he only kissed her as she was leaving. By her second visit, however, he apparently responded to the reassuring outcome of the previous time by offering a warm welcome. The worker's visits provided an opportunity for assessing his adjustment as a guide to his readiness for adoption. She could also get to know him better for greater discernment in selecting the adoptive home most suitable for him. By keeping in touch with Jimmy and the foster family, Mrs. K. could interpret his behavior to the foster mother and make suggestions as needed that prevented and relieved difficulties and promoted constructive and satisfying experiences. Thus, when Jimmy's initial honeymoon was over and he became disobedient and negativistic towards the foster mother, telling her to "shut up," Mrs. K.'s explanations to the foster mother dissipated the latter's incipient hostility and replaced it with justified pride in Jimmy's progress as illustrated by the improvement in speech. He now spoke in full sentences instead of isolated words, although his pronunciation was still unclear. After about two months Mrs. K. began more open preparatory discussion about finding Jimmy an adoptive home, although some clarification had been attempted ever since the outset of contact. Thus, he had begun to call his foster mother "mommy" and Mrs. K. records: "I said to Jimmy that Aunt Marie was not his mommy, that I was looking for a mommy and daddy for him and that when I found a mommy and daddy I thought Jimmy would like we could then go and visit them and then come back to Aunt Marie's, and if Jimmy did like this mommy and daddy we could go back there again and he could stay there forever. Jimmy said that he did not want to visit anybody and I said that we were not going now, that I was only looking for them and when I found them perhaps he will then want to go to visit. Jimmy looked at me questioningly and then smiled at me and nodded his head." At another session, by which time Jimmy had finally come to calling the foster mother Aunt Marie, worker reports: "I said to Jimmy that I knew he liked it here and he would want to stay. I also told him that Aunt Marie liked him but that she and Uncle Peter were not his mommy and daddy and they kept him and looked after him and liked him, but I wanted him to have a mommy and daddy so that he could stay with them all the time, and therefore we may have to go to visit them. Jimmy said 'No' and busied himself instead of listening to me. I kept on repeating the sentences in very simple words and then Jimmy again, as once before, looked up at me and smiled." During this period Jimmy was developing very well, physically and socially. Some increase in bed wetting and temper outbursts became apparent and some limitation of concentration span troubled Mrs. K. Despite the worker's interpretive and guidance efforts the foster mother, more accustomed to younger children, did not handle the boy's growing aggressiveness too well. This probably contributed somewhat to his symptoms just mentioned, but another source no doubt was the anxiety provoked by the case worker through her repeated preparations for adoptive placement to which Jimmy reacted with renewed separation anxiety, clinging to his immediate known world—that of the foster family. In the long run, however, it was felt better for Jimmy to eundre this deliberately incurred anxiety, with much in the relation with Mrs. K. to sustain and gratify him, than to expose him to worse emotional consequences through repressed conflicts, emotional unpreparedness and a sense of non-participation in his own life plan. However, it was felt important to avoid protracted anxiety through delay in adoptive placement once Jimmy was felt to be ready for it.

Psychiatric consultation had been sought for prognostic evaluation of his residual symptoms which, in addition to those mentioned, included car sickness, fear of the bogeyman, and fear of being bitten by animals, as well as a tendency to bite other people himself. Despite unknowns in Jimmy's early history and his subsequent shifts, prognosis was considered reasonably favorable. Psychological examination revealed a score of average intelligence with evidence to suggest higher potential. Since the test was undertaken when the child was physically under par with a head cold, the likelihood of his actual ability exceeding the score is the greater.

By the end of what I have called the second phase of case work Mrs. K. took Jimmy to the CAC office from the foster home (entailing a train ride since the foster home is in a suburb and the office in New York City). Jimmy was prepared for this trip well in advance and had come to look forward to it, but only after he had actually clamped his hand over Mrs. K.'s mouth when she began to talk again about a new family. He recognized the CAC office and the toys he played with during his first few interviews with considerable pleasure and sense of continuity. "A man and a lady" dropped in while he was playing there and he accepted them as a matter of course. Actually they were prospective adoptive parents viewing the child for possible adoption. According to her promise, Mrs. K. journeyed back with Jimmy to the foster home, thereby emphasizing her trustworthiness to him. The couple did not wish to proceed further with Jimmy due to their persistent preference for a much younger child, but the trip seemed to liberate Jimmy somehow, perhaps through successful facing and surviving some thing he had dreaded.

The last month of Jimmy's care by the CAC may be regarded as phase three of his case work and was carried out by another worker, Mrs. S., because Mrs. K. had to leave the agency. Mrs. K. prepared Jimmy for this change and explained her departure to him. The youngster took this transfer very well, partly due to the skill of the new worker, partly because of Mrs. K.'s handling of the shift, and to a large extent, I think, because he really grasped that Mrs. K., Mrs. S., and the CAC office which he had just revisited, were all part of the same supportive team, one member of which could therefore somewhat represent another on his behalf, so that the legacy of good feeling built up through the months with Mrs. K. was available to Mrs. S. In any event, Mrs. S. telescoped the over-all time of phase three by seeing Jimmy very intensively. No doubt this played a role too in his responsiveness to her, since Mrs. K. had visited him much less frequently and for shorter periods. Mrs. S. saw Jimmy four times within five days, spending a morning or afternoon with him each time on pleasurable outings. Mrs. S. reports: "I told him I was the lady Mrs. K. had told him about and that I was coming to see him instead of Mrs. K., etc. He nodded his head in acceptance. As time went on in my contacts, I told him that I was going to find a mommy and daddy for him.

He did like to hear this. Interestingly enough though, during this week when I was seeing so much of Jimmy he never once wet the bed. At times when I was reading to him, or if I hugged him, he would pick up my hand and bite me. He also gave me a few 'socks'. He related easily and loved the attention he was given by me. He expressed many fears such as of a bogeyman, was afraid to pick up a book that had fallen off the porch because 'rats would come out and bite me'. I brought him a circus book one day and while he liked the story, he was afraid each animal pictured would bite him.''

On the fourth outing within the five day period, Mrs. S. told him that she would be coming to see him again three days from then and would bring some friends with her, a man and a lady. He nodded assent to this. Mrs. S. meanwhile had discussed Jimmy with Mr. and Mrs. N. who were extremely eager to see him as soon as possible. In the words of Mrs. S., ''Jimmy was a little shy in the beginning but he soon warmed up to Mr. and Mrs. N., the toys they brought helping in this. He was intrigued with Mr. N.'s green car and he wanted a ride, so we went to the park I had taken him to before (again the stress on the familiar). He bit Mr. and Mrs. N. a few times, for which I had prepared them.'' After the visit Mrs. S. was in touch with the N.'s. At first Mrs. N. had a little reservation because of Jimmy's poor speech, but three days later she had come to think of the speech difficulty as an insecurity symptom and with Mr. N. felt very positive and comfortable about Jimmy as their son. They visited Jimmy again, giving him a holster with two guns and a cowboy hat which he had greatly longed for. Once he got them he wouldn't take them off and even slept with them. After this visit Mrs. N. was positive she wanted Jimmy and felt she had exaggerated the speech difficulty before and now was easily able to understand him. (Note earlier comments about subjective correspondence between liking the child and liking his ''defects.'') Mrs. S. and the N.'s visited Jimmy for the third time on the following day, on which occasion the N.'s took him out in the green car which Jimmy liked very much. He seemed quite comfortable in leaving with them, without Mrs. S., although when he returned he wanted to know where she was to tell her about what they had done.

''I spoke to Jimmy about the N.'s and he told me he liked them. I told him they didn't have any little boy but wanted one very much, that they would like to have him for their little boy if he would like this. He shook his head 'Yes' and then hid his

415

face in my lap. I told him about their house in the country, the ride in the car to get there, the bed he would sleep in, etc. and he listened very carefully.'' Mrs. S. had arranged with the N.'s for Jimmy's placement with them for the very next day, feeling that readiness had been established and prolongation would be more anxiety-provoking for Jimmy.

When Mrs. S. and the N.'s arrived Jimmy was dressed in his cowboy equipment, with clothes and toys packed, eagerly awaiting their arrival. He had continued dry at night throughout this period of meetings with the N.'s. ''We played a while in the house and finally Mr. and Mrs. N. asked Jimmy if he was ready to go with them, and he ran for his things, ran out to the car and was all ready to go. He waved good-bye to us very gayly and seemed very comfortable in going off with Mr. and Mrs. N.''

Phase three of case work with Jimmy, then, was concentrated within a nine-day period starting with Mrs. S.'s first visit and concluding with adoptive placement. Both the acceleration of the last period of work and the patient, slow-going pace of the earlier months seem clinically helpful in terms of the child's progress. Excerpts from Mrs. N.'s letters to Mrs. S. right after Jimmy joined them and during the next few months convey the flavor of the postplacement experience and attest to the agency's effective selectivity of adoptive parents and case work with them preparatory to actual placement, which constitute an all-important service to Jimmy and other Jimmies.

Five days after placement Mrs. N. wrote, ''Jimmy is going through the various stages of adjustment much faster than expected. He called us mommy and daddy from the moment we arrived. When we take a walk or go visiting we have to know 'where my house is' (need for reassurance—V.W.B.). We have some difficulty changing clothes and so far pajamas have not been worn. He hasn't had a bath but does clean up quite well. (Is he afraid if he takes off his clothes to take a bath or change to pajamas that he will be unprotected and defenseless, or perhaps does he fear the loss of his new clothes if he lets go of them?—V.W.B.) He had a few mild temper outbursts lasting about five minutes when he got very tired because a rabbit trap was set up for twenty minutes and no rabbit would come to it. If too many of his friends (three) should come at once to the house, he shuts the door of his room so that 'they can't take my toys.' For a day or two he didn't like me and wouldn't share his daddy with me. His resentment and hostilities are taken out on old logs and rocks and pieces of lumber, and less frequently on us. His doll shares some of it. And tonight he got a plastic Shmoo about his size, which bounces back when you punch it. He enjoys that immensely. He often asks to be told a story. The greatest thrill we got was when he saw his daddy the first evening after the day's absence. Words could not express his joy at the reunion." A few days later Mrs. N.'s letter reported a victorious bath, less frequent and less intense biting, and a let-up on his initial excessive and exclusive appetite for sweets. By the following month Mrs. N.'s letter indicates that Jimmy is sharing his toys more easily because he seems much less afraid that he will lose them. His temper outbursts are less frequent and more controlled. "His fear of a bogeyman is actually a fear of the dark. We have tried to help him overcome it, but that will take more time." Although preferring to wipe out every reminder of life other than that in their present family, Mrs. N. overcomes her disinclination of speaking with Jimmy about Mrs. S. because she can see the value of a more realistic continuity for Jimmy and, grateful to the agency, she accepts its continued interest and responsibility for the next months prior to legal adoption. Mrs. N. reports that Jimmy loves to hear about all his relatives "those he has seen as well as those he hasn't seen. He brags to the other children about his grandmas, grandpa, cousins, etc." (Is not this an expression of hunger for belongingness on the part of a child who never had any relatives at all?—V.W.B.) When the family moved to the city for the winter from the country where Jimmy first joined them and spent his first months, the N.'s recognized and understood renewed expressions of anxiety. Another move might mean a dreaded separation as in the past. The N.'s decided to tell him the story of his adoption. "We call it the 'Jimmy Story.' He enjoyed the story very much, especially when details were mentioned that he remembered. . . . he has been wearing pajamas for the last ten days or so."

Four months after placement Mrs. S. reports: "He bites his nails once in a while, but not as often as he did in the beginning. He was afraid of the animals when the N.'s took him to the zoo so they haven't repeated this though he seems to be less afraid of dogs now and loves kittens and cats. He no longer gets car sick. Temper tantrums occur on occasion when Jimmy is very frustrated, but they are much milder and less frequent. He is happy, loves to help around the house, and has moved the hands on the clock to where they should be when Mr. N. comes home in order to make his daddy come home sooner. He plays very well with other children, speaks as distinctly as is normal for a child his age, and no longer bites people. His concentration span is excellent and he can entertain himself with his toys for long periods of time.''

Several references have been made already to case work with prospective adoptive parents in terms of the agency's responsibility to them as clients in their own right, and in relation to the children's welfare by optimum selective home finding. A most desirable trend has been under way for some time in a number of adoption agencies toward more and better case work with adoptive applicants. It is to be hoped that the field in general will increasingly make the necessary adjustments in administration, personnel and staff qualifications to further extend this development. This trend, concerned as it is with unconscious motivations, attitudes and conflicts, is probably due in large measure to the general integration of psychoanalytic concepts into case work from which it certainly derives much of its rationale and method. Gains in psychological insight also account for a parallel shift in the weighting of factors sought in "desirable" adoptive homes. Emotional capacities for parenthood rather than economic advantages per se, for instance, are considered more important and, of course, are harder to ascertain.

Several important aspects of case work with adoptive parents as developed in the agency with which I am connected have been well described in articles by Brown (5), Michaels (21), and Brenner (3), so that it would seem needlessly repetitious to review this in detail. In general, case work with this type of client attempts several functions. Selective assessment, of course, is the main one entailing diagnostic skills of a high order. However, in line with the well known principle that diagnosis and therapy are to some extent inseparable processes, a case worker can help as well as appraise. It is true that these clients come to the agency seeking a child, not therapy, so the help must be within the context of the adoption situation. Adoption for these couples may be viewed as a gradual sequential process. The case worker enters into this process at several stages along the way, her functions varying somewhat with each. Only some of those who embark on this sequence with the agency actually reach their original goal of adoption. They may withdraw themselves or be refused a child by the agency at any of the successive steps, although every effort should be made toward disqualification as early in the progression as clinically possible in order to minimize false hopes and resultant greater trauma.

What then are we looking for in adoptive parents and how should we look for it? In this subtle complex realm of parental potential there can be no simple checklist of qualifying and disqualifying items, nor any single rule of thumb method for differentiating, on behalf of the children for whom the agency is responsible, those who may be most or least suited for successful adoptive parenthood. We can neither ignore our responsibility to use existent knowledge and skills toward such appraisals, nor delude ourselves into a sense of infallibility regarding our judgments in areas where so much remains unknown or controversial. In general, we seek couples whose relationship with each other is mutually satisfying but which will be enhanced, rather than upset, by the addition of a child. We seek couples whose conscious and unconscious motivations to adopt are relatively free of neurotic conflict and compatible with warm, mature love for the child as an individual in his own right. We seek couples who have come to terms enough with their feelings about their childlessness to accept adoption in lieu of biological parenthood with maximum comfort and minimum fear, shame or resentment. In short, we seek couples who are on good adult terms with themselves and each other, who are ready for adoption psychologically and situationally, and whose desire for children stems from emotionally healthy needs and capacities. And not infrequently, in the course of searching for those attributes through case work interviews, opportunities arise whereby the case worker can use her skill and insight therapeutically—still within the adoptive context—so that inhibiting anxieties or self-doubts may be relieved and latent capacities released sufficiently to make a decisive difference in a couple's ability to move into adoption successfully.

From the outset of contact another way the worker assists is by furnishing realistic information about adoption since applicants usually approach the agency with a varying number of misconceptions and false expectations. The client's reactions and use of this data at the initial interview, or any subsequent stage, not only has value for him by way of preparation for adoption experience, but may offer diagnostic indications of such relevant personality factors as flexibility and the degree of realistic dominance over the irrational elements in his mental life. It is not infrequent that such factual confrontation results in couples discovering for themselves that they cannot really

419

accept a child other than their own, or that they are in much less agreement about wanting a child than either had let the other, or sometimes even himself, know until then. The value of maladjustment prevention by self-withdrawal for such couples is obvious, as well as for the child they might have obtained and probably would have, had they sought independent adoption.

The reasons for the couple's childlessness, what it means and has meant to the husband and wife, and how it affects their feelings toward themselves, each other, and their motivation to adopt should be carefully explored. Naturally, we try to reach behind the clients' conscious attitudes, cognizant of the deep feelings and conflicts entailed, and the profound psychic interconnections between reproductive incapacity and the total personality. The question of whether the impaired fertility afflicts the husband, wife, or both, is of considerable psychodynamic significance. Likewise, the psychological implications of absolute sterility, as in hysterectomy, for example, are different than for relative infertility. As part of intake procedure, our agency routinely requests a confidential letter from the couple's physician stating the cause or causes of childlessness, its treatability, and the prognosis for future childbearing.

Psychogenic sterility, or more accurately, functional infertility, may be symptomatic of unconscious neurotic conflicts closely related in these clients to repressed motives, anxieties and fantasies underlying the conscious wish to adopt. Studies so far have been mainly limited to female psychogenic sterility. Hypotheses as to the specific physiological mechanisms involved are still speculative but the clinical experience of many of us supports Kroger and Freed's (17) statement: "Psychogenic sterility should receive more attention from clinicians because it is now recognized that emotional conflicts can produce dysfunctions in the generative organs." Psychosomatic researches by Therese Benedek (1) have pointed to interconnections between ovarian hormonal cycles and emotional manifestations; she elaborates some of the implications of these findings in a recent discussion of infertility in women as a psychosomatic defense (in the absence of causative organic pathology). "The term 'defense' is defined as an unconscious function of the ego to protect the self—the total personality—against the dangers originating within the organism; in this case the physiologic processes of the procreative functions." According to Benedek, the monthly hormonal preparation for pregnancy of the sexual cycle is paralleled by an emotional preparation which by monthly repetition normally fosters psychosexual maturation. In certain neurotic and immature women, however, this inner process is reacted to with fear and each monthly repetition builds up defenses against the repressed irrationally dreaded dangers until actual protective inability to conceive is "achieved." This should not be misconstrued to mean that all women seeking adoption with somatically unexplained infertility fit into this category and should be denied adoption. As already stressed, our evaluations cannot be made on the basis of a single factor. Repeated patterns and clusters rather than isolated instances are necessary in personality appraisal. Alertness to possibilities, however, sharpens perception of clues that may then be substantiated or refuted by further evidence.

Without wishing to attach undue importance to the topic of infertility in adoptive work, it might be of interest to pursue this discussion somewhat further. It is common knowledge that previously "sterile" women sometimes conceive shortly after adopting a child, or even during some stage of the adoption process. Systematic investigation and establishment of causal connections are still lacking essentially.* Kroger and Freed (17), referring to a study by Hanson and Rock (American Journal of Obstetrics and Gynecology, Vol. 59, pp. 311-319, 1950) state: "Hanson and Rock questioned a group of 202 women and found that adoption cannot be considered a reliable cure for sterility. Their study is interesting but we doubt the reliability of questionnaire material." Orr (23) has reported the case of a woman who became pregnant following the decision to adopt. He had analyzed both this patient and her husband. Conception had been previously unsuccessful, despite medical treatment for both husband and wife. Orr suggests how the psychodynamic realignment entailed in this women's preparation for the adoptive baby might have influenced conception. The concomitant somatic treatment received by husband and wife does not refute psychic causality in this case but renders it less conclusive. Helene Deutsch (8) devotes a chapter to psychogenic sterility in women and describes five specific types from her psychoanalytic experience, stating that she considers unconscious fear as the most frequent cause of such sterility. In another valuable chapter on adoptive mothers discussed from the psychoanalytic standpoint, Deutsch mentions three cases of women who became pregnant in connection with adoption, the first when about to

---

* Female Functional Infertility and Adoption, Viola W. Bernard, in work

adopt, the second less than a year after adopting a baby, and the third—the only one of the three whom Deutsch analyzed herself—during the first year of her adoptive motherhood. Deutsch suggests some psychodynamic explanations. Knight(16) also refers briefly to functional sterility, citing instances of childless women who sought adoption when convinced of the impossibility of conception and who became pregnant after adopting a child. He theorizes that unconscious sterility "was somehow overcome by the experience of adoption and taking care of a child."

Data from adoptive mothers studied by the writer is in general agreement with Knight, Deutsch, Orr, and Benedek. An extremely interesting instance of the reciprocal possibilities between clinical service and research inherent in adoption work in general, and the problem of functional infertility in particular, occurred a few years ago. Jacobson (15) has contributed the first detailed psychoanalytic case report in the literature of a case of sterility cured by psychoanalytic treatment. Conception occurred during the eighth month of analysis and the pregnancy and delivery were normal. The patient, a married woman in her mid-thirties, had been amenorrheic since the age of sixteen after two years of normal periods. Her sterility, thought due to ovarian deficiency, had remained medically refractory throughout the ten years of her marriage, despite strenuous conscious efforts to become pregnant. There had been no medical treatment other than psychoanalysis for an appreciable time, however, since the sterility was regarded as organically irreversible on the basis of a biopsy report of atrophic endometrium.

The patient's need and suitability for analysis had been first recognized by this writer as psychiatric consultant to the adoption agency from which the patient and her husband were then seeking a baby. Although, as well put by Michaels (21), psychiatric referral of adoptive applicants by the agency is most often unwise, even when psychopathology becomes evident, this patient was among the exceptions for whom it was indicated. The patient dramatically demonstrated unconscious fear and opposition to the motherhood she had sought so desperately by developing acute anxiety, depression and bodily symptoms when her conscious wish for the adoptive baby was realized. The baby who had been placed with the couple showed signs of reactive stress and the agency, acting on its responsibility for the child, replaced it in a more favorable home. Referred to as Mrs. A., this initial phase of the case history supplementing Jacobson's report may be found in a paper by the writer (2). In view of how much preparatory psychiatric help this patient needed in order to accept referral, it seems more than likely that progressive illness rather than the gratifying therapeutic result would have eventuated for this woman without the agency's intervention. The psychiatrist's activity included several direct interviews, as well as continuous consultation with the case worker. Although scarcely typical of day-to-day agency function, the case illustrates how analytically oriented case work with the adoptive parents can prevent or reduce serious future maladjustment for the child, as well as for the parents.

The main function of adoption work, of course, is the very positive one of helping to dispel the deep frustration of barren couples and homeless children by family formation. Concomitant prevention of greater frustrations by ill-advised adoptions is less rewarding and more arduous, but essential. Experience has proven repeatedly, for instance, that couples should not adopt while either or both are suffering from depression, for their own sakes' and the child's. Ignorant of this, many couples—urged on by their sympathetic, well-meaning friends—desperately turn to adoption in reaction to recent tragic bereavement such as the death of a child. The same misguided hope to cure depression by adoption may be seen in some mood disturbances related to sterility. In either case, the decision about adoption should await recovery from the depression, for placement during it is in clinical violation of everything known about the psychopathology of depression, popular misconceptions to the contrary, and leads to added rather than lessened misery. Recently bereaved parents adopting a "replacement child" cannot help but relate to him with rejection and ambivalence. His value for them as a substitute for the deceased child entails rejection of him in his own right; hostility for surviving and displacing their own child is almost inevitable, often complicated by guilt feelings toward the latter should they let themselves love the newcomer for himself. Stampeded by great pressure from the community and their own compassion, workers have been misled into rushing such emergency placements through, often waiving the ascertainment of history data and precrisis personality which might even have been disqualifying had adoptive application preceded the occurrence of tragedy. Of course it is true that most adoptions, for the parents, are attempts to substitute for their own children that could not be born or who could not survive. But this adjustment through substitution works out far better when the adopted child is felt as replacing the otherwise lost opportunity to experience family life and parental role, rather than as a replacement of a specific child.

Adoptive placement is also contraindicated while a couple is emotionally preoccupied by insistent craving for conception and is in the midst of active medical measures to achieve it. This does not mean that the agency should unrealistically expect couples to eradicate a longing for biologic parenthood from which, after all, the soundest urge toward adoption derives its force. What is meant, however, is illustrated by a couple seen recently who pleaded for an adoptive baby at the same time as they frantically intensified efforts to achieve conception by every method at once, including hypnotism and artificial insemination. They should be dissuaded from considering adoption until, should they ultimately fail to achieve the much preferred natural pregnancy, they can accomplish the inner adaptation whereby rechanneling of their needs and yearnings permits preponderant fulfillment rather than frustration by adoption; otherwise they cannot help but resent adoption as a narcissistic defeat and the adopted child as a symbol of that defeat. Insufficiently resolved conflicts about their fertility can impair the adoptive parents' relation to their child in many subtle ways. Some such parents find it too difficult to tell the child about his adoption, even though doing so is generally recognized as best for the child. Not infrequently their disinclination, rationalized as kindness to the youngster, is rooted in retained, acute feelings of shame and guilty anxiety about infertility so that "telling" about adoption means revealing too painful a defect. For such parents the adopted child may be valued far less for himself than as a narcissistic compensation for a persistent sense of narcissistic injury. The child inevitably disappoints such a parent whose expectations are irrationally high, whereupon adoption provides an all-too-ready rationalization for rejection, i.e., "He's not really my child."

Hopefully, reference to some of these frequently seen hazards will not give rise to false pessimism about adoption. The case of Jimmy and Mr. and Mrs. N., presented earlier, typifies the brighter aspects. Results of placement outcome for the fifty children followed up by Brenner and Hartley (4) were on the whole very encouraging. Retrospective study of mistakes in the cases of the relatively less successful outcomes have already led to improved practice. In order continually to improve the bases for predictions in this field, more such detailed follow-up studies are desirable, preferably with larger samples. Brenner's discussion of the characteristics of the fifty couples in relation to the placement outcome is of particular interest in this matter of adoptive parent selection, although one might have wished it possible to have included data as to how the child's inborn tendencies and reactions to preadoptive experience influenced parental attitudes, in turn so crucial for the child's adjustment. In the same study David M. Levy developed a rating scale for adoptive homes in an attempt to provide a standard scheme for observation as a research tool for further investigations. Levy selected six areas of the parent-child relationship which he thought reflected conditions which contribute to children's growth and emotional security. These are "affection, admiration and criticism, ease or tension, patience and indulgence, freedom and time spent by the parents with the child." These six qualities were rated by case work observations on a six-point scale ranging from "insufficient" to "excessive," and a scoring system was worked out based on low desirability for both extremes. The method admittedly involved qualitative judgment in evaluating what was too little or too much in each of the parent-child areas. However, Levy set up definitions as guides and reports that three independent clinicians experienced in adoption work—a social worker, psychiatrist, and psychologist —used the scale and came out with the same answers. As a further check, the best and worst homes, as evaluated by the social worker, were found to have been picked up by the six-item scale. Despite a number of sizable limitations recognized by the authors, the instrument is to be welcomed as a promising methodological advance for extending research.

For adoptive parents the first sight of the child suggested to them by the agency is a profound and culminating experience. For an older child, the same is true although he is usually protected against possible rejection by the couple's seeing him before he meets them as possible parents. We have already viewed the child's side of the experience through the story of Jimmy and Mr. and Mrs. N. Some of the implications for the prospective parents were described by the writer (2) some years ago. The first meeting represents a major stage in facing the actuality of parenthood. As the adoption thus materializes into reality many couples find the realization and happiness they had anticipated. Occasionally, however, latent conflicts with marked anxiety and rejection of the child are aroused, in contrast to previous manifest attitudes. Although always

425

distressing for the client, these reactions may or may not prove serious. The case worker and couple need to re-evaluate the wisdom of adoption for them and here again the case worker's insight and help can be decisive in enabling some to move on comfortably to adoption and others to face their previously unrecognized deep-seated opposition to adoption in order that they may withdraw with minimum trauma. Certain common patterns as well as significant differences in the underlying conflict solutions were described.

Insight derived from psychoanalytic principles enlarges the adoption worker's view of her own role and personality dynamics in relation to her professional work. While this is true for all social worker-client interactions, the specifics of what is at stake for her triple clientele—adoptive couple, natural parents, and children—and the vital way these bear on her own basic experience are especially acute and profound in the adoption field. Realization of the psychological cruciality of the relatively final family relationships the worker helps bring about or prevent, and of her personal emotional resonance to the fundamental urges, frustrations, conflicts and gratifications with which she daily deals, heightens her sense of responsibility, with resultant satisfactions and anxieties as well. Relief from such anxieties may understandably be sought by some workers' need to blind themselves to their own subjectivity and to the psychological requirements of their clients, instead of the more desirable, though taxing course of maximum awareness and thereby maximum effectiveness and safety for themselves and their clients.

Aside from professional training and acquired case work skills, adoption work makes high demands in terms of personal stability and maturity. Unconscious conflicts and attitudes linked to the worker's own early family relationships, psychosexual development, and experiences or lack of them as wife and mother are under constantly bombarding stimuli inherent in the case material. A certain amount of the worker's psychic energy goes into the continuous task of self-scrutiny and disengaging the client and herself from what can otherwise be her unconsciously rationalized expression of hidden needs deceptively distorting her desired objectivity. Because the emotional substance of adoption is so powerful for all concerned, touching on the deepest human longings, deprivations, and fears, the social worker participating in these profound and intricate human processes may experience reinforcement of constructive sublimations and adaptations or intensification of neurotic propensities, depending on the many variables of individual personality functioning. As Clothier (6) states: "Whatever the inner need may be that leads the social worker into her profession, that need is the motivating force or energy which makes her usefulness possible. Like any elemental force or power the inner need that seeks solution can operate socially or destructively."

Naturally the specific ways in which adoption workers may project their own unconscious feelings into their jobs are innumerable. Extremes of sympathy or hostility toward any one of the sets of clients may be regarded as warning signals of possible inner involvement calling for self-exploration. A few rather frequently occurring patterns might be mentioned as illustrative. Overpunitive and condemning reactions, overt or disguised, toward the unmarried mother may stem from unconscious envy of the latter's "sexual freedom" and/or childbearing achievement based on a sense of personal thwarting. Or, the unmarried mother may represent a threat to the outcome of a worker's inner battle between conscience and forbidden impulse so that by invoking social penalties on the externalized transgressor self—the unmarried mother—the worker may unconsciously seek this roundabout way to strengthen her own inner defenses. On the other hand, depending on the balance of inner conflicting forces, the unmarried mother may unconsciously stand for a different aspect of self, in arousing the worker's vehement championing in terms of self-rescue and exoneration. Particularly strong and deep-rooted personal feelings may be set off by the unwed mother's decision about keeping or surrendering her child for adoption. Is the worker unconsciously tempted to rob the unwed mother of her baby? In fearing this form of baby-snatching in herself, must she overcompensate by denying needed appropriate help toward clinically indicated adoption in the name of "passive technique?" Or perhaps her hostility, through identifying with the baby, is mainly due to remobilization of early abandonment terrors.

The worker's childhood feelings toward parents often exert an understandable regressive influence on her reactions to adoptive parents and may combine with an overidentification with the child to be placed. The possibilities of unconscious childish fantasy fulfillment, wishful as well as fearful, add to the inner pressure under which the worker labors. Can any parents be perfect enough? Or, swinging over to her inner view

427

of the parents' view, can any child be perfect enough? Are parents figures to be compulsively obeyed or defied, looked up to or looked down on, or competed with? Do the unconscious implications of power in the worker's role and the residual fantasies of omnipotence over those early omnipotent figures—parents—significantly intrude on the realistic current situations? On behalf of the child for adoption, is the fear of possible rejection too great to risk placement? How do the worker's own feelings about the children she herself mothers, or wants to mother, or does not want to mother, affect her unconscious feelings of envy or vicarious gratification in helping relieve the adoptive parents' childlessness. Brenner (3), in fact, suggests that the lag in application of "sound psychiatric case work principles for evaluating adoptive parents . . . is partly the result of our unconscious fear of examining our own feelings about parents."

Certainly the multiple and often conflicting professional loyalties, as Clothier (6) has stressed, which the case worker in this field strives to harmonize, are unusually great. Instead of a single client's problem, the adoption worker serves the needs of several, i.e., natural parents, adoptive parents, and children for adoption. Although the child traditionally is regarded as the primary client whose needs are paramount, our knowledge of the interdependence of family relationships leads toward maximum consideration for all concerned as in line with the best interests of the child. As McCleery (20) has properly stressed, the agency, through supervision and administration, can contribute significantly to helping the worker "find a way of handling his anxieties so that they will not be passed on to the children or the parents."

Although the natural parents constitute another major group of adoption agency clients, as already mentioned, they will not be discussed further in this presentation. Most of them, though not all, are unmarried mothers and space does not permit doing justice to the wealth of clinical data concerning them. Furthermore, their needs are so multiple (medical, financial, case work, shelter care, etc.) that the adoption agency should be but one, and by no means the central resource of interrelated community services offering comprehensive coverage.

A final phase of case work function on behalf of adoptive parents and children is that of supervision prior to legal adoption. The term "supervision" reflects the child-protective aspect but not the casework function. A term less suggestive of old-style authoritative snooping would seem preferable and in line with professional progress. The case worker visits the newly formed family periodically during the first six months or year after placement, her functions differing somewhat in an infant placement from that of an older child. For the latter, relationship with the child as well as the parents is of importance. Most children are apt to react to her with ambivalence. On the one hand the worker, granted a good preadoption relationship, represents continuity, familiarity and security for the child. Adjusting as he must to a whole new world, her visits can signify her continued protective support and interest. On the negative side, however, the child may see the worker as a "taking away" person because of her role in his previous separations from natural parents or foster homes. Her visit therefore may threaten the treasured permanence of his new-found home. With understanding reassurance, most workers can sufficiently minimize the anxiety to salvage her security value for him. Some ambivalence toward the worker is almost always felt by the adoptive parents as well. A good preadoptive relationship is usual, heightened by very warm feelings in reaction to obtaining the long-desired child. On the other hand, the worker represents an obstacle to the healthy and desired process of becoming a self-contained independent family unit. The agency's legal right to remove the child, if deemed necessary for its welfare, is also a source of some anxiety. With careful preadoptive selection and preparation recourse to this power of removal is seldom necessary, but on occasion it is invoked, as in the case of Mrs. A., the mother described earlier, who was referred for analytic treatment and later bore her own child. An up-to-date discussion of the purposes and methods of supervision is to be found in a report of interagency meetings in New York City (25). As regards the case work function, the group agreed as to the value of help related specifically to the adoption situation. They were not in total accord as to the desirability of case work service for the less specifically adoptive aspects of family life. It seems to me, however, that no hard and fast distinction can be made between the adoptive aspects of the couple's reactions and the feelings and attitudes referable to their newness as parents. Overapprehensiveness and feelings of ineptness are common to many parents with their first baby. The new adoptive couple's anxieties around their inexperience as parents and from the special circumstance of adoption seem inseparably blended. The visiting case worker can often greatly relieve difficulties. Certainly many of these couples seek, welcome, and constructively utilize the case worker's support and guidance during these initial months, despite the degree of ambivalence already noted. Naturally there are others with different needs and resources for whom minimum postplacement agency contact is best. In my opinion the mental health potentialities of this aspect of adoptive case work have not been sufficiently explored or developed. This is due in large part to budgetary limitations. A promising innovation is being considered of offering parental guidance, individually or in groups, to adoptive couples at some period after they have legally adopted.

After legal adoption, contact with the agency is terminated. Through the years a certain number of parents and children return for specific assistance. Thus, a couple may bring their adolescent youngster who has come to want more information about his origins than the parents can satisfy. The worker differentiates her handling of this request in terms of her appraisal of the motives and feelings behind it for parents and youngster, as well as the quality of family relationships. The child's wish need not be symptomatic of any serious discontent and the worker, while protecting the natural parents' anonymity, may furnish some nonidentifying details. These, plus the parents' understanding willingness in coming, the physical tangibility of the agency, and the worker's helping attitude may meet such a youngster's need for connection with his past—an expression of his sense of ego identity formation so important in adolescence as quoted above from Erikson. Occasionally we see tragically pathological distortions of this constellation. These very disturbed young people who had been adopted in early childhood develop an all-consuming, obsessing need to locate their biologic parents who in fantasy, or even delusion, have become the idealized good parents in contrast to the adoptive "bad" parents with whom they are usually no longer in contact. The insecurities of war precipitated a number of these acute reactions among young men particularly when facing the prospect of overseas shipment to the dangerous unknown world. The personal histories of those cases known to me invariably revealed glaringly unsuitable adoptive placements. These sick youths acted out in overt form the family romance fantasy described as universal by Otto Rank and considered of special importance in the psychology of adopted children by several psychoanalysts, including Clothier (7) and Deutsch (8). When feeling disappointed or frustrated by their parents, all children are prone to imagine at some point in their lives that these disappointing parents are not their real parents, but through mysterious circumstances had found or somehow acquired them as infants. Their true parents were idealized paragons and some day the child will regain his wonderful rightful heritage and be free of these horrid, worthless people who call themselves his mother and father. Dynamically the fantasy is thought to evolve as a child's means of coping with his usual ambivalence conflicts. Two sets of parents permits his assignment of all bad feelings to one set, and all good feelings to the other, thus dealing with the problem of simultaneous love and hate toward the same parents. Normally this fantasy plays a minor and fleeting role in the child's mental life, but Deutsch, Clothier and others have shown through analysis how the coinciding with reality in adoption renders this fantasy of more compelling and central significance in the psychodynamics of the adopted child. His adoptive parents really did mysteriously find him as a baby, born of unknown parents, and thus reality seems to confirm his fantasies and thereby strengthens them, in contrast to the non-adopted child's use of reality to neutralize fantasy. Clothier emphasizes the role this plays in the symptomatology of emotionally disturbed adoptive children.

Since the child turns to the unknown fantasied parents, facilitated by the reality of adoption in reaction to feeling angry and hurt by his real-life adoptive parents, it follows that the most potent antidote to excessive and persistent pathological recourse to this escapist fantasy is a healthy, secure, satisfying relationship between the child and his adoptive parents. These are truly his real parents, as defined by cumulative experience of living together as a family. In emotionally healthy adoption —which includes of course a normal degree of mutual frustration, anxiety and hostility—the child's involvement with his biological parents remains within bounds. The extent to which case work along dynamic lines can foster this goal has been extensively described.

Perhaps some readers have become impatient by now with what may appear to them as needless exaggeration of the psychological complexity of adoption and the precautions advocated. This attitude may be bolstered by knowing of some apparently happy adoptions accomplished much more simply, either through independent adoption or social agencies with minimal case work. The personal qualifications for adoptive parents and for case workers may seem perfectionistic and the intensive psychological work with unmarried mothers and pre-adoptive children a lot of fancy nonsense. By way of reply, psychoanalysis provides a microscope whereby otherwise invisible psychic structures and processes come into view. A description of pond water in accordance with structures and movement observed in a drop under the microscope can sound unbelievable to one accustomed to water, but not to microscopes. Although hit-and-miss methods of adoptive placements sometimes do turn out well, reliance on knowledge rather than luck promises better control over the outcomes by adding to the successes and reducing the failures.

BIBLIOGRAPHY

1. BENEDEK, T. Infertility as a psychosomatic defense. Fertility and Sterility, 3, November-December, 1952.
2. BERNARD, V. W. First sight of the child by prospective parents as a crucial phase in adoption. Am. J. Orthopsychiat., 15, 1945.
3. BRENNER, R. F. The selection of adoptive parents: a casework responsibility. Child Welfare, December, 1946.
4. ——— and Hartley, R. A Follow-Up Study of Adoptive Families. New York: Child Adoption Research Committee, 1951.
5. BROWN, F. G. What do we seek in adoptive parents. Soc. Casework, April, 1951.
6. CLOTHIER, F. The social worker in the field of adoption. Ment. Hyg., 24, 1940.
7. ——— The psychology of the adopted child. Ment. Hyg., 27, 1943.
8. DEUTSCH, H. The Psychology of Women. New York: Grune & Stratton, 1945.
9. ERIKSON, E. H. Growth and crises of the healthy personality. Symposium on the Healthy Personality. New York: Josiah Macy, Jr. Foundation. 1950.
10. ESCALONA, S. The use of infant tests for predictive purposes. Bull. Menninger Clinic, 14, 1950.
11. FAIRWEATHER, M. E. Early placement in adoption. Child Welfare, 31, 1952.
12. FREUD, A. The psychoanalytic study of infantile feeding disturbances. The Psychoanalytic Study of the Child, 2:119, 1947. New York: International Universities Press.
13. HALLINAN, H. W. Who are the children available for adoption? J. Soc. Casework, 32, 1951.
14. ——— Adoption for older children. Soc. Casework, 33, 1952.
15. JACOBSON, E. A case of sterility. Psychoanal. Quart., 15, 1946.
16. KNIGHT, R. P. Some problems involved in selecting and rearing adopted children. Bull. Menninger Clinic, 5, 1941.

17. KROGER, W. S. AND FREED, S. C. Psychosomatic Gynecology. Philadelphia: W. B. Saunders Company, 1951.

18. LEITCH, M. AND ESCALONA, S. K. The reaction of infants to stress: a report on clinical findings. The Psychoanalytic Study of the Child, 3/4:121, 1949. New York: International Universities Press.

19. MALCOVE, L. Margaret E. Fries' research in problems of infancy and childhood; a survey. The Psychoanalytic Study of the Child, 1:405, 1945. New York: International Universities Press.

20. McCLEERY, S. The adoption worker's role and his personality in the professional adoption process. Child Welfare, October, 1952.

21. MICHAELS, R. Casework considerations in rejecting the adoption application. J. Soc. Casework, 18, 1947.

22. OMAN, H. G. Giving up a baby. The Survey, January, 1952.

23. ORR, D. W. Pregnancy following the decision to adopt. Psychosom. Med., 3, 1941.

24. RAINER, L. Helping the child and the adoptive parents in the initial placement. Child Welfare, November, 1951.

25. Report of the Inter-Agency Discussion Group of New York City. The process of supervision in adoptive placements. Child Welfare, November, 1952.

26. RIBBLE, M. C. The Rights of Infants. New York: Columbia University Press, 1943.

27. SPITZ, R. A. Emotional growth in the first year. Child Study, Spring, 1947.

28. ———— Relevancy of direct infant observation. The Psychoanalytic Study of the Child, 5:66, 1950. New York: International Universities Press.

29. ———— The psychogenic diseases in infancy: an attempt at their etiological classification. The Psychoanalytic Study of the Child, 6:255, 1951. New York: International Universities Press.

30. THAYER, S. W. Moppets on the market: the problem of unregulated adoptions. Yale Law J., March, 1950.

31. WIRES, E. M. Placement for adoption—a total separation? J. Soc. Casework, July, 1949.

32. WOLKOMIR, B. They are adoptable. Better Times, Welfare Council of New York City, January 31, 1947.

CHAPTER 35

Substitute Families. Adoption*

JOHN BOWLBY, M.D.

"The central paradox of work for deprived children is that there are thousands of childless homes crying out for children and hundreds of Homes filled with children in need of family life." This situation, graphically described in the annual report of the Children's Officer of an English borough, obtains in many Western countries. Yet very little serious study has been given to the problems of adoption, and it is only gradually becoming recognized as a process requiring scientific understanding and professional skill. Too often the baby's future is the concern only of a well-meaning amateur or of a health visitor trained to consider no more than physical hygiene. Once again scientific studies of the subject are conspicuous by their scarcity.

The process of adoption concerns three sets of people—the mother, the baby (almost always illegitimate), and the prospective adopters. There is skilled work to be done with each. First, help must be given to the mother to enable her to reach a realistic decision; this requires skill in making a relationship of mutual confidence with her, in understanding her personality and her social situation, and in helping her face unpalatable facts in a constructive way. Secondly, there must be an ability to assess the potentialities of the baby—no easy task and one

---

* Chapter XI of Maternal Care and Mental Health, World Health Organization, 1951.

about which there are many ungrounded assumptions. Finally, there must be an ability to predict how a couple will care for children, often in the absence of any direct demonstration of their capacities, and to help them in the initial adjustments. These are formidable tasks. Furthermore, they must be discharged reasonably quickly since all with experience are agreed that the baby should be adopted as early in his life as possible.

The evidence given in Part I of this report points unmistakably to its being in the interests of the adopted baby's mental health for him to be adopted soon after birth. No other arrangement permits continuity of mothering and most other arrangements fail even to ensure its adequacy. If the baby remains with his mother, it is not unlikely that she will neglect and reject him. The work of Rheingold and Levy has shown that if he is parked temporarily in a nursery or group foster-home his development will often suffer in some degree. Nothing is more tragic than good adoptive parents who accept for adoption a child whose early experiences have led to disturbed personality development which nothing they can now do will rectify. Very early adoption is thus clearly in the interest also of the adoptive parents. Moreover, the nearer to birth that they have had him the more will they feel the baby to be their own and the easier will it be for them to identify themselves with his personality. Favourable relationships will then have the best chance to develop.

The arguments against very early adoption are three in number:

(a) it requires what might be a precipitate decision by the mother
(b) the baby cannot be breast fed
(c) there is less opportunity to assess the baby's potential development.

Of these the first argument is the most weighty. It is clearly of the greatest importance not only that the right decision should be reached by the mother but that it should be reached by her in a way which leaves her convinced that she has decided wisely. This may take time, though, as Rome has shown, no good comes from prolonging the period of indecision indefinitely. If the mother has sought care reasonably early it should be possible for the experienced case-worker to help her reach a realistic decision either before the baby is born or soon after, since most of the factors which matter (e.g., stability of personality, realism towards the problem, and attitude towards the putative father) will be evident in her life before the birth of the baby.

If all of these are adverse the baby's birth will not change them, and the likelihood is small of the mother making a success of looking after the child. More knowledge, skill, and realism on the part of caseworkers could undoubtedly lead to wise and emotionally satisfactory decisions being reached fairly early in a large proportion of cases.

Moreover, it is in the mother's interest to make the decision to keep or part with her baby early rather than late. Unless it is reasonably clear that she will be able to care for the child, it is no kindness to permit her to become attached to him; parting is then all the more heart-breaking. Some unmarried mothers decide, after reflection, that they would prefer not to see their baby, a decision which should be respected. Rigid policies that all unmarried mothers must care for their babies for three or six months and must breast feed them have no place in a service designed to help illegitimate babies and their unmarried mothers to live happy and useful lives.

It is, of course, only when a baby is likely to be breast fed that the interruption of breast-feeding is an argument against early adoption, since if the mother is averse to such feeding or if the baby is to be deposited in a nursery or foster-home the matter becomes irrelevant. If early adoption does in fact mean depriving a baby of breast feeding it is, of course, a serious matter. Even so, to reach the correct decision regarding the best age for the child to be adopted requires the weighing of one set of medical disadvantages against another and only far more research than has been done into the adverse effects of each can permit the decision to be realistic. Meanwhile, it is unwise to assume that breast-feeding and later adoption is better for the baby's future welfare than early adoption and affectionate artificial feeding.

The third argument against early adoption—that there is less opportunity to assess the baby's potential development—is commonly used by psychologists but is the weakest of the three. It rests on the assumption that the various tests of development available in the first year of life have predictive value for the child's later development. In an exhaustive inquiry Bayley has shown that this assumption is not justified. She shows that the correlation of test performance at nine months of age with that at four years is zero and that "scores made before eighteen months are completely useless in the prediction of school-age abilities". This same conclusion is reached by Michael & Brenner in one of the comparatively few pieces of systematic re-

436

search on adoption. They carried out a follow-up of 50 adopted children when they were four years of age or over both to discover what proportion had proved successful and what were the most reliable criteria for making predictions. They conclude rather sadly that "the psychologist's findings, in this and other studies, suggest that the case-worker's tendency to assume that infant tests provide a safe index of potential development is not warranted".* Not only is this so but, as has been seen, there is a very serious danger that keeping a baby in a nursery awaiting adoption in the belief that in a few more months an accurate prediction can be made will itself produce retardation, which is then taken as evidence that the baby is inherently backward. Hence there develops the paradoxical situation in which misguided caution in arranging adoption creates a baby which at first appears, and ultimately becomes, unfitted for it.

Probably the best guide to potential intelligence is the intelligence of the parents, though for many reasons this can be no more than a very rough guide and adoptive parents like natural parents must be prepared to take a normal biological risk.

It will be seen, therefore, that the arguments against early adoption are far less strong than they appear at first sight. On psychiatric and social grounds adoption in the first two months should become the rule, though some flexibility will always be necessary to permit mothers to work their way to a satisfactory decision. If during the waiting period the baby is not cared for by his mother it is preferable for him to be cared for in a temporary foster-home rather than in an institutional nursery.

To dub a baby unfit for adoption is usually to condemn him to a deprived childhood and an unhappy life. Few are qualified to reach this decision and the grounds on which it is commonly reached today in Western countries are more often well-meaning than well-informed. For instance, many adoption agencies place an absolute bar on the children of incestuous relationships, however good the stock. Naive theories of genetics may also lead to a child being blackballed for such reasons as having a sibling mentally defective or a parent suffering from mental illness. In the days when it was the accepted psychiatric view that all mental illness was hereditary this may have been a reasonable policy. Now that this is no longer so it is unreason-

---

* The failure of infant tests to predict the future does not of course rob them of their value as an index of present development, a value which may be compared to that of the weight-chart which, irrespective of any predictive value it may have for the infant's future physique, remains a valuable guide to his physical progress during infancy.

able, except in those cases where the incidence of mental defect or illness in the family is clearly much above the average. It has already been remarked that mental tests have no predictive value in the first 18 months of life, so that some retardation, even in the absence of deprivation, need not be taken seriously unless it is very marked. Finally, the widespread assumption that children with certain physical handicaps are unfit for adoption is ungrounded, as Wolkomir has shown in her interesting paper "The unadoptable baby achieves adoption".

Three principles thus emerge from discussion of a baby's suitability for adoption:

(a) that an assessment of the child's genetic potentialities requires the opinion of a person with training in human genetics and that in no case should an adverse decision be reached without the opinion of a competent person;

(b) that psychologists should be thoroughly familiar with the predictive value of their tests and with the effects of deprivation, illness, and other environmental factors on test performance;

(c) that even if the child's state, or prognoses about his future, are not wholly favourable an attempt should still be made to see whether there may be adoptive parents who, after being given full knowledge of the facts, are prepared in a realistic mood to accept him.

The third area in which knowledge and skill is required is in the appraisal of prospective adoptive parents and in helping those who are suitable to adjust happily to the intense emotional experience of adopting a baby. Here there is no place for the amateur, whose only criteria can be outward signs of respectability, or the worker trained only in physical hygiene with the criteria of income, cleanliness, and cubic feet of air space. These criteria have led to irrelevant and fancy standards. The baby's mental health will depend on the emotional relationships he will have the opportunity to develop; and their prediction requires good knowledge of the psychology of personality and skill in interview techniques. The principles of the work are admirably discussed by Hutchinson, whose book *In quest of foster parents* should be consulted. She emphasizes the cardinal importance of estimating the real motivation behind the mother's desire to adopt a baby (it being almost always the mother rather than the father who is the architect of the plan). This motivation is often not what it appears to be and its true nature may be largely concealed from the woman herself.

"That foster parents are often searching for love or more love or a different kind of love is not disqualifying, but it is a significant clue to a richer understanding of them. The crux of the matter lies in the degree of normality and reasonableness of their love-specifications. An adoptive mother may insist, in highly rigid and explicit terms, on the qualifications which she wants and must have in a baby. It must be a girl, of specified colouring, age, intelligence, parental status, nationality and temperament. The striking factor is the tenacity with which she may cling to these specifications even after she learns that practically speaking, her conditions are unreasonable and a hindrance. A prospective adoptive father may be unwilling to deviate from his determination to have a boy who at all costs will fulfill his own frustrated ambition. Such inflexible and narcissistic requests are in contrast to the requests of the foster parent who can easily consider a reasonable range of children and does not come with terms too preconceived or irrevocable."

Those adopting these rigid and inflexible attitudes are doing so for reasons connected with their own emotional conflicts deriving from their own childhoods. In such a case the child is needed not for himself but as the solution of a private difficulty in the parents and, as might be expected, more often than not provides no such solution. The woman who has always felt unloved and who seeks love and companionship from the baby will not wish him to grow up, make friends, and marry. The woman who seeks a little girl who will achieve all that she has failed to achieve is likely sooner or later to be disappointed and to turn against her. Many other unsatisfactory motives may underlie the demand for a child. In the same way satisfactory motives may masquerade under exteriors which seem unpromising. The woman with a gauche brusque manner or the easy-going, untidy, and not too clean couple may none the less have warm hearts and prove loving and effective parents. If their motives are right much else can be overlooked.

How is the social worker to discover their true motives? Partly by inquiring how it was that they first thought of adopting a baby and partly by learning more about them as people, especially their capacity to make easy and loving relationships with others. In assessing these, three principal opportunities offer—the way they speak about other people, especially their relatives, the way they treat each other, and the way they treat the social worker. The value of these last two criteria are attested in the follow-up conducted by Michaels & Brenner who conclude: "the most fruitful area of exploration in these home studies was the marriage; the needs it filled for both partners, and the way they achieved their own satisfactions and met each others' needs within it". Yet, as Hutchinson has pointed out, this is precisely the area most commonly evaded by the interviewer who, unless thoroughly trained, feels, and is, quite incapable of making inquiries which are both useful and yet not embarrassing. Michaels & Brenner proceed:

"The relationship between client and worker also had diagnostic importance. Families who resented the worker's interest in their intimate lives or felt that their references, position, or deep need for parenthood entitled them to a child with no questions asked, often were reflecting underlying problems bearing an important relation to parental capacity. Often, too, the families who easily established a relationship with a worker, who recognized the agency's need to choose good parents for children and admitted to human qualms, problems, and imperfections, were revealing deep assets for parenthood."

The capacity to face difficulties in a courageous way and to consider soberly how best to meet them is indispensable in adoptive parents for "the ability to take some risks is essential for adoptive parenthood" as it is for natural parenthood.

"The question is not whether we can match their need surely in a child's infancy; for we plainly cannot. The question is rather what they would do with disappointment; and whether they could still function as loving parents, satisfied in their parenthood. There is no such thing, unfortunately, as a 'guaranteed adoption'; no children an agency can safely mark 'Certified'. It is vital, therefore, that parents be able to accept a child whether or not he can measure up to their hopes and wishes for him" (Hutchinson).

Flexibility and the capacity to face the truth are clearly also desiderata if the parents are to tell the child of his adoption, a practice which all are agreed is essential since sooner or later the truth will become known. Provided the parents can themselves admit the truth and do not have to cling for personal reasons to the fantasy of having produced the child themselves, there need be no great difficulty in bringing the child up from earliest years in the knowledge that he has been adopted. Complications will arise only if the natural and adoptive parents know each other. Reputable agencies usually preserve absolute secrecy on this matter, and there seems no doubt that this is essential if the adoption is not to be jeopardized.

The intense emotional experience of a parent who adopts a baby is often overlooked. Hutchinson has spoken of the "excitement, urgency and deep feeling" which often characterize the adoptive mother's attitude. To her it means not only taking possession for better or for worse of a human life and with it all that the possession of a baby means to a woman, but it may signify also the final acceptance both for her and her husband of the painful fact that they will never have a baby of their own. These are difficult and conflicting emotions which if not worked through adequately may linger to mar the parents' feelings for the baby. Once again insight based on knowledge and skill based on training are required. Similarly, knowledge and skill are necessary in the social worker when she has to tell parents that they are not suitable. Naturally, she will try to put it to them in the most palatable form to avoid distressing them more than necessary, but her principal aim must be to help them see the truth for themselves, for unless this can be achieved the prospective parents will not only feel disgruntled, but will persist in their search for a baby to adopt.

Not much is heard of the black market in babies—the process whereby would-be adopters who have been refused by reputable agencies succeed, sometimes by the payment of large sums to third parties, in securing a baby for themselves. In most countries at present this can be done by people whom all would agree are quite unfit to care for a child. It is a social and legal problem which one day will require attention, but it would be foolish to tackle so thorny a problem before the recognized machinery for adoption is in the hands of qualified people who can be relied upon to make realistic assessments of prospective parents. This will take time.

INCIDENCE OF FAVOURABLE ATTITUDES AMONG PARENTS OF ADOPTED CHILDREN AGED FOUR YEARS PLUS
(Michaels & Brenner)

Attitude of parents	Children number	%
Favourable	26	52
Fairly favourable	18	36
Unfavourable	6	12
Totals	50	100

441

It has already been remarked that prediction of how a baby will develop is an exceedingly difficult task and for this reason the matching of baby and parents is more easily desired than achieved. Moreover, so long as there are queues of parents waiting for a trickle of babies, the parents may feel thankful to get any child. Race and to some extent colouring can be matched fairly easily, and by matching social class the securing of comparable intelligence is the more likely. Until predictions of other characteristics can be validated, time spent on assessing them is largely window-dressing.

Finally, it may be asked what is the proportion of adoptions which are successful? This, of course, is a relative question, the results depending largely on the skill of the agency arranging them. What one needs to know is the proportion of successes when adoption is carried out by skilled workers. No such study seems to be available, even that by Michaels & Brenner being concerned with the outcome of adoptions arranged during a period when the agency was changing from a volunteer to a professional basis. The results of this study are given in the table above.

Regarding the unsuccessful cases, they note "No child . . . is poorly housed, clothed or fed, or treated cruelly or irresponsibly by adoptive parents. In this sense none of these homes is bad. The six homes considered unsuccessful are, rather, homes where the child is either rejected, or excessively over-protected and infantilised". In assessing the meaning of these figures variables such as the age at which the children were adopted and the criteria of success used by the investigators must be taken into account. They must be compared, also, with similar assessments of parents caring for their own children. Judged by the latter standard, so far as it is known, the proportion of successful and unsuccessful adoptions does not seem unsatisfactory. This result is in accordance with clinical experience which does not suggest that an undue proportion of adopted children are referred to child-guidance clinics. From these meagre data it may tentatively be inferred that in skilled hands adoption can give a child nearly as good a chance of a happy home life as that of the child brought up in his own home. Even so, the data are deplorably inadequate and if these problems are to be taken seriously will need to be greatly amplified.

CHAPTER 36

Some Problems in Developing Research on Adoption

DONALD BRIELAND, Ph.D.

The National Conference on Adoption held in Chicago in January 1955, highlighted two general conclusions:
1. the need for research on many aspects of the adoption process;
2. recognition of the scientific knowledge already available relating to adoption, which should and does affect social agency practice. It is easy to place emphasis on the second of these elements and to forget the first in the press of day-to-day responsibilities to get a practical job done.

Some of the problems involved in the development of adoption research can profitably be reviewed. Several assumptions underlying adoption have a bearing on possible research. The first of these concerns the acceptability of the adoption process —to society, to the child, the adoptive parents, and the natural parents.

Positive Attitudes of Society

Adoption is acceptable to society. Society considers adoption as an adequate means to provide for the rearing of children who must for some reason be deprived of growing up in a natural family. Adoption for a child is considered generally preferable to his living in an institution, and usually superior to placement in a foster home where there is no legal transfer of parental responsibilities to those persons who serve in fact as the child's parents.

Being adopted is acceptable. Children find relationships with adoptive parents rather like those of natural parents, with most of the same rewards and demands. The adopted child does not usually consider himself as being different from children who live with their natural parents, although he may have special concerns from time to time about his identity and parentage. Society tries to give full legal rights to adopted children and attaches no social stigma to being adopted.

Being adoptive parents is acceptable. Childlessness may result in varying degrees of concern ranging from little if any disappointment or anxiety to deep feelings of personal inadequacy. Having no children by choice is likely to result in criticism. Inability to have them but applying to adopt them is an active step toward having a family. Adoption offers an opportunity not only to satisfy the needs of a child, but to satisfy the need for a child. More than that, adopting a child indicates to the outside world that childlessness was not intentional.

The relinquishing of a child for adoption by the natural parents is acceptable. Under certain circumstances this serves the best interests not only of the child but also of the natural parents and of society.

These positive attitudes of society and of the persons directly concerned in adoption should facilitate the conduct of research.

A second assumption to consider is: Most adoptive parents are willing to participate in research on adoption following the completion of the period of supervision as well as during that period, particularly when they understand that the purpose of research is to improve adoption procedures in the future, and not to alter or extend agency supervision for them.

Traditionally, the reluctance of the agency to make any subsequent contact with the family has been a barrier to research and may have resulted from an unrealistic sensitivity on the parents' part. Limited efforts to request information from adoptive parents have met with good success and the interest of the agency has often been welcomed. Obviously, a program involving intensive contact that might be interpreted as continued supervision or just plain interference must be avoided. However, intelligently planned follow-up research will underscore the need to learn as much as possible about making adoptions successful rather than to suggest a desire to give advice or extended supervision. There is little reason to believe that research would be difficult to carry out because of strong parental resistance, if it is conducted with the usual emphasis on keeping individual case material confidential. The importance of the problems makes it necessary to go ahead with research, even though a certain amount of parental non-cooperation will be encountered. The success of research with clients in marriage counseling and psychotherapy, where one would expect more defensiveness than in adoption, is encouraging.

A third assumption is: Research participation by an agency can be a source of confidence to many clients. While most people know little of research methods and techniques, the word research and the notion that it implies systematic study and evaluation are very familiar.

Much of the prestige gained by research in the physical sciences also carries over to work in the social sciences, although in these areas human behavior presents a different set of problems. The participation of an agency in a research program can be presented to clients as an indication that it is keenly interested in improving its agency operation. Any agency interested in research should not have to apologize to its clients or board members for this interest, but must be careful to avoid the charge of "guinea pigism."

Obstacles in Planning Research

The assumptions that adoption is socially approved, that adoptive parents accept and even welcome occasional contact from the agency following the period of supervision, and that research participation is a source of confidence to the client affect the planning of research. If it is agreed that these concepts are valid, a number of specific practical studies in the adoption area should be feasible.

There are several obstacles frequently mentioned as important in the planning of any research, including studies of adoption. A serious problem is presented by the wide variations in agency practice. Not only do agencies do things differently but the same agency will operate in various ways as executives and staff change and as new ideas emerge. Sometimes too much stress is placed upon the possible effects of differing agency practices. While it is necessary to recognize differences, there is no reason to assume that they make research impossible. They do make it imperative that the organizations participating in studies formulate an accurate statement of their own procedures and philosophies, and describe their setting carefully to prevent inappropriate generalization of results.

Another obstacle to research which is typical of social work, as well as of clinical psychology, medicine, and other services, concerns the limitations of case records. Follow-up studies are often necessarily limited because records may not be suitable for certain research problems. All possible use should be made of present records. For many research purposes special recording methods must be set up for a particular project. We cannot expect to arrive at a prefabricated case recording system that will answer all demands of care, supervision, and research. Brevity alone would often make case recording more useful for research. Thus the planning and the results of adoption studies should have many implications for case recording practice. Some of the difficulties involved in varying agency practice and differences in case records can be taken into account through the use of several agencies to conduct parallel studies.

Another obstacle is implied by the comment that since there are so many non-agency placements, research in adoption agencies tells too little. Certainly independent placements must also be studied carefully in a comprehensive research program. At the present time, however, it is in the agency setting that the most satisfactory research can be designed involving the needed control and required parental cooperation. It seems reasonable to be interested in good agency practice first since this is generally the most acceptable way for adoption to take place. Not only do the agencies offer professional staff who have special interest in the problem, but one can also expect more cooperation from individuals who are willing to accept the safeguards to both child and parent which the agency provides.

The purpose of the remainder of this discussion is to indicate four different ways in which adoption research can be undertaken, and to present suggestive questions which such research may be expected to answer. These questions are in no way inclusive of all the important issues but provide a point of departure for research planning.

(1) *Adoption research previous to the initial interview*

Many adoptive agencies receive their first contact from potential applicants by telephone or letter. It would be helpful to case-workers to have more knowledge of the expectancies of applicants for adoption. Not only would this make possible bet-

446

ter rapport but also would indicate how well the public understands the operation and objectives of the adoption agency and might suggest, depending upon the outcomes of the research, that more effort should be made to increase public information and understanding of the work of the agency.

Perhaps agencies have been unwilling to consider research previous to the initial interview because they feel that the emotional state of the applicant would make such a project inadvisable for the client. The usefulness of the method could easily be explored first on a pilot basis.

Between the time the initial contact is made and the first interview, a questionnaire could be sent to the potential adoptive parents to be filled out anonymously and returned to an independent group such as a welfare council research division. Such an arrangement would make it impossible for applicants to be identified individually. It would be clear then that information given would not be used in deciding whether an application will be approved. However, since the prospective parents are interested in receiving a child from the agency, the percentage of returns should be higher than in the usual questionnaire study. Several general follow-up methods could be used to encourage return of the questionnaires.

Some of the areas that could be included are indicated by the following questions:

How did the couple become interested in adoption from this agency?

What advantage do they see in agency placement compared to independent placement?

What has been their previous contact with people who have adopted children through this agency and from others?

With what personal factors do the applicants feel the agency will be concerned, e.g., income, housing, health history, etc.?

How long do the applicants think it will take for a child to be placed with them?

What do they see as reasons for refusing to consider a couple as prospective adoptive parents?

What is the sex preference of a child by these applicants? Why?

How much contact do they expect to have with the caseworker and what do they see as its purpose?

What do the applicants consider to be the agency's reason for charging fees (if it does so)? What is their attitude toward the practice?

(2) *Study by follow-up of completed adoptions*

A study of completed adoptions can provide information in many areas including parent-child relationships. The questions presented below are suggestions for research involving the parent. A similar group of questions could be developed for studies on adopted children.

Parental satisfaction: Do the parents consider the adoption to be generally successful? What are their specific qualitative reactions after various periods of time? Were they satisfied with the agency supervision? What suggestions would they offer concerning supervision?

Matching: If matching of physical characteristics was an aim in the agency's practice does it appear that this was done successfully? Do the parents feel that there is a physical resemblance? If not, is it a source of concern for them?

Sibling relationships: Have there been natural children born to parents who are not clearly sterile (e.g., as a result of hysterectomy)? Have the parents tried to adopt another child? Were they successful? What can be learned about sibling problems?

Identity: Have the parents received questions from the child concerning his identity? Did the fact of adoption come up if "Where did I come from?" was asked? Has the child been told about his adoption? If so, how? Do the parents feel they have succeeded in this? Does the fact of adoption come into disciplinary situations?

Specialized help: Have the parents felt any need for specialized help with the child? Have they made efforts to seek such help, and have the efforts been successful? To what extent have these children been referred to child guidance facilities in the public schools or other community agencies?

Source of referral: Have these parents been able to provide help to other people who have wished to adopt?

(3) *Study of current adoptive placements and pending applications*

Here it is possible to bring about the greatest degree of control and to get at variables with more success than in the follow-up method, although it will mean that the research must be extended over a substantial period of time. Not only can many of the questions above be dealt with but there are additional possibilities:

Does the study of the adoptive parents provide the basis to make predictions about parent-child relationships? Can personality testing be used more successfully to predict parent-child relationships?

How important is matching to adoptive applicants?

What are the areas of concern shown by questions most frequently asked by adoptive parents in the initial interviews? What are those areas typically discussed with the caseworker at the time of regular visits?

What factors are used to determine whether or not a couple is considered a good adoptive possibility? What agreement is there from worker to worker?

Are the observations of two caseworkers who may share the responsibilities of giving help during the period of supervision valuable for gaining additional insight into the adoption process?

Is there any relationship between factors in the fertility study and the ultimate success of adoptions?

How are attitudes toward illegitimacy related to successful placements?

(4) *Follow-up of rejected applicants and those who withdraw before agency action is completed*

Much knowledge is needed of how skillful agencies are in getting couples whom they consider poor risks to give up their interest in having a child. It would also be helpful to see how frequently these clients are able to adopt by other means.

What is the expressed attitude of the applicants toward being rejected?

Were applications to other agencies made before the rejection or withdrawal? After the rejection or withdrawal?

Does the couple now have children? How were they secured?

A special research technique that has received considerable attention is electronic recording. Where it is helpful to have a verbatim record of what took place, for example, in an intake interview, this method is ideal. Although there is a period of self-consciousness during the first few minutes of recording for many clients, this does not last long. It is unusual for anyone to refuse to have material recorded once he is assured that it will be kept in confidence. No evidence has been presented that the use of recording is detrimental to the client or to the client-worker relationship. Many professional workers are probably the victims of a cultural lag since a number of clients with whom they work have access to such equipment and may use it extensively.

Difficulties come in the handling of recordings once they are made. Editing is a tedious job and may be highly subjective. Recording no doubt will have its place in adoption research although the criteria for editing recorded material must be set up carefully.

To have complete recordings of intake interviews with varying sorts of adoptive parents could indicate how various workers weight factors revealed in the interviews and their agreement on criteria of selection of adoptive families. These recordings together with face-sheet data would make it possible for caseworkers to analyze the same material. The same question might also be studied using written case records and the results compared. Problems in making decisions on applicants might be seen quite differently if there is high agreement among workers from various agencies on who are good adoptive prospects and who are not, or if they disagreed among themselves after evaluating the same interviews. Electronic recording has been considered here only as an illustration of the need to use the newer research tools whenever they are particularly appropriate.

Since there is considerable interest in adoption research, agencies should readily find adequate local resources from foundations and individuals to carry on studies. It is important that such studies be coordinated on the national level to prevent unnecessary duplication and to provide the highest degree of integrated effort.

Research on adoption should begin in those agencies which are considered to have policies and procedures representing the best methods—best in terms of current casework practice-theory. The main problem may be getting research under way with a high level of agency interest. A stumbling block comes because some of the basic problems cannot be translated immediately into the findings which are useful to the agency. Certain research projects can well be done by graduate students but in these instances difficulties result if the aims of the thesis advisory committees and those of the agency are different. Along with research that is immediately practical, agencies have an additional responsibility to cooperate in fundamental studies which may seem academic but which in the long run will make their contribution to the practical working of the agency. Likewise, staff members of colleges and universities have a responsibility to make research designs as practical as possible in the interests of the agencies that they will want to help supply data.

The need for coordination at the national level is imperative to the success of a research program in adoption.

CHAPTER 37

Implications of Psychological Testing for Adoptive Placements

LELA B. COSTIN

Social workers making adoptive placements usually feel keenly the weight of the responsibility they have undertaken at the point where a family and a baby are selected for each other. The decision as to whether a particular infant will be "right" for a particular couple looms large and most workers find themselves casting about for all possible substantiation of their decision.

Along with the information at hand about the baby's natural parents, the worker's evaluation of the child's personality development, the pediatrician's opinion based upon his regular examinations of the child, the boarding mother's wisdom gained from her broad experience in caring for different babies with differing personalities, most agencies rely also upon the psychologist's evaluation of the baby's performance on one of the infant intelligence scales—more often and more correctly termed infant development scales. Indeed, one of the important motivating factors for the psychologists' development of these tests has been pressure from workers in adoptive agencies who have wanted to understand more clearly a child's potentialities before selecting a permanent home for him. Used properly, the observations and evaluations that the psychologist makes from the administering of an infant test can be most useful to the adoptive agency; but many adoptive workers are in the peculiar position of attaching far greater significance to and making more far-reaching predictions from the test than would any psychologist informed and skilled in infant testing.[1]

Many adoption workers now attempt to use the results of the baby's performance on the infant test as reported to them by the examining psychologist as a means of predicting or estimating what the child's future intellectual abilities will be. Generally speaking, babies whose performance on the psychological test shows development above the expectation for their age levels are placed with couples where it is known academic achievement is valued and expected; those infants whose performance is at about the norm are placed with couples where there is less emphasis on intellectual achievement but where opportunity for such would probably be possible; and those infants whose performance on the test falls below what is generally expected at their age levels are placed with couples who themselves have achieved less academically and who would probably be accepting of minimum achievement from a child—and where it is known less opportunity for achievement will be offered.

These seem rather arbitrary assumptions to make, involving decisions with far-reaching effects on a child's future, particularly when we realize that such assumptions are made sometimes on the basis of a single test, and for infants at such ages as two, three, and four months.

If such is current practice in some agencies, then it follows that we should re-examine what we know of infant behavior in the light of what psychologists themselves tell us of the tests they have developed.

Let us turn first to a brief examination of the structure of infant developmental scales, and then to some of the statements of psychologists as to the value of such tests.

Structure of Infant Tests

In constructing tests that, hopefully, would measure the intelligence of infants, psychologists sought the answer to such questions as: What in infant behavior may accurately be termed "mental"? What specific behavior precedes later mental achievement? To what extent can later achievements be predicted from early, that is, infant behavior? To what extent is an infant's rate of growth affected by environmental conditions?

---

[1] This article applies to adoptive planning for infants, rather than for older children. There are, of course, a number of tests, both of intelligence and of personality structure, which are of considerable help in understanding the potentialities of school-age children.

Because the most observable developments in young children are in motor facility, infant developmental scales have included many items of this type. The tests have been standardized in much the same way as in the Stanford-Binet mental-age scale. The simple tasks that are observed include such items as the ability of infants to follow a shiny moving object with the eyes, to brush away a stimulating object, to sit alone, to pick up a small cube, and so on. These abilities can be determined for most infants at one month, two months, three months, and so on. Dr. Arnold Gesell and his students have published extensive tabulations showing just what kinds of motor performance can be expected at defined chronological ages. Psyche Cattell's Intelligence Scale for Infants and Young Children is another widely used test. There are others as well. All these tests were first devised and standardized on the assumption that maturation in sensori-motor functions and simple adaptations are intellectual functions and should be predictive of later intellectual performances.

In examining this assumption, Nancy Bayley, a psychologist who has done extensive work in an examination of the reliability of infant tests, wrote: ". . . it does not necessarily follow that individuals whose sensory acuity is great and whose simple co-ordinations are perfected more rapidly will eventually be able to respond more adequately to complex situations. In adults, simple sensory tests have only very low correlations with intelligence. It may well be true that the relationship in infants is no greater, even though, developmentally, the simple forms of behavior appear first and are components of the more complex intellectual responses which develop later. . . . We must bear in mind the possibility that behavioral development during the first year may, within rather wide normal limits, give little indication of later intelligence. Intelligence may involve characteristically 'higher' functions which have very little representation in the infant's repertory. It may be as difficult (outside of pathological deviations) to predict intelligence in infancy as it is to predict vocational aptitude or artistic genius in infancy." [2]

Evaluation of Infant Tests

In order to gain evidence as to whether infant mental tests were or were not good predictors of later intelligence, a number

[2] Nancy Bayley, "Mental Growth During the First Three Years," *Child Behavior and Development,* Roger G. Barker, Jacob S. Kounin, and Herbert F. Wright (eds.), McGraw-Hill Book Company, New York, 1943, Chapter VI, p. 87.

of psychologists, among them Furfey and Muehlenbein,[3] Bayley,[4] Shirley,[5] and Honzik,[6] followed the actual development of a group of infants from early infancy up to the period at which mental tests show reasonable stability of results from one testing to another. All report an absence of relationship between mental test standing before the age of eighteen months and later test performance. There is general agreement that it is only with the appearance of speech that the tests begin to have predictive value, and even then the amount of confidence that can be placed in the results as indices to the child's ultimate level of development continues to be small up to the age of four or five years.

In examining the data obtained from the studies that followed the development of a group of infants to school age, Bayley concluded: "From these data it would appear that prediction in the grade school from tests given at four years of age may be possible within wide classifications for most children. . . . Tests given between two and four years will predict eight and nine year performance with less success, while scores made before eighteen months are completely useless in the prediction of school-age abilities."[7]

One factor important in all testing situations assumes even greater importance in infant examinations—that of the conditions of testing. If the environmental circumstances are such that the baby does not cooperate fully with the examiner, a drastic interference with efficiency may result. It is known that the results may be sizably in error even if only one or two test items are failed as a consequence of some disturbance. The infant does not have a wide enough repertoire of responses so that chance successes or failures even out as with older children.

Improper Use of Test Results

In view of these evaluations of the reliability of infant tests, it becomes evident that for adoption workers to regard an I.Q. obtained from an infant test as predictive of a later Stanford-

[3] P. H. Furfey and J. Muehlenbein, "The Validity of Infant Intelligence Tests," *Journal of Genetic Psychology*, Vol. XL, No. 1 (1932), pp. 219-223.

[4] Nancy Bayley, "Mental Growth During the First Three Years: A Developmental Study of Sixty-One Children by Repeated Tests," *Genet. Psychol. Monogr.*, Vol. XIV, No. 1 (1933). Also, Nancy Bayley, "Consistency and Variability in Growth of Intelligence from Birth to Eighteen Years," *Journal of Genetic Psychology*, Vol. LXXV, No. 2 (1949), pp. 165-196.

[5] M. Shirley, "The First Two Years: A Study of Twenty-five Babies: Vol. II, Intellectual Development," *Inst. Child Welfare Monogr. Ser.*, No. 7, University of Minnesota Press, Minneapolis, 1933.

[6] M. P. Honzik, "The Constancy of Mental Test Performance During the Pre-School Periods," *Journal of Genetic Psychology*, Vol. LII, No. 2 (1938), pp. 285-302.

[7] Bayley, *op. cit.*, footnote 2, Chapter VI, p. 100.

Binet I.Q., or to tell an adoptive couple that the infant being offered them is going to be "just average," or, in other instances, will have ability "to get good grades in school," is completely unjustified. What we more commonly see, however, is adoption workers making rather fine distinctions from the psychological report as to whether a baby should be placed with a "good" family or an "average" family, meaning a family where intellectual achievement is valued and sought, or one where there is less emphasis upon such successes. Such labels as "good," "average," "low-average" applied in various combinations to babies and adoptive couples badly need careful scrutiny and definition.

Other workers are aware of the limited use that can be made of infant psychological tests but allow themselves to attach greater significance to the test results because of their conscientious desire to have more knowledge of the kind of an infant being offered an adoptive couple.

In writing of the use made of infant tests, Florence Goodenough says: "In one sense it may be said that in the success with which they have been used lies their greatest weakness, for too often this successful use has engendered a blind faith in all tests results to which some kind of numerical score is attached. Figures are likely to have a hypnotic effect upon most of us. Although we may know that the significance of a test score varies with the test used, the conditions under which it is given, and the age of the child tested, even the well-informed are often far too prone to feel that, once it has been calculated, an I.Q. is an I.Q. with fixed and absolute meaning. This attitude has led to two unfortunate errors in thinking. On the one hand, we have those who, on the basis of a single test, even when given at a tender age, are ready to 'diagnose' the child's present mental level, make predictions as to his future, perhaps even take action with respect to matters of vital importance for his future. On the other hand, we have those who, with equally naive confidence in the accuracy of the tests, regard every fluctuation in standing as indicating a 'real' change in the child's mental level."[8]

Proper Use of Test Results

The foregoing discussion on the limited use of infant psychological tests does not imply they should not be used in adoption

---

[8] Florence L. Goodenough, "The Measurement of Mental Growth in Childhood," *Manual of Child Psychology*, Leonard Carmichael (ed.), John Wiley & Sons, New York, 1946, Chapter 9, p. 472.

agencies, or that the test results are of no value in understanding the child available for adoption. As was stated in the beginning, the observations and evaluations the psychologist makes can be most useful to the adoption worker. But if infant tests cannot be relied upon as predictors of later intelligence, then what are the ways in which the skill of the psychologist, working through the medium of an infant test, can be of important professional help to the adoption worker in planning for a baby's permanent home?

It stands to reason that when a baby can be given a series of psychological tests rather than a single one, the results are more beneficial to the worker wanting to know more about the child and his present level of development. When a baby can be seen by the psychologist four or five times at monthly intervals, the factor of unfavorable circumstances of testing with its chance successes and failures is minimized. There is also more opportunity for the baby who is developing in "spurts of growth" or is going through a seeming "leveling off period" to show his normal rate of growth. But since most infant tests are not administered before the age of two months, and with the trend in agencies toward placing babies in their permanent homes at a younger age than formerly, such a series of tests usually is not possible before placement. In most cases the added knowledge that the psychologist has to give us must be gained from one, or at most two, testing situations.

In most cases, certainly, the testing situation will identify infants with pathological deviations in their level of development. It will also allow us to identify the child who is making less progress than others, in the sorts of development usually observed at certain ages. Perhaps one of the most usual benefits to the adoption worker is that she gains another professional observation and evaluation of the baby's development to add to her already accumulated series of observations by the baby's worker, the pediatrician, and the boarding mother. Certainly, if the psychologist is experienced and skilled in infant testing, he will have a knowledge from his observations of many infants in many testing situations. From such an examiner, the social worker often is able to gain a graphic picture of the baby's behavior as seen by another professional observer. Examples of psychological reports that add to the worker's acquaintance with the baby are as follows:

Morris, Carol
Born: 10/29/51
Exam I: 3/8/52
Age: 18-1/2 weeks
Gesell Developmental Schedules

Adjustment to Examination

Carol was an unusually purposeful and resolute baby considering her age, which was just short of 19 weeks. She had a high energy level which she seemed definitely to be directing into what she wanted to accomplish. She was clearly ambitious to do things beyond reasonable expectancy for her age level and was undaunted by the fact that, for lack of more advanced muscular control, she was hitting herself in the head with the rattle repeatedly on the rebound when banging at a 28-weeks level—hence, it was necessary to restrain her from this activity. If she lost objects, she went after the job of recovering them, and once resorted to using her mouth as a helping prehensile instrument.

Test Observations

In all four fields of behavior explored by the Gesell Developmental Schedules, maturity characteristics extended well above the nearest age level, 20 weeks, and showed the following range:

Gross motor: 24-28 weeks
Fine motor: 28 (radial rating 32) weeks
Adaptive: 24 (-)-28-32 weeks
Language: 28 weeks
Personal-Social: 20-24-28-32 (est. 28-) weeks

Among the unexpected accomplishments and efforts were 32 weeks radial rating, removal of the cube from the cup with examiner stabilizing the cup (estimated 40 weeks plus), 28 weeks banging, effort at 28 weeks transferring and 32 weeks personal-social behavior.

Summary

Carol is a baby who is pleasant, calm, resolute, goal directed, and who gives evidence of having made progress at a superior rate. She should be an excellent prospect for adoptive placement. If it is possible to follow this examination without jeopardizing her status in the placement, it would be interesting for academic and professional reasons.

James, Rodney

Born: 5/16/51

Exam I: 9/29/51

Age: 19 weeks, 3 days

Test: Gesell Developmental Schedules

Adjustment to Examination

Rodney's energy level is very high. In fact, he might be described as tending toward hyperactivity. He is large, muscular, and vigorous for his age. He is constantly in motion, straining at ambitious accomplishments. He is often on his feet and hands with body raised well above the crib level and has such a bent for locomotion that the leg on which he puts most pressure seems to be bowed. Some of the test situations had to be presented unconventionally because of his advanced postural patterns. He does not remain supine even momentarily. He is about to creep, and in order to have the rattle accepted, it was offered to him in this position, from which he reached with one hand free to accept and exploit it. In spite of the advancement, there is a restless and fairly agitated quality about Rodney's movements.

Test Observations

Rodney is generally accelerated at the age of 19 weeks. All growth characteristics range upward from 20 weeks with spots of incredibly advanced effort and successes, of which were: determined and persistent overside platform play (48w), successful securing of the ring (32w), grasping the bell by the top handle (44w), incomplete transferring effort (less than 23w), pivoting at prone (32w). Otherwise, the following ranges were generally true.

Gross motor: 24—28 weeks

Fine motor: 20—24+ weeks

Adaptive: 24+ weeks

Language: 24—28 weeks

Personal-Social: 24+ weeks

Summary

As seen at this point, Rodney's growth progress is generally accelerated. He is a somewhat agitated, restless child who seems as if he is seeking something that he does not have. It would seem important to give rather close attention to selection of a placement for him so as to meet the emotional needs that may be pushing him into such drives for accomplishment and independence.

It will be noted that on neither of these tests did the psychologist make any statement as to the baby's future intellectual capacity. The emphasis is on the baby's present level of development or maturation. In the instance of the second child, whose growth progress is generally accelerated, the examiner emphasizes not his future intellectual capacity, but his need for a home that will meet the emotional needs giving rise to this drive for accomplishment. In each case the worker is given information that helps her to know this particular baby better, but to make assumptions as to its future level of intelligence is unwarranted.

Another poignant example of the kind of important information about a baby that a psychologist can give us from the testing situation is as follows:

Allan was an attractive baby of four months when he was first seen for psychological testing. His development had been particularly gratifying to the boarding mother, the worker, and the pediatrician.

The available knowledge of the family background revealed nothing that would suggest future difficulty. Allan had been seen for regular examinations by the pediatrician who reported excellent progress in physical development. He was a vigorous baby, one who loved attention and was most responsive to it. He had been noted to be a very alert, observant baby. He had had excellent care in the boarding home, and was a happy, loved, and secure member of a family group. He smiled, laughed, cooed, loved rough play, was regarded by everyone who saw him as a wonderful baby, and by the agency worker as a most promising baby for adoptive placement.

When he was seen by the psychological examiner, the question was raised as to whether Allan might have a hearing loss since he had not responded on test items requiring hearing at the same accelerated rate as he had in other areas. Repeated psychological testing reinforced this suspicion of hearing loss. Subsequent medical examination confirmed it. The next step was to attempt to ascertain what degree of residual hearing might be present.

There was no structural defect present which the pediatrician could have noted earlier. Allan had been so alert to new situations, so observant and responsive to all other stimuli except sound, that the boarding mother and the worker had not yet become aware of his hearing loss. The psychologist, seeing the baby in a controlled testing situation and as an impartial observer, was alert to this defect.

The early recognition by the psychologist of this handicap enabled the agency to seek early specialized medical care for Allan, to help the boarding mother to an understanding of Allan's special needs, and to search for a permanent home for him which would give him the particular love, security, and opportunity he needed.

Conclusions

Certainly there is an important place in adoptive planning for psychological testing. This article is not attempting to minimize the role of the psychologist but rather to see it in proper perspective. The skill of the psychologist can be of value to us only if we free him of the expectation of giving us predictions of a baby's future intellectual level and use his knowledge for increased understanding of the baby we have now—its present level of growth and development. Perhaps at some future time infant psychological tests will be perfected to the point where they can more accurately predict intelligence at a later age but, for the present, the value of infant tests lies in the increased knowledge given us about the baby in his present state.

Perhaps the real need is for us, as adoptive workers, to reaffirm what we seek in adoptive parents—relaxed, loving, mature adults who can accept a child as he grows and develops and help him to his own particular heights. This need is clearly recognized and stated in a recent follow-up study of adoptive families: "In the study of a home and in selection of a child, workers have sometimes attempted to protect adoptive families against every conceivable problem or disappointment in their future with their child. This is most evident in the anxiety often shown by workers around matching intellectual expectancy of the child to the family's educational ambitions; or in some cases, with artistic or gifted parents, to select children who may have such promise. Actually, it is of course no more possible to protect adoptive parents against disappointments than it is to protect biological parents. Workers need to understand, as far as possible, the qualities and kinds of achievement in a child that might give an individual family special pleasure, and to take this into account in selecting a child. The important thing to assess, however, is what people do in their relationships when they are disappointed; and whether, if a child cannot meet their fantasy expectations, they will reject him, or continue indefinitely to exert rigid pressure upon him to conform, or find the experience a source of frustration and heartbreak, impairing their capacity to enjoy him as he is."[9]

A careful "matching" of intellectual abilities between parents and children, even were this possible, is no guarantee that a child will be enabled to use his intellectual abilities. There is no substitute for the qualities in parents of warmth, flexibility, understanding, enjoyment of living, and all the other components of emotional maturity. If, as adoption workers, we can find parents with these personality characteristics, we can be reasonably hopeful that, in this democracy, the children we place will find opportunities to develop their own particular abilities and potentialities for good citizenship.

[9] Ruth Brenner, *A Follow-Up Study of Adoptive Families,* Child Adoption Research Committee, New York, March, 1951, p. 136.

CHAPTER 38

The Legal Profession's Responsibility in Adoption

ALEX ELSON

It is well at the outset to restate some of the basic assumptions which give status and acceptance to the professions, including the legal profession. These are:
1. The professional person offers competency in his field, knowledge and skill which are not generally shared.
2. A professional person is not solely concerned with giving skilled services, as such, however important this may be, but is concerned with the total personality of the individual he serves. Put another way, the general welfare of the client in the full center of his social situation cannot be ignored in rendering service to him.

"Clergyman, physician, psychiatrist, nurse, psychologist, lawyer, teacher, social worker, all are involved in the giving-taking relationship. In serving they do things for, with, and to people. The recipient responds in terms of what he is and of what the services mean to him. His response embodies something of himself and something of the helper. Traditionally, the professional person has been concerned to give what he has to offer in ways which are helpful, in ways which enable the recipient to make good use of the contribution regardless of whether or not he pays for the services. Today there is an increased awareness of the total personality involved in this relationship and growing concern as to what is being 'done to' the person experiencing a professional service."[1]

3. The professional person recognizes responsibility not only to the persons he serves but to society or the community at large.

4. Responsibility of the professional person to the client and the community transcends personal gain or advancement. This concept is explicit in the oath taken by lawyers on their admission to the bar.

5. A professional person recognizes the competence and skill of other professions. Put in other terms he must know and fully accept his own limitations and how best to relate other fields of specialized knowledge to the needs of his client.

6. A professional person is continually interested in and concerned to advance knowledge and understanding in his field of interest. This involves a research approach to problems, a willingness to learn and to teach, a willingness and eagerness, if you will, to work for and accept progress.

These concepts are fundamental to the legal profession among others, but the task of the legal profession can also be sharply defined in relation to the task of the law. Roscoe Pound recently stated:

"The task of the law is to adjust relations and order conduct so as to give the most effect to the whole scheme of expectations of men in civilized society with a minimum of friction and waste."[2]

This definition has a close relation to adoptions. An adoption is a creation of the legal process. It involves unequivocal and irrevocable adjustment of legal relations, with profound and permanent implications for all concerned.

The lawyer serves as a family counselor and is jealous of his role. His advice is sought on a great variety of relational problems including those of the most intimate character. The privileged character of the relationship encourages full disclosure by the client. The fact that the lawyer will observe his confidence frequently gives the client a release, which is meaningful to him even though the lawyer plays the completely passive role of the listener. The client goes to a lawyer with his problems about his

---

[1] Charlotte Towle, *The Learner in Education for the Professions,* pp. 3-4, University of Chicago Press, 1954.

[2] *The Lawyer from Antiquity to Modern Times,* pp. 24-25, West Publishing Company, 1953.

wife, his difficulties with his children, especially when they become involved with the law, the making of his will, which for most clients is a solemn undertaking of far-reaching consequences. The lawyer advises on a wide range of subjects. He brings to bear his knowledge and experience of many years. It is not easy for him to confess his inability to advise. It is well to recognize this factor and to deal with it directly and understandingly.

A lawyer who has observed some of the disastrous consequences of misguided adoptions or attempts at adoption knows the hazards involved. But this alone does not bring recognition of the expertness which is available in a recognized child-placing agency. In some cases nothing short of actual observation of the handling of a case by a skilled child welfare worker will convince the lawyer. We must recognize that a substantial part of the legal profession is not generally aware of the nature and character of the social work profession, that it has developed special skills based on a body of knowledge developed over many years. This is true in relation not only to adoptions but to many other fields of social service. One can say that, with few exceptions, the attorneys who appreciate and recognize the special skills available in a child-placement agency are those who have been educated through the handling of the legal aspects of an adoption processed by an agency. I do not mean to suggest that they have been lectured to by social workers; though some lawyers have been lectured to by some social workers. Theirs has been the process of education by association and observation.

Although this is not the time or place to discuss what can be done about further education of the legal profession, I should like to make one suggestion, which I last made at the National Conference of Social Work in 1951 in a discussion of legal guardianship. I suggested that the United States Children's Bureau, which had taken the initiative in bringing about a discussion of legal guardianship, arrange to confer with the appropriate committees of the American Association of Law Schools relative to the important contributions of the social work profession.

In fairness to the lawyer, when he attempts to give service in most cases his motivations are in accord with professional standards. But the best motivations are not a substitute for specialized knowledge and training. Lawyers will best serve their profession and their clients if they recognize this fact.

Typical Situations Confronting Lawyer

In pragmatic terms, what are the responsibilities of the lawyer in relation to the several categories of adoption matters that come to him? First, let us consider the fairly common occurrence of a lawyer who is consulted by clients who tell him, usually haltingly and with some embarrassment, that they desire to adopt a child. He will, of course, tell them that an adoption has important legal consequences and what these consequences are. He will tell them what the requirements of the relevant adoption statute are and, in general, something of the process. But most important, he will stress the serious social and relational problems involved and make clear that he is not the person who can best advise them in this area. He will refer them to a recognized child-placement agency. This is the focal point of the interview and should the lawyer fail here, he does a great disservice to his clients, a disservice which may have damaging consequences to them and to others. The fact is that lawyers are not competent and do not have the requisite training and experience to deal with what has become recognized as a special area of social service. This is accepted by a substantial and growing part of the legal profession. But in actual practice there are many lawyers who fail to act accordingly. It is important to try to understand this.

The key problem is focused in the interview at the point that a client tells his attorney that he understands that it is difficult to secure a child. He has heard from friends of the "red tape" and "delays" involved in adoption agencies and that the agencies are "choosy." In some cases the clients have already canvassed the available agencies and have either been discouraged or rejected. They ask the lawyer's assistance in securing a child. Here the lawyer must be understanding, patient and firm. He can play a constructive role in indicating the legal limitations which apply under laws requiring licensing of child-placement agencies and which forbid lawyers or others from engaging in placement. He can explain the reasons for such laws. He can outline the hazards to the client, to the child, and to the community in what has been described as blind adoptions. It is clear that he would violate his professional responsibility if he ventured to secure a child or suggest the means of securing a child outside recognized agencies, if indeed he knows of any sources. Stated in positive terms, his professional duty is to encourage the clients to rely on the advice and guidance available to them in the recognized child-placement agencies.

Second, let us consider the role of the lawyer in an adoption which originates in a child-placement agency. Here the task of the lawyer is considerably eased. Assuming a properly handled case, the usual anxieties which surround an adoption are resolved, the agency has approved and tested techniques to bring together a sound family unit. The lawyer has the important job of making certain that all of the legal requirements of the adoption statute have been met and that the decree will be unassailable. The smaller agencies which do not have legal consultants must rely heavily on the practitioner for guidance in all legal aspects of the adoption.

Third, we come now to the most difficult situation which confronts the lawyer in the adoption process. The client advises him a child is about to be placed in his home. Usually in this situation, the doctor delivering the child has made the arrangements. The client asks that the lawyer arrange to secure the consent of the mother and to do everything necessary to complete an adoption. This situation bristles with questions. Should the lawyer accept such a case? If he accepts the case should he undertake to confer with the natural mother and secure a consent? To what extent can the client make use of child-placement agencies in the community? Are other resources available? If he secures the consent of the mother how can he protect against revocation? If investigation is required by the adoption statute, what agency will investigate? If the agency which investigates makes an adverse report what should his attitude be? These and many other questions which arise in this situation should be fully discussed in these sessions. Unhappily we must accept the fact that lawyers are often confronted with these questions. Recognized child-placement agencies are without sufficient resources to handle all children of unmarried parents available for adoption. Some doctors will, for some time to come, continue to make private placements. The legal profession cannot shut its doors to adoptive parents in these situations. The individuals involved usually have good motives.

The basic problem is that the method is wrong. How can the lawyer best protect the child, the natural parents, the adoptive parents and the community? The fact is that the lawyer can only function as a lawyer. This is a hard fact, but it is inescapable. He can provide his experience and knowledge to bring about hopefully an adoption decree which will withstand attack. In all other areas he walks on quicksand. If he is fortunate, he can complete the legal process; he can seldom have the satisfaction of knowing whether the new family which he has legalized will experience a normal range of happiness.

Fourth, there is the problem of the unmarried mother who presents herself to the lawyer for help in planning for her unborn child. The problem here is almost exclusively a social problem, assuming a situation in which the father is unknown or in which there is no desire to establish obligation to support. The duty of the lawyer is clear. The client should be referred to the appropriate social agency in the community so that she can be helped to make the best plan for herself and her unborn child.

Role of Judges

It can be said that apart from seeing that the requirements of the statute are met, the judge in the adoption process is most strategically placed to protect parties involved assuming the existence of a good adoption statute. This is especially true of the independent placement. Those of us who have followed the judicial process know that in very few cases does a judge upset an independent placement. This is not said in criticism of the judges, who are, as a general rule, keenly interested in the child. The fact is that the case comes to the judge too late, usually months after the mother has relinquished the child and a new family unit has been formed. Thus, the case comes before the court without the benefit of an objective and expert appraisal of the situation.

The court may be of great assistance in the more gross cases by establishing a pattern of searching inquiry with the aid of competent caseworkers and by giving weight to the recommendations.

In the process of discussing some of the problems confronting the practicing lawyer, I have perhaps given a more negative portrayal of the role of the legal profession than is justified. The legal profession not only has recognized the proper role of the lawyer, but has used its disciplinary proceedings to discourage the small minority of lawyers engaged in the black market who have forgotten their professional obligations. More important, the legal profession has been active in securing improvements in adoption and related laws throughout the history of the adoption process.

CHAPTER 39

What the Adoption Worker Should Know About Infertility

RICHARD FRANK, M.D.

In the selection of adoptive families, agencies draw primarily from childless couples. Leading child-placing agencies require thorough medical exploration of infertility as precedent to an application to adopt a child. It is, therefore, essential that adoption workers understand what an adequate infertility work-up comprises.

Sterility and infertility are terms which are often used interchangeably. Reference to the dictionary, however, reveals that these terms cannot be so used. Sterile is defined as "incapable of producing." It describes a condition that is unalterable. Infertile is defined as "non-producing," a functional state, temporary or reversible. In other words, sterility is permanent, produced by absence or removal of the gonads or by the absence, removal or blocking of such organs as transport the sex cells or are necessary to provide growing space for the fertilized egg. It is an irreversible condition. Infertility is frequently temporary, often relative, and is curable, the outlook depending on the underlying causes.

The causes of infertility are so manifold that their discussion is best carried out together and along with the description of an adequate infertility examination. Methods of treatment will be discussed briefly, and finally some suggestions will be made for integration of the medical findings into the adoptive picture.

It has been said that "knowledge is but a small island in the vast sea of the unknown." As our knowledge grows, the shore lines of this island increase, that is, our contact with the unknown is ever increasing. This applies so well to our field under discussion. Tremendous strides have been made in the diagnosis, treatment and study of infertility, resulting in the fact that today a thorough infertility study should demand much more in the way of observation and specific examinations than we so frequently see being done. Relatively few years have passed since it was recognized that the male is responsible in from forty to fifty per cent of infertility cases. And it is only in recent years that the male has become gradually less resistant to an infertility investigation. This is an important step forward, because an infertility study must include a study of both partners in all details, and the heretofore casual semen examination of the male, resulting in his exoneration because a few motile sperm cells were visible under the microscope, has given way to a detailed study such as the female has undergone for many years already.

Medical History Reveals Disorders

A careful and thorough medical history of both partners will reveal absence or existence of systemic disease, such as diabetes, renal disease, thyroid disorder or nutritional aberrations which may shed light on the infertile state. Glandular disorders, expressed in menstrual irregularities, or in the male in arrest of the sexual development may be of importance.

A general physical examination often leads to discovery of obvious causes of infertility. Undescended testicles in the male, arrested development of the female genital organs, generalized bodily signs of glandular disorders in either partner can in this way often be detected or at least suspected, and further study thus initiated. In other instances pathological conditions may be discovered that were without symptoms and, therefore, were unknown to the patient. Laboratory tests, including a test for syphilis, a basal metabolism, a complete blood count, and a urinalysis, round out the general examination needed by both partners.

From the outset, the gynecologist advises the couple who come for help because of childlessness that a thorough and careful infertility investigation cannot be done hurriedly. The cyclic nature of the female reproductive system demands that certain tests be carried out only once a month, and if they have to be repeated, another month or two may have to go by. The couple must know that certain observations have to be carried out and that a total work-up may easily take six months, during which time one of the partners or both may have to be seen by the doctor at three- to four-week intervals.

From this point on, the method of investigation varies for male and female, because the function of the respective reproductive glands is now in question. It is logical to begin with a semen examination, as it entails the least discomfort to the couple. As we progress to testing tubal patency, doing endometrial biopsies and other necessary tests, certain, however minimal, pain or potential danger may be encountered. This then is the reason why we usually advocate the semen examination as the first test. Certain precautionary measures are to be observed to obtain a reliable result. The specimen must never be collected or submitted in a condom which contains certain chemicals that frequently kill sperm cells. It should not be older than two or three hours, and should be kept cool during this period. The observations must include:

1. the amount of the total specimen in ccm.,
2. the degree of viscosity,
3. thenumber of sperm cells per ccm.,
4. the percentage of motile cells,
5. the degree of motility expressed from one to four plus,
6. the percentage of abnormal sperm cells, and finally
7. the kind and amount of other cells present.

Only specimen that have undergone such detailed scrutiny are acceptable in an infertility study. It is not possible to give a lower limit for a sperm count below which an egg cannot be fertilized. As much or more depends on the motility and survival time as on the total number of sperm cells present. Not infrequently two or more semen specimen have to be examined before a favorable or unfavorable opinion can be given.

Test Tubal Patency

Many times a couple will present x-ray pictures as evidence that the woman's tubes are patent. She has been informed by her physician of this fact, visible on the films. The conclusions that her tubes are therefore normal for purposes of transporting the

471

egg and the sperm are, however, fallacious. The function patency of the Fallopian tubes can only be ascertained by the "Rubin" test, an office procedure, in which the passage of carbon dioxide gas through the Fallopian tubes is tested under conditions which permit the gynecologist:

1. to observe the pressure which is needed to drive carbon dioxide gas through the tubes,
2. to register the degree and amount of contractions of the muscular covering of the tubes during the test,
3. to take notice of the occurrence of immediate or delayed shoulder discomfort after the test.

At times it may be necessary to repeat the tubal patency test two or more times before a definite answer can be given. Tubal patency varies at different times of the menstrual cycle, and the best time must be chosen for performing the test. This is just before or at ovulation time when the tubal musculature is most relaxed and spasm least likely to occur. The x-ray visualization of the tubes should be reserved for cases where patency cannot be demonstrated by the Rubin test and where we may gain more information as to where in the tubes the obstruction is located. The primary testing of tubal patency by means of injecting a radio-opaque medium into the tubes and taking x-rays is not acceptable as proof that the tubes are normal.

Observation of Ovulation

For many years the keeping of a basal body temperature (BBT) chart has been used to obtain an impression whether the woman under investigation is ovulating. The procedure is as follows: Each morning upon awakening the woman takes her temperature according to the directions given her, and she charts the result daily. This results in a curve which in a normal ovulating woman has two phases: a low one for about twelve to fourteen days after the menstrual period, followed by a rise at about the fourteenth day and a higher phase which persists until onset of the next menstrual period. The keeping of this BBT record under the supervision of the physician is very important as it gives the latter much valuable information. Such a chart should however, never be construed to be a timetable for the couple as to when the best time for conception is at hand during any given month. This emphatic statement is made for two reasons:

1. nobody—not even the expert—can interpret the BBT curve until the monthly cycle has been completed and the "timing" would be poor guesswork indeed,

2. by trying to follow a "timetable" the spontaneity of the sex
   life is badly shaken, and a psychological factor may possibly
   be added to the infertility problem at hand.

The temperature readings must be taken for a period of three to
six months before the observing physician can draw any conclusions from them.

Another test to observe the presence of ovulation in a given
cycle is the endometrial biopsy, carried out as an office procedure.
In this test a small strip is removed from the lining of the uterus
and examined under the microscope. The test must be carried
out close to the day when the menstrual flow is to begin, and the
tissues obtained must be carefully prepared for the microscopic
examination or the findings may be misinterpreted. It takes more
than a good pathologist to interpret an endometrial biopsy as
this interpretation has to be carried out in the framework of
other findings in the individual patient.

Even though the sperm may be plentiful and normal in every
respect, it may become inactive if the secretions of the female
genital tract are inimical to it. We know that the secretions of
the vagina are never favorable to the survival of sperm cells,
but that the secretions of the cervix—the lower portion of the
uterus—undergo cyclic changes which only at certain times of
the month are favorable to sperm cells. The knowledge that the
cervical glands produce secretions which favor survival and
transport of sperm cells around the time of ovulation is utilized
for the compatibility test. Within two hours after intercourse,
secretions are removed from the cervix and examined under the
microscope for the presence of motile sperm cells. If they are
present, the test is favorable; if absent, and the test performed
at the correct time of the cycle, this hostile environment for the
sperm population has to be improved.

Treatment of the Couple

Proper treatment of the infertile couple begins at the first
visit when the patients are advised what to expect from an
infertility work-up, and how long it will take before a final
answer can be given. The reasons for each test are outlined to
them, and both husband and wife should leave the first interview
knowing that there is no "miracle-drug" cure for them, that
hormone shots or pills only rarely are indicated in the rational
treatment of infertility, and that their chances to reach their
goal are good until proven otherwise by the outcome of the
tests. Reassurance should be the keynote at every visit and at

473

every test. It is of importance to advise patients of the outcome of each test as it is performed. This should not be construed in terms of jubilant unjustified enthusiasms when certain tests are favorable, nor as unnecessary pessimism, if certain tests should be below par. But the results should be explained in the light of the functional variations to which any test of a physiological nature is exposed.

Dietary deficiencies may need correction. A high protein diet with an increased vitamin intake is often advisable. Thyroid medication is indicated when the basal metabolsm or clinical manifestations indicate lack of thyroid substance. Iron is prescribed if anemia is found during the blood examination. In short, all factors which are found to be below par are corrected, because a poor semen picture, or poor ovulation response, may well be due to a general debilitated state. In the male, chronic infection of the prostate gland may have to be eradicated. In the female, drugs to remove spasm of the tubal musculature are often found indicated and are helpful. Infection of the cervix must be treated by cautery or other appropriate means to improve the survival time of the sperm cells in the uterus.

The question frequently arises as to when a couple should consider undergoing an infertility investigation, and it is usually accepted that one year of married life without use of contraceptives should pass, before an infertility work-up should be started. Another question raised is how long a couple should remain under investigation or treatment? If a factor or factors are found that will make conception impossible, the couple should be so advised and the investigation terminated. There are definite limits to our therapeutic ability, and it must be clearly stated that the use of hormones to produce or increase sperm production is strictly experimental, and that no sound basis exists at this time for such treatment. The same pertains to any hormonal treatment of absence of ovulation. There is today no known hormone which will, in the human female, stimulate or produce ovulation. In our endeavor to find such agents, we conduct clinical research in the course of which patients are given hormones. They must understand, however, that such treatment is entirely experimental and should be used only after all conventional means of treatment have failed.

If all tests are within the range of normal, the period of observation should extend over six to twelve months. During this time the above-mentioned steps toward improving the various factors are taken. At the end of that period, it is usually advisable to have a conference with the couple, explaining the satisfactory outcome of the study, and pointing out to them that another six to twelve months should pass without the possible anxieties involved in monthly observations and tests. If at the end of that period, now a total of three years, no pregnancy has occurred, plans for adoption should be discussed.

Psychological Reasons for Infertility

The term "functional infertility" is frequently used in lieu of a better term for a childless couple who have undergone all infertility tests and the entire period of observation without bringing to light any organic or physiological pathology. And still no pregnancy occurs. It is in such couples especially, that we look for psychological reasons of the infertility. The field of the psychological influence on infertility is practically untouched. Even though almost everybody knows some couple who achieved a pregnancy after adopting a baby and tries to make the adoption responsible for the "relief of tension" which caused the pregnancy, the work of Rock and others puts these experiences strictly in the category of "chance." There is no question that many an infertile couple has psychological difficulties; it can also hardly be denied that undergoing an infertility study over a prolonged period of time and wanting a child desperately, can scarcely prevent the average couple from becoming anxious. The real connection between physiological processes like ovulation and emotions has not been solved, and it is hardly within the framework of this discussion to dwell on it further.

It may now be appropriate to make some suggestions to integrate the medical findings into the adoption investigation. If sterility, as defined in this presentation, is known in a couple applying for adoption, no further medical investigation is necessary, over and above the criteria of general physical and mental health which have always been required in any adoption study. If infertility factors are presented as the basis of the adoption request, it seems logical that a strict yardstick must be applied to the evaluation of the results as they are presented to the agency. A detailed medical questionnaire should be returned by every applying couple. The information should include all the points raised in this discussion. Agencies would do well to have on their staff a consultant gynecologist, who is an interested expert in infertility. The adoption worker should have occasion to discuss the infertility picture of every applicant with this consultant. It seems furthermore feasible that every adoption agency should have on hand a referral list of gynecologists who are interested in infertility and willing to cooperate with the agency to obtain or to complement the necessary study, so that couples are not deprived of the possibility of natural parenthood because they have been unable on their own to find a competent infertility expert. This is not to be construed as a devaluation of the practicing physician, but only as expression of the ever-increasing amount of specialized work needed in an infertility study.

CHAPTER 40

Psychiatric Considerations in Foster Home Placement and Adoption[1]

RALPH D. RABINOVITCH, M.D.
SARA DUBO, M.D.
VALERIA F. JURACSEK, M.D.

We are pleased to have this opportunity to discuss with you some issues of concern to all of us in the field of child placement. Our remarks will be for the most part concerned with psychiatric implications for casework in the area of foster home placement and supervision. Our observations stem from an integrated study of children in foster homes, carried out in Michigan in a collaborative project involving the Children's Service of the Neuropsychiatric Institute, University of Michigan, and the Michigan Children's Institute, our State foster home placement agency. The value of our study, we believe, lies in its truly multi-discipline approach and it is evident that there is a great need for pooling all our resources in the study of placement and adoption. In this project, which covers the study of approximately one hundred children in foster care, Clarence Ramsay, director of the Michigan Children's Institute, and Doris Wencke,

[1] This report, read at the Annual Meeting, New York State Welfare Conference, 1952, by Doctor Rabinovitch, covers one section of a study carried out with the aid of a grant from the Horace H. Rackham Fund, University of Michigan Graduate School.

assistant director, met with our group from the Neuropsychiatric Institute which included Winifred Ingram, clinical psychologist, and Dorothy Engel, research social caseworker, along with the present authors.

A detailed study of the background and longitudinal adjustment of each child was made, the placement agency studied its involvement and practices in the case, the foster mother was interviewed by a worker from outside the agency, two psychiatrists interviewed each child in an attempt to probe the inner life, and the clinical psychologist complemented these studies with projective tests. The data itself proved of interest but equally valuable, we believe, was the opportunity for each of us to meet with experienced workers in the related fields, in pursuit of a definitive goal. It seems to us that this multidiscipline approach, which unfortunately is more often talked of than practiced, has not been sufficiently applied outside the child guidance clinic field. The psychiatrist has a definite role to play in the placement agency but he must be really integrated in its functioning and must give up any concept of autonomy if his work is to be of optimal value. As psychiatrists, all involved over a number of years in the work of placement agencies, we have been taught many of the practical lessons of the field through the patient guidance of many experienced caseworkers. It is not always easy for the psychiatrist to learn these practical lessons and we might say that we are grateful to those of you who take the time to orient us. We may meet your teaching with some initial resistance because sometimes we feel called upon to be the teachers but realities gradually penetrate and we become better psychiatrists because of our contacts with you. We cannot overstress the importance of integration of our fields in such areas as foster home placement, institutional care and adoption. The psychiatrist, working directly in the field, can, we hope, bring to you some further insights into the inner life of children separated from their natural families and into the psychologic meaning of various types of placement. This paper will attempt to do this. There is probably little new in our observations; we doubt that our findings will tell you very much that you do not already know or at least feel, but we hope that they will serve to crystallize feelings that have not been sufficiently formalized in our placement work philosophy. There is in fact a surprising paucity of contributions in the area of philosophy underlying child placement. Placement workers are probably too busy to philosophize which in some ways is all to the good but we have probably reached a point in our progress at which increased introspection is indicated. We have drawn some rather broad general conclusions from our case material; these are not presented as definitive but with the hope that they will stimulate discussion and further research, so much needed in the placement field.

The Meaning of Separation

First we should like to discuss the problem of diagnosis as it affects placement, especially diagnosis of the child's relationship capacity that dictates his special needs in placement. Relationship capacity will in large measure depend upon the earlier opportunities provided in the child's first years for a primary mother relationship. Most children referred for placement have had some meaningful primary relationship and are anxious and conflicted because traumatic distortions have invaded their relationships with their natural parents; these children are neurotic in reaction to their life experience. Others exhibit much less in the way of neurotic conflict, are relatively unanxious and seem to have a paucity of inner life and fantasy. We shall refer at some length to these differential criteria later in this paper.

Many of the children in our group have known their parents and have had an opportunity in the early years to relate and identify with them, being separated later, after the age of three or four years. One of the striking observations in our material is the confusion and concern that so many of these children express regarding the initial separation from the natural parents. It is often difficult for us as adults to avoid the pitfall of adult projection when we think of children and this occurs at every level. For example, it is rather startling to find some professional workers, in their consideration of psychosexual development, still interpreting the Oedipus complex as implying a four-year-old boy's wish for adult sexual intercourse with the mother. This is an adult projection of the type that many psychoanalysts have warned against in recent years. Thus, Adelaide Johnson[2] points out: "There is no compelling reason to think that the child has a strong impulse to walk or talk at three months yet such an assumption is as defensible as the assumption that the child has a powerful impulse for intercourse at four years." Psychosexual development occurs at the child's level of biologic growth and mother-son relationships at four

---

[2] Johnson, Adelaide, McF.: "Some Etiological Aspects of Repression, Guilt and Hostility." *Psychoanalyt. Quart.* 20:511, 1951.

years must be viewed from the child and not the adult developmental level.

An analogous tendency to project adult standards still prevails when we consider children in their family setting. The level of apparent neglect or the traumatic reality in the home may be evident to the adult and may provide a clear indication for separation, but children tell us a very different story. Identified with the parents and the family unit the child tends to find extenuations for difficulties and often he genuinely cannot understand the adult's concern for his welfare. The worker may see himself as the child's protector; in the child's fantasy this same worker may well be a kidnapper. This problem was brought into sharp focus for us in our work with a twelve-year-old displaced child from Europe whose parents were killed in Nazi Germany. The boy was brought to America and placed in an excellent adoptive home in which he acted out intense hostility, at times reaching the point of violence. In therapy he indicated the major source of his conflict; although intellectually he knew that his parents had been killed he maintained the feeling that the adoptive parents were kidnappers and had stolen him from his natural parents. Such fantasies are common and will be referred to again in our remarks on problems of adoption.

By and large it would seem that we have failed to recognize as fully as we might the primary significance of family to the child and the biological roots of needs in this area. In their productions children tell us with remarkable regularity of their need to be with family and there is little correspondence in this feeling to what the family actually has to offer the child. The implication for casework is clear; separation should be effected only when every reparative resource has been brought to bear. When separation is necessary it is not sufficient to just talk of preparing the child; it is essential to probe the child's feeling about separation and to allow him an affective response in the protection of a meaningful casework relationship.

Guilt, Restitutive and Extenuating Fantasies

Content material on the fantasy life of children who have been separated from their families indicates some interesting mechanisms that children evolve to explain realities too traumatic for the ego to integrate. There is a strong tendency, revealed in our case studies, to relate separation to a specific event and to take personal responsibility for the separation. This is not surprising in view of what we know of children and their fantasies. They tend to think concretely and in specific terms so that abstractions are avoided and explanations are found in specific situations. One of us (S. D.) has described, in a study of the psychologic aspects of tuberculosis in children, the explanations that tuberculous children give for their having contracted the disease. "Although they are aware of the specific agent and the source of infection in their home, in our group discussions we are told: 'It's my fault because I didn't take care of myself'; 'I didn't obey my mother so it's my fault'; 'I got TB because I stayed out late'; 'I didn't come home at the right time or eat the right foods' ".[3]

Time after time we find the foster children of our study expressing similar concrete explanations for their separation and assuming responsibility for it. Thus ten-year-old Walter, in placement for five years, discusses his natural mother: "She was real nice. She fed us all the time. Three meals a day; every place she went she took us. She gave us money but she wasn't very rich. Dad didn't make much money so once in a little while we had a dime or so. My mother and father parted and I stayed with my father, then I went to my grandmother's. It was daddy's fault. He went to other people's houses, other women's houses. I was with him once when he had a trucking business. I remember once he stopped at another woman's house and she gave me a banana. I don't know how my ma found out. She was mad and then she parted. I was very sad. I wanted to be with my ma and my dad. My ma didn't want me because I went with my dad and stopped at that house. She wanted my brother, she didn't want me. You see I look like my dad and we stopped at that house." This five years after the separation.

Jerry, in foster placement for four years, and now eight years old tells us smiling, when we ask how many mothers he has had in his life: "Just one, you can only have one mother, your own mother. My mother was just like any other mother, only sometimes she didn't feed me like she should. I was only four years old once and I got mad one day and I tried to make me some pancakes and I messed it all up. So she just went off and left me. I'm sorry about those pancakes. Then I had to leave my sister and now she's in a hospital with TB. I always dreamed I was back home. Then in the morning I'd wake up and I'd be mad because I wasn't. Now I just want to see my mother and see how she looks."

[3] Dubo, Sara: "Psychiatric Study of Children with Pulmonary Tuberculosis." *Am. J. Orthopsychiat.* 20:520, 1950.

Alice had lived with her grandmother for two years from age six to eight and in a foster home from age eight to ten. As she plays with a mother doll she associates as follows: "My mother was real nice. She got married three times. Every night she'd give me money for a show. One day she told me not to take my sister's doll to school and I took it and fell on the ice and broke it. Now I dream how nice she was to me and how she kept me then and I'm sad about my mother. I want to go back. I don't think they'll ever let me go back, the social worker. I think when I get big I'll want to go home and I won't know the way and I'll feel scared."

George, deserted by his mother at age five and now seven, recalls his quarrels with his mother: "She used to tell me to stop throwing pillows at my brother and I always said yes, but I threw too many pillows and she went away. I think I saw her yesterday in the bus. I went up to the lady and said are you my mother and she didn't answer me or nothing. Do you think it was my mother?"

These productions are typical of children who have known their parents and established meaningful relationships with them, and then have been separated, sometimes precipitously. It is evident that in these cases the child has not reached a comfortable solution of his primary family relationships and we can expect that these confusions and lingering preoccupations will affect his adjustment in the foster home and in life at large. Again there is an implication for casework. Given an opportunity, children will discuss these inner problems and it is therapeutic that they do so. To share their fear and guilt with an interested and meaningful adult is therapeutic in itself and the reassurance that the worker can provide is further helpful. We do not propose at this time to go into casework techniques; we plan to at a later date when our entire group reports on our study in more detail. But some general principles are implicit in this material.

We should like to stress again that the group of children just described have established meaningful relationships with parents before the time of separation. They have internalized and preserved an image of the natural parents which serves as a focus for identification. It would seem that this identification with internalized parent images is much more meaningful than any identification occurring with the foster parents with whom the child is actually living. At times we have probably overstressed in our study of these children the actual situation in the foster home failing to give sufficient attention to this vital inner factor. Keeping alive this interest in the natural parents, encouraging the fantasies about them and allowing the child to find extenuations for the causes that led to separation will in the long run help rather than impair adjustment in the foster home. From our study we conclude that the commonest cause of failure in placement with these particular children is the fact that they are haunted by unresolved guilt, by uncertainty and by worry about the natural parents, and these inner preoccupations do not allow for the integration of new substitute relationships. We realize that there are many practical problems facing the placement worker as she tries to help the child in this area, questions as to the advisability of the child visiting with the natural parents and of maintaining the child in the foster home while the basic problems are resolved. The caseworkers in our group have given attention to these matters and will discuss them in a later paper. There are of course no easy solutions but our practices must insofar as possible be guided by these psychologic realities.

Problems of Identity and Identification

Another group of children in foster care can be differentiated. These are the children who also have established primary relationships through gratification in early mothering, and have achieved the capacity to relate, but who have no conscious memory of their natural parents, never having known them or having been separated early. Many adopted children are in this group. Here the problem for the child is often to achieve some sense of identity. We use the term 'identity' as distinct from 'identification'. *Identity* is a conscious concept and refers to the child's ideas about his origin and the meaning of his name to him. *Identification* represents an unconscious process through which the child patterns himself after the parents or parent substitutes with whom he grows. The sense of identity is more basic and is frequently undermined in children who have uncertainty about their background. It is difficult to conceive of comfortable ego development in the latency and adolescent years when some knowledge of identity is lacking. Our case studies indicate the tragic confusion of children who have such uncertainty. Alice, perplexed and troubled, tells us: "I got a couple of mothers but I think Aunt Jane is really my mother but I don't know. Do you know?" Peter, age nine, discusses his name: "I don't know about that. I think they gave it to me." 'They' refers to the placement agency. Johnnie, age seven, anxious and depressed, is much confused by the difference between a real mother and a foster mother. After much thought he finally tells us: "We just keep going from one place to another to find out what is the real mother; when you get used to a place it's the real mother." Another nine-year-old boy puts it more simply: "One's good and the other's bad."

Again with these children we find that the parent does not have to be present in the child's life for him to develop a concept of identity. Explanations can be given, questions answered and sometimes backgrounds manufactured to satisfy the child's need to know his origin. Children tend to cling to such explanations and they lead to sustaining fantasies which meet a deep and basic need. When we fail to answer the basic questions of identity for the child the confusion tends to spread to all relationships and some of these cases resemble schizophrenic children in their diffusion and uncertainty. These lost, amorphous and rootless children are among the most tragic we see, rather empty in content and so little motivated toward a future because they have no past. To keep alive a concept of the past is the job at hand.

The Affectionless Child

There is a third group, the most challenging and yet discouraging to work with—those children who do not appear to have the capacity for depth relationships and social identifications. To provide a historical background for this discussion may we review for you some of the research findings regarding personality growth in children. In 1937 David Levy[4] pointed out the correlation between the lack of emotional response in children and the absence of continuous mothering in infancy. Suggesting the relationship between later inability to relate and primary affect hunger Levy wrote: "The power of maternal love may be seen most clearly in life histories where it is absent —a kind of ablation experiment." In 1940 Lawson Lowrey[5] reported on a larger ablation experiment, presenting longitudinal studies of 28 children raised during their first year or two years in an institution where they have received virtually no direct mothering. His clinical observations led Lowrey to the following formulation: "The conclusion seems inescapable that infants reared in institutions undergo an isolation type of experience, with resulting isolation type of personality, characterized by unsocial behavior, hostile aggression, lack of patterns

484

for giving and receiving affection, inability to understand and accept limitations, marked insecurity in adapting to environment." In 1943 Goldfarb[6] presented his first comparative study of children raised in infancy in institutions and those raised in foster homes; from this and later studies he concluded: "It would appear as though the early group experience of the institution children is a highly isolating one. The emotional and intellectual deprivation resulting from the absence of adults produced a series of distinctive personality traits. These children continue to be different from a group of children with continuous family experience even as late as adolescence and even after a long period of foster family and community contact."

Lauretta Bender,[7] drawing upon her experience with some 8,000 children referred for study to the Psychiatric Division of Bellevue Hospital, confirmed and amplified these earlier findings. Summarizing the concept of psychopathic disorders in children she writes: "It is not a hereditary or constitutional defect. It is caused by early emotional and social deprivation, due either to early institutional or other neglectful care or to critical breaks in the continuity of relationships to mother and mother-substitutes." A comprehensive synthesis of present knowledge regarding these effects of early deprivation can be found in John Bowlby's excellent World Health Organization Monograph of 1951.[8]

Along with these retrospective or reconstructive studies in which disturbance in older children has been traced back to earlier deprivations, there have been confirmatory direct observations of infants and young children. The present emphasis in psychoanalytic research is on ego psychology and the direct observation of infants and children, with particular concren with the emotional aspects of infancy. For example, Spitz[9] has

[4] Levy, David M.: "Primary Affect Hunger." *Am. J. Psychiatry*, 94:643, 1937.

[5] Lowrey, Lawson G.: "Personality Distortion and Early Institutional Care." *Am. J. Orthopsychiatry*, 10:576, 1940.

[6] Goldfarb, William: "Infant Rearing and Problem Behavior." *Am. J. Orthopsychiatry*, 13:249, 1943.

[7] Bender, Lauretta: "Psychopathic Conduct Disorders in Children." In *A Handbook of Correctional Psychology* (R. M. Lindner, Ed.). Philosophical Lib., New York, 1947.

[8] Bowlby, John: *Maternal Care and Mental Health.* World Health Organization Monograph, Series No. 2, World Health Organization, Geneva, 1951. (New York, Columbia University Press.)

[9] Spitz, Rene A.: "Hospitalism." *The Psychoanalytic Study of the Child*, 2:113, 1947.
————————: "Anaclitic Depression." *The Psychoanalytic Study of the Child*, 2:313, 1947.

reported on hospitalism and anaclitic depression, describing the direct effects on infants of maternal deprivation or loss of the mother. In an outstanding study Therese Benedek,[10] considering the psychosomatic implications of the mother-child unit, points out the manner in which the infant develops a sense of confidence in his world: "Through the rhythmic repetition of the gratification of its physiologic needs the infant develops to the perception that the source of the need is within and the source of gratification is outside the self." In an earlier paper we have suggested the importance of these investigations: "Continued research into the emotional aspects of infancy holds perhaps the greatest promise for psychiatry today . . . The implications of these research approaches extend far beyond the area of psychopathic development, providing a potential frame of reference for scientific assessment of many theoretical formulations. They may allow us ultimately to broaden the concept of constitution beyond predestination and anthropometric levels to an understanding of basic individual differences in primary needs that can be met through preventive efforts."[11]

It would seem then that there are ample clinical and research data to enable us to delineate the clinical syndrome of the child with limited capacity to establish personal and social identifications and also to relate the disorder to a definitely known cause, the factor of absence or gross limitation or distortion of mothering in the infancy and early childhood periods. The implications for casework from these findings are clear. On the basis of these studies there has been a strong trend to provide for neglected or abandoned infants, a close, continuous relationship with a gratifying substitute mother in a foster home in place of an institutional experience. There is still however progress to be made in this area and we can hope that in the coming years even greater emphasis will be placed on this need for early placement with earlier adoption placements and the development of increasing foster care programs for infants for whom adoption for one reason or another cannot be carried out.

But with all our hopes for the future there is a present need to be met and you in the placement field not only have these children to study but also to maintain in placement, with all the practical problems involved in that task. Older children, deprived

[10] Benedek, Therese: "The Psychosomatic Implications of the Primary Unit: Mother-Child." *Am. J. Orthopsychiatry,* 19:642, 1949.

[11] Rabinovitch, R. D.: The Concept of Primary Psychogenic Acathexis, in "Psychopathic Behavior in Infants and Children," Round Table, 1950. *Am. J. Orthopsychiatry,* 21:231, 1951.

in infancy, have taxed the resources of our agencies probably more than any other group, and have contributed to innumerable placement failures. Experience indicates that many of these children, because of relationship limitations, do not become a part of the foster family and are so little gratifying to the foster parents. Their conceptual thinking is shallow and their inner life empty, as the following representative productions indicate. You will note how different these are from the productions of the neurotic children, described earlier.

An eight-year-old girl, totally neglected in her first three years, tells us, in discussing her mother: "I got a couple of mothers. Mildred is my mother because she buys me clothes and stockings." There seems to be no further concept of a natural mother and no further preoccupation. The only dream she was ever able to recall was the following: "I dreamed I owned the Institute and my sisters owned it and we got the meals and everything." Johnnie, age twelve, who had spent his first seven years in an institution, was found to be totally confused and to demonstrate virtually no concept formation. Talking about his mother he tells us: "I lived one place one day, one place another day. I lived six places where I lived and I forgot them. Boy a nice place this, a nice build-up." When asked what the agency initials MCI meant, he replied, after much thought: "I don't know; I think it means nervous." The most tragic fact was that not only did he not know anything about the agency that had full responsibility for him, but he seemed to lack the inner need to know. Alice, age nine, severely deprived in infancy, found it difficult to distinguish people from animals in her thinking. When a group of children returned from a trip to the circus and were asked to name their favorite animal, several picked the elephant, others the lion, still others the horses. After careful consideration Alice expressed her preference: "Clyde Beatty". Bill, age eleven, had spent his first three years in an institution because his mother had tuberculosis. He returned to her when he was three years old and from then on remained continuously with the family. Because of delinquency he was sent to a psychiatric hospital at age eleven. Asked what made him most lonely away from home, he replied: "I miss my bicycle most." With some suggestion he was able to change his opinion to "I miss my mother most." When asked which he really missed most, he replied, after a struggle, "I miss my mother more; I knowed her longer."

These are typical productions of affectionless children and

there is no group whom we see in clinical practice more tragic and less reachable. Generally they do not respond well in direct psychotherapy. They do not enter into a therapeutic relationship with the psychiatrist or the caseworker and there is so little anxiety that one can utilize in treatment. We believe that our study may prove helpful in suggesting a program in these cases. First however we should like to consider the problem of planning placement according to diagnosis both of the child's needs and capacities and of the foster parents' personality and needs.

Foster Parents, Givers and Receivers

In our work in the placement field in general we have still not learned to use foster parents sufficiently as allies of the agency and in fact as auxiliary therapists in our planning for disturbed children. So often in the past we have been concerned primarily with the motivation of the foster mother in particular, attempting to determine just why she wants a foster child. In a recent paper Irene Josselyn and Charlotte Towle[12] point out the fallacy of assuming that, having determined the motivation, we can then predict the outcome. Originally the motivation may have seemed dubious, but in the case of so many such foster parents, regardless of the motivation the outcome has been excellent. Many other factors are of course involved, and must be taken into account as we assess the suitability of a home for a particular child. One essential factor is the level of relationship expectation or need of the foster parents, perhaps more essentially, the foster mother. In this regard we can, in a general way, define three groups of foster mothers:

1. Foster mothers able to give warmth freely and able to provide a mothering experience for the foster child; in return requiring an affective response from the child and some return of warmth in order to gratify their own needs.

2. Foster mothers capable of giving much love and providing an atmosphere of warm mothering while at the same time not requiring a return of affection.

3. Foster mothers who gain satisfaction not from the emotional or affective relationship with the child, but rather from the child's conformity to their demands in terms of behavior.

The first group, those who handle the child largely through a give-and-take of warmth and feeling, generally work well with

---

[12] Josselyn, Irene: "Evaluating Motives of Foster Parents" (with a discussion by Charlotte Towle). *Child Welfare*, 31:3, 1952.

case-workers and accept therapeutic guidance. Not so for the last group, as many workers know; they tend to be protective of their role as foster mothers, generally uncommunicative with the agency and often resentful of the worker's interest which is interpreted as interference. This latter group of controlling mothers is probably somewhat larger in number than we sometimes think or like to think; they do however fill a definite need in the case load of every agency when what they have to offer is used insightfully.

Earlier we referred to the importance of placing children according to diagnosis both of the child and the foster family. We can, we believe, fit the diagnostic groupings of children described earlier with this general scheme of groupings of foster mothers. Place the aggression-inhibited, anxious and guilt-ridden child in the controlling, emotionally sterile foster home and trouble is invited. Place the affectionless, relatively empty child, who cannot give, with a foster family that requires meaningful affective responses and an equally disturbing situation ensues. Diagnosis is of course never an end in itself but if in this way we can plan insightfully both for the needs of the children we place and for those of the foster families with whom we place them, then such diagnosis is not only helpful but in fact essential.

At this juncture a word of caution is in order. Diagnosis of the affectionless or psychopathic child must be made with care and on the basis of the child's inner life rather than his behavior. Unfortunately the term 'psychopathic' still tends to be used as a synonym for delinquent behavior regardless of the etiology of the behavior pattern. We have considered the differential criteria for diagnosis of neurotic and affectionless children in a previous paper (R.D.R.[13]); we include these brief remarks here to stress the importance of careful diagnosis as a guide to planning for individual children.

Assuming that the diagnosis is accurate, we can expect the affectionless child to have poor inner resources for goal-directed behavior and planning, and to adapt socially more by mirroring the behavior of others than by responding to inner feelings. Because of these factors social patterning is vital for these children and we must provide an environment that will offer clear-cut directives and controls. Our best results with these children have been obtained through placement in homes which are essen-

[13] Rabinovitch, Ralph D.: "Observations on the Differential Study of Severely Disturbed Children." *Am. J. Orthopsychiat.* 22:230, 1952.

tially controlling and with foster parents who require little in the way of depth of emotional response.

Implications for Adoption Practices

Much of the material discussed thus far relates to the adoption field as well as that of foster placement. At a meeting some time ago an adoption worker commented that a young man of twenty-two had recently returned to her office at the agency, much troubled, and insisting that he be told the identity of his natural parents. Another worker at the meeting commented that this was deplorable and a sign of a poor adoption. How mistaken she was. One must expect the adopted child to be pre-occupied with background and original identity whether the adoption be good or bad. Such preoccupation must be expected as adopted children learn the realities of birth, of continuity of family and of heredity. Many children react to the knowledge that they have been adopted by deep concern with their original identity and we might well give more attention to the problem of helping the adopted child find answers to these basic concerns. In the guise of making easier the adopted child's acceptance of his status too often adoptive parents have accomplished just the opposite. Sometimes, explaining the adoption, they tell the child that they chose him above all others and therefore love him all the more. They may tell the child that they walked through the nursery and saw many children but picked him because they knew at once that he was the boy they wanted. Told such stories, what is a child's reaction? Frequently he is stimulated to wonder who left him in that nursery and why and the whole purpose of the adoptive parents' explanation is distorted. There is a need for us to look into techniques of helping adoptive parents share the reality of the child's basic identity with him, a problem often very difficult for these parents.

Finally we should like to stress one more implication for adoption from this material—the earlier the adoptive placement the better. As Bowlby[14] points out, all the evidence at hand indicates "unmistakably that it is in the interests of the adopted baby's mental health for him to be adopted soon after birth. No other arrangement permits continuity of mothering and most other arrangements fail even to ensure its adequacy." A number of contraindications are often suggested to early adoption but we can, we believe, on the basis of our present knowledge, rule these out. In general, intelligence tests have virtually

---

[14] Bowlby, John: *op. cit.* page 101.

no predictive value when given in the child's first eighteen months of life, and our earlier tendency to depend on these tests in considering a child's suitability for adoption has been most unfortunate. An excellent discussion of these problems is to be found in Bowlby's monograph.

This report has covered one aspect of our project, the psychiatric implications for foster home placement and, secondarily, for adoption practices. We should like to stress again that our material has led us to some rather broad conclusions most of which are not new but which we feel merit reiteration and further investigation as we attempt to arrive at a more definite philosophy in our placement work.

In a later report our group plans to discuss in some detail casework techniques suggested by our data. One general finding can be mentioned briefly at this point. Regardless how positive and how meaningful the foster home experience may be for the child, the placement worker and the agency play a larger role in the child's fantasics than many of us have tended to think. In our cases we find so often that the worker is viewed as the bridge between the child's past and his future which he hopes some day may include his natural parents again. Twelve-year-old Peter summarizes this dynamic relationship between child and worker when he tells his worker, sitting with her in her office: "Some day I may have to go to a different home but I know you're always here." Mildred, age 11, reveals a deeper, pervasive level of fantasy when she tells us of her worker: "She took me away from my mother. She'll take me back."

CHAPTER 41

Criteria for Predictability

JULIUS B. RICHMOND, M.D.

Although in fact we have little reliable knowledge concerning predictability, our practices necessarily must make positive use of what knowledge we have along with our convictions concerning desirable practices. Lest anyone have any doubts concerning the sparsity of basic information on prediction, one need only point to the repeated emphasis by the geneticists participating in this conference that, with all their scientific rigor and precision, there are relatively few clearcut, decisive answers they can provide for us. Little wonder that in the less well developed research areas of the social and psychological sciences we have even fewer precise answers.

This is intended to emphasize that in adoption practice we serve as clinicians. In dealing with a single human being or group our scientific knowledge must be blended with clinical judgment; thus we are practitioners of an art—not a science. This does not mean that our clinical skills must remain an enigma without objective evaluations. Increasingly social scientists and other researchers are finding ways of looking into our professional transactions with a view toward better understanding and, in turn, better practices.

The contribution of the pediatrician to predictability in adoption procedure is heavily weighted biologically. As Dr. Samuel

Karelitz pointed out the genetic information available (all too meager usually) may alert the pediatrician to some possible abnormalities in the infant. Consultation with a geneticist may be particularly helpful in these instances or those in which an abnormality of presumably genetic background is detected. For those agencies which cannot have a geneticist available on a continuing basis, the pediatrician is the logical person to make the determination concerning the desirability of consultation.

Now that we have become increasingly aware of the potential impact of certain occurrences during the prenatal period, the prenatal history becomes more meaningful to the pediatrician. The occurrence of German measles and perhaps other virus diseases during the first third of pregnancy and maternal diabetes or even the pre-diabetic state portends a higher incidence of congenital anomalies in the fetus. Rh and other blood group incompatibilities, the age of the natural parents, and whether or not a previous baby had been born with an anomaly are significant factors.

Lest we develop an overconcern about congenital malformations it is appropriate to mention that many anomalous babies are eliminated early in pregnancy in the form of spontaneous abortions or miscarriages. Also it is estimated that about 20 per cent of fetal deaths in the third trimester of pregnancy and 15 per cent of those in the newborn period can be attributed to gross malformations.

Two groups of babies destined to have biological problems may not be detected by the pediatrician early:

1. the group that has abnormalities of internal organs which cannot be detected by the physical examination, such as abnormalities of the urinary tract, biochemical disorders, and even some heart disorders;

2. the group that has degenerative disorders which may have a genetic background, but which do not become apparent until later in life, such as degenerative disorders of the central nervous system, liver, or other organs.

With all of these hazards, however, the advantage insofar as congenital anomalies are concerned is clearly in favor of the adoptive parent over the natural parent. Adoptive parents have the more obvious anomalies eliminated for them through the agency's supervision. Natural parents of course must accept whatever the outcome of the pregnancy.

A few words on prediction of the outcome of physical disorders are appropriate. Many conditions which we thought of as fatal or hopelessly debilitating have a considerably changed outlook today. Let us remember that many of the cardiac surgical procedures which are routine today are but ten years old or less. Although we can not make definitive predictions, our research on these children and children with other anomalies provides much hope which heretofore did not exist. Babies who once would have had a certain death because of incomplete formation of the gastrointestinal tract now can go on to normal development after surgery. We know much more about the potentialities for the child with cleft lip or palate than we knew in years gone by. And one could extend this list. Research endeavors provide an everchanging—and more hopeful—outlook.

The examination of the newborn infant by the pediatrician is significant not alone for detection of anomalies and possible effects of the birth process. It provides opportunities for an evaluation of general vitality, and particularly for performing the first neurological examination. The baby's posture, activity, feeding, and sleeping patterns have meaning. The serial examinations of the infant, preferably by the same physician over a period of weeks or months, may permit earlier detection of neurologic and developmental disorders than previously. Greater refinement in examination methods is desirable and it is anticipated that further research will provide us with better criteria for predictability concerning central nervous system development.

Since this conference has been much concerned with earlier placement of infants, a few words on the significance of the early experiences of infants are in order to separate research data from professional practices which are not based on direct evidence. Much of our current concern about early placement has developed from the observations of the impact of maternal deprivation on infants. Most of these studies are drawn from observations on infants who have undergone separation, generally of a severe variety, in the latter half of the first year.

The effects of more minor degrees of separation and more subtle changes in physical care, such as would occur in most agency-conducted adoptive programs in this country, are less well known. I mention this not because I lack conviction about the desirability of a continuing, close, primary relationship with parental figures. Indeed much of the research with which I am currently concerned is based on the hypothesis of the late Dr. Margaret Gerard which implies that children who develop illnesses which we classify as psychosomatic have had uncomfortable experiences in infancy. We need much more direct evidence, however, to know just how much or how little we are traumatizing young infants by providing foster mothers—particularly multiple foster mothers. Also the timing of these potential traumata in the life of the baby may have considerable significance on later personality development.

For example, biologic maturation may have real influence in determining whether separation from a mother figure may go smoothly or not. To use visual maturation as an example, a baby generally develops a capacity to visually identify the mother figure between three to six months (an individual variation perhaps influenced by stimulation). Thus, with natural parents, when this recognition develops the baby begins to manifest separation anxiety when the mother leaves him with a stranger although this may not have occurred earlier. Does this imply that a baby adapts more readily to mother substitutes during the early portion of the first year? We do not know, for we are aware of the fact that the baby "perceives" the kind of care which he receives prior to this visual maturation. Further researches on the effects of the "smoothness" or "difficulty" in early care will be helpful in providing us with data drawn upon which to base our practices.

Since we are concerned with "teamwork" in the development of criteria for predictability, it is well to emphasize that teamwork should realistically provide an opportunity for effective sharing of thoughts among the members of the team. This can never be full and complete when the various members of the professional staff do not meet together to discuss each case. A written record can never serve quite the same purpose. During the course of such staff conferences each member of the team grows in stature and learns something of the thinking of people in related professional fields without giving up any of his own professional identity.

Our greatest advances in adoption practices are destined to come from research which will in turn facilitate the development of increasingly better practices. In addition, research in the setting of an adoption agency offers a rich opportunity to learn some basic information concerning personality development through the observation of the results of various types of early infant and child care. Thus the research carried on in adoption agencies can potentially make far-reaching contributions to psychiatric thought as well as to adoption practice.

CHAPTER 42

Anthropology and Adoption Practice

H. L. SHAPIRO, Ph.D.

A title like the above would suggest at once to an anthropological group that my subject might be the distribution of the custom of child adoption in primitive societies with possibly some reference to its function in the social organization of these communities. As I think of it this is a subject not without its interest and one that might repay some attention. But it is, however, not the one I am going to consider. I have assumed—or to be more accurate I have been instructed—that I am to talk about the national, cultural and racial factors in properly and wisely placing children for adoption in our own country. In an earlier generation such considerations might not have arisen, or if they did, were disposed of on less systematic lines than are regarded as desirable today. This change in attitude is the consequence of the growing conviction that the welfare and development of the child is the primary concern of agencies responsible for their placement and not simply satisfying the desire of a couple for a child or the mere transference of a child from institutional to familial care. As psychological nuances in a child's life are increasingly explored and their significance emphasized, it is no wonder that conscientious agencies seek to forestall any of the grounds for conditions of incompatibility that might provoke undesirable situations or episodes in the life of the child.

There has, therefore, grown up a conviction that a reasonable matching of parents and child in as many attributes as possible is likely to reduce conflicts, incompatibilities, rejections or other disturbing elements in the parent-child relationship.

It is not my purpose to question this direction of adoption practice. I assume that the wise and experienced worker who has to weigh all the factors, many of them imponderable and subtle, in the fitness of a particular couple for a particular child will know how to carry the matching technique and when to ignore it for over-riding reasons. Moreover, my own experience in this field does not qualify me to make any judgment on adoption practices. I shall speak only as an anthropologist evaluating the factors of culture, nationality and race as I understand them to enter the picture.

Minimizes Cultural Differences

A clear understanding of the fundamental distinction between genetic and acquired attributes will automatically help clarify what is pertinent to the matching procedure. As everyone knows, groups and populations differ from each other in a number of ways. Consequently the individual members of such groups in so far as they share the characteristics of their groups will also differ, usually in the same directions as their group. Now such differences cover a wide gamut but they are obviously not equally significant or important for matching purposes. For the present I think we need only distinguish the characteristics that are learned or acquired during any individual's lifetime from those which he inherits through his parents' germ plasm. The former obviously are such things as language, religion, customs, values, certain kinds of behavior patterns—in short, cultural attributes. In one sense we have little choice in our acquisition of these characteristics since we are conditioned to accept them by the full pressure of family and society. Who in his right mind refuses to learn the language of his family and country and insists on the exercise of a choice of a foreign one? The important thing however, is that none of us is born with these characteristics, we must learn them or be conditioned by them. This means that they are not inherent and that they are readily available for acquisition by individuals who join the group. In matching, therefore, it may be anticipated that no more difficulty would be encountered in a young child learning or acquiring the cultural attributes of the adoptive parents than would a natural child learning from his own parents and their culture. We may,

I think, safely dismiss cultural differences as of little or no importance in this context. The only circumstances in which I can conceive of their demanding serious consideration are in cases where the child has passed beyond his early formative stage and thus acquired fixed habits of thought or behavior that might conflict with those of his adoptive parents.

From my previous distinction it will be evident that many nationality differences are also merely cultural ones and can be dismissed with them. Nationality is in great measure the sharing of a common tradition which consists of such things as language, literature, values, customs, political institutions, etc. To many people, however, nationality conveys or is used to carry the notion of race. This is inexact although racial differences may sometimes parallel nationality. Perhaps I can make the distinction and usage clearer by some examples.

> The racial differences between Norway and Sweden are negligible although a feeling of nationality separates these two countries. Similarly Britain and France are separate and distinctive national entities, but their racial heritages have much in common.

Racially, the overlap of the two nations is considerable and it would be easy to find nationals of the one country physically indistinguishable from those of the other on racial grounds. Of course, as nationalities are more and more widely separated geographically the tendency is for racial differences to increase since they have, by virtue of their geographic distance, been subject to increasingly different genetic histories and influences. Thus Italians and Chinese differ both in nationality and race. We may consider from this that insofar as nationality differences are cultural, they can be ignored in adoption practice since the differences are not inherited and the nationality of the child will not affect his ability to adjust to another nationality pattern.

Wisdom of Selection by Race

The confusion in the usage of nationality comes in when racial differences also exist between nationalities. In such instances we are not dealing with acquired characteristics but inherited ones that should be classed as genetic in the two-fold division suggested above. It is, I surmise from my own experience, in just this area that most of the difficulties lie. In many states it is forbidden by law to place children of one race in a family of another. Besides these legal prohibitions, there are the sociological situations and the attitudes toward race that

498

create or may engender hostility, rejection or other undesirable psychological elements in the child's development. And to avoid these it is generally regarded as good practice to match the race of the child and the parents.

Racial characteristics are, as everyone knows, genetic in origin and are, therefore, inherited through the parental germ plasm. They are given to us at birth and we can do nothing to change them during our lifetime. Races, however, contrary to common opinion, are not and have never been homogeneous or uniform as far as the members of a racial group are concerned. Within each group there is a considerable degree of genetic variation which expresses itself in a variety of possible combinations. This genetic variation arises from mutations in the genes. Some that are especially adapted to the environment in which the population lives tend to be preserved and increase through natural selection. When the races have been isolated from each other for long periods of time the accumulation of genetic difference tends to increase so that although the races may vary within their own limits they do not overlap to any considerable degree. Recognition is consequently easy. The major racial divisions of mankind are of this order. There are, however, many minor divisions where isolation has not been as complete or when it is recent and thus has not had time to provide for the independent accumulation of genetic differences. In these instances the difference is small which means that the overlap is large and individual recognition or classification is not always easy. Here the stereotype of a group tends to obscure the variation that normally exists within it. A member of such a group, regardless of his own appearance, is often identified with the stereotype even though he may genetically fall within the range of another group. The ''racial'' differences between various white groups overlap in this fashion.

Problem of Inter-racial Background

Perhaps the most difficult decision facing the agency in the field I have been discussing has to do with the mixed bloods— the children of matings between individuals of different major races. In particular I am referring to Negro-White children. The agency, sensitive to social attitudes expressed by or imagined to exist in the community it serves, is highly sensitive to this problem. Now although the racial distance between Negroes and Whites is considerable and presents no problem whatever as far as classification or recognition is concerned, this distinction is one that does not survive where miscegenation takes place. The isolation that in a sense created the differences is now replaced by contact that tends to break them down. Gene flow comes into play and the genes characteristic of Negroes and of Whites are interchanged. If the process of mixture with Whites continues over several generations, the offspring become progressively more like Whites in their appearance and in the genes they possess. Thus a continuum is created that spans the two races and obliterates the sharp division that originally existed. One might well ask when does a Negro strain become white if it continues in this way to absorb more and more "white" genes. The biological answer, if there were one, would however be of little help since the problem is largely one of attitude. If a child were predominantly white in phenotype or appearance, which in this instance would also imply the same for the genotype, the community might still regard him as Negro if any trace of Negroid origin remained. And even where an individual were white enough to "pass," the discovery of his origins would affect his classification status quite definitely in some communities and perhaps more subtly in others. Thus it is clear that existing racial attitudes are not based on biological grounds and that the problem in matching is not a purely biological one. Clearly, where the classification of a racially mixed child is concerned, the sociological attitudes of the community and the adoptive parents must be taken into account. The specific practice might well vary according to those conditions.

The "Genes" Story

One of the fears commonly expressed by white parents in adopting mixed children that in appearance might pass as White is that such children are likely in their own marriages to produce offspring with distinctly Negro characteristics. There is no genetic basis for this assumption. If such a child marries a white individual, there would not be enough of an accumulation of "Negro" genes to produce a Negro child. The child receives half of its genes from each parent, thus it could at most receive only those "Negro" genes carried by one parent and none at all from the other. But more probably it would inherit from its mixed parent even less than that parent possesses. Thus such a child would be even "whiter" than the mixed parent.

The detection of Negro ancestry in a child of mixed origin presents no difficulty when Negro traits are well defined. The difficulty arises when the amount of Negro admixture is so slight that its effect is subtle and elusive as far as appearances are concerned. In those cases there is no alternative to consulting someone experienced in such determinations. Unfortunately there are no infallible or universal laboratory tests. Since the cases difficult to analyze racially are precisely those that are predominantly white and must therefore have many more white genes than Negro, they are the least likely to retain the identifiable genes more characteristic of Negroes than Whites. For example, sickling of the red blood corpuscles is found in Negroes and not in Whites. Even in American Negroes it occurs in about only eight per cent. Thus many Negroes would not have the characteristic at all, and as admixture with White increases the frequency of occurrence would diminish. Consequently it is not likely to be found in children who are already predominantly white. This is true also for the blood groups found more commonly in Negroes than Whites. In most instances it is necessary, therefore, to rely on morphological characters and on the judgment of an experienced investigator.

We are accustomed in our cliches about race to attribute specific personality and psychological characteristics to certain races. As a consequence, some concern is frequently felt that conflicts on this score might also arise between adoptive parents and child when they are of different racial origins. The only psychological quality that has been explored to any great extent on a racial basis is intelligence as measured by various standardized tests that involve both verbal and non-verbal responses. The scores on these tests are apparently influenced in varying degree by education, milieu and other environmental factors. To some extent, therefore, differences between races subjected to divergent influences can be discounted as non-genetic and non-racial. Whether all the difference can therefore be attributed to non-genetic factors is still controversial. But in any event the difference is relatively small compared to the range within any racial group. In other words, overlapping is very considerable and as a result the intelligence tests lack the specificity to be found in anatomical racial characters. It would be a rash person indeed who would attempt to identify someone by I.Q. alone. All this adds up to the conclusion that high and low I.Q.'s may be found in all racial groups. And, as far as we can judge, personality types similarly are not restricted to any one race.

To some extent the problems of race I have been discussing are those created by the social environment in which we live. Are we to continue in adoption practices to classify children who are predominantly White as Negro because they have some remote Negroid admixture? Here is an ethical problem that goes beyond a scientific judgment. It is one that the agencies must examine.

CHAPTER 43

Moppets on the Market: The Problem of Unregulated Adoptions

STUART W. THAYER

The market for babies is a sellers' market. As a result, a few individuals make money by selling babies as they would sell goods. Contrary to popular impression, however, "black market" placements—independent[1] adoptive placements in which a third party makes a profit—are not common. By far the greater number of adoptions are the product of independent placements arranged without profit by well-meaning parents, friends, relatives, doctors, and lawyers.[2] Only in about one-fourth of the

---

[1] An "independent" placement is one made without the aid of an authorized child-welfare agency. Authorized agencies include state welfare departments and private agencies which they license and supervise. The welfare department usually has authority to license private agencies to engage in child-placing work. See, e.g., MICH. ANN. STAT. § 25.358(3) (Henderson, Supp. 1949); S.D. Laws 1939, c 168, § 3. Only a few states, however, require that all adoptive placements be made through these authorized agencies. See pages 731-4 infra.

[2] This conclusion is based upon information received in response to a questionnaire sent to the welfare departments of the various states. Replies were received from thirty-five states and the District of Columbia. As to the extent of "black market" trading in babies, the following statements are typical. "[W e]do not believe there is much of this activity in Texas. . . . What we have seen referred to as the 'grey market' is much more prevalent in this State. It involves placements by physicians, lawyers, ministers, midwives, who are often well-meaning, but who cannot, of course, offer the protection of agency services." Communication to the YALE LAW JOURNAL from Mr. John H. Winters, Executive Director, Texas Department of Public Welfare, dated January 3, 1950, in Yale Law Library.

"For the most part, intermediaries in independent placements are physicians, nurses, lawyers and friends of the mother or friends of the petitioners who participate sometimes

cases are placements made by authorized child-welfare agencies, which are best equipped to protect the interests of all by seeing that the right child gets in the right home.[3]

When adoptions are the product of independent placements, the blind frequently lead the blind. Good intentions are no substitute for trained and experienced personnel. The interests of the child, as well as those of the natural and adoptive parents, may be lost and unprotected in a humanitarian mist. The problem is becoming acute, for adoption is increasing by leaps and bounds. Adoption petitions were filed for approximately 50,000 children in 1944, a three-fold increase over 1934.[4] And recent

directly and other times indirectly in the placements. It is our belief that for the most part these intermediaries are persons who have known of the petitioners' desire for a child, or know of the mother's interest in relinquishing or releasing a child for adoption, but we do not consider that they are actively engaged in child placing from a commercial standpoint." Communication to the YALE LAW JOURNAL from Miss Loa Howard, Administrator, Oregon Public Welfare Commission, dated January 18, 1950, in Yale Law Library.

It appears that the bulk of independent placements are made by parents and physicians. An analysis of 2,587 independent adoptions which were approved by the California welfare department in 1948, for example, revealed that 43.8 percent of the placements had been made by parents and 25.6 percent had been made by physicians. Communication to the YALE LAW JOURNAL from Miss Myrtle Williams, Director, California Department of Social Welfare, dated November 30, 1949, in Yale Law Library.

Although "black market" placements are not frequent, it is a common practice in independent placements for adoptive parents to pay the doctor's fee and the hospital expenses of the natural mother. A study of 992 children placed independently with non-relatives in Florida in 1947-8 disclosed that in at least 45 percent of the cases both the doctor's fee and the hospital costs had been paid by the adoptive parents. WARD, ANALYSIS OF ADOPTIONS IN FLORIDA 1943-49, p. 10 (mimeographed, 1949). The situation in other states is similar. Louisiana, for example, reports that "there are a very large number of cases which although not strictly 'black market' involve the payment of support to the girl during the period of her pregnancy or confinement as well as various presents under the guise of providing the girl with an adequate wardrobe, helping her find a job, giving her rail fare back to her home town, etc." Communication to the YALE LAW JOURNAL from Mr. Lawrence E. Higgins, Commissioner, Louisiana Department of Public Welfare, dated November 9, 1949, in Yale Law Library.

[3] A Children's Bureau (Federal Security Agency) study of 9,000 children for whom adoption petitions had been filed in fifteen states in 1944 disclosed that slightly more than a quarter had been placed in the adoptive home by an authorized agency; another quarter had been placed independently with unrelated persons; and approximately a half were being adopted, with the aid of an agency, by stepparents and other relatives. Zarefsky, *Children Acquire New Parents*, 10 CHILD 142, 143 (1946). The proportion of adoptive placements made by authorized agencies varies substantially from state to state, however. Thus Maine reports that of the total number of adoptions made in that state in 1948, only 9 percent involved placements by authorized agencies, whereas in Louisiana authorized agencies handled 48 percent. Communications to the YALE LAW JOURNAL from Miss Lena Parrott, Director of Child Welfare, Maine Department of Health and Welfare, dated November 14, 1949, and from Mr. Lawrence E. Higgins, Commissioner, Louisiana Department of Public Welfare, dated November 9, 1949, both in Yale Law Library.

[4] In 1944 twenty-two states reported a total of more than 16,000 children for whom adoption petitions had been filed. On the basis of this figure the Children's Bureau estimated that in that year petitions had been filed for approximately 50,000 children throughout the country. Zarefsky, *supra* note 3, at 142. In the six states for which comparable statistics were available, the number of children for whom petitions were filed in 1944 was more than three times as great as in 1934. *Ibid.*

figures indicate another 40 to 50 percent increase in the last five years.[5]

Most of these children are adopted at an age when they are far too young to look after their own interests. A recent Children's Bureau survey indicated that at the time of the filing of the adoption petition, 62 percent were under six, 26 percent were between six and fourteen, and 12 percent were between fourteen and twenty-one.[6] This extreme youth also makes it inordinately difficult for potential adoptive parents or any untrained layman to make an intelligent decision, to foresee future problems latent at the time of adoption.

In an effort to protect all parties, most states have passed laws providing for an increased administrative and judicial supervision over adoption generally. These laws vary considerably in effectiveness and in strictness of enforcement, but the best reflect the procedure of authorized adoption agencies. Their procedure, while not wholly standardized, eliminates much of the hazardous guesswork inherent in casual independent placements, and substitutes an informed professional judgment which may offer the best hope for family happiness.

The Practice of Authorized Adoption Agencies

Authorized adoption agencies are of three general types: state welfare departments, private agencies engaged solely in adoption work, and private agencies whose adoption activities are only one part of a general child-welfare program. In many states the welfare department's adoption service merely supplements private facilities,[7] but in one state that department is

---

[5] The Children's Bureau is at present collecting data on the number of petitions filed in 1948. Preliminary examination of some of the reports where comparable data are available for 1944 indicates that adoption petitions have increased between 40 and 50 percent since that time. Communication to the YALE LAW JOURNAL from Miss I. Evelyn Smith, Consultant on Foster Care, Social Service Division, Children's Bureau, dated November 22, 1949, in Yale Law Library.

[6] Zarefsky, *supra* note 3, at 143. This information was available for 8,764 of the 9,000 children for whom adoption petitions were filed in fifteen states in 1944. Almost half of the children were being adopted by stepparents and other relatives, and such children usually are older than others being adopted. Therefore the proportion of young children being adopted by non-relatives was even greater than the figures indicate. *Ibid.*

[7] *E.g.*, Maine, Nebraska, Washington. In a few states placements are also made by county adoption agencies. California, for example, amended its adoption law in 1947 to authorize the licensing of county adoption agencies by the state welfare department. CAL. CIVIL CODE § 225m (Deering, 1949). The county adoption agencies are reimbused by the state for their entire administrative costs and for a portion of the costs of caring for children relinquished to them. Communication to the YALE LAW JOURNAL from Miss Myrtle Williams, Director, California Department of Social Welfare, dated November 30, 1949, in Yale Law Library.

the sole agency making adoptive placements.[8] A few private agencies in large cities are adoption agencies exclusively, providing care only for children made available for adoption.[9] But the great majority of private agencies placing children for adoption are general child-welfare agencies, whose purpose is to provide all types of care for dependent, neglected, or delinquent children.

Many of the children under the supervision of a general welfare agency are not available for adoption. Some are away from their families only temporarily.[10] Other children, though likely to remain under the agency's care for a longer period, are unavailable for adoption because their parents have neither abandoned them nor consented to their adoption.[11] Some children are not adoptable because of serious mental and physical defects. For all these children who cannot be placed in adoptive homes, the agency must provide some alternative form of care, either in private families or in an institution. Many of them are placed in boarding homes, private homes in which the agency pays the cost of the child's basic maintenance.

The children who *are* available for adoption come under the supervision of an authorized agency in a variety of ways. Some are orphans and foundlings. Others have been removed from their homes and placed under agency guardianship by a court order because they were neglected or mistreated by their parents. But a far greater number are voluntarily surrendered to the agency, most often by unwed mothers. Illegitimate children account for about 60 percent of all children adopted,[12] and if adoptions by stepparents and other relatives are excluded, this figure runs even higher. Thus, one of the adoption agency's main responsibilities is to provide prompt, sympathetic, and skillful service for the unmarried mother.[13] If she is undecided

---

[8] Arkansas. Communication to the YALE LAW JOURNAL from Mrs. Henry Bethell, Commissioner, Arkansas Department of Public Welfare, dated December 27, 1949, in Yale Law Library.

[9] Wilson, *What the Layman Does Not Know About Adoption*, 26 CHILD WELFARE LEAGUE OF AMERICA BULLETIN 13, 14 (June 1947).

[10] In a typical instance the child's mother is being divorced and remarried, after which the child will return to her. See LOCKRIDGE, ADOPTING A CHILD 28 (pamphlet ed., 1948).

[11] Stougaard, *Unsound Talk About Adoption*, 27 CHILD WELFARE 17 (November, 1948).

[12] The Children's Bureau study of 9,000 children for whom adoption petitions were filed in fifteen states in 1944 revealed that 58 percent of the children were illegitimate. Zarefsky, *supra* note 3, at 144. An earlier Bureau study of 2,041 adoption petitions filed in nine states in 1934 disclosed that 61 percent were for illegitimate children. COLBY, PROBLEMS AND PROCEDURES IN ADOPTION 10 (Children's Bureau Publication No. 262, 1941).

[13] See *Social Workers Look at Adoption*, 10 CHILD 110 (1946) for an appraisal of agency shortcomings in this respect.

about surrendering her child for adoption, the agency explores with her the alternatives, including temporary placement in a boarding home. Often a mother who has surrendered a child immediately after its birth later finds that she is in a position to care for the child. A reputable agency accepts a surrender only after the mother herself has decided that adoption is the best plan. But once a child is deemed available for adoption, four procedures are carried out: an investigation of the natural parents, a study of the child, an evaluation of the prospective parents, and a supervised probationary period.

Investigation of the Natural Parents

If a child's parents are known—that is, if he is not a foundling —the agency seeks information about his family background. An unmarried mother is asked to disclose confidentially to the agency the name of the child's father, so that the agency can investigate both the maternal and paternal histories. Some agencies regard a child as unsuitable for adoption if his family history discloses pathological conditions which some medical opinion views as hereditary.[14] But most agencies feel that little is known about what conditions are inheritable, and that no child should be excluded from adoption solely on the basis of his assumed hereditary background.[15] A child whose family history is spotted with feeblemindedness, epilepsy, or psychoses, needs special scrutiny, but his family background is only one of many elements to be taken into account before a final decision is made as to whether he is adoptable.[16]

Study of the Child

Most agencies place the child in a pre-adoption boarding home for at least three months as soon as he comes under their

---

[14] See Lippman, *Suitability of the Child for Adoption,* 7 AMERICAN JOURNAL OF ORTHOPSYCHIATRY 270 (1937); TEAGARDEN, CHILD PSYCHOLOGY FOR PROFESSIONAL WORKERS 30-68 (1940).

[15] See Clothier, *Placing the Child for Adoption,* 26 MENTAL HYGIENE 257, 259-61 (1942); Theis, *Case Work in the Process of Adoption* in 69 PROCEEDINGS OF THE NATIONAL CONFERENCE OF SOCIAL WORK 405, 409 (1942); Wolkomir, *The Unadoptable Baby Achieves Adoption,* 26 CHILD WELFARE LEAGUE OF AMERICA BULLETIN 1 (Feb. 1947).

[16] Various studies have explored the relative influence of heredity and environment upon the mental development of adopted children. See *e.g.,* Freeman, Holzinger, & Mitchell, *The Influence of Environment on the Intelligence, School Achievement, and Conduct of Foster Children,* 27 NATIONAL SOCIETY FOR THE STUDY OF EDUCATION YEARBOOK 103 (1928); Burks, *The Relative Influence of Nature and Nurture upon Mental Development,* 27 *id.* at 219; Leahy, *Nature-Nurture and Intelligence* in 17 GENETIC PSYCHOLOGY MONOGRAPHS 235 (1937); SKODAK, CHILDREN IN FOSTER HOMES: A STUDY OF MENTAL DEVELOPMENT (1939). The results of these and other studies are summarized in BROOKS & BROOKS, ADVENTURING IN ADOPTION 172-9 (1939), and TEAGARDEN, *op. cit. supra* note 14, at 41-53.

care.[17] During this period the agency tries to get as complete a picture of the child as possible—physically, mentally, and psychologically.[18] The first step is a thorough medical examination.[19] A child may still be adoptable though suffering from congenital abnormalities, such as blindness or deafness, or from a disease like syphilis, tuberculosis, or diabetes. But the agency must know these medical facts in order to provide immediate treatment. Eventually it may pass the child on to adoptive parents who, fully informed of the child's condition, still wish to adopt him and have the means to provide him with proper medical care.

It is equally important that the agency have an estimate of the child's intelligence, maturity level, and rate of development. For children two years of age and older the Stanford-Binet intelligence test is most commonly used. But many of the children adopted are younger than two, and for them no Stanford-Binet test is available.[20] Increasing use is being made of the diagnostic tests developed by Gesell and others at the Yale Child Development Clinic for children ranging from four weeks to three years. The Gesell system sets up test situations for each of the four major fields of behavior—motor, adaptive, language, and personal-social.[21] A particular child's patterns of behavior in each of these fields is observed and then compared with norms appropriate to his age.[22] Thus the Gesell system, unlike the Stanford-Binet, is not limited to a single inclusive formula. But regardless of which system is used, the tests are the beginning and not the end of diagnosis. The child's rate of development may change when he is placed in a more favorable environment.[23] In the last analysis the diagnostician must weigh all the qualifying considerations, including medical history, previous environment, and the performance of the child.

---

[17] Clothier, *Adoption Procedure and the Community,* 25 MENTAL HYGIENE 196, 206 (1941). Some agencies have experimented with the practice of transferring the child from his present home to his permanent adoptive home without the use of an interim temporary placement. Oshlag, *Direct Placement in Adoption,* 27 JOURNAL OF SOCIAL CASEWORK 229 (1946).

[18] Pendleton, *Agency Responsibility in Adoption,* 19 FAMILY 35, 37-8 (1938).

[19] See Clothier, *Some Aspects of the Problem of Adoption,* 9 AMERICAN JOURNAL OF ORTHOPSYCHIATRY 598, 605 (1939).

[20] See TERMAN & MERRILL, MEASURING INTELLIGENCE (1937).

[21] GESSELL & AMATRUDA, DEVELOPMENT DIAGNOSIS 7 (2d ed. 1947).

[22] *Id.* at 111. A separate rating is determined for each of the four fields of behavior. Only when the child's maturity in all fields is at nearly the same level is it deemed permissible to assign an overall maturity level and a general rating. *Id.* at 114.

[23] Jenkins, *Adoption Practices and the Physician,* 103 AMERICAN MEDICAL ASSOCIATION JOURNAL 403, 405 (1934); Clothier, *Placing the Child for Adoption,* 26 MENTAL HYGIENE 257, 262 (1942). And see articles cited in note 16 *supra.*

If on the basis of the physical and mental tests a child is found to be unadoptable, he either remains in the agency, is placed in a boarding home, or, if he is definitely feeble-minded, he may be committed to a state institution. A child whose adoptability is uncertain remains under agency care for further testing and observation until a final decision can be made. However, after a child is adjudged adoptable, the sooner he is placed the better. Children adopted at an early age have a far greater chance of normal adjustment.[24]

Evaluation of the Adoptive Parents

Many agencies have ten times as many applicants as they have children available for adoption.[25] The agency must first determine, on the basis of interviews and a home study, which of the applicants are fit to be adoptive parents.[26] Then, from its list of suitable adoptive parents on the one hand and its list of available children on the other, the agency must "match" parents and child.

In the interviews the caseworker explores with the applicants their motives for adoption. The experience of agencies has shown that certain motives on the part of adoptive parents lead to an impossible situation for the child: the husband or wife thinks that adopting a child is the solution to an unhappy marriage; a couple wants an adopted child merely as a playmate for a child of their own; the family doctor has recommended adoption as a cure for the wife's nervousness.[27] The caseworker looks for applicants who regard an adopted child as something more than a satisfaction of their own needs, who recognize him as a separate personality with needs of his own.[28]

The adoptive parents must have not only the will but the power to give the child a fit home.[29] This means a state of rea-

---

[24] See THEIS, HOW FOSTER CHILDREN TURN OUT 113-118, 163 (1924).

[25] Michaels, *Casework Considerations in Rejecting the Adoption Application,* 28 JOURNAL OF SOCIAL CASEWORK 370 (1947). This figure is corroborated by reports received from various states in response to a questionnaire. See note 2 *supra.*

[26] See, generally, Harral, *The Foster Parent and the Agency in the Adoption Process* in 68 PROCEEDINGS OF THE NATIONAL CONFERENCE OF SOCIAL WORK 411 (1941); Brenner, *The Selection of Adoptive Parents: A Casework Responsibility,* 25 CHILD WELFARE LEAGUE OF AMERICA BULLETIN 1 (Dec. 1946).

[27] Clothier, *Some Aspects of the Problem of Adoption,* 9 AMERICAN JOURNAL OF ORTHOPSYCHIATRY 598, 610 (1939); Clothier, *Placing the Child for Adoption,* 26 MENTAL HYGIENE 257, 265-6 (1942); Gillean, *The Responsibility of Private Child Welfare Agencies for Adoptions,* 17 CHILD WELFARE LEAGUE OF AMERICA BULLETIN 1 (June 1938).

[28] Jenkins, *supra* note 23, 404.

[29] *Id.* at 404-5.

509

sonable health and a life expectancy sufficient to cover the child's growing years. Mental deficiency, drug addiction, epilepsy, alcoholism, or any chronic and incapacitating disease disqualifies an adoptive applicant. Prospective parents must also be capable of providing the child with the necessities of life and with a minimum of educational advantages. Once this basic financial requirement is met, high-income applicants are not necessarily favored over low-income ones.[30]

If the applicant couple is childless, it is important to know whether they are likely to have a child of their own. The subsequent birth of a natural child often places an adopted child in a disadvantageous position, because the need for which a child was adopted has been filled.[31] Hence many agencies request childless couples to be examined by a gynecologist, and if there is a reasonable possibility of a natural child, their application may be rejected.[32]

Some agencies make a preliminary sifting of applicants on the basis of certain fixed standards. One of the leading agencies in New York City, for example, automatically rules out all women over thirty-five, all men over forty, and all persons who have children of their own.[33] Some agencies refuse to consider single persons or couples with two or more adopted children.[34] Most agencies, however, follow what seems to be the more desirable practice of judging each case on its own merits. An unmarried, divorced, or widowed person deserves consideration, even though a family environment is usually more promising. A couple in their forties may on occasion offer the best home for a particular child, despite the fact that preference might normally be given to younger couples.

If an application is accepted, it is followed by a home study. In evaluating a home the caseworker attempts to get a careful diagnostic picture of the applicants as prospective parents.

---

30 For example, two-thirds of the children placed by the Free Synagogue Child Adoption Committee, one of the leading adoption agencies in New York City, are placed in families with annual incomes of less than $6,000. FREE SYNAGOGUE CHILD ADOPTION COMMITTEE, WHERE A FELLER HAS A FRIEND. See also N. Y. Times, Jan. 10, 1950, p. 37, col. 5.

31 Clothier, *Placing the Child for Adoption*, 26 MENTAL HYGIENE 257, 267-8 (1942); Jenkins, *supra* note 23, at 405; Rathbun, *The Adoptive Foster Parent*, 23 CHILD WELFARE LEAGUE OF AMERICA BULLETIN 5, 6-7 (Nov. 1944).

32 McCormick, *The Adopting Parent Sees the Child in* STUDIES OF CHILDREN 133, 134 (Meyer ed. 1948).

33 Communication to the YALE LAW JOURNAL from Miss Roberta Andrews, Assistant Director, Spence-Chapin Adoption Service, New York City, dated March 6, 1950, in Yale Law Library.

34 Michaels, *supra* note 25, at 370.

She makes several visits to the home, and also talks with relatives and friends of the family. Her investigation attempts to bring to light any serious personality defects or any evidences of marital incompatibility that might threaten the child's security.[35] The agency wants couples who are mature and emotionally well adjusted.

Once a home has been approved generally, the "matching" process begins: the agency must decide which children and which parents are best suited to one another. Physical, mental, psychological, and religious factors are taken into consideration. An effort is made to see that the child's features and general appearance do not differ too much from those of his adoptive parents. An agency usually selects adoptive parents of the same race and religious faith as that of the child. Some state statutes make this mandatory, others are merely suggestive.[36] Insofar as possible, a child of superior intelligence is placed in a home with intellectual interests and educational advantages. But this is never the main consideration; a child with a high I.Q. may be placed with persons of only average intelligence if the caseworker believes that the child will be well adjusted in his new home and that the applicants will make good adoptive parents.

---

[35] Clothier, *Placing the Child for Adoption*, 26 MENTAL HYGIENE 257, 266 (1942).

[36] Texas specifically prohibits the adoption of white children by Negroes and of Negro children by whites. TEX. ANN. CIV. STAT. art. 46a, § 8 (Vernon, 1947). Montana and Louisiana require that the petitioner and the child be of the same race. MONT. REV. CODE ANN. § 61-127 (Choate & Wertz, 1947); LA. GEN. STAT. ANN. §§ 4827, 4839.26 (Dart, 1939). The Nevada adoption statute is inapplicable to any "Mongolian" except in the cases of an adult "Mongolian" seeking to adopt a "Mongolian" child. NEV. COMP. LAWS § 9484 (Hillyer, 1929). Indiana, Washington, and the District of Columbia, although not prohibiting interracial adoptions, require that the petition include facts as to race. IND. STAT. ANN. § 3-116 (Burns, 1946) ("color" of child); WASH. REV. STAT. ANN. § 1699-7 (Remington, Supp. 1943) (race of petitioner and child); D.C. CODE § 16-201 (1940) (race of petitioner and natural parents).

Religious restrictions take a variety of forms. Several states require that a court, when practicable, select adoptive parents of the same religious faith as that of the child or his natural parents. *E.g.*, ILL. ANN. STAT. c. 4, § 4-2 (Smith-Hurd, Supp. 1949) ("whenever possible") N.Y. SOCIAL WELFARE LAW § 373 ("when practicable"); R.I. Laws 1946, c. 1772 (absolute requirement "if there is a proper or suitable person of the same religious faith or persuasion as that of the child available to whom orders of adoption may be granted"; otherwise "when practicable"). A few states require that information regarding the religion of the prospective adoptive parents and of the child be set forth in the petition. *E.g.*, IOWA CODE § 600.1 (1946); MD. ANN. CODE art. 16, § 85F (Flack, Supp. 1947); PA. STAT. ANN. tit. 1, § 1 (Purdon, Supp. 1948). Some states require that reports submitted to the court by the state welfare department or other agencies include information as to race and religion. *E.g.*, CONN. GEN. STAT. § 6867 (1949) (religion); GA. CODE ANN. § 74-411 (Supp. 1947) (race and religion).

These statutory restrictions, especially those forbidding interracial adoptions, raise a serious constitutional question under the "equal protection" clause of the Fourteenth Amendment. *Cf.* Perez v. Lippold, 32 Cal. 2d 711, 198 P.2d 17 (1948), 58 YALE L. J. 472 (1949) (California anti-miscegenation statute held unconstitutional as violative of "equal protection" clause). Even those statutes which are merely suggestive raise the possibility that an unconstitutional criterion is sought to be applied.

Probationary Period

Most agencies require a probationary period of a year in the adoptive home before the adoption is legally consumated. The purpose is twofold: to help adoptive parents integrate the child into their family life, and to make certain that the child is developing normally. During this period an important task of the caseworker is to help adoptive parents clarify their own thinking about what explanation of adoption they will give to the child.[37] All agencies insist that the child be told of his adoption.[38] Practice varies widely, however, as to how much information about the child's background should be given to adoptive parents, and through them, to the child himself.[39] Some agencies tell the parents as little as possible, particularly material of a negative nature. Others believe that adoptive parents should be told everything they wish to know except the names of the child's natural parents.[40] But all agree that the adoptive parents should at least have full knowledge of the child's medical history, and of any pathological condition in his family history which may be inheritable.[41]

Throughout the probationary period the caseworker maintains contact with the home and observes the success of the placement.[42] If at the end of a fair trial the child is not making a reasonably satisfactory adjustment, the placement is terminated. A doubtful placement may require that the probationary period be extended. If a reexamination of the child produces favorable results and the placement is judged to be successful, the agency gives its consent to the adoption.

The Regulatory Problem

When a child is placed independently, the safeguards of agency practice are lacking and the risks of adoption are in-

---

[37] See Rautman, *Adoptive Parents Need Help, Too,* 33 MENTAL HYGIENE 424 (1949).

[38] Eppich & Jenkins, *Telling Adopted Children* in STUDIES OF CHILDREN 96 (Meyer ed. 1948).

[39] Because of the confidential nature of adoption records, over half the states have provisions protecting such records from public inspection. Berkley & Colby, *Problems in Safeguarding Adoptions,* 23 JOURNAL OF PEDIATRICS 344, 349 (1943). Access is usually limited to "parties in interest" or "parties to the action." *Ibid.* The Children's Bureau recommends that all adoption records, including those of state welfare departments and of any other agencies participating in the adoption, be made available only on court order. ESSENTIALS OF ADOPTION LAW AND PROCEDURE 24 (Children's Bureau Publication No. 331, 1949). As to changes in birth records following adoption, see FEDERAL SECURITY AGENCY, THE CONFIDENTIAL NATURE OF BIRTH RECORDS 6-8 (1949); Colby, *Progress in Adoption Legislation,* 16 SOCIAL SERVICE REVIEW 64, 72-3 (1942); Huffman *A First Protection for the Child Born out of Wedlock,* 11 CHILD 34 (1946).

[40] Lippman, *supra* note 14, at 273.

[41] Clothier, *Placing the Child for Adoption,* 26 MENTAL HYGIENE 257, 271 (1942).

[42] Jenkins, *supra* note 23, at 407.

creased many-fold. Since the identities of natural and adoptive parents are seldom concealed from one another, adoptive parents are frequently harassed by a mother who has changed her mind and wants her child back. Or the child may be mentally deficient. This danger is particularly acute in the case of independent placements with non-relatives, often made when the child is less than a month old, because feeblemindedness can rarely be detected under the age of three months. Furthermore, no systematic effort is made to study the home before placement or to select the home best suited to the particular child. In short, the natural parents may be high-pressured into hasty and ill-considered decisions to surrender their child, the adoptive parents may enter the arrangement blindly, and throughout the placement process the child himself is a helpless pawn.[43]

In order to minimize these risks, regulatory legislation should extend to all adoptions the careful procedures of the more competent authorized agencies. The statutes should protect three sets of interests. They should protect the child from separation from natural parents who might give him a good home if sufficient help were available to them, and from adoption by persons unfit to rear a child. They should guard the natural parents from hurried decisions to give up their child, made under strain and duress. Finally, they should protect the adoptive parents from assuming responsibility for a child whose mental and physical condition is questionable, and from interference by the natural parents after the child has been satisfactorily established in his new home.

Existing laws are of two types: adoption statutes proper, which govern the court proceeding; and placement statutes, which regulate the placing of children in homes in contemplation of adoption. In most states the pattern of regulation under these statutes is seriously deficient.

---

[43] The need for adequate safeguards in adoptive placements was demonstrated in a study conducted in 1945 by Dr. Catherine S. Amatruda of the Yale Child Development Clinic. Dr. Amatruda undertook to analyze the results of 100 independent placements and 100 agency placements. Her standards were modest. A child was regarded as a good adoption risk unless it was mentally retarded or had serious personality defects. A family was regarded as suitable unless the investigation disclosed a highly unstable marriage, serious psychiatric difficulties, alcoholism, prostitution, wife beating, or drug addiction. Of the hundred independent placements, only 46 were satisfactory; 26 were questionable at best; and 28 were definitely undesirable. The hundred agency placements, on the other hand, had brought about a satisfactory situation in 76 instances; a questionable situation in 16; and an undesirable situation in only 8. YALE CHILD DEVELOPMENT CLINIC, REPORT OF CURRENT ADOPTION PRACTICES IN CONNECTICUT — INDEPENDENT AND AGENCY PLACEMENT (mimeographed, 1949). See also Colby, *Protection of Children in Adoption* in 65 PROCEEDINGS OF THE NATIONAL CONFERENCE OF SOCIAL WORK 146, 155-6 (1939).

Adoption Statutes

Adoption was unknown to the common law and was not authorized by statute in Great Britain until 1926.[44] The earliest adoption statutes in the United States permitted adoption by means of a deed, without court procedings of any kind.[45] A Massachusetts statute of 1851[46] was the first to require a formal judicial proceeding.[47] Adoption by deed persisted in other states for many years thereafter, but such provisions have gradually been repealed, and today every state requires that adoption be by judicial proceeding.[48]

Jurisdiction and Venue

Since most adoptions are of minor children, jurisdiction of adoption proceedings is best vested in a court accustomed to handling children's cases. But this is not what the law of some states provides. In Utah, for example, although juvenile courts have had forty-five years' experience handling children's cases, adoption remains in the hands of the district courts.[49] In New York, three sets of courts—county, surrogate's, and children's—preside over adoptions.[50] Children's courts have jurisdiction over an adoption proceeding only when the child is delinquent, neglected, or dependent,[51] and as a result they handle a rela-

---

[44] 2 ABBOTT, THE CHILD AND THE STATE 164 (1938). The original British statute, 16 & 17 GEO. 5, c. 29 (1926), was followed by the Adoption of Children (Regulation) Act, 1939, 2 & 3 GEO. 6, c. 27, providing for the registration of adoption societies. Because of the war, the operation of the latter statute was suspended until June, 1943. See *New Adoption Regulations in England,* 17 SOCIAL SERVICE REVIEW 369 (1943); *Adoption Problems in Great Britain,* 24 CHILD WELFARE LEAGUE OF AMERICA BULLETIN 10 (April 1945).

On the history of adoption generally, see 2 ABBOTT, *op. cit. supra,* at 164-228; BROOKS & BROOKS, *op. cit. supra* note 16, at 93-110; GALLAGHER, THE ADOPTED CHILD 19-28 (1936); PECK, ADOPTION LAWS IN THE UNITED STATES 1-2 (Children's Bureau Publication No. 148, 1925); Brosnan, *The Law of Adoption,* 22 COL. L. REV. 332 (1922).

[45] Oler, *Construction of Private Instruments Where Adopted Children Are Concerned: I,* 43 MICH. L. REV. 705n.1 (1945).

[46] Mass. Acts & Resolves 1851, c. 324.

[47] Oler, *supra* note 45, at 705 n.1; Kuhlmann, *Interstate Succession by and from the Adopted Child,* 28 WASH. U. L. Q. 221, 22-3 (1943).

[48] Texas was the last state to enact this requirement. Until 1931 a person could legally adopt a child in that state by filing with the county clerk a written statement of adoption and, if the natural parents were living, a written transfer of parental authority. TEX. REV. CIV. STAT. arts. 42, 44 (1925). See *Note,* 18 TEX. L. REV. 523 (1940). Despite a 1931 statute requiring that all adoptions be by judicial proceding, TEX. ANN. CIV. STAT. art. 46a (Vernon, 1947), adoption by deed continued to be widespread for several years thereafter. WOOLFORD, THE ADMINISTRATION OF ADOPTIONS UNDER TEXAS LAWS 1936, p. 20 (1938).

[49] UTAH CODE ANN. § 14-4-7 (1943). The Utah juvenile courts were created in 1905. See UTAH COMP. LAWS § 720x (1907).

[50] N. Y. Domestic Relations Law §§ 109, 110.

[51] INFORMAL OPINIONS OF THE ATTORNEY GENERAL OF NEW YORK 252 (1944).

tively small percentage of all New York adoption cases.[52]

About a third of the states limit venue in adoption actions to the county or district in which the petitioners reside.[53] Many states permit the action also to be brought where the child resides, especially when the petitioners are non-residents.[54] Some states further provide that when the child is in the custody of a child-welfare agency, the proceeding may be brought where the agency is located.[55] These multiple-venue provisions seem unwise. A court must pass judgment on the qualifications of petitioners as prospective parents, and, in some states, must supervise their home during a probationary period.[56] It thus would appear desirable to limit the action to the place where they are known and where their home is located. Only in exceptional cases should they be permitted to bring the action outside the county or district in which they reside, and in no event outside the state of their residence.[57]

Consent

Every state requires that the consent of certain parties be obtained before an adoption may be approved by the court.[58] The consent of the child is generally mandatory if he is above a specified age, usually twelve or fourteen.[59] Most states provide that if the petitioning adult is married, which is the usual case,

---

[52] Of a total of 1,079 adoptions granted in twelve upstate New York counties in 1946, 45 percent were granted by surrogate's courts, 44 percent by county courts, and 11 percent by children's courts. STATE OF NEW YORK, REPORT OF THE SPECIAL COMMITTEE ON SOCIAL WELFARE AND RELIEF OF THE JOINT LEGISLATIVE COMMITTEE ON INTERSTATE COOPERATION (Assemblyman Harold C. Ostertag, chairman) 29 (Legislative Document No. 51, 1948) (hereafter cited as OSTERTAG REPORT).

[53] LEAVY, THE LAW OF ADOPTION SIMPLIFIED 30-3 (1948). See, e.g., CAL. CIV. CODE § 226 (Deering, 1949); MONT. REV. CODE ANN. § 61-132 (Choate & Wertz, 1947).

[54] Leavy, op. cit. supra note 53, at 30-3. See, e.g., COLO. STAT. ANN. c. 4, § 1 (1935); MASS ANN. LAWS c. 210, § 1 (Supp. 1948).

[55] E.g., FLA. STAT. ANN. § 72.08 (Supp. 1948); MD. ANN. CODE art. 16, § 85B (Flack, Supp. 1947).

[56] See pages 730-1 infra.

[57] If all states were to limit venue in this manner, one problem might arise: a disproportionately large number of adoptable children in big cities and a corresponding shortage of adoptable children in other areas where the need might be greater. This could be remedied by authorized agencies in metropolitan centers transferring some of their adoptable children to agencies located elsewhere, with the receiving agency reimbursing the transferring agency for expenses already incurred.

[58] LEAVY, op. cit. supra note 53, at 40.

[59] Id. at 40-2. A few states set the age at ten years. E.g., MD. ANN. CODE art. 16, § 85G (Flack, Supp. 1947); MICH. STAT. ANN. § 27.3178(543) (Supp. 1949). Louisiana and South Carolina are the only states which do not require the consent of the child under any circumstances.

his spouse must either consent to the adoption or join in the petition.[60]

Under ordinary circumstances a child may not be adopted without the consent of his natural parents, or, if he is illegitimate, without the consent of his mother.[61] But every state prescribes certain conditions under which parental consent is not required. Typically consent may be omitted when the parents (a) have abandoned, deserted, or neglected the child; (b) have been deprived of the child's custody by a court of competent jurisdiction; (c) have voluntarily surrendered the child to an authorized child-welfare agency; (d) are habitual drunkards; (e) cannot be found or are unknown; and (f) have been deprived of civil rights or imprisoned for a felony.[62] In many instances, however, there has been no prior judicial determination of whether the parents are guilty of misconduct. As a result, the judge in the adoption proceeding is faced with two questions: whether the natural parents have so conducted themselves that they should be deprived of a child's custody, either temporarily or permanently; and whether the child should be adopted by the petitioners. These questions are quite distinct; the unfitness of the natural parents does not establish the fitness of the petitioners. Yet if the two issues are part of the same proceeding, it is difficult to keep them separate.[63] A satisfactory solution is found in the Wisconsin adoption statute, under which the termination of parental rights is decided in a separate proceeding and becomes no part of the adoption action.[64]

Where the consent of the parents is not necessary, somebody else must usually give consent in their stead—the child's legal guardian or next of kin, a "next friend" appointed by the court, or an authorized agency to whom the child has been surren-

[60] 4 VERNIER, AMERICAN FAMILY LAWS 340 (1936). See, *e.g.,* IDAHO CODE ANN. § 16-1503 (1948) (consent of spouse required); MASS. ANN. LAWS c. 210, § 1 (Supp. 1948) (spouse must join in petition). Several of the states requiring joinder make an exception for stepparent adoptions. *E.g.,* TEX. ANN. CIV. STAT. art. 46a, § 1 (Vernon, 1947); WISC. STAT. § 322.01 (1947).

[61] LEAVY, *op. cit. supra* note 53, at 42.

[62] 4 VERNIER, *op. cit. supra* note 60, at 341. As to the consent required when the natural parents are divorced, see Colby, *Protection of Children in Adoption,* 65 PROCEEDINGS OF THE NATIONAL CONFERENCE OF SOCIAL WORK 146, 152 (1939); Note, 91 A.L.R. 1387 (1934).

[63] See Note, 14 U. OF CHI. L. REV. 303, n.16 (1947); Colby, *Protection of Children in Adoption,* 65 PROCEEDINGS OF THE NATIONAL CONFERENCE OF SOCIAL WORK 146, 152-3 (1939).

[64] WIS. STAT. § 322.04(2), 48.07(7)a (1947). Following the termination of parental rights the court may, if it chooses, transfer the "care, control and custody" of the child to an authorized agency, which then has authority to consent to the child's adoption. *Ibid.*

dered.[65] Little may be gained by permitting a "next friend" to give consent. A Children's Bureau study in 1936 revealed that courts often regarded such appointments as a mere formality. One Rhode Island judge, for example, said that he usually appointed "someone in the room," who merely signed the petition and made no investigation. In Wisconsin the courts usually appointed an attorney, who received a five-dollar fee from the county for his services.[66] The Alabama-type statute offers a much better solution. It provides that whenever the consent of the parents is unnecessary and the child has no guardian, responsibility for giving consent rests with the state welfare department.[67]

The statutes of many states are inadequate in other respects. A number of them make no provision whereby parents may voluntarily surrender all rights in a child to an authorized agency.[68] And some states, though permitting surrender, make no provision for dispensing with the consent of the parents in a later adoption proceeding.[69]

There is great diversity among the states as to the form which consent may take. The Utah statute has the most stringent requirement, that all consents must be signed before the court in which the petition is filed.[70] Other states require that consents be signed before any judge of a court of record, except when the child is legally the ward of an authorized agency.[71] In a far greater number of states, however, the sole requirement is that consents be acknowledged before a notary public or other officer

---

[65] The Maine statute is typical in this regard. It provides: "If there are no such parents, or if the parents have abandoned the child and ceased to provide for its support, consent may be given by the legal guardian; if no such guardian, then by the next of kin in the state; if no such kin, then by some person appointed by the judge to act in the proceedings as the next friend of such child. . . . In [cases of surrender to an authorized agency or to the state welfare department] the consent to adoption hereinbefore provided for may be given by such incorporated society, asylum, or home, or state department of health and welfare, and the consent of the parents or parent of said child shall not be required." Maine Laws 1945, c. 60.

[66] COLBY, PROBLEMS AND PROCEDURES IN ADOPTION 94-5 (Children's Bureau Publication No. 262, 1941). Such practices still persist in some states today. ESSENTIALS OF ADOPTION LAW AND PROCEDURE 15 (Children's Bureau Publication No. 331, 1949).

[67] ALA. CODE ANN. tit. 27 § 2 (1940). North Dakota has a similar provision. N.D. REV. CODE § 14-1104 (1943).

[68] E.g., Pennsylvania, South Carolina, Texas.

[69] E.g., R.I. GEN. LAWS ANN. c. 373, § 2 and c. 420, § 3 (1938).

[70] UTAH CODE ANN. § 14-4-8 (1943).

[71] E.g., MICH. ANN. STAT. § 27.3178 (543) (Supp. 1947) (must be signed before a probate or juvenile court judge); WIS. STAT. § 322.04(4) (1947) (must be signed before a judge of the county in which the parent resides or the child was born); N.D. Laws 1949, c. 130, § 1 (same).

authorized to take acknowledgments.[72] And some states are even more lax: they require simply that consents be "in writing,"[73] or fail to specify any form in which they are to be given.[74] This laxity may be harmless when an authorized agency is participating in the case. It is dangerous in other circumstances. Natural parents, and particularly unwed mothers, are often prevailed upon to release their children for adoption before they have fully considered the matter, sometimes even before the child is born. To prevent undue influence or precipitate action, an adoption statute should require that all consents be signed in the presence of a judge or a representative of the state welfare department.[75]

Investigation and Trial Period

In recent years, a highly significant development in the law of adoption is the requirement of a "social investigation" before the court may act upon the petition. The investigation includes an inquiry into the reasons why the natural parents are surrendering their child, into the child's family history, environment, and physical and mental condition, and into the suitabilty of the prospective adoptive parents to rear the child. In short, it is a codification of the practice of authorized adoption agencies. Today thirty-five states and the District of Columbia make a social investigation mandatory, while six other states provide that it may be made in the discretion of the court.[76] Approximately two-thirds of these states vest responsibility for making

[72] *E.g.*, FLA. STAT. ANN. §72.14 (Supp. 1948); Maine Laws 1949, c. 173; NEB. REV. STAT. § 43-106 (1943); VA. CODE ANN. § 63-351 (1950).
[73] *E.g.*, ARIZ. CODE ANN. § 27-203 (1939); N.H. REV. LAWS c. 345, § 2 (1942); ORE. COMP. LAWS ANN. § 63.402 (1940).
[74] *E.g.*, ALA. CODE ANN. tit. 27, § 3 (1940); D.C. CODE § 16-202 (1940); MINN. STAT. ANN. § 259.03 (1947).
[75] California requires that consents be signed in the presence of a representative of the state welfare department or of a licensed county adoption agency. This requirement is waived, however, when the adoption is being made by a stepparent or has been arranged through an authorized agency. CAL. CIVIL CODE § 226 (Deering, 1949).
  Courts divide as to whether a natural parent who has given his consent may revoke it before a final decree of adoption has been entered. See Notes, 32 MINN. L. REV. 496 (1948); 26 N.C.L. REV. 293, 294-5 (1948); 138 A.L.R. 1038 (1942); 156 A.L.R. 1011 (1945)
[76] Colorado, Idaho, Mississippi, Oklahoma, South Carolina, and Wyoming are the only states which make no provision for a social investigation of any sort. Maine, Maryland, Montana, Nebraska, Nevada, and Pennsylvania provide that it may be made in the court's discretion. See, *e.g.*, MONT. REV. CODE § 61-133 (1947); NEB. REV. STAT. § 43-107 (1943); PA. STAT. ANN. tit. 1, § 3 (Purdon, Supp. 1948). Oregon leaves the making of an investigation to the discretion of the state welfare department. ORE. COMP. LAWS ANN. § 63-401 (Supp. 1947). Under this provision the welfare department investigates every adoption petition filed in the state except when the placement has been made by an authorized agency. Communication to the YALE LAW JOURNAL from Miss Loa Howard, Administrator, Oregon Public Welfare Commission, dated Jan. 18, 1950, in Yale Law Library. All other states and the District of Columbia make a social investigation mandatory.

or arranging for the investigation in the state welfare department, or require that it be made by an authorized public or private child-welfare agency.[77] In the remaining states the court may designate a probation officer or other officer of the court, an agency, or "any suitable person" to make the investigation.[78]

The majority practice is clearly superior. Judges have neither the time nor the training to make the investigation themselves. When the matter is left entirely in their hands, adoption petitions are often filed and granted in a single day.[79] It is not enough to require that the investigation be made by somebody other than the judge; reports submitted by attorneys and other persons appointed by the court tend to be inadequate.[80] The most satisfactory requirement is that all adoption petitions be investigated by caseworkers from the state welfare department or from an agency it designates.

Most states require that once the investigator has submitted his report and recommendation to the court, the court hold a hearing before acting upon the petition.[81] It is a serious deficiency in many adoption statutes that they make no provision for disposition of the child if the petition is denied.[82] As a result, judges often grant an adoption or allow the child to remain in the adoptive home even though they find the placement undesirable.[83] An adoption statute should provide specifically that if the petition is denied and the child is not already in the permanent custody of an authorized agency, the judge should certify the case to the court having jurisdiction to determine the custody of children.[84]

[77] E.g., DEL. REV. CODE §3550 (1935); N.M. STAT. ANN. § 25-202 (Supp. 1949); VT. STAT. § 9942 (1947).

[78] E.g., ILL. ANN. STAT. c. 4, § 3-1 (Smith-Hurd, Supp. 1949); S.D. CODE § 14.0406 (1939); WASH. REV. STAT. ANN. § 1699-10 Remington (Supp. 1947).

[79] A study of 206 adoptions in four Indiana counties in 1939, for example, disclosed that in 150 cases the petition had been granted on the same day it was filed. 7 INDIANA DEPARTMENT OF PUBLIC WELFARE, QUARTERLY STATISTICAL SURVEY 12 (April-June, 1941). The Indiana adoption statute was amended in 1941 to require a social investigation by an authorized agency. IND. STAT. ANN. § 3-118 (Burns, 1946).

[80] "When studies are made by social agencies either public or private, complete investigations are made. When made by an attorney or other persons of the Judge's choice, they tend to be meager and incomplete." Communication to the YALE LAW JOURNAL from Miss Clara Willman, Supervisor, Children's Services, Washington Department of Social Security, dated Nov. 14, 1949, in Yale Law Library.

[81] 4 VERNIER, op. cit. supra note 60, at 296.

[82] E.g., Kansas, Montana, Utah.

[83] OSTERTAG REPORT, supra note 52, at 25-6.

[84] For statutory provisions of this type, see, e.g., OHIO GEN. CODE ANN. § 10512-21 (Page, Supp. 1949); FLA. STAT. ANN. § 72.28 (Supp. 1948).

Nineteen states expressly provide for appeal of adoption decrees. Zacharias, Judicial Review of Adoption Decrees, 23 CHI-KENT. REV. 233, 237 (1945). For an analysis of the statutes and decisions on this point, see id. at 236-45.

About a fourth of the states provide that if the court approves of the adoption, it shall issue an interlocutory rather than a final decree.[85] There is then a trial period, usually of six months or a year, during which the child lives in the adoptive home.[86] The person or agency which made the original social investigation visits the child at periodic intervals, and at the end of the period reports its finding to the court. If the court is satisfied that the adoption is in the best interests of the child it issues a final decree. Most of these states give the court discretion to waive the trial period if it sees fit, especially when the placement has been made by an authorized agency.[87]

Placement Statutes

Placement statutes, which regulate the placing of children in homes in contemplation of adoption, are an adjunct of adoption statutes. An adoption statute, though it embodies all the modern safeguards, including a social investigation as a part of the adoption proceeding, has one main defect: the investigation frequently comes at too late a point. When a child is placed independently the investigation is made only after an adoption petition has been filed, often not until the child has lived in the home for a year or more.[88] In the meantime, emotional ties have

[85] LEAVY, *op. cit. supra* note 53, at 54-6. Several other states make the issuance of an interlocutory decree discretionary with the trial court. *E.g.*, CONN. GEN. STAT. § 6867 (1949); MD. ANN. CODE art. 16, § 85J (Flack, Supp. 1947). Furthermore, nearly half the states, although having no provision for an interlocutory decree, require that the child must have lived in the adoptive home for a specified period (usually six months or a year) before the court may approve the adoption petition. LEAVY, *op. cit. supra* note 53, at 54-6. See, *e.g.*, NEB. REV. STAT. § 43-109(1) (1943) (six months); UTAH CODE ANN. § 14-4-14 (1943) (one year). In these states, however, there is usually no supervision of the home during this period, unless the placement has been made by an authorized agency.

[86] *E.g.*, ARK. STAT. ANN. § 56-108 (1947) (six months); FLA. STAT. ANN. § 72.19 (Supp. 1948) (not more than one year as fixed by court); MICH. STAT. ANN. §§ 27.3178(546)-(547) (Supp. 1949) (one year).

[87] *E.g.*, OHIO GEN. CODE ANN. § 10512-18 (Page, Supp. 1949); VA. CODE ANN. § 63-355 (1950).

Courts generally hold that an adoption decree may be annulled on the same grounds as any other decree. See Note, 2 A.L.R.2d 887 (1948). But over a third of the states make special statutory provision for annulment of adoptions. The most common formula is that the adoptive parents may seek annulment if the child develops feeblemindedness, insanity, epilepsy, or venereal disease from causes existing at the time of the adoption and not then known to the adopting parents. BROOKS & BROOKS, *op. cit. supra* note 16, at 132. See, *e.g.*, IOWA CODE § 600.7 (1946); UTAH CODE ANN. § 14-4-13 (1943).

[88] Many states provide that the child must have lived in the prospective adoptive home for a period of six months or a year before the adoption may be approved by the court. See note 85 *supra*. And in many cases an adoption petition is not filed until the child has lived in the home for a period exceeding the statutory minimum. Lukas, *Babies Are Neither Vendible Nor Expendable*, 5 N.Y. CITY BAR ASS'N RECORD 104 (1950); Townsend, *Placement and Protective Services in Adoption*, 75 PROCEEDINGS OF THE NATIONAL CONFERENCE OF SOCIAL WORK 331, 334 (1949).

been formed between the child and his new parents—the child has become a part of the adoptive family. Courts are reluctant to break those ties by denying the adoption petition, even though an investigation at this late point may disclose that the placement is unsatisfactory. Judges realize that a child uprooted from one home and transferred to another is subject to considerable trauma. Hence they often think it wiser to approve an unsatisfactory placement rather than to remove a child from the surroundings with which he has become familiar.[89] In this circumstance the investigatory process has failed to accomplish its purpose.

Legislatures have sought to plug this hole by enacting three types of placement statutes: those outlawing independent placements, in whole or in part; those requiring judicial or administrative approval before an independent placement may be made; and those authorizing administrative investigation once a child has been placed independently. The results are not encouraging.

The statutes of eleven jurisdictions provide that no person except a natural parent, a guardian, a relative, or an authorized agency may place a child in a home in contemplation of adoption.[90] These statutes have proved almost completely ineffective. The exception made for natural parents opens the door to all types of independent placements. Evasion of the statute is simple; a third party who arranges a placement can easily make it appear that the placement was made directly by the natural mother.[91]

---

[89] OSTERTAG REPORT, *supra* note 52, at 25; Colby, *Protection of Children in Adoption*, 65 PROCEEDINGS OF THE NATIONAL CONFERENCE OF SOCIAL WORK 146, 154 (1939); Seeley, *Adoptions: Maryland's Better Way*, 37 SURVEY GRAPHIC 255, 258 (1948).

[90] Alabama, California, District of Columbia, Montana, New York, North Dakota, Oregon, South Dakota, Texas, Virginia, and Wisconsin. See, *e.g.*, CAL. CODE § 224q (Deering, 1949) (parents and authorized agencies); N.Y. SOCIAL WELFARE LAW § 374(2) (parents, guardians, second degree relatives, and authorized agencies); D.C. CODE § 32-785 (Supp. 1949) (parents, guardians, third degree relatives, and authorized agencies).

[91] The reluctance of law-enforcement officials to prosecute under a statute of this type is well illustrated by a recent opinion of the attorney-general of Wisconsin. The Wisconsin statutes provide that "no person, other than the parent or legal guardian, and no firm, association or corporation, and no private institution shall *place, assist, or arrange* for the placement of any child in the control and care of any person, with or without contract or agreement, or place such child for adoption, other than a licensed child welfare agency"; and that "no person conducting or in any way connected with the conduct of any maternity hospital shall *in any way directly or indirectly offer to dispose of* any child or hold himself out as being able to dispose of children in any manner." WIS. STAT. §§ 48.37(1), 48.45(1) (1947) (emphasis added). In an opinion addressed to the director of the state welfare department, dated July 24, 1948, the attorney-general of Wisconsin spoke as follows: "You have submitted a number of types of cases of irregular placements and inquire in each case whether the facts show a violation of one or the other of the above statutes.

"A. The physician who confined Miss A, an unmarried mother, learned that she

---

But the statutes of eight states are apparently much more rigid, and prohibit *all* independent placements except when made with relatives.[92] In two of these states—Utah and New Jersey—the attorney-general has nullified the statute by ruling that it does not apply to natural parents.[93] The statutes of the other states, though purporting to require that all placements with non-relatives be made through authorized agencies, have been notably unsuccessful. In Indiana, for example, over half of all placements are made independently; in Maine independent placements accounted for 91 percent of the total in 1948.[94] Officials are loath to prosecute when authorized agencies are already heavily overburdened.

had expressed a wish to place her child for adoption. He therefore informed Mr. and Mrs. Y, who were patients of his, that he knew of a child that would be available for adoption. He gave the name of the adoptive parents to the mother. They made arrangements to transfer the child to them upon discharge from the hospital. The adoptive parents sent a relative to meet the mother outside the hospital and the relative transported the child alone to the prospective adoptive home.

"B. The physician who confined Miss B, an unmarried mother, learned that she had expressed a desire to place her child for adoption. The physician told the mother that he knew a desirable adoptive home. He communicated with the proposed adoptive family, telling them about the child and suggesting that they employ an attorney. Subsequently, the attorney visited the mother and obtained the mother's consent. Upon discharge from the hospital the mother and child were met by the adoptive parents who took the child to their home.

"In case A it is our opinion that on the narrow fact situation presented no successful prosecution could be maintained. While it could be argued that one who gives information gratuitously to the parties performs a material act of 'assistance,' it is our view that unless more could be shown it would be impossible to obtain a conviction. If the physician, in addition to informing the prospective adoptive parents of the existence of the child, actively promoted the placement, there would be a clear violation. But just passing on the information is insufficient in our judgment to warrant a prosecution. The doctor could always say that nothing he did prevented the parties from using proper channels in obtaining the placement. Nor was the act of the relatives in taking possession of the child for the adoptive parents, after the arrangements had been made, sufficient in our judgment to warrant prosecution.

"In case B it is also our view that the physician should not be prosecuted for merely giving the information, particularly since he suggested employment of an attorney. The attorney, according to the facts stated, merely performed a legal service in obtaining the mother's consent and did not 'assist' in or 'arrange' for the placement in the sense meant by the statute." 37 OPINIONS OF THE ATTORNEY GENERAL OF WISCONSIN 403, 405-7 (1948).

92 Colorado, Georgia, Indiana, Iowa, Maine, New Jersey, Tennessee, and Utah. See, *e.g.*, Tenn. Acts 1949, c. 127, § 11 (no exceptions); GA. ANN. CODE § 99-201 (1937) (second degree relatives); IOWA CODE § 238.25 (1946) (fourth degree relatives).

93 Communication to the YALE LAW JOURNAL from Mr. John F. Larson, Director, Bureau of Services for Children, Utah Department of Public Welfare, dated Nov. 15, 1948, in Yale Law Library; Communication to Mr. Sanford Bates, Commissioner, New Jersey Department of Institutions and Agencies, from Mr. Walter D. Van Riper, Attorney-General of New Jersey, dated Aug. 14, 1946, photostatic copy in Yale Law Library. A recent New Jersey decision confirmed the attorney-general's ruling. *In re* Moffett, 5 N.J. Super. 82, 68 A.2d 479 (1949).

94 Communications to the YALE LAW JOURNAL from Mr. E. M. Dill, Administrator, Indiana Department of Public Welfare, dated Dec. 5, 1949, and from Miss Lena Parrott, Director of Child Welfare, Maine Department of Health and Welfare, dated Nov. 14, 1949, both in Yale Law Library.

A few states have sought to control independent placements by requiring approval of the welfare department or a court order before a child is placed in a home in contemplation of adoption.[95] Those statutes which require a court order make no provision for an investigation before the order is issued.[96] But this is a minor problem compared with the extent to which the statutes are disregarded entirely. The Ohio law, for example, provides that no placement of a child under two years of age may be made without written consent of the state welfare department or commitment by a juvenile court. A study of adoption practices in sixty-one Ohio counties in 1938 disclosed widespread violation of this provision by parents, doctors, nurses, maternity homes, lawyers, authorized agencies and even by juvenile courts which did not have proper jurisdiction over some of the children whom they had placed.[97] Yet there have been few prosecutions for violation of the statute.[98]

Four states require that whenever a child is placed independently for adoptive purposes, either the person who places the child or the person who receives the child must notify the state welfare department.[99] The department is given authority to investigate the case and, if it finds that the child has been placed in an unsuitable home, to take the child into its custody. But in three of these states the investigation is discretionary with the department,[100] and in the one state which makes an investigation mandatory, the present case-load is over 200 investigations per caseworker.[101]

Evidently, a state cannot rid itself of independent placements by outlawing them. The ultimate answer to the problem may be a requirement that all placements be made through authorized

[95] *E.g.*, MICH. STAT. ANN. § 27.3178(552) (Supp. 1949) (court order); MO. REV. STAT. ANN. § 9616 (Supp. 1949) (court order); Neb. Laws 1949, c. 204, § 1 (court order); OHIO GEN. CODE ANN. § 1352-13 (Page, 1946) (consent of welfare department or court order for children under two years).

[96] Except for Michigan.

[97] MULLINNIX, OHIO ADOPTION STUDY 28-30, 38-9, 42, 178 (mimeographed, 1941).

[98] *Id.* at 144; Communication to the YALE LAW JOURNAL from Judge J. H. Lamneck, Director, Ohio Department of Public Welfare, dated Nov. 22, 1949, in Yale Law Library.

[99] MD. ANN. CODE art. 88A, § 16H (Flack, Supp. 1947) (receivers must notify welfare department); MASS. ANN. LAWS c. 119, § 14 (Supp. 1948) (placers and receivers); N.H. REV. LAWS c. 130, §§ 17-8 (1942) (receivers); R.I. GEN. LAWS ANN. c. 373, § 3 (1938) (placers). Kentucky provides that any person who places a child for adoption without first notifying the welfare department and obtaining its consent is guilty of contributing to the neglect of the child. KY. REV. STAT. § 405.370 (1948).

[100] Massachusetts, Maryland, and New Hampshire.

[101] Communication to the YALE LAW JOURNAL from Mr. Lawrence C. Cole, Administrator, Children's Division, Rhode Island Department of Social Welfare, dated Nov. 22, 1949 in Yale Law Library.

agencies, which would be given enough money and large enough staffs to handle the additional load. At present, however, no state seems ready to put up the necessary funds.

Meanwhile, probably the most satisfactory check on independent placements would be to pass and *enforce* a statute providing that every person who receives a child into his home and intends to provide it with permanent care must register with the state welfare department. The registrant should be required to file a report setting forth facts about the child, the natural parents, and the manner in which the child was obtained. An investigation by the welfare department should be mandatory. The department, if it regards the placement as unsuitable, should be authorized to apply for a court order terminating it. There should be subsequent investigations until the child is formally adopted or reaches the age of sixteen.[102]

A registration scheme of this sort would involve substantial outlays. But being less complete, it would cost much less than a program requiring that all placements be made through authorized agencies. Since a child would go directly from his former home to his adoptive home, an agency would not have the expense of supporting him for a period of a few months to several years. Investigation of the adoptive parents and of the child would be less complete, and therefore less expensive, than if an agency had arranged the placement. Adoptive parents rather than the agency could pay the doctor's fee and hospital expenses of the natural mother.

In addition to passing registration statutes, states should promptly outlaw independent placements in which a third party makes a profit. The New York legislature recently enacted such a statute, making it a misdemeanor for the first offense and a felony for subsequent offenses to give or receive compensation for placing out a child.[103] The statute specifically exempts payments to authorized agencies and payments by adoptive parents to cover the "reasonable and actual" medical fees and hospital expenses of the natural mother.

---

[102] Various civic organizations in New York, including the Society for the Prevention of Crime and the New York City Committee on Adoptions, are seeking enactment in that state of a bill with substantially these provisions. N. Y. State Assembly, Bill No. 2347, introduced by Assemblyman Rabin, Feb. 22, 1949. The bill failed of passage at the 1949 session, but renewed efforts are being made to secure its passage at the current session.

[103] N.Y. PENAL LAW § 487-a. The first information under this statute was returned on Dec. 5, 1949, against Irwin Slater, a New York attorney. N.Y. Times, Dec. 6, 1949, p. 38, col. 6.

Registration and anti-profiteering laws would be improvements but not cures. The basic difficulty in the field of adoption is a shortage of applied community resources. Additional facilities are required not only for the placement of children in adoptive homes, but for the care of unmarried mothers as well. Case work service, financial assistance, and medical and confinement care are essential.[104] Yet at present community services for the unmarried mother are inadequate in the extreme. Her problem is particularly acute if she has left her home town; often her care cannot be financed from public funds because of legal limitations on residence, and private funds are not available because private agencies give preference to local applicants.[105] As long as the community ignores her needs she will continue to place her child through unauthorized sources or, far worse, resort to abortion to keep from having the child at all. An adequate program of assistance would avert unsatisfactory adoptions, increase the supply of children for deserving persons to adopt, and relieve the underworld abortionist of most of his business.

Adoption agencies themselves are partially to blame for the fact that three out of every four adoptions are independently arranged. Some agencies have too rigid a notion of what constitutes an adoptable child.[106] At times an overly cautious attitude leads them to pass up valuable placement opportunities.[107] A few agencies still disqualify adoptive applicants on a superficial basis.[108] But these practices are not typical. One of the most encouraging signs at present is the extent to which agencies are moving toward more flexible standards.

Generally, agencies have the will but they do not have the way. Most of them are supported entirely by private funds; in

[104] See, generally, MORLOCK, A COMMUNITY'S RESPONSIBILITY FOR THE CHILD BORN OUT OF WEDLOCK (mimeographed, 1949); MORLOCK & CAMPBELL, MATERNITY HOMES FOR UNMARRIED MOTHERS (Children's Bureau Publication No. 309, 1946); Brenner, *What Facilities Are Essential to the Adequate Care of the Unmarried Mother?*, 69 PROCEEDINGS OF THE NATIONAL CONFERENCE OF SOCIAL WORK 426 (1942); Brower, *What Shall I Do With My Baby?*, 12 CHILD 166 (1948).

[105] INDIANA DEPARTMENT OF PUBLIC WELFARE, SUMMARY REPORT OF ADOPTION AND UNMARRIED MOTHER STUDY 7 (mimeographed, 1946); NEW YORK CITY COMMITTEE ON ADOPTION IN NEW YORK CITY 11-12, 33-4 (1948); OSTERTAG REPORT, *supra* note 52, at 55-7.

[106] MULLINNIX, *op. cit. supra* note 97, at 114, 185; OSTERTAG REPORT, *supra* note 52, at 58; Johnson, *Why Babies Are Bootlegged*, 77 SURVEY 176 (1941).

[107] Theis, *Case Work in the Process of Adoption*, 69 PROCEEDINGS OF THE NATIONAL CONFERENCE OF SOCIAL WORK 405, 408-9 (1942).

[108] See page 721 *supra*.

only a few cities, such as Chicago, Cincinnati, and New York, are part of their expenses paid by the city government.[109] In an effort to increase their facilities, agencies are experimenting with the practice of charging fees to adoptive parents.[110] But this will always be a limited source of private funds if adoptive applicants are to be chosen on the basis of their qualifications as parents and not on the basis of their incomes. Hand in hand with an expansion of private facilities there must be an expansion of public facilities as well. State welfare departments, financed by state funds and federal Social Security grants,[111] make few direct placements and often lack the personnel to investigate independent placements.

The need for sound adoption practices is great and is steadily increasing. It is time the states moved to meet it.

---

[109] BROOKS & BROOKS, *op. cit. supra* note 16, at 113; NEW YORK CITY COMMITTEE ON ADOPTIONS, *op. cit. supra* note 105, at 18; POLIER, EVERYONE'S CHILDREN, NOBODY'S CHILD 216 (1941).

[110] Some agencies charge a flat fee, often of $100 or $150. See Carlton, *An Adoption Agency Looks at Fees,* 23 CHILD WELFARE LEAGUE OF AMERICA BULLETIN 4 (Feb. 1944); Foster, *Fees for Adoption Service,* 74 PROCEEDINGS OF THE NATIONAL CONFERENCE OF SOCIAL WORK 344 (1948). A number of agencies, however, have a graduated scale geared to the income of the adoptive family. The Spence-Chapin Adoption Service of New York City, for example, charges adoptive parents a fee of $100 to $450, depending on their circumstances. SPENCE-CHAPIN ADOPTION SERVICE, 1948 ANNUAL REPORT (1949). The Free Synagogue Child Adoption Committee of New York City recently established a schedule ranging from a $200 fee for incomes below $3,500, to a $1200 fee for incomes above $15,000. N.Y. Times, Jan. 10, 1950, p. 37, col. 5.

[111] The Social Security Act of 1935 authorized an annual appropriation of $1,510,000 to be alloted to the states for the development of child-welfare services. 49 STAT. 633 (1935), 42 U.S.C. § 721 (1946). In 1946 Congress increased the authorized annual appropriation to $3,500,000. 60 STAT. 986 (1946), 42 U.S.C. § 721 (1946) The allotment is made by the Federal Security Administrator on the basis of plans developed jointly by him and state welfare departments. *Ibid.*

A
FORWARD
LOOK

A Forward Look

Everyone knows a little about adoption. But most people need to know more. Children who need new parents because their own parents cannot carry the responsibility for them, are deeply in need of the whole community's concern. Many people take it for granted that every protection is given to this helpless group of children. Unfortunately, this is not the case.

Several factors influence the overall adoption program in any community and may prevent the carrying out of good adoption practices. One alarming factor is the lack of any authorized adoption service in many communities throughout the country. Where agency service is not available it is hardly surprising that independent placements flourish.

Even where agency service is available, there is often a lack of trained staff equipped to give adequate service in adoption. Perhaps the staff is well qualified but too few in number to meet the needs in the community; or the staff working in adoption may not be qualified to give this service. In evaluating the ability of an agency to give good adoption service it is essential to consider not only the professional training, experience, and personality attributes of the caseworkers, but also the size of caseloads assigned, the quality and quantity of supervision, the availability of psychiatric and psychological services, the existence and kind of in-service training program available, and the social philosophy of the administrators and board of directors in the agency since they control general policies. Weakness in any one of these areas may cause agency failure to provide good adoption services.

Not long ago it was estimated that there were probably 5,000 children in foster care in New York State who could be placed for adoption if adoption services were available.[1] These are only a few of the thousands over the country who could profit from adoption. When these facts are better known and interpreted to local communities and state legislatures, the need for funds to provide resources will be met and the children who need adoption will be identified and plans made for them.

A serious shortage of qualified caseworkers exists in every area of social work at the present time, and adoption service is not exempt from this handicap. The combination of high professional standards (at least two years of graduate study to complete professional training) and relatively low pay in the field of social work has tended to deter many persons from entering this field of work and has even drawn some away from it to better paid occupations. Without highly skilled and mature staff adoption work cannot fulfil its obligation to the persons vitally involved in the process.

In addition to the availability of adequate staff the adoption program is vitally affected by its financial support. The unwed mother often needs financial help, children needing adoption almost always require a temporary period of boarding care while plans are worked out or legal obstacles removed, and expensive medical care is necessary for some children. Budgetary limitations affect an agency's services in these areas and its ability to carry out what the staff knows are desirable procedures. Without adequate financial support they may require an unmarried mother to prosecute a putative father to obtain financial aid, or require the exploration of the possibility of support from relatives, even when this may not be good casework planning and may ruin a helpful relationship with the unwed mother.

Laws and regulations are sometimes based on rejecting and punitive attitudes of communities and legislators toward unmarried mothers and inadequate parents. There is a tendency to feel that if help is made easy it encourages undesirable behavior in parents. Judgmental attitudes on the part of the community toward these nonconforming individuals will probably not be changed until there is more general understanding of

---

[1] New York State has established a special adoption program which has changed this situation very considerably.

what causes these particular problems. But surely help, financial or otherwise, should not be withheld from a child because of weaknesses in his parents.

Agencies exist to serve people and administrative policies should be such that they facilitate this service. This has not always been true in adoption agencies and in too many agencies is still not true. All too often restrictive and unrealistic policies discourage those who need the services from applying and cause some of those who apply to withdraw their request for service.

Policies which sometimes affect the unmarried mother adversely include: waits for initial appointments, restriction of services to residents of a limited area in which contributions are solicited, financial support policies, referrals to several agencies and individuals to obtain the service needed, refusal to accept a relinquishment until a baby is declared adoptable, delayed placements of the child. Policies which adoptive applicants find it difficult to accept include those relating to maximum age, long waiting lists with no assurance of getting a child, definite proof of sterility and considering a doctor's statement on infertility insufficient, inflexible matching policies, and closed applications.

Legal problems are another area in which obstacles may be so great that it is difficult for an agency to work out adoption for a child even when it is the most desirable plan for him. In many localities attorneys and courts are reluctant to take the necessary action to make a child available for adoption even though the child is critically neglected or abandoned by his own parents. The laws traditionally favor the rights of parents rather than those of the child and a court's decision cannot always be based entirely on the future well-being of the child. "Yet [guardianship] is not an absolute right of the parents but a trust which at all times must be exercised for the child's benefit. It must yield to the child's interests and welfare."[1]

One of the most important factors influencing adoption for a number of years has been the discrepancy between the number of families wanting to adopt a child and the number of children legally available for adoption. With ten or more families applying to adopt for every child legally available for adoption it was impossible for adoption agencies to meet the demand for children. It was this inability to meet the demand, as much as

---

[1] Guardianship, Children's Bureau Pub. No. 330, p. 166.

anything else, which caused criticism of adoption agencies. Recently there seems to be a tendency in the opposite direction. A number of agencies are concerned about the decrease in applications for adoption of normal white infants. If this experience continues until it becomes a national trend there may be a need for radical changes in publicity material on adoption agencies.

These are only a few of the many problems faced by adoption agencies and their solution is not easy. Not all criticisms of agency adoptions are justifiable. Many result from misunderstanding on the part of the public of the function and goals of the agency and what it is able to do with the resources and staff available. It is incumbent upon agencies to help the public to a better understanding of the service they are giving not only to the children under care but to the natural parents, adoptive parents and the community as a whole.

Safeguarding adoptions requires: services to the parents when their need is greatest to help them determine the best plan for the child and themselves; an evaluation as early as possible of the need for permanent placement and the inability of parents to resume care of the child; knowledge of the child and his background in order to select a home for him that will be suitable; a search for adoptive homes which can meet the needs of children requiring adoption; a study of the prospective adoptive parents to determine their capacity for parenthood; a period in the adoptive home under supervision of an agency prior to legal adoption in court; services to children placed independently in adoptive homes; wide disseminaton of information regarding services available in the community; community efforts to provide essential services; cooperation of social, medical, and legal professions in determining feasible solutions to the problem of eliminating practices that do not safeguard children placed in adoption; and enactment of state legislation which will protect the legal and social interests of the children and adults concerned.

Until the above safeguards are assured, agencies and communities must continue to reexamine their services to children, natural parents, and adoptive parents. They should work toward the goals of (1) emphasizing services to parents in order that children may continue to live in their own homes whenever possible, (2) reviewing their caseloads to determine which children need adoption or can be freed for adoption; (3) eliminating unnecessary restrictions; (4) reducing the period of delay before a permanent plan is made for a child; (5) providing agency service for more children needing adoption, especially difficult-to-place children; (6) handling more effectively requests from adoptive applicants and interpretation of the reasons why many "good" families may find it impossible to obtain a child; (7) reexamining the standards applied to adoptive homes; (8) expanding state-wide indices and the exchange of information about children available for adoption and families interested in adopting a child, between agencies within a state (twenty-two states now have such adoption exchanges); and establishing an adoption resource exchange between states; (9) resolving differences between agencies and physicians and lawyers through joint planning which considers the interests and aims of all groups; and (10) developing broad citizen interest and participation in planning and supporting adoption and related programs. This last goal is most important since only increased public understanding and support will bring improved adoption services.

When these goals have been reached, social workers will have less concern that children are being separated from parents because services are not available to help the parents, or that children are kept in boarding homes and institutions so long that they are not considered for adoption until too late. Then our communities will have the assurance that before an adoption placement is made, parents have been helped to carry out their parental responsibilities to the fullest degree of which they are capable; and that an adoption home to assure the child a permanent home and family, is provided at the time when the need is first evidenced. Then more adoptive parents will have the children they want; more children will have the homes they need.